Microeconomic Reform in B

Microeconomic Reform in Britain

Delivering Opportunities for All

HM TREASURY

Foreword by Gordon Brown
Chancellor of the Exchequer

Edited by Ed Balls, Chief Economic Adviser to the Treasury,
Joe Grice, Chief Economist and Director, Public Services and
Gus O'Donnell, Permanent Secretary

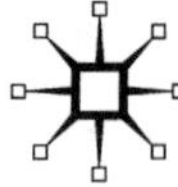

First published 2004 by
PALGRAVE MACMILLAN
Houndmills, Basingstoke, Hampshire RG21 6XS and
175 Fifth Avenue, New York, N.Y. 10010
Companies and representatives throughout the world

PALGRAVE MACMILLAN is the global academic imprint of the Palgrave Macmillan division of St Martin's Press LLC and of Palgrave Macmillan Ltd. Macmillan® is a registered trademark in the United States, United Kingdom and other countries. Palgrave is a registered trademark in the European Union and other countries.

ISBN 1-4039-1249-1 hardback
ISBN 1-4039-1250-5 paperback

This book is printed on paper suitable for recycling and made from fully managed and sustained forest sources.

A catalogue record for this book is available from the British Library.

Library of Congress Cataloging-in-Publication Data
Microeconomic reform in Britain : delivering opportunities for all / H.M. Treasury ; foreword by Gordon Brown ; edited by Ed Balls, Gus O'Donnell, and Joe Grice.
p. cm.
Companion volume to : Reforming Britain's economic and financial policy.
Includes bibliographical references and index.
ISBN 1-4039-1249-1 (cloth) — ISBN 1-4039-1250-5 (paper)
1. Great Britain—Economic policy—1997- 2. Microeconomics. I. Balls, Edward. II. O'Donnell, Gus, 1952- III. Grice, Joseph (Joseph W.) IV. Great Britain, Treasury. V. Reforming Britain's economic and financial policy.

HC256.7.M53 2003
330.941—dc22

2003065840

10 9 8 7 6 5 4 3 2 1
13 12 11 10 09 08 07 06 05 04

Printed and bound in Great Britain by
Antony Rowe Ltd, Chippenham and Eastbourne

Contents

List of Tables vii
List of Figures viii

Foreword by Gordon Brown, Chancellor of the Exchequer xi

Introduction 1

1. Overview: Key Principles For Policy Making 5

Part 1 Raising Productivity in the UK

2. UK Productivity Gap and the Foundation for Government Policy 23
3. Trend Growth 44
4. Enterprise and Productivity Challenge: Government Policy to Date 65
5. The Regional and Local Dimensions 88
6. The Environment 122
7. European Economic Reform 145
   Annex 7.1 – The EMU Assessment: Supporting Studies 167

Part 2 Full Employment and the Labour Market

8. Historical Performance of the UK Labour Market 175
9. Welfare to Work 188
10. Making Work Pay 208
    Annex 10.1 – The Economics of Tax Credits: Inactivity Participation and Labour Supply 227
    Annex 10.2 – The National Minimum Wage 232

Part 3 Tackling Poverty and Promoting Opportunity

11. Supporting Families and Children 241
12. Promoting Saving Throughout Life 266
13. Security and Independence in Retirement 281
14. Tackling Poverty: A New Global Deal 298

Part 4 World Class Public Services

15. Public Services Productivity: An Analysis 325
16. Public Service Reform 345
17. Public Investment and Capital Appraisal 362

18. Conclusion: Constrained Discretion – The New Model 379

Notes 388
Glossary of Key Microeconomic Terms 399
List of Abbreviations 404
Bibliography 408
Index 423

List of Tables

2.1 Decomposition of the productivity gap, 1999 33
3.1 Real GDP growth between 1972 and 2002 55
3.2 Labour productivity growth rates, 1950–1999 56
3.3 Contributions to trend output growth 63
6.1 Development and implementation of economic instruments 134
6.2 Examples of government policies to address market failures 137
10.1 National Minimum Wage rates since its introduction 217
10.2 Comparison of levels of minimum wages across countries, end 2002 218
10.3 Adult minimum wages as a percentage of full-time median earnings, mid 2002 218
10.4 Number who stood to benefit from the introduction and subsequent increases in the NMW 219
10.5 Weekly Minimum Income Guarantees 224
10.6 The effect of the Government's reforms on high marginal deduction rates 226
12.1 Individual characteristics from 1992 to 2000, by earnings level and pension choice in 2000 270
12.2 Correlation between housing wealth and pension status in 2000 271
16.1 Major public service reforms since 1997 352
17.1 Proceeds of sales of fixed assets, 1991/92–2002/03 370

List of Figures

2.1	Productivity gap with the US 1991–2001	26
2.2	Output per worker 1990–2001	26
2.3	International comparisons of productivity, 2002	27
2.4	The total factor productivity gap, 1999	28
2.5	Relative capital intensity, 1970 and 1999	29
2.6	Changes in labour input by hours and quality, 1986–98	31
2.7	Employees by skill level	31
2.8	The 'enterprise gap', 2002	37
3.1	Economic (Business) cycle	45
3.2.	Trend and observed non-oil GVA	48
3.3	Annual growth in average hours worked	57
3.4	Annual growth in the employment rate	59
3.5	Annual growth rates in population of working age	61
5.1	Within-region dispersion in GDP per head	90
5.2	Relative regional GDP per capita	91
5.3	Decomposition of regional GDP per capita gap with UK Average, 1999	93
5.4	Employment and productivity in UK regions	94
5.5	The regional productivity gap, 1999	95
5.6	ILO unemployment rate by region	96
5.7	Highest qualification, 2001	98
5.8	Education by region	99
5.9	Skill levels: disparities within/between regions	100
5.10	Manufacturing capital expenditure per worker and manufacturing GDP per worker, 1997	101
5.11	Expenditure on R&D performed in UK businesses, 2001	102
5.12	Number of R&D firms in the South West by sub-region, 2001	103
5.13	Business start-ups by region per 10,000 resident adults	105
5.14	Business start-ups (VAT registrations) in the North East	106
6.1	Emissions of greenhouse gases, 1990–2012	140
6.2	Days when air pollution was moderate or higher, 1987–2002 (provisional)	141
6.3	Total road traffic volume, 1970–2002	141
6.4	Rivers of good or fair chemical quality, 1990–2001	142

6.5	Population of wild birds, 1970–2000	142
6.6	Percentage of new homes built on previously developed land, 1989–2001	143
7.1	GDP per person employed and employment rate, 2002	148
7.2	Total and female employment rates, 2002	149
7.3	Total and older worker (aged 55–64) employment rates, 2002	150
7.4	EU employment rates and the Lisbon Agenda targets	151
7.5	The 'enterprise gap', 2002	156
7.6	R&D as per cent of GDP	159
7.7	Percentage of firms reporting increased competition from elsewhere in the EU, as a result of the Single Market	162
7.8	State aid to industry by Member State, 1991–2001	164
8.1	Employment and ILO unemployment	177
8.2	Lone parent employment rate by age of youngest child	179
8.3	Working age claimants of incapacity-related benefits, 1979-97	182
8.4	Changes in the way households organise their work	183
8.5	Claimant rate, UK regions, April 1997	185
8.6	Total and average hours worked, 1992-97	187
9.1	Long-term unemployment, youth and 25+	191
9.2	Employment and ILO unemployment	194
9.3	Earnings and unemployment	195
9.4	Total and average hours worked	196
9.5	Lone parent employment rate	199
9.6	Working age claimants of incapacity-related benefits, 1979–2002	202
9.7	Percentage activity and employment rates for population of working age	204
9.8	Children in workless households, 1990-2002	205
10.1	Wage bill impact in the low paying sectors of the October 2001 Uprating of the NMW	221
10.2	Average net gain from an increase in the National Minimum Wage to £4.50	222
10.3	Gains to work for different households with one child	224
10.4	Gains to work for people aged 25 and over without children	225
10A.1	Individual labour supply choice in the presence of a non-convex and non-linear budget set	228
10A.2	Impact of the WTC on choice of labour supply: non worker	229
10A.3	Impact of the WTC on choice of labour supply: worker	230

10A.4 The minimum wage in a competitive model 233
10A.5 The minimum wage in a monopsony model 236
11.1 Percentage of children in low income households in the European Union 246
11.2 Children in low income households by family type, 1979 and 2001–02 247
11.3 Gains for families with children as a result of tax credits and other children's measures introduced between 1997 and 2004 252
11.4 The widening mortality gap between social classes 258
11.5 Investment in housing as a percentage of GDP 260
11.6 Permanent dwellings completed in Great Britain 261
11.7 Children in low income households 264
12.1 Households' savings ratio, 1963-2002 267
12.2 Distribution of net financial wealth in 2000 268
13.1 State Second Pension accrual rates, compared to SERPS 285
13.2 The Pension Credit 287
13.3 Overall gains for pensioner families from pensioner policies, by income decile 290
15.1 Healthy life expectancy within the UK's main competitors 328
15.2 Health expenditure and life expectancy 329
15.3 Distribution of service performance across local authorities 330
15.4 Distribution of service performance by service area 330
15.5 Local authorities' use of resources and their services' performance 331
15.6 Operating costs for major Registered Social Landlords in England, 2002 332
15.7 Unit costs by probation area, 2001–02 332
17.1 Distribution of public sector assets, March 2002 363
17.2 Public sector net investment, 1975–1998 364
17.3 Gross fixed capital formation, by government sector, 1969–1997 365
17.4 The sustainable investment rule, 1989–2009 367
17.5 Public investment in public services, 1997–2006 367

Foreword

Gordon Brown

Since 1997, our Government's central objective – the heart of our vision for a prosperous Britain – has been to promote opportunity and security for all.

Our first priority was to address our country's chronic macroeconomic instability. And as the companion volume to this book, *Reforming Britain's Economic and Financial Policy: Towards Greater Economic Stability*, set out, putting in place a wholly new fiscal and monetary framework – including the independence of the Bank of England and new fiscal rules – was a crucial step towards meeting this goal and has already produced real benefits – unemployment has fallen to levels not seen since the 1970s, while inflation and interest rates remain at historic lows, and Britain has experienced the longest period of sustained peacetime growth since records began over 130 years ago.

But a sound macroeconomic framework is a necessary but not sufficient condition to achieve, in what is an increasingly competitive global economy, a Britain where there is opportunity and security not just for some but for all. That is why, since 1997, we have also introduced policies which aim to improve the supply-side of the economy. Our approach has been to make the UK more productive by promoting, on the one hand, competition, enterprise, science and skills while on the other hand, reforming the welfare system and public services as a route to a more efficient and fairer Britain in which every individual can realise their potential.

This book focuses on the agenda for microeconomic reform in those areas – setting out what has been achieved over the last seven years and the challenges for the way ahead. And it tackles important questions about the relationship between individuals, government and markets – acknowledging that whilst in some areas it is clearly in the public interest for markets to have an enhanced role, in others market failures need to be addressed to make markets work better – and in some cases markets cannot safeguard the public interest. Equally, we must put the case for a reformed and renewed public sector with clear and long-term objectives, devolution of power and transparent mechanisms for accountability.

The context for this book is the growing competitive challenges of the global economy. Within twenty years half the worlds manufactured exports – from cars and clothes to computers and microchips – may be produced outside Europe, Japan and America in low wage developing countries. Up to five million British, European and American jobs could end up outsourced – offshore in countries like China and India as they strive to become the world's second and third largest economies. And even today China's significance to the global economy is that every year it, on its own, is adding as much output as the whole of the G7 put together.

For Britain this means recognising that there is no escape from uncompetitiveness by resorting to loss making subsidies, artificial barriers or protectionist shelters. Indeed, the price of failure is not a long period of slow decline but sectors going under altogether. And the opportunity for us is that as low cost, low value production comes under increasing pressure, the high valued added, high tech, high skilled, science-driven products and services are the key to wealth creation in the future.

So to succeed in this modern global economy we need to enable markets to work better and create an environment in which firms can operate effectively and in which they have the certainty to invest in the future. At the same time, if we are to make the most of the potential of open trade, we also need greater flexibility as we respond to new technologies and adjust to shifts in consumer demand. The more we are internationally interdependent, and thus the more our regions face intense global competition, the more successful will be the regions and localities that have the flexibility to adapt to change.

This new approach has led to fundamental changes in direction not just in macroeconomic policy but in microeconomic policy. Since 1997 by strengthening the competition regime we have encouraged firms to innovate and minimise costs, which advances the public interest through providing better quality goods and services for consumers. We have put in place a new industrial policy – replacing the old centralisation of national champions, picking winners or offering special subsidies to loss makers with a level playing field for all. We are celebrating the entrepreneurial culture – opening up opportunity for those with ideas and dynamism, and reducing regulation where is does not serve the public interest. Investment in science is now a central priority. And instead of the old protectionism, we advocate open markets and free trade.

At the same time, the new realities of fast changing labour markets mean there is a constant need for retraining and up-skilling by the British workforce. Instead of thinking of employment policy as maintaining people in old jobs even when technological and other change is inevitable, it is by combining flexibility – helping people move from one job to another – with active intervention to provide skills, information and financial support that is the best route to full employment. As a result of the New Deal and our other employment programmes, there are 1.7 million more people in work now than in 1997. And the next stage of the New Deal is to help people move from low skilled work to higher skilled work – including a second chance for adults without basic skills to learn through further education, distance learning or work-based training.

A modern global economy also requires a more modern welfare state that responds to the needs of working families while protecting the most vulnerable, including children and pensioners. The world has moved on a great deal from when Beveridge set out his plans in 1942, but the principles which underpin the welfare state remain the same: opportunity for people to improve their circumstances and those of their families; security to protect people from undue hardship that can arise from life events; and the responsibility of everyone to make the most of the opportunities on offer. The new welfare system puts into practice these principles – transforming the passive and reactive system of the past into one which provides support for all, alongside the right incentives for people to move into, and progress in, work.

Taken together, these reforms are not only supporting but enhancing markets in the public interest. But we must also have the courage to recognise where markets do not work well and lead to outcomes which are inequitable, inefficient or both – and hence where market failure can be dealt with best through public provision.

But even when a market is inappropriate, old command and control systems of management are not the way forward. Instead, our significant and sustained investment in Britain's public services must be tied to reform and results – and in doing this, we have to develop decentralised models for public provision that respond to people's needs, extend choice and get the balance right between efficiency and equity. The modern challenge is to move beyond old assumptions under which equity was seen to go hand in hand with uniformity; or diversity appeared to lead inevitably to inequality. Instead we should seek the maximum amount of diversity consistent with equity.

As a result, we are now stepping up our efforts to pioneer decentralised public service delivery to ensure greater freedom and flexibility for local providers; and empowering Regional Development Agencies, local authorities and the private and voluntary sectors to deliver services in innovative ways which meet local needs.

All this opens up a challenging agenda for reform – and one which is continually evolving as technology and rising expectations challenge each generation's vision of what is possible and best. But as this book suggests, it is an agenda which can meet the contemporary challenges of competitiveness and equity – creating a Britain where instead of enterprise thriving at the cost of fairness or fairness at the cost of enterprise, we can advance both enterprise and fairness together and provide opportunity and security for all.

Chancellor of the Exchequer

Introduction

This book provides a comprehensive guide to the extensive microeconomic reforms implemented since 1997 to realise the UK Government's goals: a stronger, more enterprising economy and a fairer society.

It is a companion volume to *Reforming Britain's Economic and Financial Policy: Towards Greater Economic Stability* (Balls and O'Donnell 2002) and offers a detailed account of a programme of reforms which together constitute a comprehensive strategy to lock in the stability needed to support steady growth by pursuing both enterprise and fairness for all.

Building on the foundations of monetary and fiscal reform, the reforms in microeconomic policy described provide the framework for expanding national wealth, protecting the environment and promoting opportunity and security for all. The Government's approach to raising the sustainable rate of productivity across all sectors and income groups, supporting families, and tackling poverty is presented, together with a detailed account of the reform of the delivery of public services.

This volume is designed to be a resource for students of economics and politics, bringing together work which underpins current British economic policy-making.

While we have tried to take a comprehensive approach, there may be some aspects of microeconomic reform of interest to the reader which are not covered here. These readers should consult the Treasury web page (www.hm-treasury.gov.uk), and other government departments (for example the Department of Trade and Industry: www.dti.gov.uk and the Department for Work and Pensions www.dwp.gov.uk) for relevant papers.

Chapter 1 provides an overview of the reforms implemented since 1997, which are discussed in the succeeding chapters. It explains why the Government decided on this course of action, and its major reform objectives, and how they relate to the policies it subsequently developed.[1]

Part 1 of the book – Chapters 2 to 7 – focuses on *Raising Productivity in the UK*. It describes the productivity challenge, known as the productivity gap, faced by the UK and sets out the Government's approach to raising levels of productivity across all sectors and income groups. Chapter 2 quantifies the UK's productivity performance and highlights the gap in performance between the UK and other major economies. Chapter 2 also explains the practical and theoretical causes of this gap, at both the national and the firm levels, and sets out the policy framework that has been put in place to address the problem. Chapter 3 provides a macroeconomic context and explains why microeconomic reforms have concentrated on improving productivity and the labour market. It sets out the basic concepts related to trend output growth and its applications in economic analysis and policy-making.

Chapter 4 describes the programme of microeconomic reform to tackle barriers to productivity growth. It sets out the microeconomic policy reforms designed to promote productivity through strengthening each of the five productivity drivers identified in Chapter 2: competition, enterprise, science and innovation, skills, and investment.

Chapter 5 deals with the regional dimension of productivity issues, setting out analysis of regional variations in economic performance in the UK. It demonstrates how policy has been shaped to improve the productivity not only of those countries and regions that have historically had the highest growth but also that of the least productive regions. Chapter 5 also looks in greater detail at policy measures at the local level.

Chapter 6 introduces the environmental dimension to the issues discussed previously in the book, making sure that the important challenges of sustainable development and quality of life are given the priority they deserve. It discusses the different types of market failures that can impact upon the environment and the range of policy tools that the Government can use to address them. Chapter 6 concludes by describing some of the measures put in place to date and discusses how progress against the Government's environmental objectives can be evaluated.

The European dimension of the Government's microeconomic reform agenda is discussed in Chapter 7. The chapter describes the United Kingdom's approach to economic reform in the European Union and briefly sets out key developments in EU reform history and the UK's view on priorities for action. Annex 7.1 gives summaries of the 18 supporting studies, which were published alongside the Chancellor's announcement of the results of the Treasury five tests assessment of membership of the single currency on 9 June 2003. Many of these cover microeconomic issues relevant to the different chapters of this book.

Part 2 of the book covers *Full Employment and the Labour Market*, and comprises Chapters 8–10. Part 2 discusses important reforms to the labour market, implemented with a view to achieving the goal of employment opportunity for all: the modern definition of full employment. Chapter 8 sets out historical trends in the labour market which have formed the basis of the development of the strategy. Chapter

9 describes how the Government is addressing the historical weaknesses of the UK labour market discussed in Chapter 8. It explains how the Government's welfare to work strategies have been developed around the fundamental premise that work is the best route out of poverty and into greater levels of productivity for the UK as a whole and that new rights should be matched with responsibilities. This section concludes with Chapter 10, which explains the emphasis on ensuring that work pays. It illustrates how the combination of the National Minimum Wage and tax credits have helped to tackle structural unemployment. Together these changes amount to the biggest single change in financial support for families since the Beveridge reforms of the 1940s. Annexes 10.1 and 10.2 then sets out the economic theory underpinning tax credits and the Minimum Wage respectively.

Part 3 of the book looks at *Tackling Poverty and Promoting Opportunity*, and comprises Chapters 11–14. It looks at the measures that have been introduced aimed at securing fairness and social justice at home and tackling poverty both in the UK and overseas. Chapter 11 analyses child poverty in the UK, and describes how the policy has been shaped to address its root causes. The strategy pulls together a number of areas of Government activity: helping people into work, supporting those who cannot work, providing high quality public services, and supporting parents and work-life balance. Chapter 12 follows with a discussion of the policies introduced to promote savings throughout the life-cycle, while Chapter 13 then sets out the policies introduced to provide security for today's pensioners, whose scope to help themselves is limited, and to enable and encourage those of working age, tomorrow's pensioners, to plan and provide for their own retirement.

The final chapter in Part 3, Chapter 14, looks at the international dimension, analysing how the UK can help to address poverty on a global level. This chapter is drawn from, and updates, speeches by the Rt. Hon. Gordon Brown MP, Chancellor of the Exchequer – to the New York Federal Reserve and to the Press Club, Washington DC – and provides an overview of the key principles underpinning the Government's approach to tackling global poverty.

Part 4 of the book focuses on delivering *World Classs Public Services*. While the first part described government policies to deliver productivity improvements across the private sector, Part 4 recognises that there remains a significant productivity challenge in the delivery of public services. Accordingly, Chapter 15 discusses the importance of improving public sector productivity and assesses how it can be measured. It explains the market failures and equity considerations associated with public services, the justification for government funding and provision of services and the problems which must be overcome to increase public sector productivity. Chapter 16 then sets out the framework for improving public service performance, focusing on three key policy building blocks and describing how they combine into a single framework. It shows how the framework has informed policies towards the key public services and gives examples to demonstrate how the range of reforms in the public services fit into this framework.

The final chapter in Part 4, Chapter 17 sets out the strategy of increasing investment in the country's infrastructure and explains how the extra resources being invested in public services are being matched with reforms to ensure that the quality of investment is raised.

Finally, Chapter 18 concludes, drawing together the key themes that cut across both this book, and its companion volume on macroeconomic policy making, and the common principles that have guided the Government's microeconomic interventions.

It is expected that many readers will use this book as a work of reference. Such readers will want to dip into various chapters without necessarily reading all the others. For this reason, we have tried to make the chapters as self-contained as possible. This means that there may be a degree of overlap in the material covered.

The editors would like to thank all Treasury officials past and present, too numerous to mention personally, who have worked on developing and implementing these policies since 1997. Many of these officials have been responsible for commenting on various chapters in this book. We would like to register our particular thanks to Jonathan Lepper, Hilary DeVries and Matthew Gilbert and our thanks to Antonia King, James Bowler, Atalay Dabak, Catherine Frances, Priyen Patel, Bryn Welham, Stephen Evans, Duncan McKinnon, Ilona Blue, Justin Tyson, Charlie Pate, Mostaque Ahmed, Fiona Richie, Andrew Walker, Lindsey Sullivan, Oliver Crane, Andrew Field, Jeremy Skinner, Conrad Smewing, Julie Fry, Rebecca Lawrence, Daniel Gordon, Sue Connaughton, Richard Hughes, Ed Miliband, Spencer Livermore, Shriti Vadera, John Battersby, Beth Russell, Rebecca Ingarfield, Balvinder Chowdhary, Jean-Christophe Gray, Stuart Glassborow and Alex Dawtrey for their work in bringing this book together.

1
Overview: Key Principles for Policy-Making

This chapter sets out the conceptual framework that underpins the Government's approach to reforms in microeconomic policy that are described in the remainder of the book. The chapter draws on the Chancellor of the Exchequer's speech 'A Modern Agenda for Prosperity and Social Reform' to the Social Market Foundation.

Introduction

The Government's objective is to deliver high and stable levels of growth and employment, with opportunity and rising living standards for all. There are three pillars to the Government's approach to economic policy: delivering macroeconomic stability, tackling the supply-side barriers to growth and delivering employment and economic opportunities for all.

The companion book to this publication, *Reforming Britain's Economic and Financial Policy: Towards Greater Economic Stability* (Balls and O'Donnell 2002), set out the Government's approach to achieving its macroeconomic goals and the principles which underpin its macroeconomic policy-making. A sound macroeconomic framework is a necessary but not sufficient condition to achieve, in what is an increasingly competitive global economy, a Britain where there is opportunity and security for all. So the Government has also sought to promote, on the one hand, competition, innovation, and the enterprise economy, and on the other hand, a modern welfare state and world class public services as the routes to an efficient and fair Britain in which individuals can realise their potential. So this book focuses on the two remaining policy pillars and the Government's approach to meeting its microeconomic objectives. This chapter provides an overview of the conceptual framework that underpins microeconomic policy.

Principles underpinning Microeconomic Reform Agenda

Formulating the long-term microeconomic agenda has meant answering the fundamental questions about the respective roles of markets and government in helping individuals and firms reach their full potential. In almost every area – the future of the Private Finance Initiative, health care, universities, industrial policy, savings policy, welfare reform, economic reform in Europe and public services reform – the question is, at root, what is the best relationship between individuals, markets and government to advance the public interest. The issue is whether the public interest – opportunity and security for all and the equity, efficiency and diversity necessary to achieve it – is best advanced by more or less reliance on markets or through substituting a degree of public financing, control or ownership for the market. Where the best route involves public sector provision, there is a further issue of whether there can, or should, be contestability.

The nature of the Government's microeconomic reforms has depended upon an assessment of where markets should have an enhanced role, where market failures should be addressed, to make them work better in the public interest, and what are the limits to markets.

Markets are a powerful means of advancing the public interest. It is therefore important to strengthen markets where they work and to tackle market failures where they occur. Promoting the market economy helps achieve the goals of a stronger economy and a fairer society. But, at the same time, it is important to recognise that there are some areas where markets are not appropriate and where market failure can only be dealt with through public funding or provision of services.

Consistent with this thinking, the microeconomic reforms are underpinned by the following principles:

- A strong economy and fair society should not only support but positively enhance markets where they can operate in the public interest.
- A recognition, applying that same public interest test, that there are limits to markets, and in these circumstances public funding

or provision may be the more equitable, efficient and responsive solution.

- Acceptance that government failure should not simply replace market failure. Where markets fail, government intervention should be targeted at addressing the specific market failure to make markets work in the public interest. Public service provision should operate within a performance framework that ensures efficiency, equity and personalised choice.

The remainder of this section looks in more detail at these three basic tenets within the Government's four major microeconomic goals:

- raising the sustainable rate of UK productivity growth;
- sustaining a higher proportion of people in employment than ever before;
- building a fairer society; and
- delivering high quality public services.

The following pages summarise the conceptual framework that underpins these goals and focuses on the role that market and non-market solutions will play in delivering them. More in-depth discussion of the goals and the policies enacted to achieve them is in the main text of the book.

Raising the sustainable rate of UK productivity growth

Productivity growth, alongside high and stable levels of employment, is an important determinant of long-term economic performance and rising living standards. Increasing the sustainable rate of UK productivity growth is central to the Government's economic strategy.

The UK has historically experienced low rates of productivity growth by international standards. Macroeconomic instability and microeconomic failures have inhibited competition, enterprise and innovation, and discouraged firms and individuals from long-term investment in human and capital resources.

Properly functioning markets can deliver productivity growth efficiently and equitably. A pro-competition policy delivers greater choice and lower prices to consumers and encourages businesses to be more innovative and creative. It also helps UK companies to compete abroad. Sheltering domestic goods and services markets through subsidies or other forms of protectionism would cause long-term damage, lessening the ability of UK companies to maintain their global competitiveness.

Therefore, the Government's industrial policy aims not to second guess, relegate or replace markets but to enable markets to work better without undermining their dynamism. The aim is to harness the initiative, creativity and innovation which can come from the decentralisation and dynamism of properly functioning markets.

Putting in place a pro-market, pro-enterprise policy can create both a more efficient and a fairer society, delivering opportunity for all. For example, in regional terms, balanced economic growth is not only in the interests of the least prosperous regions but in the interests of regions where prosperity can bring congestion, overcrowding and overheating. A skills and education policy which draws on the talents of not just some but the widest range of people and their potential will not only be the most efficient from an employer's perspective but also the most equitable for society. Likewise, by removing entry barriers, for example lack of access to capital, it is possible to widen economic opportunities for lower-income groups and unemployment black spots where the enterprise culture is weakest.

So the role of government in raising the UK's sustainable rate of productivity is not only to support but positively enhance markets in the public interest. Policy is therefore directed to ensuring dynamic properly functioning markets with fair and accurate information possessed by consumers; fair competition between many suppliers, with low barriers to entry and free mobility of capital and labour.

By contrast, where markets fail, the role of government is to actively tackle that market failure. Market failure exists when the competitive outcome of markets is not efficient from the point of view of the economy as a whole. Put another way, markets fail when the private returns which an individual or firm receives from carrying out a particular action diverge from the returns to society as a whole – resulting in a too much or too little of the activity being carried out. Market failures can be classed into four generic categories as follows:

- *Externalities*: spill-over effects which occur when actions by a firm or individual create benefits or costs that do not accrue or are not borne by that firm or individual. For example, training provided by one firm benefits future employers as well as that firm.
- *Market power*: where competition is hindered firms can reduce efficiency and innovation and set higher prices without being corrected by the market.

- *Information*: a lack of information hampers the efficient functioning of the market.
- *Poor regulation*: excessive or unnecessary regulation obstructs and efficient market functioning.

Government policy looks to correct these market failures in the most efficient and equitable way.

Policy is also focused on the need to promote opportunity for all – every individual and business and every locality. For individuals, the aim is to raise pupil attainment across the education system and set a framework to ensure government, individuals and employers each tackle deficiencies in the skills base. For businesses, the aim is to expand and facilitate choices at each stage of an enterprise's development. For localities, the aim is to increase the productivity and realise the potential of every region, city and locality with the ambition of raising the performance of under performing areas so that all, and particularly disadvantaged communities, can share in rising prosperity.

This new regional policy rests on two principles. First, it aims to strengthen the long-term building blocks of growth, innovation, skills and the development of enterprise, by exploiting the indigenous strengths in each region and city. Second, it is bottom-up not top-down, with national government enabling powerful regional and local institutions to work by providing the necessary flexibility and resources.

To achieve these aims, the Government has pursued a wide-ranging strategy to tackle the barriers to productivity growth and to close the productivity gap. Microeconomic reform aims to remove barriers that prevent markets from functioning efficiently, allowing firms and workers to maximise their productive potential at each stage of their development. The reforms target historic weaknesses in five key drivers of productivity performance:

- strengthening the *competition* regime, to encourage firms to innovate and minimise costs, and to deliver better-quality goods and services to customers;
- promoting *enterprise*, to help new and established businesses start up, develop and grow, especially in disadvantaged areas;
- supporting *science and innovation*, to utilise the potential of new technologies and to develop more efficient ways of working;
- improving *skills*, through better education for young people and greater training opportunities for those already in the workforce; and

- encouraging *investment* to improve the stock of physical capital in all sectors and industries.

While the ultimate aim of these interventions is to raise the long-term growth potential of the UK economy, it is critical to our long-term well-being that this growth is environmentally sustainable. The Government's approach to protecting and improving the environment is based upon the same conceptual framework that underpins the strategy for improving the UK's productivity performance. Correcting environmental market failures helps to ensure that the productivity of natural resources is maximised alongside the productivity of other inputs.

Market failures can exist where the costs of environmental damage are not reflected in prices of goods and services; where environmental improvements can only be achieved by society acting collectively rather than individually; or where decision-makers do not have clear information about how best to reduce their costs. If the Government intervenes to correct these market failures efficiently, it will achieve better environmental outcomes as well as greater overall economic efficiency. In any intervention, the benefits must justify the costs. These economic instruments can provide incentives for behaviour that protects or improves the environment, and can enable environmental goals to be achieved at the lowest cost and in the most efficient way.

Increasing employment opportunities for all

In 1997, the Government set out its aim of extending employment opportunity to all in a changing labour market. The goal is to ensure a higher proportion of people in work than ever before by 2010.

At the time, the labour market was characterised by a number of severe problems, many of which had developed over long periods. Despite five years of economic recovery, aggregate levels of unemployment were still high, especially compared with those seen before the 1980s. Over two million people were unemployed on the International Labour Organisation (ILO) definition, while long-term unemployment remained high by historical standards. Many unemployed people had drifted into economic inactivity, often on disability-related benefits, and never returned to work, even as the economy recovered.

Rather than being a solution to these problems, the welfare system had become a positive barrier to moving people into work. There were obligations to seek and be available for work only for the registered unemployed but these were not matched by the support and guidance that many needed to find jobs – especially after extended periods of detachment from the labour market. There were no obligations or opportunities for the 4 million people classed as "inactive" which included 1 million lone parents and 2.5 million sick and disabled.

And for many people, especially those lower down the income scale, the structure of the tax and benefit system meant that work did not pay more than benefits. For a couple with one child and one partner entering full-time work at a typical entry wage, the gain to work was just £30 a week. Meanwhile many of those in work were discouraged from working longer hours or taking a better job by a tax and benefit system that, in many cases, withdrew more than 70 pence for every extra pound they earned.

The Government's strategy approach has been for moving people from welfare into work and improving the overall performance of the UK labour market based upon:

- *maintaining a stable macroeconomy* and the right conditions for sustained job creation, avoiding excessive cyclical fluctuations that leave people detached from the labour market;
- *moving from a passive to an active welfare state* combining rights and responsibilities;
- *ensuring that work pays* more than benefits by reforming the welfare system to address the unemployment traps that had existed;
- *encouraging progression in work* by reforming the tax and benefit system to reduce the number of people on high marginal deduction rates, in addition to promoting lifelong learning; and
- *promoting a flexible labour market* by equipping people to cope with change and ensuring the institutional flexibility to respond to shocks and deliver high levels of employment across the economic cycle.

At the heart of this strategy for tackling unemployment and wider worklessness is the principle of work for those who can. All working age benefit recipients operate within a work-focused system of advice and support – the New Deals. This "employment first" principle is underpinned by an implicit contract between the government and the individual balancing the rights and responsibilities of each. This balance between rights and responsibilities forms the basis of the New Deals. For the individual, the presumption is that those capable of working should actively seek and be available for work. This obligation to seek work is matched by a commitment from the Government to provide jobseekers with the skills, guidance and opportunities that they need to find work.

This support is tailored to the needs of the individual jobseeker through one-on-one attention from a personal advisor.

Financed by a windfall tax on privatised utilities, the New Deal for Young People was launched in 1998 to end long-term youth unemployment. The achievement of this goal almost two years ahead of time enabled the Government to extend the New Deal to long-term unemployed, older workers, lone parents and the disabled.

The New Deals have helped to reduce long-term unemployment to levels last seen a generation ago and deliver a substantial rise in the employment levels of key groups like lone parents. The new Jobcentre Plus goes further generalising the employment first principle across the whole benefits system so that work and benefits advice are integrated in one place and provided to all.

If the New Deal's active, work-focused, policies are to be effective, they must be backed by a guarantee that work will pay more than benefits. Since 1997, the Government has taken a range of steps to strengthen work incentives – especially for those on low incomes. In 1999, the National Minimum Wage was introduced to ensure that work provides a fair minimum income. The NMW has been complemented by reforms to the tax system (the 10 pence starting rate of income tax and reforms to the National Insurance system) and to the benefit system (the introduction of the Working Families Tax Credit and the new Working Tax Credit) to improve work incentives. As a result of these changes the Government has substantially increased both the gains to moving from welfare into work and enhanced the economic incentives for individuals to progress in work.

Box 1.1 Flexibility and microeconomic reform

In the modern global economy, flexible labour, product and capital markets are vital to ensure that the economy is responsive and that economic shocks do not have long-lasting effects, so that high and stable levels of output and employment can be maintained. Were the UK to join EMU, the need for flexibility would be even greater, as the ability to adjust interest and exchange rates would no longer be available at the national level.

A sufficient level of wage flexibility is vital to eliminate imbalances between supply and demand; relative price adjustment is a particularly important mechanism to allow changes in competitiveness between countries, and a flexible and integrated capital market can provide the financial instruments that help consumers and firms stabilise their consumption following a shock. These issues are covered in detail in the assessment of the Five Economic Tests for EMU membership, and are discussed in Annex 7.1.

Microeconomic reform is also aimed at delivering a flexible labour market that has the ability to adjust to changing economic conditions in a way that maintains high employment, low inflation and unemployment, and continued growth in real incomes. An efficient and flexible labour market, that creates jobs, increases competitiveness, and raises productivity, is essential to the UK.

Building a fairer society

Economic strength must be underpinned by fairness and social inclusion, so that every individual has the chance to fulfil their potential, regardless of their circumstances. Since 1997, the Government has sought to reform the welfare state to ensure an equal chance for everyone to share in rising national prosperity.

The old welfare system was failing on many counts. It was passive and reactive, delivering poor-quality, fragmented services. Welfare benefits were seen as being mainly for the poor, and vulnerable groups, notably children and pensioners, were left behind as others benefited from rising living standards.

Although the world has changed greatly since Beveridge published his report in 1942, the principles which form the basis of the Government reforms to the welfare state remain those of:

- *opportunity* for people to improve their circumstances and those of their families;
- *responsibility* of everyone to make the most of opportunities, for example through employment.; and
- *security* to protect people from undue hardship that can arise from life events;

As described in the previous section, the Government's reforms to the tax and benefit system have been targeted at removing the barriers to individual advancement and providing people with the opportunity to reach their full potential. For those of working age, the National Minimum Wage, reforms to tax and NICs, and the Working Tax Credit have helped to reduce the high marginal deduction rates that people used to face when they moved into work or sought to increase their hours. For families with children, the Government has helped parents to balance their work and family lives with record increases in maternity pay, enhanced support for childcare and record levels of investment in childcare provision. For pensioners, the Government has brought forward proposals to simplify the tax system to provide individuals with greater choice and flexibility about how they save for retirement and introduced the new Pension Credit which will guarantee pensioners a minimum income while, for the first time, rewarding pensioners for having saved.

Enhanced levels of welfare support have been matched by an increase in the responsibilities of the claimant. For those of working age, all those capable of work are expected to actively seek and be available for work, and all benefit recipients operate within a work-focused system of advice and support. For pensioners, the Minimum Income Guarantee brings all pensioners income up to a guaranteed minimum entitlement, and those that contribute towards the National Insurance system over their working lives are entitled to the Basic State Pension and, in many cases, to the Second State Pension. Above this foundation the Government provides a framework of tax incentives, information to enable individuals to choose their preferred level of income in retirement and save accordingly over their working lives. To help individuals find the best way to save, the Government has provided a suite of simple, low-risk savings products such as the Child Trust Fund, Savings Gateway, Individual Savings Account and Stakeholder pension, which are tailored to each stage of a person's life cycle.

Underpinning this enabling framework has been a commitment to enhance the security and protection that the welfare state offers to the most vulnerable groups and reverse the legacy of child and pensioner poverty that the Government inherited in 1997. In its first five years, the Government used the full range of policy levers at its disposal to tackle child poverty including increased Child Benefit rates by 25% in real terms, the introduction of the Working Families Tax Credit, and an 80% increase in income support levels for children under 11. However, this support for families was provided through several different instruments and is administered by different parts of the government. From April 2003 all income-related support for children has been integrated into one credit – the Child Tax Credit. Similarly for pensioners, from October 2003, the new Pension Credit will incorporate the Minimum Income Guarantee into a single credit which guarantees an individual pensioner a minimum income of £102.10 per week for singles and £155.80 for couples while rewarding those with modest saving.

These reforms are more than just a technical improvement in the way the Government delivers benefits to families and pensioners. The Child and Working Tax Credits and Pension Credit represent a philosophical break with the old view of a welfare system designed to transfer resources from working taxpayers to long-term benefit recipients. In its place, these policies put into practice the principle of progressive universalism – support for all, and most support for those who need it most. This approach is built on the foundation of universal benefits such as Child Benefit and the Basic State Pension. However higher universal benefits on their own would not tackle the problems of poverty and inequality, unless they reached levels which were simply not affordable. On the other hand, restricting income-related help to narrow means-tested benefits for those out of work would undermine work incentives and fail to reflect the reality that everyone needs support from time to time.

Box 1.2 The role of taxation

The primary purpose of taxation is to raise revenue to be spent on the Government's priorities. The Government is committed to maintaining a modern and fair tax system which ensures that everyone pays their fair share while minimising the compliance burden on households and businesses. But the tax system can also play a wider role, for example, in tackling market failures, enhancing incentives and promoting fair outcomes. In some cases, such as certain environmental or transport taxes, their revenue yield may even be a secondary consideration, for example, in the case of the Climate Change Levy the revenue raised is recycled to business. As discussed in greater detail in the different sections of the book the tax system plays an important role in:

- *Promoting productivity and growth.* Alongside support for lifelong learning and direct funding of scientific research, the Government has used the tax system to capture the positive externalities that come from research and development through the R&D tax credit and to bolster entrepreneurship through Enterprise Management Incentives.
- *Protecting the environment.* Environmental taxes can help to address environmental market failures and are frequently used in conjunction with incentives and spending programmes which are themselves often financed with revenues recycled from the tax – as in the case of the climate change levy and landfill tax.
- *Tackling poverty and supporting families*, through tax-benefit integration. The system of child and working tax credits, together with reforms to the structure of income tax and NICs, has improved work incentives, increased support for families right up the income scale and provided a modern, responsive system of family support.
- *Encouraging people to save*, through the system of tax incentives for retirement and other forms of saving. Alongside better information and measures to extend working lives, the Government has brought forth proposals to simplify the system of pensions tax relief and introduced new, simpler tax-favoured savings products to strengthen the system of retirement provision.

Progressive universalism – by integrating the tax and benefit systems – enables the tax system to be far more dynamic and responsive to people's changing needs and circumstances over their life cycle, without forcing people onto stigmatising benefits. In this way, the tax system can reflect the reality that for most people, there will be times in their life when they simply pay tax to support services and contribute to the needs of the nation, and there will be other times when they will need to make a net withdrawal from the Exchequer. Instead of a narrow means-tested benefits system aimed at the poorest families, a tax credit system can support to the changing needs of a broad majority of families. This support and advice is delivered through high-quality, integrated, client-focused services, such as Jobcentre Plus and the Pension Service, tailored to people's circumstances.

Delivering high-quality public services

The Government has set a goal to deliver world-class public services through sustained increases in investment and matched by reform to ensure that taxpayers receive value for money. Strong and dependable public services extend opportunity, tackle poverty, ensure security and improve the quality of life for all. They also lay the foundations for a successful, high-productivity, economy.

The Government's approach to public service delivery starts with an understanding of the role of markets. As set out in Part 1, the Government is committed to advancing markets where they are in the public interest. A clear and robust defence of markets must be combined with a clear and robust recognition of their limits. Despite the benefits of the market in certain circumstances there are limitations to its effectiveness. For most consumer goods, markets adjust to preferences and thus demand and supply on a continuous basis. Where market failure does exist governments can intervene to ensure the price mechanism is working. But there are some situations where the market failures cannot be corrected through market enhancing government intervention. One example would be where there are externalities and clear social costs that cannot, even with the use of economic instruments, be fully captured by the price mechanism. Another would be where there are multiple distortions in the price and supply disciplines, or in the availability of proper information, and where the removal of one distortion to create a purer market may turn a second-best outcome into a third-best outcome. Examples of such market failures occur in the provision of health care and education.

In healthcare, for example, as the Chancellor observed in his speech to the Social Market Foundation (2003), the consumer is not sovereign: use of healthcare is unpredictable, information is asymmetric and can never be planned by the consumer in the way that, for example, weekly food consumption can.

Nobody can be sure whether they need medicinal treatment and if so when and what. Furthermore, the range of potential costs of necessary medical treatments can be enormous. In every society this uncertainty incentivises the pooling of risks as individuals, families and entire societies will seek to insure themselves against the eventuality of being ill. The question is then – on efficiency grounds – what is the best insurance system for sharing these risks?

In 2002 when the Government examined the funding of health care it concluded that, with uncertainty about risk, insurers often have poor information on which to base their risk assessment of the customer; that as a result of these uncertainties – and, with many citizens considered too high a risk, too expensive and therefore excluded – there are serious inefficiencies in private pricing and purchasing. As the Chancellor said in his Social Market Foundation speech, on efficiency and equity grounds private insurance policies that by definition rely for their viability on multiple exemptions or loopholes and can cover only some of the people some of the time should not be preferred against policies that can cover all of the people all of the time.

The Government also concluded, on efficiency as well as equity grounds, that the case for such a comprehensive national insurance policy was greater now than on its inception in 1948 when the scientific and technological limitations of medicine were such that high cost interventions were rare and thus health care, compared with now, relatively inexpensive.

The existence of multiple market failures also makes the case for a central role for the public sector in the provision of healthcare. In health: price signals don't always work; the consumer is not sovereign; there is potential abuse of monopoly power; it is hard to write and enforce contracts; it is difficult to let a hospital go bust; and we risk supplier induced demand. Consequently the provision of such goods by the market will lead to neither the most efficient nor the most equitable outcome, jeopardising the delivery of opportunity and security for all.

Command and control systems of public service management employed in the past had serious drawbacks; in particular they lacked devolution, transparency and accountability. Decentralised means of delivery can be more responsive to local needs and circumstances and can thus deliver a more efficient, equitable and customer-responsive outcome. This includes contestability between providers – including, where appropriate, the private sector – on the basis of cost and efficiency. The aim is to secure the most cost-effective basis for our public services, and, in certain circumstances the private sector in partnership with the public sector – a PPP – will provide the best method of doing this.

By matching the attainment of ambitious national standards with the promotion of local autonomy, the Government has sought to reform public service delivery to better promote both efficiency and equity. Its approach is based on the constrained discretion model – an approach to policy making that enhances credibility, and therefore the effectiveness of policy, by ensuring the objectives of policy are clear and the way in which those objectives are pursued is clear. The key principles for a framework of credible 'constrained discretion' are:

- clear and sound long-term policy objectives;
- pre-commitment, through institutional arrangements and procedural rules; and
- maximum openness and transparency and clear accountability.

At the macroeconomic level this concept was applied to monetary policy in giving independence to the Bank of England in 1997. The Bank is constrained by the Government's inflation target but is granted discretion to respond flexibly to changing economic conditions. At the microeconomic level, constrained discretion has been operationalised through the move away from centralised, top-down decision making in public services. This gives those at the point of delivery freedom and flexibility: first, to tailor services to reflect local needs and preferences; second, to develop innovative approaches to service delivery and raise standards; and third, to remove bureaucratic controls which hamper delivery. But maximising local freedom and discretion has to be consistent with equity. Local autonomy needs to be constrained by appropriate accountability mechanisms and defined service standards to ensure it does not lead to increased inequality between people and regions. The corollary to greater local autonomy is greater local democratic oversight and increased accountability.

So the approach to the provision of public services has been to move towards:

- devolution to regions, localities and communities;
- a focus on outcomes and results;

- long-term, usually three-year, allocations of funding based on thorough analysis of consumption and investment requirements;
- breaking down departmental boundaries to see how consumer needs can best be met; and
- national targets set in public service agreements within which local authorities, hospitals, departments and others have the incentive to innovate and the discretion to do so.

Conclusion

The relationship between individuals, markets and communities is constantly evolving as technology and rising expectations challenge each generation's vision of what is possible and best.

The principles that underlie the Government's approach to microeconomic reform are based upon recognition of the power of markets together with an understanding of their limits. The aim of microeconomic reform is to achieve the goals of a stronger economy and a fairer society by strengthening markets where they work in the public interest, to tackle market failures where they occur whilst recognising that there are some areas where markets are not appropriate and where market failure can only be dealt with through public funding or provision of key services. But when a market is inappropriate, policy design must set out how to avoid the trap of simply replacing market failure with state failure. A more decentralised systems that matches the attainment of ambitious national standards with the promotion of local autonomy can shape both efficiency and equity.

This book sets out the policy measures that have been taken to advance this agenda, together with the economic debate which has helped to promote those policies.

Part 1
Raising Productivity in the UK

2
The UK Productivity Gap and the Foundation for Government Policy

This chapter sets out the main determinants of economic growth and describes the historic productivity gap between the UK and other countries. It then explores the underlying reasons for this productivity gap and describes the Government's approach to reducing it. The chapter ends by setting out the 'five drivers' of productivity.

Introduction

The Government's central economic objective is to achieve high and stable levels of economic growth and employment. Productivity growth, alongside high and stable levels of employment, is an important determinant of long-term economic performance and rising living standards.

The UK has historically experienced low rates of productivity growth by international standards. Macroeconomic instability and microeconomic failures have inhibited competition, enterprise and innovation, and discouraged firms and individuals from undertaking long-term investment in human and capital resources. Against this backdrop, increasing the sustainable rate of UK productivity growth is central to the Government's economic strategy. As this chapter shows, the Government's strategy for achieving improved productivity is based on improving both the macroeconomic environment in which businesses and individuals operate, and on reducing market failure through targeted microeconomic policies. And there are early signs that the UK's performance has strengthened in recent years and that progress is being made towards improving our performance relative to our competitors.

Why worry about productivity?

Growth in the output of an economy is determined by two factors: the growth in the number of people who are working; and growth in the amount they each produce, that is, in how productive they are. Box 2.1 below sets out the various measures of productivity.

Box 2.1 What is productivity?

Productivity is a measure of how effectively the economy uses resources to generate economic outputs. Productivity is therefore measured in terms of the relationship between inputs and outputs. There are several measures of this relationship. Their main characteristics, as well as the differences between them, are set out below.

Labour productivity measures look at the output produced per unit of labour input. The most common indicators are output per worker and output per hour worked. *Output per worker* has the advantage of being easy to calculate because the data on total output and employment are readily available. It can also be related directly to total output growth, which is equal to growth in output per worker multiplied by the growth in employment. *Output per hour*, on the other hand, measures the productivity of an hour of labour input. Its main advantage is that it is not influenced by the number of hours worked over a given period, and consequently takes account of part-time work and time not spent working.

Both output per hour and output per worker relate to only one factor of production: labour. But there are others factors in the production process. Productivity can increase, for example, if capital is substituted for labour, as happens when robots are used in assembly lines or when automatic teller machines are installed. Since capital is an important input into the economy, there are measures which attempt to capture its effects.

Total factor productivity (TFP) attempts to measure the output produced from a unit of combined inputs, where the inputs are generally defined as labour and capital. TFP measures the efficiency with which capital and labour can be used to produce output.

Despite its strengths, using TFP to measure productivity has a number of disadvantages. First, given the way it is calculated, it can be argued that TFP is just a measure of residuals, since it captures what is left over after accounting for the contribution of labour and capital inputs to the production process. Secondly, and very important for practical reasons, using TFP requires us to have accurate measures of capital stock, for which the data are sometimes insufficient or unreliable. For this reason, TFP is not always the most appropriate measure of productivity to use.

All of these productivity measures have advantages and disadvantages, and give different insights into the nature of productivity. The Government uses output per worker as the central measure for assessing the productivity gap.

The UK's record on the first of these measures, employment growth,[1] has been impressive over recent years. UK labour market performance now compares favourably with previous periods, and is strong by international standards. Employment growth has averaged 1.1per cent per annum in 1997–2002; in the third quarter of 2002, the UK employment rate for working age adults was 74.5 per cent.

As a result of this growth in employment, the UK unemployment rate[2] stood at only 4.9 per cent in autumn 2003, close to its lowest rates since the 1970s and the lowest in the G7 for the first time since the 1950s. In total, nearly 1.7 million extra people were in work in autumn 2003 than in spring 1997. Although there is more to be done to make the goal of employment opportunity for all a reality, all UK regions have an employment rate significantly higher than the EU average, with the UK's employment rate the highest of the G7 industrialised nations.

The productivity of the UK's economy has historically lagged behind those of other economies, and are lower than those of the US, France, and Germany. In the post-war years, countries such as France and Germany experienced higher levels of labour productivity growth than the UK. Although labour productivity *growth* in the UK has often been faster than in the US – with the exception of recent years when US productivity growth has accelerated – the US has generally managed to maintain a higher *level* of labour productivity than the UK. Figure 2.1 shows the UK's productivity gap with the US from 1991- 2001.

The Government's central measure of productivity is output per worker, a measure that is both relatively straightforward to quantify and directly related to the objective of raising the economy's trend rate of growth. The scale of the gap between the UK's productivity and its competitors' productivity can be seen in comparisons using output per worker: in 2002, output per worker in the US – the world's most productive economy – was 31 per cent higher than in the UK. Output per worker in France was 14 per cent higher than in the UK and in Germany it was 5 per cent higher.

In order to be meaningful, however, international comparisons of productivity should be made over the longer term to ensure that the effects of the economic cycle do not distort comparisons between countries and because interventions at national level to improve productivity typically take some time to have an influence. Figure 2.2 shows that since 1990, the gap in productivity levels between the UK and France has narrowed significantly while the gap between the UK and Japan has closed completely. This pattern is not, however, repeated in comparisons with

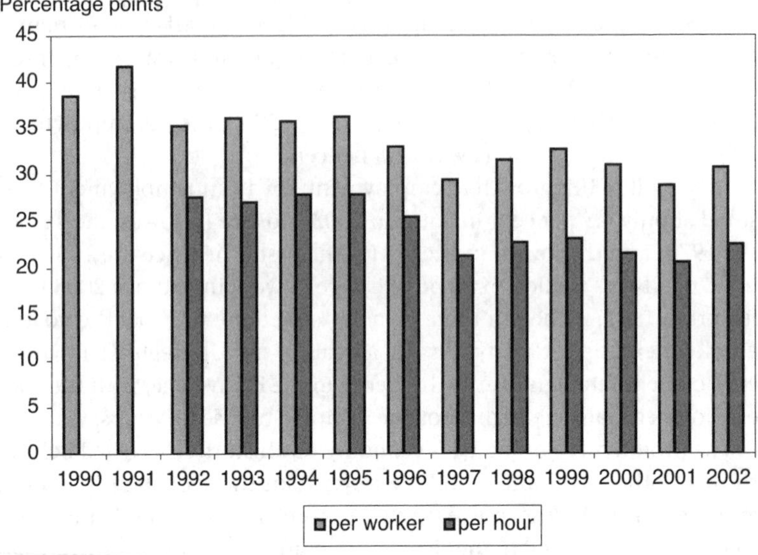

Source: ONS/HMT

Figure 2.1 Productivity gap with the US, 1991–2001

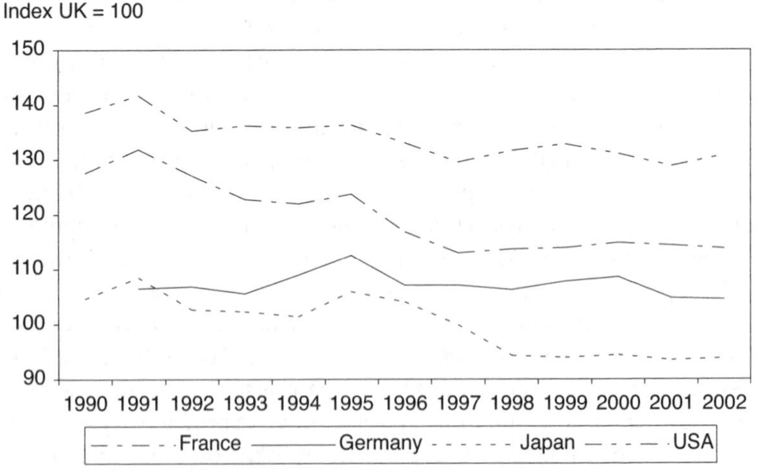

Source: ONS/HMT

Figure 2.2 Output per worker, 1990–2001

the US or German economies. In particular, the productivity gap with the US has widened in recent years.

The relative performance of different countries can vary depending on which measure of labour productivity is used, because those employed in the US and the UK tend to work more hours than in the Continental European countries. Nonetheless, comparisons of output per hour worked also show a significant gap between the UK and other major economies. In 2002, the US registered 26.3 per cent higher productivity per hour worked than the UK; France registered 25.2 per cent; while the gap with Germany was 24.6 per cent.[3] This is shown in Figure 2.3.

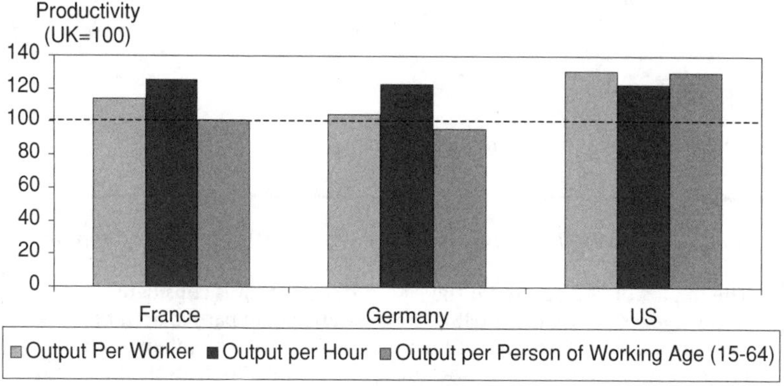

Source: Output per worker and output per hour (experimental) measures based on OECD/ONS data. Output per person of working age: HMT estimate based on ONS data.

Figure 2.3 International comparisons of productivity, 2002

Figure 2.4 shows the productivity gap for the UK expressed in terms of total factor productivity. The gap between the UK and its competitors is smaller (and negligible for France and Germany) for TFP than for other measures. This is explained by the UK's relatively low capital stock.

Closing the productivity gap by achieving a faster rise in productivity than in other countries is a long-term challenge. The growth in output per worker has varied in recent years. In 2000, it averaged 1.6 per cent across sectors. The latest figures show productivity growing at an annual rate of 2.1 per cent, its highest rate of growth since the second quarter of 1998. Furthermore, following recent methodological improvements, detailed in Chapter 3, most recent estimates of productivity growth in terms of output per hour suggest that recent performance has been better than previously thought. These most recent estimates indicate that pro-

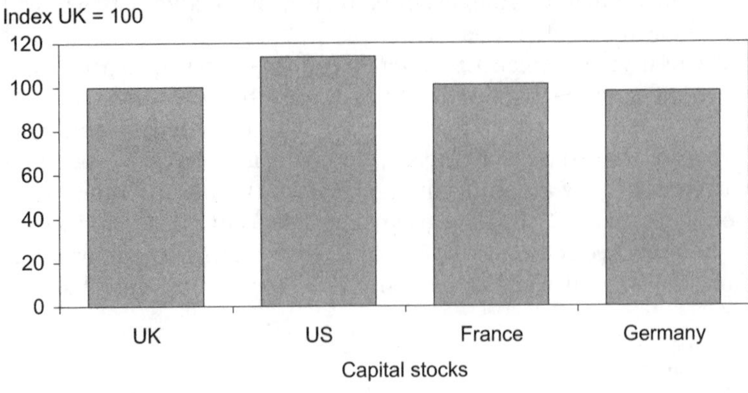

Source: NIESR (O'Mahony 2002).

Figure 2.4 The total factor productivity gap (1999)

Box 2.2 The impact of possible UK entry to EMU on UK productivity

The impact of EMU entry on the UK's productivity was considered as part of the five tests assessment (HMT Treasury 2003a), in particular in the fifth test on growth, stability and employment. EMU membership could enhance productivity over the medium term by increasing trade and investment and by stimulating competition. EMU entry could also boost productivity by encouraging specialisation, as highlighted in the EMU study *EMU and business sectors*. Trade is a key way of exploiting gains from specialisation in terms of comparative advantage, which shifts the allocation of resources from less to more productive sectors or enterprises, and economies of scale, raising the productivity and living standards of trading partners. The EMU study *EMU and trade* found that the UK's trade with the euro area could increase between 5 to 50 per cent. An increase in trade at the top end of this range could result in UK output being around 9 per cent higher over 30 years within EMU. These gains are conditional on the achievement of sustainable and durable convergence between the UK and the euro area.

Competition is important to assessing how EMU membership could affect UK productivity in the longer term, since competition increases the incentive for firms to innovate and helps to shift the allocation of resources from less to more productive enterprises. The EMU studies *Prices and EMU* and *EMU and business sectors* examine how EMU membership could affect competitive pressures. Competitive pressures across a large single market have contributed to higher productivity levels in the US as discussed further in the EMU study *The United States as a monetary union*. (For further details on the five tests and accompanying studies, see Annex 7.1)

ductivity growth between 1997 and 2001 was 2.44 per cent in terms of total output per hour. This compares to previous estimates of 2.14 per cent and represents a substantial increase from the figure over the last economic cycle (1986 to 1997), which was 2.05 per cent.

Finally, should the UK decide to enter EMU then such a move could potentially have an impact on UK productivity and the productivity gap as Box 2.2 describes.

Understanding the productivity gap at the national level

The factors affecting the productivity gap between the UK and its competitors fall into three categories:

- physical capital;
- human capital; and
- innovation and technological progress

Physical capital

Growth in an economy relies heavily on investment in physical capital to augment the productivity of labour.[4] In the past, the capital stock of

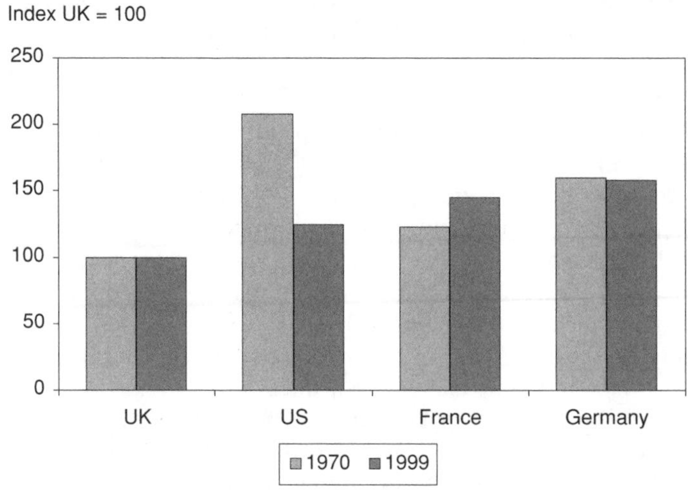

Note: relative capital intensity is measured as capital per hour worked.

Source: NIESR (O'Mahony and De Boer, 2001).

Figure 2.5 Relative capital intensity, 1970 and 1999

firms and the stock of public infrastructure in the UK have been well below those of its main competitors. This shortfall has been a major part of the explanation of the UK's relatively poor labour productivity, and reflects years of low investment in both the public and the private sectors.

Figure 2.5 sets out the ratio of capital to labour in the UK in 1970 and 1999, relative to that of the US, France, and Germany[5]. The UK's weak position on capital per hour worked is a long-standing one. In 1970, the UK had lower capital per hour worked than each of the other comparator countries and in 1999 its position remained unchanged. The US, in 1999, had 25 per cent more capital stock per worker than the UK, France has 40 per cent more, and Germany 60 per cent more.

Recently, however, greater certainty that the macroeconomic environment will remain stable has helped foster a positive climate for investment in physical capital. Although direct measures of the cost of capital are not available,[6] yields on UK Government bonds – a useful indicator – have fallen sharply since 1997, and the differential with, for example, Germany has significantly narrowed. In the 2002 Spending Review, the Government also announced plans to increase total UK investment in public services to over £46 billion by 2005–06, compared with £23 billion in 1997–98.

Although there is still a long way to go, further investment in the economy is likely to promote productivity growth and build on the early signs of improvement in the UK's productivity growth rate.

Human capital

The contribution of labour to growth depends on both its quantity and its quality. Increasing the proportion of the population that is working is key to increasing economic growth and prosperity. So too is increasing the skills of the workforce, since a skilled workforce is likely to be more productive than a less skilled one, and so itself be a source of growth.[7] Furthermore, high levels of human capital make both economies and firms better able to assimilate new ideas.[8]

Figure 2.6 sets out estimates of the respective direct contributions of increased labour quantity and labour quality to economic growth in different countries between 1986 and 1998[9]. It shows that, in the UK and France, changes in labour quality may be as important as changes in quantity in explaining recent growth performance.

Figure 2.7 compares the labour quality of the UK workforce with that of the US and Germany[10] according to whether they have higher skills (a university-level degree or above) or intermediate skills (a vocational qualification above high-school level but below degree level).[11] The

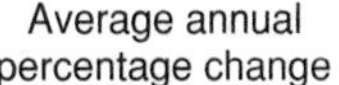

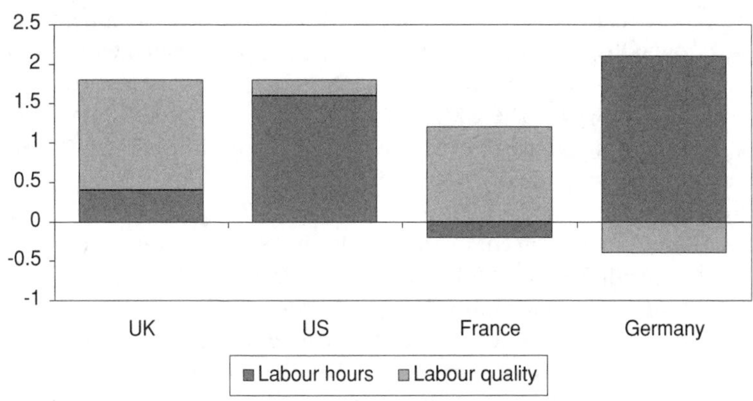

Source: HM Treasury (2001a)

Figure 2.6 Changes in labour input by hours and quality, 1986–1998

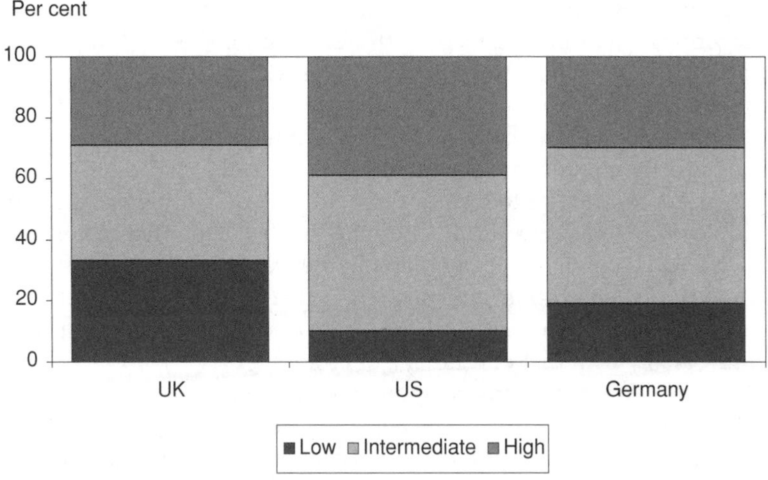

Note: International comparisons of workforce skills are complicated by the difficulty of establishing equivalences between countries with widely different education systems. The data used here is drawn from OECD (2001) which, unlike previous studies, compares both work-related and academic based qualifications across countries.

Source: OECD (2001).

Figure 2.7 Employees by skill level

evidence suggests that the UK suffers from significant skills shortages, especially at the intermediate and higher skills levels. As Figure 2.7 shows, Germany has far more workers with intermediate skills, and fewer with low skills, than the UK. On the other hand compared with the US, the UK lacks highly skilled workers.

Overall, however, the UK's education and training performance has shown some encouraging signs in recent decades, with skills levels across the population gradually improving. The proportion of young people entering the workforce with the equivalent of 5 GCSEs at A*-C grades has risen from 24 per cent of 16 year olds in 1979 to 52 per cent in 2003. Between April 2001 and July 2002, over 300,000 adults improved their literacy and numeracy skills. The proportion of 11-year-olds achieving the standard expected for their age increased by 12 per cent in English and 11 per cent in Maths between 1997 and 2003; and in 2000 around 43 per cent of the UK's 18–21 year-olds went into higher education. The UK now has the highest first-degree graduation rate in the EU.

Innovation and technical progress

Innovation and technical progress are important factors in determining economic growth.[12] Productivity growth relies on a continual stream of inventions and innovations of both new technologies and improved working practices. New ways of working provide a source of efficiency gains, enabling workers to operate more effectively and providing firms with greater opportunities to use labour and capital inputs in ways which maximise their productive potential.

A major contributor to technical progress is expenditure on research and development. Historically, the share of GDP dedicated to R&D in the UK was only slightly lower than in other countries. Over the 1990s, however, this proportion generally fell, increasing slightly towards the end of the 1990s. As a result, in 1999 R&D spending in the UK compared unfavourably with that of other major economies.

The dissemination of Information and Communications Technology (ICT) is also likely to have a considerable, although as yet not totally quantifiable, impact on productivity. There is evidence to suggest that the recent increases in labour productivity in the US have been partly caused by increased business investment rates, focused especially on ICT-related capital, and most notably the Internet and e-commerce. In the UK, in comparison, computing equipment makes up a relatively small share of the overall capital stock. Nevertheless, that share has been growing by over 33 per cent a year over the period 1996–98, almost double the growth rate experienced in the UK 1991–95.

Accounting for productivity differences at national level

A good deal of research has focused on which of the key factors – physical capital, human capital, innovation and technological progress – account for countries' different growth performances. The basic approach that has been used is known as 'growth accounting'.

Table 2.1, based on work by O'Mahony and De Boer, divides the labour productivity gap[13] with the US and Germany, into the components of physical capital and TFP.[14] It shows that physical capital accounts for a sizeable element of the productivity gap between the UK and Germany. The UK's productivity gap with the US, in contrast, is explained primarily by differences in TFP.

Table 2.1 Decomposition of the productivity* gap, 1999 (per cent)

		US	Germany
Physical capital		31	55
TFP		69	45
Of which:	*innovation*	65	17
	skills	0	14
	other	4	14
Total productivity gap		100	100

* Labour productivity measured as output per hour worked.

Source: Crafts and O'Mahony (2000)

It is possible to use growth accounting methods to break down TFP further into elements such as human capital and technological progress. Although there are methodological difficulties associated with creating such breakdowns, the disaggregation of TFP by economists is instructive. Crafts and O'Mahony's research indicates that different factors account for the UK's TFP gap with different countries. Skills, for example, seem to be more significant in explaining the gap with Germany, while innovation – proxied by R&D expenditure – appears very significant in accounting for the UK's productivity gap with the US.

At national level, it therefore appears that certain conclusions can be drawn about productivity in the UK:

- macroeconomic stability has contributed to an increase in business investment in the UK,[15] but despite this the physical capital stock per hour worked in the UK remains considerably below that in all its major competitors;

- the UK's human capital stock is deficient in comparison with the US in terms of the numbers of workers with higher skills, and in comparison with Germany in terms of intermediate and vocational skills; and
- the rate of technological progress in the UK could also be improved.

Variations in productivity between firms

Firm and plant-level analysis[16] reveals that there is a wide distribution of productivity among UK firms, with a long tail of firms in each sector in the UK that are substantially less productive than UK leaders.[17] For example, research shows that the most productive manufacturing plants, in terms of output per worker, are five and a half times as productive as the least productive plants.[18] In the service sector, there is evidence of even wider productivity dispersion, as much as double that in manufacturing.[19]

If under-performing firms were to be more successful at adopting established best-practice techniques from the leaders in their sector, potential productivity gains in the UK economy could be very large. Haskel and Martin (2002) estimate that overall manufacturing productivity could be increased by between 8 per cent and 10 per cent by raising poor performers to the median productivity level in their industries. Since variation in the service sector is larger, the gains in the service sector of getting to best practice might be larger than those in manufacturing.

An examination of the performance of firms over time reveals a more complex picture. Some firms improve their performance, others fall behind, and a large number of firms enter and leave the market. However, the evidence shows that the productivity performance of firms that survive is relatively consistent over time. The most productive firms in each sector tend to remain productivity leaders, while the least productive usually only catch up slowly and frequently remain relatively unproductive.[20] Low productivity firms also have relatively high probabilities of exit.

Factors driving productivity growth at the level of the firm

At the firm level, there are two forces that account for productivity differences between firms: differences in the inputs used by firms – including physical capital, human capital, managerial and entrepreneurial ability, and technology; and differences in the competitive environment firms face.

(i) Physical capital

Empirical studies have found a high correlation between firms' physical capital intensity and productivity. A study by Oulton (2000) shows that UK firms with foreign owners typically operate with 50 per cent more capital per worker than comparable UK firms, and suggests that in most areas of manufacturing this explains their greater labour productivity. In the service sector, variations in capital intensity explain a significant amount of the productivity gap between foreign-owned and domestically-owned firms.

(ii) Human capital

A second key determinant of labour productivity in firms is human capital. Human capital includes workers' education, skills, and training, which can be acquired both on and off the job. The skill level of a firm's workforce has a large positive impact on the labour productivity of the firm. More productive plants in an industry have a higher proportion of skilled workers than less productive plants. Indeed, the top 20 per cent of businesses in the UK have on average 4.4 times higher labour productivity than those in the bottom 20 per cent, and between 30 per cent and 70 per cent higher levels of human capital.[21] In both services and manufacturing, the evidence shows that growing firms, innovators,[22] and larger firms spend more on training than stable or declining firms, non-innovators, and smaller firms.

A lack of entrepreneurial and managerial ability is also likely to be a particular constraint on the ability of firms to grow and improve their productivity performance.[23] A series of studies has found that the degree of managerial experience in new firms is positively associated with their growth rates.[24] There is also evidence to suggest that changes of ownership can promote productivity growth, with firms experiencing above-average productivity growth for several years after their ownership changes.[25] Furthermore, it has been found that the productivity of a plant is positively related to the productivity of the firm to which it belongs, in both its level and its growth rate.[26] This suggests that firms are frequently able to transfer key knowledge and skills to their individual plants and facilitate the introduction of new technology and best-practice techniques through effective management.

Together, differences in physical capital and human capital – including management and entrepreneurialism – explain around 60 per cent of the productivity gap between domestically owned firms and US-owned firms. They explain nearly all of the gap with other foreign-owned firms.[27]

(iii) Innovation and technological progress

The third critical input into production is technology, which includes innovations in best-practice techniques. Spending on Research & Development (R&D) is associated with a high rate of productivity growth and innovation.[28] The evidence from small to medium-sized enterprises in the UK shows that there are substantial variations in spending on R&D between firms,[29] with medium-sized and manufacturing firms more frequently engaging in R&D than smaller firms and those in the service sector.

The three inputs that firms use – physical capital, human capital, and technology – cannot be considered in isolation. There are strong complementarities between them, and for firms to maximise their productive potential they need to invest in them all. For example, firms' ability to implement innovations and employ best-practice techniques is dependent on the ability of their workers to understand new technologies and transfer their knowledge into improved working practices. Research finds strong complementarities at firm level between workforce skills and the rate at which firms adopt new technologies.[30] Similarly, technological progress is frequently embodied in a firm's capital stock, so investment in physical capital is an important contributor to the dissemination of new technologies.[31]

Furthermore, innovative activity at firm level tends to persist over time. Firms that have been successful innovators in the past can build on their success and increasingly outperform their competitors.[32] This suggests that investment in R&D, combined with investment in physical and human capital, not only improves firms' current productivity performance, but also creates a platform from which they build future success.

(iv) The competitive environment

In addition to the inputs used by firms, competition plays a central role in driving firms' productivity growth. It encourages them to innovate by reducing slack, putting downward pressure on costs, and providing incentives for the efficient organisation of production. Competition also drives the reallocation of resources away from inefficient firms to more productive competitors and new entrants. Research shows that competitive pressure in a sector has an impact on firm efficiency and productivity growth rates. For example, firms that have growing market shares and supernormal profits – both indicators of market power – achieve lower future productivity growth.[33]

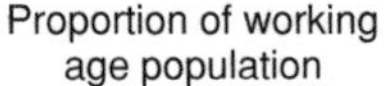

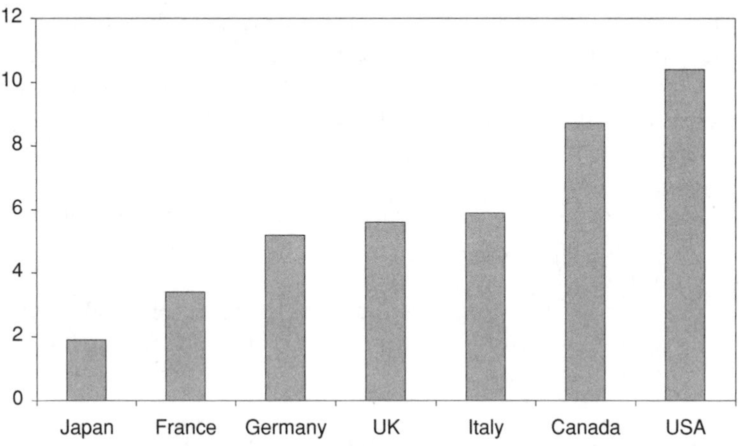

Source: HM Treasury (2002a)

Figure 2.8 The 'enterprise gap' in 2002: the proportion of the working-age population who are involved in starting or growing a new firm (under 42 months old)

Competition is affected by a number of factors. Entrepreneurialism is a key source of competitive pressure. The numbers of people starting a business in a country and the rate at which individuals invest in start-up companies that they do not own are highly correlated with growth.[34] The number of new entrants in a market, and the threat of new entry, can stimulate innovation.[35] Figure 2.8 shows the rate of involvement in starting or growing a new firm in the UK and other competitive countries. In the UK, the formation of new firms; the closure of less productive rivals; and the transfer of resources between existing plants and firms, have accounted for around half of labour productivity growth and as much as 90 per cent of total factor productivity growth over a 12-year period.[36] It is therefore significant that, although levels of entrepreneurship in the UK are close to the EU average, the US has business start-up rates which are nearly twice as high.[37]

Market failure and its impact on productivity

The analysis so far has indicated that all participants in the economy – businesses, workers, investors and others – have a role to play in raising productivity. The Government's strategy is to provide the best environment for participants to maximise their productive potential by allowing effective and efficient markets to operate. Where markets work well, they are a powerful means of advancing productivity growth efficiently and equitably. This point is illustrated by considering the potential productivity benefits of effective and efficient product, capital and labour markets. Effectively functioning product markets create:

- competitive pressures that increase the economy's output by keeping prices down;
- ensuring that firms innovate; and
- ensuring that firms minimise their costs of production by combining factor inputs in the form of labour and capital in the most efficient way.

Similarly, well-functioning capital markets ensure that firms have adequate access to the capital they need to operate efficiently and to grow. Individuals also need access to finance to invest in their own human capital. Efficient capital markets therefore promote economic growth in four ways. They:

- ensure that firms are able to finance potentially viable investments;
- provide funds for firms to innovate;
- enable shareholders to place incentives on firms to maximise the efficiency of their operations; and
- allow people to maximise their productive potential by borrowing against their future earnings to pay for the acquisition of skills and training.

Effective labour markets not only tackle the underlying causes of deprivation and inequality, but also generate growth by:

- allowing employment to rise to meet the demands of a growing economy for increased output;
- ensuring the economy is able to adjust rapidly to take advantage of new growth opportunities; and
- rewarding workers according to their performance and skills.

But it is also important to recognise that markets have imperfections and failures. Where these occur, there can be a negative effect on the economy and productivity growth, to the detriment of society.

Market failures can be classed into four generic categories as follows:

1. Externalities:

One type of market failure occurs when actions by a firm or individual create benefits or costs that do not accrue entirely to that firm or individual. In these cases, the overall benefit or cost of the market activity diverges from the benefit or cost borne by the firm or individual undertaking the activity. The activity produces a 'spill over', which can be good or bad. A classic example of a negative spill over would be the pollution caused by production, the costs of which are not borne by the producer responsible for it. (See Chapter 6 for further discussion of environmental externalities.) A positive spill over, on the other hand, could result from a company investing in training its employees, who could later take their skills elsewhere for the wider benefit of the economy. These spill over effects are known as 'externalities'.

Externalities can reduce the incentives to act in ways that might improve productivity. For example:

- Research and development often generates knowledge that is difficult to appropriate, such that the benefits of one firm's R&D activity might be shared free by other firms. This may discourage R&D activity (see Box 2.3).
- Training produces skills that are transferable – a firm that invests in an employee's training will not reap the rewards of that investment if the employee moves jobs. This could act as a disincentive to invest in training and raising skills levels.
- Firms or individuals can free ride on other firms' or individuals' investment in public goods; for example, infrastructure such as transport can often be freely used by all firms and individuals. This encourages each firm to wait for someone else to invest, and so if the market is left entirely to itself the outcome might be insufficient investment in transport.

2. Market Power:

Market failures also occur where firms are in a position of market power as a result of a lack of entry into the market by other firms or by an inability of consumers to substitute one product for another. This can restrict competition. Restricted competition can limit productivity growth by reducing firms' incentives to use existing assets efficiently and to innovate.

Box 2.3 An example of private and social returns diverging: R&D

Private and social returns to R&D can deviate from each other because of market imperfections such as spill over effects. R&D creates new knowledge. It is an investment from which other firms can benefit, and the returns may not be fully appropriated by the firm making the investment. This means that social returns to R&D often exceed private returns and that, as a result, individual companies are likely to invest less than might be optimal from the point of view of the economy as a whole.

Seminal work in this area was carried out in the US by Zvi Griliches,[38] who concluded that social returns to R&D were in the order of 40% and about one and a half times the private return. It has been argued that these estimates may understate the social returns to R&D[39] for a number of reasons. For example, they ignore the fact that R&D yields further benefits to the economy by generating new growth opportunities[40] – a point underlined by the models of endogenous growth.

This evidence bears out the claim that there are market imperfections such that the market left to its own devices would under-invest in R&D.

3. Lack of information:

Lack of information can reduce the efficient functioning of markets. For example, if workers are not fully aware of the benefits they will gain from training, they might under-invest in their training. This could have a long run effect on their productivity.

4. Poor regulation

Effective and well-focused regulation can play a vital role in correcting market failures, promoting fairness and ensuring public safety. However, unnecessary or poorly implemented regulation can be an obstacle to flexibility, restricting competitiveness and employment growth, stifling innovation and deterring investment.

The framework for government policy

Where there are market failures which impact the UK's rates of investment in physical capital, human capital, technological innovation and competition, government can improve productivity through a framework of appropriate targeted policies.

As noted earlier, there are two strands to the approach:

- to provide a stable *macroeconomic environment* within which firms can make critical long-term decisions with greater certainty and, consequently, at lower cost; and

- to make markets work through a series of carefully directed and designed *microeconomic reforms.*

Macroeconomic stability

Macroeconomic stability remains a cornerstone of the Government's economic policy and is key to ensuring that firms have the right incentives to invest in their productivity. Full details of the policy are set out in the companion volume to this book, *Reforming Britain's Economic and Financial Policy: Towards Greater Economic Stability* (Balls and O'Donnell 2002).

Macroeconomic stability is critical for individuals and firms to plan, save, and invest, making it pivotal in improving productivity. The high volatility of inflation and output in the UK over the last 30 years held back economic growth in the UK. A broad consensus now exists that macroeconomic stability is essential for maximising long-term economic growth.[41] Past policies may have facilitated short-term growth, but did so by sacrificing long-term stability and creating an inflationary and uncertain environment, which deterred firms and individuals from investing in the future.[42]

Since 1997 the Government has introduced a new framework for the operation of macroeconomic policy. Monetary and fiscal policy are now highly transparent, based on clear rules and targets, and underpinned by legislation. As the Chancellor of the Exchequer has set out, this acts as a discipline on policy-makers, preventing them from setting macroeconomic policy on the basis of short-term political considerations.[43] As a result, a platform of economic stability has been created upon which the economy can grow.[44]

Microeconomic reforms

In addition to securing macroeconomic stability, there is a need to intervene at the microeconomic level to improve the UK's productivity and build on the secure macroeconomic environment.

The approach, as discussed in *Productivity in the UK* (HM Treasury 2000c), focuses on five priority areas which are of particular importance in determining firms' and the economy's productivity and which follow from the analysis presented earlier. They are referred to as the *five drivers of productivity growth*, and are as follows:

1. *Investment* in physical capital – which raises labour productivity directly by providing the equipment and infrastructure with which

workers operate. It also contributes to raising productivity by facilitating the introduction of new technology.
2. *Improving skills and human capital* – human capital directly increases productivity by raising the productive potential of employees. The evidence shows that firms with highly skilled employees and experienced managers invest more in physical capital and are better at introducing new technologies and innovative work practices.
3. *Science and innovation* – innovation and technological progress through R&D and investment in human and physical capital have strong positive impacts on the rate at which technological and best-practice techniques are adopted.
4. *Competition* – competition reduces slack and makes a continuous stream of innovations a critical ingredient to business success. It provides strong incentives for firms to adopt best-practice techniques and engage in innovative activity, and hence increases productivity.
5. *Enterprise* – enterprise creates competitive pressure because entrepreneurs who start up new firms introduce innovative practices and new technology and challenge incumbents' performance.

Government policy is based on strengthening these key drivers in order to improve Britain's productivity performance. The specific policies are examined in Chapter 4.

Conclusion

This chapter has shown that productivity is an important determinant of overall economic growth. Historically, the UK has had a productivity gap with its major competitors but there are early signs that the UK's performance is improving.

The productivity gap has been explained with reference to a combination of factors, including the limited physical capital stock in the UK; weaknesses in the UK's skills base compared with competitors. Historically the UK has had a productivity gap with its major competitors, but there are early signs that the UK's performance is improving.

At a national level, these differences can be accounted for by the differences in the inputs firms use (physical capital, human capital and technology) and the differences in the competitive environment firms face.

The analysis suggests that the Government can improve productivity through a framework of appropriately targeted policies on both a macroeconomic and a microeconomic level. Microeconomic reforms are based on improving firms' access to inputs of production to raise their productivity and in creating a competitive environment in which they are encouraged to do so. These reforms are aimed at strengthening the five drivers of productivity: investment in physical capital; improving skills and human capital; science and innovation; competition; and enterprise. Demonstrable progress has, however, been made towards improving these key drivers. For example, the creation of a stable macroeconomic environment to better promote enterprise and the significant improvement of the UK's competition regime. It is now considered one of the world's best according to the 2003 Global Competition Review. Policies aimed at further improving these key drives form the basis of the discussion in Chapter 4.

3
Trend Growth

This chapter provides an explanation of overall economic performance which illustrates why microeconomic reforms have concentrated to a large extent on improving productivity and the labour market. It sets out the basic concepts related to trend output growth and its applications in economic analysis and policy-making, explains how trend growth is defined and estimated using different methods, and gives an analysis of the decomposition of trend growth and projection of its components.

Introduction

The rate of trend (or potential) growth is the rate at which the output of the economy can grow, on a sustained basis, without putting upward or downward pressure on inflation. Many factors influence the observed rate of economic growth. Some, such as changes in confidence, demand conditions in the UK's trading partners, and the stance of monetary and fiscal policy, have temporary effects on economic growth. Other factors, such as the growth of productivity and the rate of growth and structure of the population, have permanent effects. This chapter focuses on the latter.

This chapter begins by setting out the basic concepts related to trend output growth and its applications in economic analysis and policy-making. It then explains how trend growth is defined and estimated using a range of methods. The final section explains the importance of labour productivity growth in the medium to long term and gives an analysis of the decomposition of trend growth and projection of its components. The chapter is intended to show why improving productivity and the labour market is crucial to overall performance and thus why the microeconomic reform agenda has concentrated on these areas.[1]

Analytical underpinnings of trend growth

The output path that the economy can sustain over the medium term without generating upward or downward pressures on inflation is commonly referred to as the economy's trend (or potential) output path. Thus the economy's potential or trend growth rate is the rate it can sustain, starting on trend, with inflation remaining stable. Over the short to medium term, the actual level of output tends to cycle around the trend level of output. This is called an economic (or business) cycle.

Figure 3.1 shows the different stages of an economic cycle. The cycle in the graph starts at point **A**; actual output is above its trend level during the time period from point A to point B (half-cycle), thus placing upward pressure on inflation during this period. The second half of the cycle starts at point **B** and continues until point **C**, which is the end of the whole cycle. During the period from point B to C, in which actual output is below its trend level, there is downward pressure on inflation. The growth rate of output over the intervals A to X and Y to C exceeds the trend rate, and over the interval X to Y the actual growth rate is below the trend rate. Figure 3.1, of course, is stylised. In practice, cycles will tend to be less smooth and less symmetric.

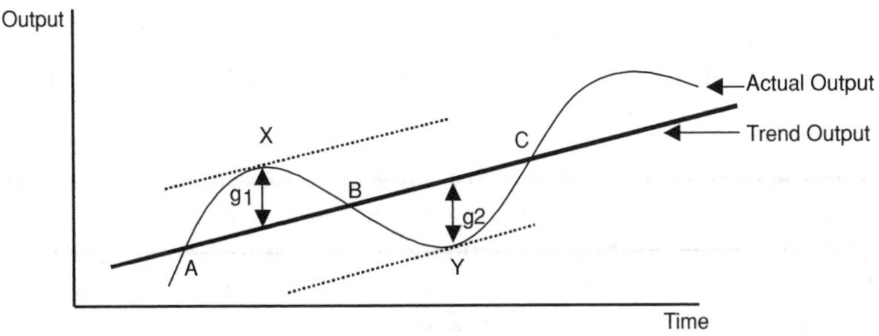

Figure 3.1 Economic (Business) Cycle

The importance of estimating trend growth

Measures of trend output and trend growth play a key role in setting macroeconomic policy both in the short term and in the medium term.

For example, in the short term, the Bank of England's Monetary Policy Committee needs an assessment of the economy's sustainable productive capacity when deciding what level of interest rates is necessary to meet the Government's inflation target.

In assessing the outlook for inflation, policy-makers often compare the current and forecast levels of output with an estimate of the trend path of output. If actual output is greater than trend output (the period from point A to B in Figure 3.1), a positive output gap is said to exist (g1). In these circumstances, competition for increasingly scarce resources is likely to place upward pressure on inflation. If actual output is less than trend output (the period from point B to C), there is a negative output gap (g2). The greater availability of unutilised resources helps to put downward pressure on inflation. When the actual level of output is equal (or close) to trend (at points A, B and C), domestically generated inflation should be broadly stable.

A similar assessment is required in the fiscal policy context. Reliable estimates of the trend output, trend growth and the output gap play an important role in the conduct of fiscal policy, and they are necessary primarily to:

- ensure that the public finances are placed on a sound and sustainable footing by taking account of, and abstracting from, the temporary impact of the economic cycle and by providing a robust assessment of the structural, or underlying, prospects for the public finances in the medium term; and
- provide an estimate of the spare capacity in the economy so that fiscal policy can play a role in supporting monetary policy over the economic cycle.

From the medium-term perspective, these measures can be used to make an assessment of the underlying or structural position of the public finances, i.e. the position of the public finances if the economy was on its trend growth path. This abstracts from cyclical influences. Because revenue and spending are highly sensitive to the level of actual output, short-term cyclical factors can mask the sustainability of the public finances, causing them to appear superficially healthier (weaker) when the economy is operating above (below) trend than they really are.[2]

A good example of this is the misinterpretation of the economic situation and health of the public finances at the end of the 1980s. With the economy at the peak of the cycle and the public finances in surplus[3] over the 1987–89 period, projections of future revenues and expenditure, and hence of the underlying state of the public finances, were over-optimistic because they failed to recognise the degree to which the economy was over-heating and the consequent cyclical boost to the public finances. Most of the improvement in economic conditions was seen wrongly as a structural, rather than cyclical, change in the performance of the economy. The underlying trend rate of growth which the economy could sustain without rising inflation was over-estimated and the output gap was implicitly thought at the time to be negative, implying spare capacity in the economy. Indeed Nelson and Nikolov (2001) have estimated that views in 1988–89 equated with an output gap approaching –4 per cent. However, the output gap was actually in excess of 4 per cent with the economy overheating. At least in part, this reflected over-optimism about the impact of supply-side reforms throughout the decade coupled with the observed fact that the output was growing rapidly without rising inflation. However, it is possible for growth to exceed its trend rate in the early upswing phase of the economic cycle without an immediate increase in inflation.

These over-optimistic assumptions on the state of the economy and the public finances, as well as on the future economic prospects, led to inappropriate macroeconomic policies. Fiscal policy was loosened with tax cuts totalling £9.5 billion in the 1988 and 1989 budgets. The relaxation of fiscal policy contributed to the dramatic deterioration in the public finances in the following years as the cycle unwound, with the fiscal deficit on current budget reaching 6.2 per cent of GDP in 1993–94 and public debt eventually roughly doubling.

The lessons from this experience led the Government to adopt an approach whereby, in order to take account of this forecast risk, it deliberately uses a cautious assumption for trend growth for the purpose of projecting the public finances and setting fiscal policy. This means that the trend growth rate assumed for projecting the public finances is set at a rate which is a quarter of a percentage point lower than the neutral view. The result of this is a need regularly to review the neutral estimate of trend growth. And in order to take account of the effects of the economic cycle on the public finances, the Treasury began publishing *cyclically-adjusted* estimates of the key fiscal indicators in July 1997.

Estimating trend growth

The Treasury's approach to estimating trend growth, i.e. the on-trend points approach, is only one of several that could be used. Other methods include the use of statistical filtering techniques, or methods based on economic models, such as production functions. The results from these different methods depend fundamentally upon the assumptions on which they are based. This section outlines the various possible approaches, and the following section looks in more detail at the one the Treasury has decided to use. Figure 3.2 shows the observed and trend levels of non-oil gross value added (GVA) over the past 20 years. This is in contrast to the smoother hypothetical curve illustrated in Figure 3.1.

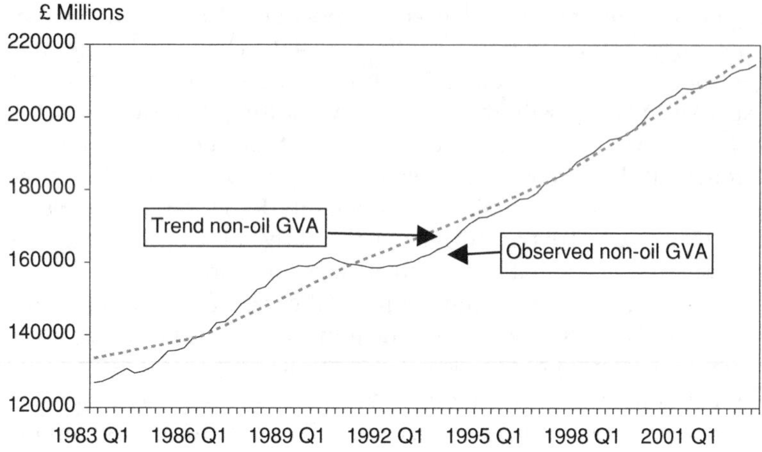

Note: GVA estimates are Chained Volume Measures

Source: HMT Estimates and ONS

Figure 3.2 Trend and observed non-oil GVA

The on-trend points approach

This requires the estimation of points where the economy is on trend. Trend output growth can be calculated from the annual average growth rate between these points.

Once the on-trend points are identified and the trend rate of output growth is calculated between these points, the next step is to decompose the change in trend output over the period into each of its components. Trend output can be decomposed into the average amount produced per hour worked multiplied by the average number of hours worked per person in employment times the employment rate times the population. In other words, the trend rate of output growth over the period equals the product of the growth rates of:

- trend labour productivity measured as output per hour worked;

- trend average hours worked per person;
- trend proportion of the working-age population in employment (employment rate); and
- the working-age population.

The projection for trend growth can then be built up from the projections of the components. This approach – which is the one the Treasury uses – is discussed further in the next section.

Trend growth estimates from statistical filters

Statistical filtering techniques are a common method used to determine trend growth because they are relatively simple to apply and easily replicated.[4] A widely used approach is to apply the Hodrick-Prescott (H-P) filter. The H-P filter is used, for example, by the European Commission as one of its methods of calculating trend output.

The H-P filter is a univariate statistical filter that decomposes a time series into two components: a long-term trend component and a stationary cycle.[5] It then estimates trends by minimising the difference between the observed series and its trend subject to a smoothness constraint, a parameter commonly known as lambda. This parameter tunes the smoothness of the trend; the greater the degree of smoothness (lambda), the closer the trend path will be to a straight line; the lower the lambda, the closer the 'trend' series is to the observed one.

Using the H-P filter, estimates of trend output will tend to be much smoother than actual output and will vary over time, flatter in some periods and steeper in others. The fact that the estimated trend can vary continuously over time is what makes the H-P filter different from a deterministic trend estimated over the whole sample period. However, a series of deterministic trends estimated over sub-periods (for example, representing growth between on-trend points as in the Treasury approach) would also give varying estimates of trend growth over a long sample period, reflecting periods when growth was lower or higher than the full sample average.

The H-P filter has the advantage of being simple to apply. However, it also has a number of disadvantages, including a variability in trend estimate caused by the filter's dependency on the output data and the smoothness constraint imposed, and an inability to detect breaks in trends.

Production function estimates of trend growth

The production function approach is also widely used – for example, by the International Monetary Fund (IMF), the Organisation for Economic

Cooperation and Development (OECD), the Bank of England and the European Commission – to estimate trend (or potential) output. One key advantage is that it provides a clear link between output and its determinants and so can be used to estimate future trend growth based on forecasts of the components. It can also be used to estimate the impact of structural change on trend growth, based on an assessment of the impact of the change in the determinants. It also has its foundations based firmly in economic theory.

The production function approach relates the level of output (GDP) to the level of technology and the inputs that are used to produce it. While, in principle, the technique could handle any number of inputs, the estimates of trend growth from the IMF, the OECD and the European Commission consider only two inputs, labour and capital. There are many different possible functional forms for the production function, but the most widely used one is the Cobb-Douglas. The Cobb-Douglas production function has a number of desirable properties and it is straightforward to estimate. It also offers a convenient decomposition of changes in labour productivity into the effects of capital deepening (change in capital per worker) and a residual, representing technical progress, known as total factor productivity (TFP) growth.

Notwithstanding its attractive features, there are a number of practical problems with implementation of the production function approach. In particular, the underlying determinants (potential labour and capital inputs) are unobservable and have to be estimated.

Examples of approaches used by other institutions

The National Institute of Economic and Social Research (NIESR) uses an approach based on a macro-model which includes a production function and takes account of influences that can be easily predicted, such as population changes.

Goldman Sachs' technique is similar to the Treasury's. They use coincident indicators to establish on-trend points in a cycle, and then deterministic linear trends between the on-trend points are used to estimate trend growth (Walton and Binsbergen 2002). As in the Treasury approach, this implies that between on-trend points the trend component of output is just a linear function of time, so the trend rate of growth is constant.

Treasury Methodology

The Treasury's methodology for estimating trend growth was set out in detail in HM Treasury (1999b). Output is measured excluding oil and gas extraction[6] since, while the oil and gas sector significantly affects output, it has little impact on the sustainable level of employment or activity. Over past cycles, trend output growth is calculated as the annual average growth rate between points when the non-oil economy is judged to have been on-trend.

Determining on-trend points

On-trend points represent the dates when actual output is believed to have been at the trend level so that there was no change in the degree of inflationary pressure in the economy. On-trend points are estimated using a wide range of survey and other information.[7]

In the 1999 *Pre-Budget Report,* the Treasury provisionally judged the economy to be on-trend in the first half of 1997 (the average of the first and second quarters) and in mid 1999 (based on the data available up to the third quarter of 1999). Further analysis of a range of indicators suggests it is likely that the economy was again on, or very near, trend in the third quarter of 2001, as evidenced from Box 3.1, completing a half-cycle which began in mid 1999. The previous cycle was judged to have run from the second quarter of 1986 up to the first half of 1997.

The Treasury has based its assessment of the trend rate of growth for the recent past on analyses of the period running from the first half of 1997 to the third quarter of 2001, comprising one-and-a-half cycles, instead of the shorter period given by the last complete provisional economic cycle which took place between the first half of 1997 and mid 1999. The length of the cycle is important for the purpose of estimating the trend rate of growth. The shorter the cycle, the more sensitive will be the corresponding estimated trend rate of growth and the contributions of components to revisions. The longer the cycle, the more robust will be any estimate of the trend rate of growth of the economy between the on-trend points.

Decomposing the change in trend output

Having established on-trend points, trend growth can be decomposed into the constituent parts outlined earlier in the chapter:

$$\text{Output} = \text{Productivity} * \text{Average hours worked} * \text{Employment rate} * \text{Population}$$

where productivity is measured as output per hour worked; average hours are calculated per person, the employment rate is the proportion

Box 3.1 Summary of the evidence that 2001Q3 is an on-trend point

The charts below show how the output gap has evolved on the assumption that 2001Q3 is an on-trend point. A wide range of evidence has been used to verify it. The data include surveys of capacity utilisation produced by the Confederation of British Industry (CBI) and British Chambers of Commerce (BCC).

Most of these indicate an on-trend point in the second half of 2001, but cannot clearly distinguish between Q3 and Q4. Moreover, in recent years these surveys have tended to have a lower correlation with the output gap. The **BCC capacity utilisation indicators** for the manufacturing and service

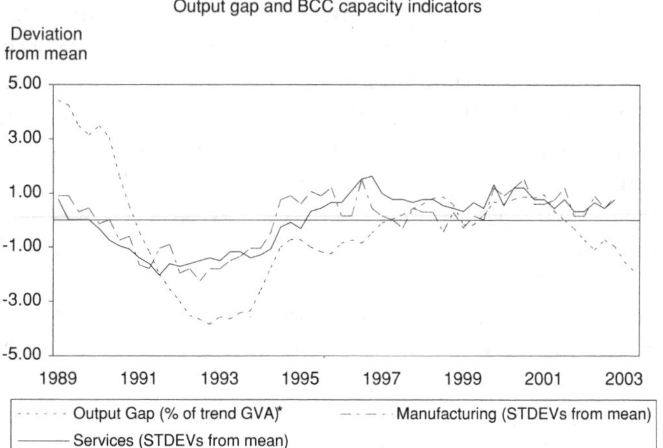

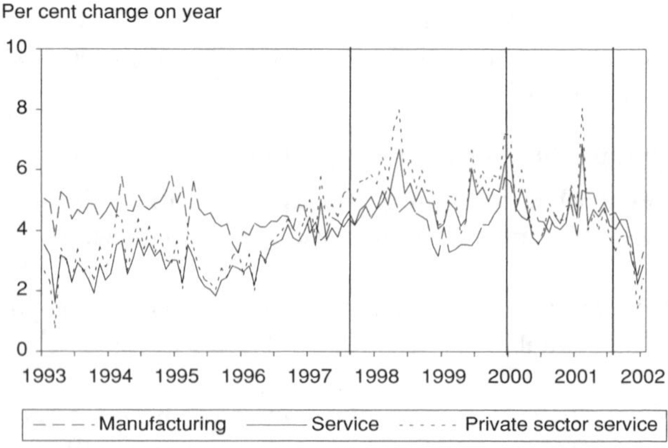

sectors have remained above their long-run levels[1] since 1999Q1 and 1995Q1 respectively, but the services indicator in 2001Q3 was close to the levels observed at the on-trend points in mid-1999 and in 1997H1. The BCC indicators of difficulties in recruiting labour in manufacturing and services were also around the levels at the previous two on-trend points.

One of the clearest indicators in favour of Q3 is the growth in average earnings. This indicator, 4.4 per cent in 2001Q3, was very close to its average since 1991 (4.5 per cent) and the 4.5 per cent sustainable rate deemed consistent with inflation target and trend productivity growth. However, it fell to 3.4 per cent in 2001Q4 and has remained below the average since then, suggesting that the economy has been below its trend level. This pattern is even more pronounced for private sector earnings in services, where the rate of growth fell to 3.6 per cent in 2001Q3, below its average since 1991 (4.4 per cent), and below 3.0 per cent in the following quarter. Another good indicator of the cyclical position of the economy is unit wage cost data. In 2001Q3 unit wage costs grew at 3.8 per cent per annum, which is comparable with previous on-trend points (3.2 per cent in 1997Q2 and 1999Q2). Finally, it should be remembered that, since earnings data are based on annual increases and not current settlements, any turning points will tend to be lagged, thus adding further weight to the argument in favour of Q3.

[1] The long-run levels of the BCC indicators are not well-defined as the back-run of data is relatively short.

of the working-age population in employment, and the population is the working-age population.[8]

The main purpose of this decomposition is to make forward projections. Of course, many factors influence the trend rate of economic growth, but arithmetically they can all be attributed to these four elements. An example of this is the impact of higher investment, which is likely primarily to affect labour productivity.

Projecting the components of future growth

The projection for trend growth from the last on-trend point is built up from the projections of the components. Once recent trends in the key variables that determine trend growth are identified, it is necessary to examine how these will change over the next few years.

Growth in labour productivity

The Treasury's approach is to base any estimated increase in productivity only on clear evidence of what has happened in the past, rather than on an expectation of what might happen. As such, the neutral estimate of the contribution of underlying productivity growth to projected trend output growth is based on an assessment of trend growth in output per hour over the recent past. Underlying productivity growth is defined as the rate that would have occurred if the employment rate had been constant. The underlying rate for the recent past is projected forward and then adjusted for anticipated changes in the employment rate to give a projection of actual trend productivity growth for use in the trend growth forecast. The distinction between actual and underlying trend rates of productivity growth is a reflection of new employees' tendency to have lower than average productivity (related to 'learning effects' and marginal unskilled workers' tendency to have relatively low productivity). Thus, when the employment rate is increasing it will tend to depress actual productivity growth and vice versa. Econometric evidence[9] suggests that the ratio of new to average worker productivity is approximately 50 per cent, which is broadly consistent with data on relative entry wages, and the Treasury's adjustment of actual trend productivity growth reflects this result.

The approach makes no allowance for possible productivity growth improvements as a result of new policies. Some recent developments such as the Government's microeconomic reforms and the new macroeconomic framework, which has resulted in a less volatile macroeconomic environment, as well as the new policies to raise public sector productivity and the growing importance of information and communications technology (ICT), are likely to raise trend labour productivity growth in the future. However, there is considerable uncertainty as to when and how much these developments might influence productivity growth figures. Hence, the cautious approach employed by the Treasury.

There are nonetheless good reasons to anticipate some increase in trend productivity growth relative to the past as a cumulative result of such factors:

1. *Macroeconomic stability and investment.* The new macroeconomic framework, as described in Balls and O'Donnell (2002), has resulted in a less volatile macroeconomic environment which is more conducive to investment and long-term planning in the economy.[10] Table 3.1 shows that growth in output has been much more stable during 1997–2002 than the other periods in the table, with the standard deviation less than a third of that over the whole period.

2. *The productivity agenda.* The approach to improving the UK's long-term productivity performance rests on delivering macroeconomic stability and implementing microeconomic reforms to remove the barriers which prevent markets from functioning efficiently.

Table 3.1 Real GDP growth* between 1972 and 2002

	Mean (%)	Standard Deviation
1972–1982	1.68	0.030
1982–1992	2.44	0.020
1992–2002	2.66	0.012
1997–2002	2.80	0.008
1972–2002	2.34	0.023

Figures are consistent with Blue Book 2003 data set.
* Four quarter growth rates in GDP at constant prices (SA). Underlying data is subject to revision by the ONS.

Source: ONS

3. *The growth of ICT*. In the US, rapid growth in ICT investment has been followed by a rise in productivity growth. In the UK, ICT investment accounted for 15 per cent of total investment in 1999. While a pick-up in productivity similar to that in the US might be expected, it has not been seen in the data so far.

4. *Government policies to raise public sector productivity.* The policies to raise public sector productivity suggest another reason why productivity might turn out higher than projected. The approach is set out in Part 4.

The growth of public sector employment could have a negative impact on measured productivity growth since the level of measured labour productivity in the public sector is typically lower than in the private sector. So an increase in the share of public sector employment will tend to depress measured labour productivity growth. This is probably partly a measurement issue, if increases in public sector productivity, which are difficult to capture, are not fully reflected in measured output. The 2003 Pre-Budget Report includes a brief discussion of the issues related to measuring real government output and productivity (see Box A4 of HM Treasury 2003l). To investigate such measurement issues, Sir Tony Atkinson was commissioned in December 2003 to undertake a review of the future developments of measures of government output, productivity and associated price indices with a view to advancing the existing methodologies.

Since productivity growth contributes directly to trend output growth, increasing its growth rate is a crucial challenge. Productivity did not fare as well in the UK as in some other major countries in the second part of the twentieth century, and despite the latest data showing significant improvements in the trend rate of productivity growth between 1997H1 and 2001Q3 in comparison with the previous full cycle (1986Q2 to

1997H1), it is still important further to raise productivity growth and close the productivity gap between the UK and some of its major competitors.

Since productivity growth contributes directly to trend output growth, increasing its growth rate is a crucial challenge. Given that productivity did not fare as well in the UK as in some other major countries in the second part of the twentieth century, the challenge of raising productivity growth becomes even more important. Table 3.2 provides an international historical comparison and shows that labour productivity growth has been faster in France and Japan than in the UK for most of the post-war period, allowing those countries to catch up and surpass the UK's labour productivity levels. The UK has, until recent years, generally seen faster productivity growth than the US, although the US has maintained a much higher level of labour productivity.

Table 3.2 Labour productivity (output per hour) growth rates (per cent per annum), 1950–1999

	1950–73	1973–99	1989–99
UK	2.70	2.17	1.93
France	5.01	2.59	1.33
USA	2.40	1.08	1.47
Germany*	n/a	n/a	2.70
Japan**	6.30	2.90	2.16

*Data available from 1989 for unified Germany
** Data available from 1953 to 1998

Source: O'Mahony (2002)

Growth in average hours worked

Over time, as the economy becomes richer and real disposable incomes rise, it is possible that people will choose to have more leisure time and work less, although some economies, like that of the US, are characterised by high working hours. In France and Germany, on the other hand, people tend to work fewer hours. This means that the productivity gap expressed on a *per worker* basis between the US and, say, France, is much greater than the gap in *per hour* productivity.

To estimate the future trend in average hours worked, it is necessary to understand past changes by identifying the key drivers and assessing whether they are likely to persist into the future. For example, the rate of decline in hours worked was higher between 1997H1 and 2001Q3

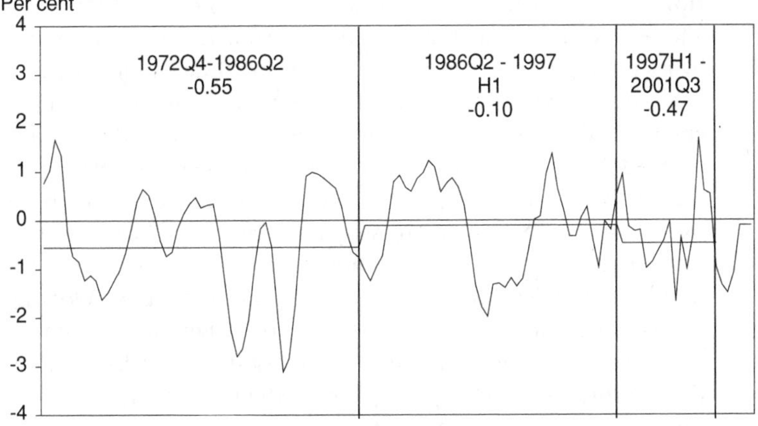

Source: ONS (LFS)

Figure 3.3 Annual growth in average hours worked

(both dates when the economy is judged to have been operating at its trend level) than during the previous 1986–97 cycle.

The late 1990's decline is not a simple story of a shift in favour of part-time employment acting to drag down average hours worked: indeed, the share of part-time employment in total employment has been very stable since 1996 at just under a quarter. Moreover, average hours worked by employees working part-time have risen, and the fall in overall average hours worked has been driven by a fall in full-time average hours. However, while it is not possible to explain fully why the number of hours worked declined from the mid-1990s, it is likely that a number of one-off factors accounted for a significant part of the decline, such as reduced self-employment, rising numbers of students, and reforms to working-time regulations:

- *Self-employment.* The self-employed tend to work above-average hours. The share of self-employment in total employment fell between spring 1997 and spring 2000, partly accounted for by a large fall in the share of self-employment in the construction sector, but has been stable since.
- *Students.* Students tend to work relatively short hours and the rising share of 16–24-year-old students in total working-age employment has contributed to the overall fall in average hours worked.

However, as already noted, the average hours of part-timers as a whole rose, indicating that the effect of students was outweighed by increasing hours of non-students in part-time employment.

- *Tax and benefit reform.* Tax and benefit reforms may have encouraged some lower-income earners to reduce their hours because they needed to work fewer hours to maintain their living standards. Reform of employers' national insurance contributions (NICs) may also have increased the incentive to employ two instead of one person for given hours.
- *Reforms to working time regulations.* The European Union Working Time Directive introduced in the UK in April 1999 will have tended to reduce average hours at the upper end of the hours distribution, though this was also happening before 1999 and it is unclear how far this is just a reporting effect.

In addition, growth in services relative to the manufacturing and agricultural sectors will have tended to reduce average hours, though the decline in employment in these sectors is by no means a new development.

Projections of the average number of hours worked must determine which of the factors explaining past changes are still relevant and which have run their course. For example, some of the factors identified above that have tended to reduce average hours worked in the late 1990s are likely to be no longer relevant. In particular, the share of self-employment has stabilised since spring 2000. Moreover, the effects of exceptionally strong employment growth and certain specific policy changes (such as the Working Time Directive) have probably largely run their course, and growth in the share of students in total employment has stabilised since 1999.

Hence, there would be a case for assuming that average hours worked might remain stable, or even increase, over the medium term. However, this would have to be set against the weak downward trend over the 1986–97 cycle.

Growth in the employment rate

Trends in the employment rate – the proportion of the population of working age in employment – need to be taken into account alongside the size of the working population and average hours in considering the total contribution from labour to growth in output. Figure 3.4 shows annual growth rates in the employment rate and the changes in cyclical averages since 1972. When the employment rate is changing, it can contribute to output growth rate. Changes in the trend employment rate

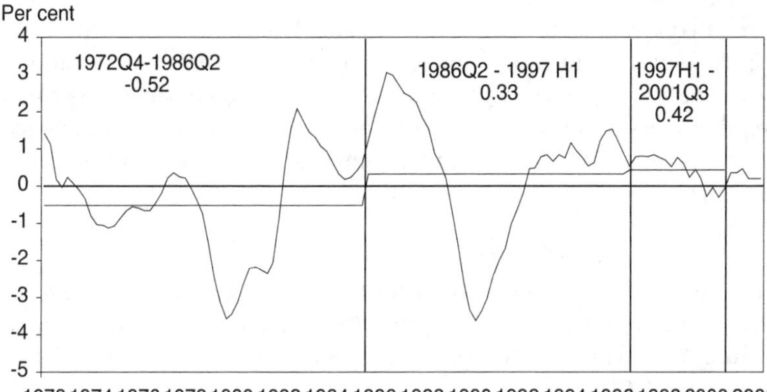

Source: ONS (LFS)

Figure 3.4 Annual growth in the employment rate

can be decomposed into those arising from a change in inactivity rates (or, equivalently, activity rates) and those arising from a change in the rate of unemployment that is consistent with stable inflation (the Non-Accelerating Inflation Rate of Unemployment, NAIRU):

- *Activity rates*. Treasury projections for the working-age activity rate identify the trends in labour market activity rates for different age and gender cohorts and project them forward taking account of changes in the composition of the working-age population.
- *NAIRU*. Variations in the NAIRU need to be allowed for because they affect the level of the employment rate that is sustainable without changing the degree of inflationary pressure in the economy. A decline in the NAIRU would imply the actual rate of unemployment could fall by the same amount. Hence the employment rate could rise by an equivalent amount without increasing inflation.

Nickell and Quintini (2002), for example, apply the now fairly standard model entailing a three-way trade-off between unemployment, changes in inflation and the balance of payments, and thus define the equilibrium rate of unemployment (the NAIRU) as the rate consistent with stable inflation and a zero balance of payment deficit. This view is embodied in the method widely used to estimate the NAIRU, adjusting the actual rate of unemployment up (down) if inflation is rising (falling) or if the balance of payments is in deficit (surplus). Changes in the estimated levels of the NAIRU are explained by changes in factors such as: the replacement ratio[11] and benefits system; collective bargaining power of the employed (trade unions); the (mis)match between the skill requirements of job vacancies and the available skills of unemployed job searchers; employment taxes; competition policy; and minimum wage legislation.

Growth in population of working age

The Treasury bases its projections for the population of working age on the population estimates and projections made by the Government Actuary's Department (GAD). The latest of these were published in December 2003.

Within projections of population growth, and net migration apart, the numbers in each age group for those of working age over the next ten years are likely to be well-estimated, as the number of children that will enter the workforce and the number of people who will come up for retirement depend only on death rates of people who are alive now. The main uncertainty over the projections concerns the assumptions about net migration.

Migration's contribution to the growth in the population of working age in the UK has been significant over the past decade. Net migration accounted for approximately 75 per cent of the growth in population of working age over the period 1992–2002. A particular difficulty with projecting net migration is that it is partly affected by policy. The design of the immigration regime will affect both the number and the activity rates of immigrants. However, immigration to the UK is not entirely a policy variable. Immigrants from other EU countries comprise over a quarter of the total, and they fall outside the immigration regime. It is likely that net migration from EU countries will be related to work opportunities, the economic cycle and higher education opportunities.

The Treasury adjusts the GAD's assumptions on the basis of latest developments, economic and otherwise, to reach its projection of working-age population growth.

The approach in practice: changes to trend growth assumptions

Any change to the Treasury's trend output growth projection can be attributed to one, or a combination, of the following factors:

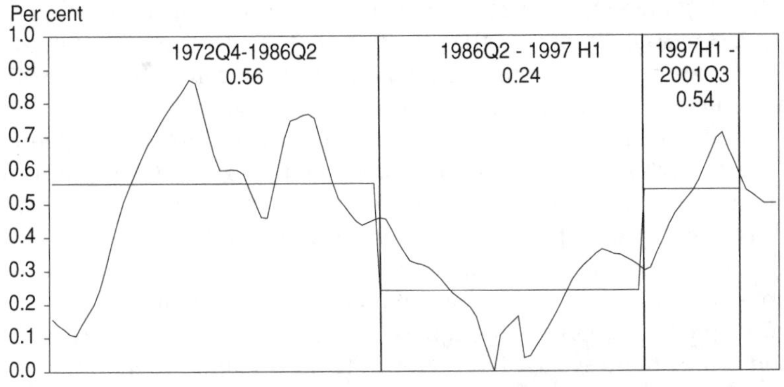

Source: ONS (LFS)

Figure 3.5 Annual growth rates in population of working age

1. Revisions to the methodology and/or assumptions for calculating trend growth.
2. Historic data revisions and/or change in the dating of on-trend points resulting in a different estimate of trend underlying productivity growth in the reference period (ie between two on-trend points over the recent past), which is then used to derive the trend actual productivity growth projected forward.
3. Changes in the projections of other components of trend growth.

The 0.25 percentage point increase in the Treasury's neutral projection of trend output growth at the time of Budget 2002 is an example of this. At the time the reference period used to derive the underlying productivity growth projection was extended to run from 1997H1 to 2001Q3 (instead of 1997H1 to mid 1999). This ensured a more robust estimate taking all latest data into account and better reflecting the latest economic environment. The change in the reference period, combined with data revisions at the time, resulted in a 0.2 percentage point increase in the estimate of underlying trend productivity growth, from 1.9 per cent derived based on the 1997H1 to mid 1999 period, to 2.1 per cent based on the 1997H1 to 2001Q3 period.

Contributions to the trend output growth projection from employment rate and population growth were revised up by 0.2 percentage points in total (0.1 percentage points each) in Budget 2002. These upward revisions arose from data revisions and a switch to the LFS measure of employment rather than the workforce jobs measure previously used. This switch to the LFS measure improved the consistency of the decomposition in the sense that the hours, employment and population components were all based upon the same, and more familiar, LFS measures.

Another major improvement at the time of Budget 2002 was to refine the Treasury's approach to decomposition of trend growth. The previous method involved decomposing trend output growth into three constituent parts (productivity per worker, employment rate and population growth). Thus, it did not take into account variations in hours worked. The new approach represented an analytical refinement of the previous approach by expressing productivity on an hourly basis and adding trend average hours growth to the decomposition. Although the contribution from the average hours worked component was negative, this was more than offset by the upward effects from other components.

Overall, a combination of these changes and methodological improvements resulted in an increase of 0.25 percentage point in the neutral trend output growth projection from 2.5 per cent in the 2001 Pre-Budget Report to 2.75 per cent in the 2002 Budget. However, projections of the public finances are still based on a deliberately cautious trend output growth assumption, 0.25 percentage points below the neutral view. As required by the Code for Fiscal Stability, the National Audit Office (NAO) has audited a trend growth assumption of 2.5 per cent per year for the public finance projections for the 2001Q4 to 2006Q4 period. The Comptroller and Auditor General has concluded that this assumption is 'reasonable and cautious' (NAO 2002).

Since Budget 2002, the ONS has introduced substantial upward revisions to past GDP data in Blue Book 2003. These revisions were driven mainly by methodological improvements such as the annual chain-linking of the National Accounts (see HM Treasury (2003l) for a detailed discussion of the Blue Book 2003 data revisions) and by new information from surveys. As shown in Table 3.3, this had the effect of boosting the estimated trend rate of growth between the adjudged on-trend points in the first half of 1997 and the third quarter of 2001. Over this period, the Blue Book 2003 data yield an annual trend rate of output growth of 2.9 per cent, revised up from the previous estimate of 2.6 per cent at the time of Budget 2003.

There have been no significant revisions over the same period to the estimated trend growth rates of average hours worked or employment, so the increase in the trend rate of output growth is primarily reflected in the productivity growth component. Therefore, the estimated growth rate of underlying trend output per hour between 1997 and 2001 has increased to 2.7 per cent, 0.3 percentage points higher than estimated at the time of Budget 2003.

Table 3.3 Contributions to trend output growth*

	Estimated trend rates of growth, per cent per year					
	Trend output per hour worked		Trend average hours worked	Trend employment rate	Population of working age	Trend output
	Underlying	Actual				
Over the recent past (1997H1 – 2001Q3)						
Budget 2003	2.35	2.14	–0.47	0.43	0.50	2.61
PBR 2003	2.65	2.44	–0.47	0.42	0.54	2.94
Projection						
Budget 2003	2.35	2.25	–0.10	0.20	0.50	2.75
PBR 2003	2.35	2.25	–0.10	0.20	0.50	2.75

* More detail and explanation on the decomposition of trend growth can be found in the Annex A of 2003 Pre-Budget Report (see Table A2).

Source: HM Treasury (2003l)

A mechanical application of the Treasury's trend growth methodology would project forward this increase in trend productivity growth, which, with other trend growth components unchanged, would raise the trend output growth projection well above the existing 2.75 per cent neutral assumption. However, after weighing up all the considerations relating to the estimated current output gap and the components of the trend growth projection, and continuing to take a cautious approach to productivity prospects, the existing 2.75 per cent trend output growth projection was retained as the neutral judgement in the 2003 Pre-Budget Report. However, the data revisions further increase confidence that the 2.75 per cent assumption is consistent with the economy's potential.

Conclusion

This chapter has introduced the concepts of trend growth, economic cycles and the output gap, and briefly explained the relationships between these concepts and inflation. It highlights their relevance to macroeconomic policy, forecasting and public finance, and suggests that reliable estimates of trend growth and the output gap are indispensable in setting monetary and fiscal policy.

The chapter also outlines the various ways of estimating trend growth including H-P filters, production functions and the Treasury's own approach. H-P filters are unable to provide more than a rough guide for estimates of trend growth, and they will be subject to significant end-point/forecasting problems that limit their usefulness to policy-makers. Many international organisations, namely, the IMF, OECD and the European Commission, all use production functions. However, this technique, while firmly based in economic theory, is not without its drawbacks. The Treasury's preferred approach decomposes past trend growth into its components and then combines projections of each of these components to reach an estimate of future trend growth.

Measuring trend growth correctly is important to ensure that the public finances are sound and sustainable and that fiscal policy is set appropriately to support monetary policy. The decomposition involved in the Treasury's approach to estimating trend growth is important because it highlights the key areas the Government must address –employment and productivity – if it is to increase the rate of trend growth in the future.

The remainder of Part 1 of the book discusses further the agenda for raising productivity in the private sector, Part 2 looks at the issue of employment and the labour market, and Part 4 returns to the issue of productivity but from a public sector perspective.

4
Enterprise and the Productivity Challenge: Government Policy to Date

This chapter describes the Government's programme of microeconomic reform to tackle barriers to productivity growth. By strengthening each of the five productivity drivers – competition, enterprise, science and innovation, skills, and investment – identified in Chapter 2.

Introduction

So far, the analysis set out in Part 1 has explained why productivity is a key determinant of trend growth and shown that in the past UK productivity performance has been weak compared with other major economies. In Chapter 2 it was argued that this poor historic performance can be broadly explained by the presence of market failures in some areas of the economy, and suggested that a framework of carefully targeted microeconomic policies, aimed at addressing the market failures, could improve productivity. This chapter focuses on these reforms, based on the five drivers of productivity – competition, enterprise, science and innovation, investment, and skills and human capital – discussed in the previous chapter. The following chapter sets out the Government's approach to regional productivity.

The Government's approach is based on the premises that it is important to: minimise the dangers of policy being impeded by imperfect information; ensure strong and well-designed guidance for those tasked with delivering policy; and create transparent institutions to maximise public accountability. Consequently, the microeconomic reform agenda has benefited from consultation with employers (including the CBI) and employees (including the TUC). The Government has also commissioned a number of independent reviews on institutional investment, retail savings, universities and the role of non-executive directors. These are discussed below.

The following sections discuss key policy interventions, designed to strengthen the five drivers of productivity growth: competition; enterprise; science and innovation; investment; and skills and human capital.

Competition

Competition policy is important not just because consumers need to be protected but also because a well-formulated policy can create the incentives for business to increase the rate of productivity growth. So the Government has taken steps to strengthen the UK's overall competition regime, building a framework for the competition authorities to address anti-competitive behaviour and reforming the regulatory system. Wide-ranging investigations into the banking industry and the new cars market have also been conducted.

The Competition regime

In the past, competition policy largely relied on the Restrictive Trade Practices Act 1976 (RTPA) and the Fair Trading Act 1973 (FTA). These instruments were ineffective and outdated. 'Anti-competitive agreements', for example, were defined mainly by reference to the form that agreements took rather than their effect on the market concerned. As a result, time was spent scrutinising innocuous agreements, while agreements that may well have been anti-competitive often fell outside the scope of the legislation. Furthermore, the absence of financial penalties for breaches of the RTPA, along with weak investigative powers of the Office of Fair Trading (OFT), provided little incentive for parties to curb anti-competitive activities.

To strengthen UK competition policy, two major pieces of legislation have been enacted in recent years. First, the Competition Act 1998 came into force on 1 March 2000 and gave the OFT powers to tackle anti-competitive practices and abuses of market dominance, and brought the UK regime in line with the key competition articles of the European Union regime.

Second, and building on this platform, the Enterprise Act 2002 brought forward a further package of reforms designed to boost levels of competition across the UK economy. The competition provisions in the Enterprise Act include:

- criminal penalties for individuals engaging in hard-core cartels;
- removing Ministers from the decision-making process on competition issues, thereby giving full independence to the UK competition authorities and freeing them from political interference;
- modernisation of the merger control regime so that decisions are taken against a clear economic test of 'substantial lessening of competition';
- reform of the provisions allowing the Competition Commission (CC) to deal with complex monopoly situations, including a new, more flexible reference test (enabling the OFT to refer such markets to the CC); and
- improving redress mechanisms for third parties harmed by anti-competitive behaviour.

These changes provide the UK with a strong legislative framework for competition. The competition authorities have also broadened their focus and have received additional resources to deliver the reforms. The OFT has taken on a new, more proactive, role in investigating markets that may not be working well. Market studies may be carried out where the OFT suspects that a particular market is not working well for consumers, and can be undertaken in response to a 'super-complaint' made by a designated consumer body. To date, thirteen such investigations have been launched. Investigations have been completed into the market for extended warranties, which has now been referred to the CC, and into consumer information technology services. As well as looking at markets and practices, the Enterprise Act also strengthened the role of the OFT to examine the impact of regulation on competition. A study into the pharmacy market (Office of Fair Trading 2002) was the first to examine specifically the impact of Government regulations on competition in the market. The OFT published a report in January 2003 proposing that regulations controlling the entry into the market of new providers of pharmacy services should be removed. The OFT made a strong case that the regulations impeded competition and reduced benefits for consumers. But given the current shortage of pharmacists and the objective to give pharmacies a strong role in the modern NHS, the Government did not believe that it was the time to move to a fully deregulated system. Instead, it proposed to move cautiously in the direction recommended by the OFT, changing the controls on new entry to allow for additional provision. David Clementi is currently undertaking an independent review of the regulatory framework of legal services with an aim to promoting competition.

As part of the drive to improve competition and minimise regulatory burdens on financial markets, the Financial Services Authority (FSA) assumed powers and responsibilities under the Financial Services and Markets Act (FSMA) 2000. This completes a major institutional reform that simplifies the regulatory environment and embodies principles of good regulation. The Act gives the OFT and the CC new powers to scrutinise the competition effects of financial services regulations. The OFT is currently assessing the impact of the FSMA on competition to date as part of a wider review of the Act. The role of the FSA is discussed further in Chapter 13.

Regulation

Effective and well-focused regulation can help to correct market failures, promote fairness, and ensure public safety. But unnecessary or poorly enforced regulation can restrict competition, stifle innovation, and deter investment. To address this, the aim is to minimise unnecessary burdens on business by empowering the competition authorities to challenge anti-competitive regulations, increasing the scrutiny of new and existing regulation, and improving the implementation of regulation to reduce administrative costs on small firms.

The OFT has a clear mandate to review the competitive impact of new and existing regulations, to help boost competition in the economy, and to identify regulations which may not be working in the best interests of consumers and businesses. Since October 2001, the OFT has scrutinised, and advised the Government on, more than 100 proposed regulations.

Banking

In 1998, the Government asked Don Cruickshank, a former Director General at the Office of Telecommunications, to conduct an independent review of competition in banking (Cruickshank 2000). The promotion of effective competition and the avoidance of concentrated market power in the banking sector is crucial to the performance of the wider economy. The review concluded that banking markets lacked effective competition and that, as a result, consumers and small firms were being overcharged. Following the report, in Budget 2000, the

Government committed itself to open up and oversee access charges to payments systems. It also referred the supply of banking services to small and medium-sized enterprises (SMEs) to the CC. In its final report, the CC found that a complex monopoly was operating in this market and identified a number of practices carried out by eight main clearing banks in the UK which restrict or distort competition and operate against the public interest; in particular, the four largest banks were able to charge excessive prices in England and Wales. The CC recommended a number of remedies – including greater transparency of prices, measures to ease switching of accounts, and a requirement to offer interest on accounts or free banking to SME customers of the 'big four' banks[1] in England and Wales – to address these problems. The Government accepted those proposals, which are now in force and being monitored by the OFT.

Utilities

To increase competition amongst utility providers, the Government has fully liberalised energy markets in the UK, with all types of customers free to choose their own supplier. For domestic consumers, average prices in real terms fell by 10 per cent for gas and 19 per cent for electricity between 1997 and 2002. For industrial users, electricity prices fell by 22 per cent in real terms, even when the climate change levy[2] is included. The number of companies generating electricity has risen considerably from six at the time of privatisation to over 30 by October 2002. Competition is also forcing companies to work harder to attract and retain customers. By June 2002, 8.3 million domestic electricity customers (34 per cent of market) had switched suppliers, so had 7.1 million domestic gas consumers (36 per cent of the market). Increased competition has also reduced the need for regulation, and price controls were removed from domestic gas and electricity supply in April 2002. The Office of Gas and Electricity Markets has now removed price controls from 70 per cent of regulated activities.

The Government's Energy Policy White Paper[3] was published in February 2003, and set out the next steps for secure and sustainable energy over the long term.

A key component of ensuring a competitive provision of utilities is to empower customers who use or are affected by these services. This means that customers must have information they need. Practical tools and information is made available to the consumer, for example through Consumer Direct, a national telephone consumer helpline, developed with £30 million of public funding. Work is ongoing to enhance the public information and education resources provided by the Trading Standards Departments, the OFT, and various consumer bodies.

Enterprise

Enterprise creates competitive pressure because entrepreneurs who start up new firms introduce innovative practices and new technology and challenge incumbents' performance. Start-ups and small businesses (in particular) are therefore key contributors to productivity growth. The small business market does, however, suffer from a number of market imperfections that need to be addressed if it is to function effectively and provide potential productivity improvements.

Policy to encourage enterprise has therefore focused on simplifying the tax system and reducing compliance burdens on businesses and investors. The approach is based on building a more entrepreneurial culture, creating a favourable environment for businesses to grow and prosper, tackling specific barriers that inhibit successful enterprise, and taking extra steps to raise levels of enterprise in disadvantaged areas, where these barriers are typically greatest.[4]

External support can also play an important role in helping small firms to achieve their potential by improving their access to advice and information. There is strong evidence[5] that a key constraint on small firms' ability to grow successfully is the lack of internal management development, for example, when they start to require more specialised skills. Good-quality business support can play a key role in helping firms manage this transition. The Small Business Service (SBS) was launched on 3 April 2000 to ensure that government support for small business is improved in terms of both quality and coherence. The SBS has developed a framework for taking forward government policy for small business, based around seven core strategies[6], and emphasising its role in championing the needs of small business throughout government.

Business tax

To provide stability and flexibility for business, to allow the UK to compete effectively internationally, and to ensure that successful enterprises are rewarded, significant reforms have been made to the business tax regime.

The tax system needs to be both competitive and fair. To create a favourable location for investment, the tax system should complement business competitiveness, not stifle it. The Government has reformed the tax system to remove tax distortions, so that decision-making is driven by commercial factors rather than by tax considerations, and promoting productivity by tackling market failures. But competitiveness needs to be balanced by fairness, ensuring individual businesses pay their fair share of tax in relation to their commercial profits and compete on a level playing field. Likewise, if the tax system is the best policy instrument, in a particular case, it needs to be used to correct for market failures that impose wider costs on society.

The key objectives for turning these principles into practice are:

- maintaining a low-rate, broad-base system, which facilitates decision-making that is driven by commercial factors, while better aligning taxable and commercial profits;
- reducing tax distortions and market failures;
- removing outdated rules and regulations that impose unnecessary administrative costs and place constraints on businesses' ability to restructure and reinvest; and
- countering tax avoidance, ensure that businesses pay their fair share of tax and do not gain an unfair competitive advantage through artificial tax planning.

Since 1997, the Government has reduced the main rate of corporation tax to 30 per cent. In addition, in 2000 it introduced a lower starting rate for the smallest companies. As a result of changes in Budget 2002, around 150,000 small companies no longer pay corporation tax, providing further support and incentives to new and growing companies.

Another key part of the programme is to modernise and reform the business tax environment in order to ensure that businesses decisions are made for commercial, rather than tax, reasons. The Government has consulted with business, first in August 2002 (HM Treasury 2002f) and then in August 2003 (HM Treasury 2003m), on how to maintain and build on the UK's position as an internationally competitive location for business and make further progress on removing tax distortions. Pre-Budget Report 2003 brought forward proposals on amending the transfer pricing rules and extending relief for the expenses of managing investments. An earlier consultation, implemented in Budget 2002, introduced a new regime for the taxation of intellectual property, goodwill, and other intangible assets to encourage companies in the knowledge-based economy and an exemption regime for capital gains and losses on most substantial shareholdings.

To improve incentives for long-term investment, significant reforms have also been made to the Capital Gains Tax (CGT) regime. This has included introducing a generous CGT taper relief[7] for business assets to encourage investment and entrepreneurial activity, giving the UK a CGT regime more favourable overall to enterprise even than that of the United States. These changes align the system more closely with entrepreneurial investment cycles[8]. The definition of business assets has also been widened to ensure that the benefits of the CGT business assets taper regime are available to a broader range of shareholdings.

Capital and regulation

There are also market imperfections in the capital markets to which small businesses have access. Those with high growth potential still have difficulty raising small amounts of risk capital. Action has been taken to address this funding gap by launching Regional Venture Capital Funds in every English region, providing extra investment of £270 million. The Government also intends to introduce Enterprise Capital Funds, a variant of the American Small Business Investment Company programme, to invest a mix of private and public sector funds in small companies with growth potential. To improve the administration and take-up of the Small Firms Loan Guarantee Scheme, the scheme has been opened up to wider groups of businesses, including in the catering and retail sectors and is the subject of an independent review that is examining the effectiveness of the scheme. To encourage investors into the finance gap, the Enterprise Investment Scheme and Venture Capital Trust tax incentive scheme have been enhanced.

Fairly and proportionately enforced regulation helps to ensure that honest businesses – the vast majority – are not subject to unfair competition from the unscrupulous few. However, unnecessary or poorly implemented regulation can stifle innovation and enterprise. According to research based on the OECD International Regulation Database (Baygan and Freudenberg 2000), the formalities and costs involved in establishing a new business in the UK are among the lowest in the industrialised world.

To ensure that regulations are communicated as effectively as possible, a new Start-Up Guide for new businesses is being launched. The Small Business Service is also leading a cross-government project to develop new online and interactive services available through a single portal, which will allow business users to see at a glance what is relevant to them, to prioritise effectively, and where appropriate to carry out related transactions.

Higgs Review and changes to the Combined Code

The Higgs Review[9] (Higgs 2003), which reported in January 2003, examined the role and effectiveness of non-executive directors. Following a consultation period, its recommendations have now been substantially incorporated into a revised Combined Code, which outlines best practice standards for boards of directors. This applies to reporting years starting on or after 1 November 2003[10].

Non-executive directors play a central role in corporate governance in the UK – mitigating agency problems by helping to align management and shareholder interests and by reducing information asymmetries through enhanced disclosure. The Higgs report concluded that the existing framework of corporate governance, though essentially sound, should be strengthened. This would involve enhancing the quality and role of non-executives, stronger boards with better processes, and better linkages between directors and shareholders.

The Combined Code[11] operates on a 'comply-or-explain' basis. Companies are required under the Listing Rules to state how they have applied the principles of the Combined Code and whether they have complied with each provision, but they have the flexibility not to comply where appropriate, and then to explain this to shareholders.

A key element of the revised code has been to change the balance of non-executive directors, so that half of a large listed company's board should be independent of management[12]. The definition of director roles has been clarified, and that of director independence stiffened. In addition, the code states that the roles of chairman and chief executive should be separated and that a chief executive should not go on to become chairman of the same company. These measure are intended to reduce scope for conflicts of interest by reinforcing both board independence and the division of responsibility between directors and management.

The revised code expands the role of non-executives in liaising with shareholders. Non-executive directors are expected to maintain contact with major shareholders to understand their issues and concerns and should expect to attend meetings if requested by major shareholders. This is expected to improve information flows and the transmission of shareholder requirements.

The revised code also seeks to improve the quality of non-executive directors and improve scrutiny of their performance. This is to be achieved by a significantly more rigorous and transparent appointment process, new directors induction and professional development requirements, and by formal evaluation of the performance of the board, its committees and of individual directors. In addition, the Higgs report identified a need for appointments to be drawn from a wider pool. Evidence collected for the Review indicates that non-executive directors are predominantly white males nearing retirement age. Since then, the Tyson report on the recruitment and development of non-executive directors[13] has investigated ways in which companies might draw on broader pools of talent to enhance board effectiveness.

Enterprise in deprived areas

There are significant imperfections in the small business market in deprived areas. A key element of enterprise policy is to recognise these imperfections and develop policy to correct them. For example, social attitudes and the business environment cause specific market failures and can result in significantly higher barriers to enterprise within the UK's disadvantaged communities. Moreover, it is in these communities that the benefits of enterprise will have the greatest social impact. A range of policies has been implemented (HM Treasury 2002a; 2003g) concentrated in approximately 2,000 Enterprise Areas, the most deprived areas across the UK. They form part of the broader strategy for neighbourhood renewal, which is discussed in Chapter 5.

Building an enterprise society

An example of the type of market imperfection discussed above is the lack of entrepreneurial and educational experience available to broad cross sections of society.

The need is therefore to work towards achieving a society in which people from all backgrounds consider and act upon enterprise opportunities. Just under 5.4 per cent of the population in the UK is involved in entrepreneurial activity, compared with almost 10.5 per cent in the US (Reynolds et al. 2002). In February 2002, the Davies Review (Davies 2002) of enterprise and the economy in education reported to the Government on the steps needed to promote a better understanding in secondary schools of business, the economy, and enterprise. The review made 15 recommendations, which the Government intends to implement in full. These include investing more in enterprise education such that all young people will have five days of enterprise experience before they leave school, providing new guidance for teachers on enterprise learning, along with new teaching materials; establishing a national benchmark of enterprise capability among young people; and a stronger emphasis on enterprise in Office for Standards in Education (Ofsted) inspections.

Work-related learning will be part of the 14–19 curriculum for all students by 2005. A National Council for Graduate Entrepreneurship is being set up to promote entrepreneurship through universities and higher education institutions as a viable career choice for graduates. The Government also recognises the important contribution of voluntary, community and other not-for-profit organisations in raising awareness of enterprise opportunities, and in providing support, encouragement and guidance to those starting out in business for the first time. Accordingly, it is supporting the work of a number of organisations, many of which are particularly active in the two thousand Enterprise Areas, for example: the Young Enterprise initiative; the Prince's Trust; the Enterprise Insight initiative; and the Business Volunteer Mentors Association.

Science and Innovation

Innovation and technological progress through R&D and investment in human and physical capital have strong positive impacts on the rate at which technological and best-practice techniques are adopted, as discussed below. The Pre-Budget Report 2002 announced two complementary reviews: the DTI Innovation Report and the Lambert review of business-university interaction. Together they aim to provide a strategy for improving the UK's comparative innovation performance and enable business-university interaction in the UK to provide a greater contribution to UK growth. Following wide consultation with key stakeholders, the reviews published their final reports in December 2003. The Lambert Review concluded that there are significant benefits to be gained from business-university collaboration. The Innovation Report notes the UK's excellent science base and track record and among its main proposals is a £150 million National Technology Strategy.

Science

The science and engineering base provides two key outputs: research knowledge and highly trained personnel. Both contribute directly to the UK's capacity to generate value through technological and business innovation. The UK competes in an increasingly global market for science and research. Maintaining the UK's historically strong tradition of scientific excellence and a good supply of new ideas and talented people requires a concerted effort by government to support the science base.

A comprehensive new approach to boosting the UK science base has been put in place by increasing the funds earmarked for capital investment and improved infrastructure in higher education, increasing funding for university research through Research Councils and through Funding Councils, and improving the career paths for academic scientists. The Government is also providing increased funding for knowledge transfer between universities and business, in order to promote the exploitation of new ideas and skills to the market.[14] By 2005–06, the Science Budget, including Research Council expenditure and the Higher Education Innovation Fund, will have risen to £3 billion, compared with around £1billion in 1997. Parallel support for research in universities through the Funding Councils will have risen from around £2 billion to £5 billion over the same period. The Higher Education White Paper of January 2003 introduced reforms to enable the best of UK university research departments to compete in a global market.

Business Research and development investment

To address market imperfections and thereby to create direct incentives for commercial R&D investment in the UK, two new tax credits for small and large companies have been introduced. The R&D tax credit for all small and medium-sized companies[15] was introduced in April 2000. The credit increases the 100 per cent relief for current spending on R&D to 150 per cent and allows companies not yet in profit to claim payable credit, worth one-quarter of the R&D they are undertaking. In 2000–01, the Government invested £80 million in R&D through the small companies' tax credit. Take-up has continued to rise as the Government collaborates with business in developing guidance for the credits and considers options for changes to improve their operation.

The introduction of a 125 per cent credit for larger companies in Budget 2002 has extended this incentive to invest in R&D to all firms. Both small and large companies can also claim a 100 per cent First Year Allowance for capital expenditure incurred on R&D. To encourage closer links between industry and universities, the tax credit is also available for R&D that large companies undertake in partnership with universities, charities, and certain other not-for-profit research organisations. These tax measures are complemented by DTI and Office for Science and Technology (OST) programmes aimed at specific sectors, technologies and research disciplines, designed to stimulate collaborative applied research between business and the science base, for example the LINK scheme which funds collaborative research between universities and companies.

Information and communications technology (ICT)

The adoption of leading-edge technologies is also a key aspect of innovation. Recent studies of US growth performance have emphasised the role of ICT in driving productivity growth, through firms both producing and using these technologies. Comparisons expenditure on ICT indicate that the UK trails the US but leads France and Germany.[16]

In the communications industry, the Government is introducing reforms through the Communications Act. It is also active in encouraging the uptake and use of ICT. For example, it acts through its UK Online campaign as a source of advice and assistance to help firms and others make the most of new technology. Ninety per cent of UK businesses now have internet access, and broadband use has doubled in the past year.[17]

One potential key input for ICT is the radio spectrum, a valuable national asset. Market-based incentives have been introduced for the efficient allocation and use of the spectrum, through auctions for some licences and pricing for others. The Government commissioned an independent review of radio spectrum management by Professor Martin Cave of Warwick Business School. The recommendation of this review, which was to move further and faster towards a spectrum trading market, has been accepted and is being implemented. Better use of the finite radio spectrum resource is being made through the wider use of market-based management tools so that all users face incentives to promote efficiency and innovation.[18]

Investment

Growth in the economy depends heavily on investment in physical capital.[19] Analyses of UK productivity performance relative to other competitor countries (for example, O'Mahony 1999), discussed in Chapter 2, suggest that a large part of the UK's productivity gap with other countries can be largely accounted for by relative deficiencies in physical capital.

Improvements in macroeconomic stability should have an impact on investment across the UK. By reducing the cost of borrowing and providing more certainty about future macroeconomic conditions, the reforms should help to encourage businesses of all sizes to invest. Equally, the new fiscal framework has removed the historical bias against public sector capital investment; as a result the Government aims to increase public sector net investment from its target of 1.8 per cent of GDP in 2003–04, to 2 per cent of GDP by 2005–06 and to 2.25 per cent by 2007–08. Recent evidence suggests that macroeconomics policy has served to encourage business investment in recent years. For example, a CBI survey (Goddon 2001) found that the required rates of return for investment projects in the manufacturing sector have fallen since the mid 1990s. The study concludes that this finding 'could well reflect reduced [economic] uncertainty, consistent with greater stability in the broad economic environment. It would mean a great willingness to invest'.

The tax system will also affect firms' investment decisions and hence can hold back productivity growth. A series of reforms are being undertaken in order to improve the climate for long-term investment. First the Government has reduced corporation tax rates, providing companies with greater access to retained profits (Bond and Meghir 1994a; 1994b), which are usually the cheapest way to finance new investments. Second, payable tax credits on dividends have been abolished, thereby removing the distortion that encouraged firms to pay out dividends rather than to retain them in the firm.

The provision of venture capital has been facilitated through schemes such as Venture Capital Trusts and the Enterprise Investment Scheme, and the introduction of the Corporate Venturing Scheme to increase the availability of venture capital from corporate investors.

The importance of macroeconomic stability in underpinning investment and the role of investment in driving productivity is examined in detail in the EMU investment test and in the EMU study, entitled *EMU and business sectors* (see Annex 7.1 for further details).

Infrastructure

Targeted reforms in planning, housing, transport, and airports have contributed to tackling market imperfections in the provision of infrastructure. This has helped boost investment in infrastructure. Those reforms are discussed further below.

An effective *planning system* is vital for successful and speedy development. The Government's proposals for reform of the planning system have proceeded in two stages: the Modernising Planning agenda (DETR 1998) and the Sustainable Communities initiative, Delivering through Planning (Office of the Deputy Prime Minister 2001). Using the planning legislation (Planning and Compulsory Purchase Bill 2003), the Government has proposed reforms that include clearer and briefer central government guidance, statutory Regional Spatial Strategies[20] to guide the pattern of development at regional level, more flexible local development plans, and a simplified compulsory purchase system to assist necessary development where owners are unknown or unwilling to sell at a reasonable price. As described in Chapter 5, it is also proposed that Business Planning Zones will be established to facilitate business development in local areas. The intention is also to speed up the process for consideration of major infrastructure projects that make a significant contribution to economic growth. Consideration is also being given to how public inquiries into such projects can be made more efficient.

A key role of the planning system is to enable the provision of new homes in the right place and at the right time. This is important to ensure that everyone has the opportunity to live in a decent home and to maintain the momentum of economic growth, which requires that houses be available for those moving to take up new employment opportunities. Regional planning bodies and local planning authorities are therefore expected to provide sufficient housing opportunities to meet the likely housing requirements of their areas. The issue of imbalance in the housing market is discussed further in Chapter 5, which sets out the aims of Kate Barker's (member of the Bank of England's Monetary Policy Committee) review of issues underlying the lack of supply and responsiveness of housing in the UK – the Interim Report was published in December 2003.

Good *transport links* have an important role in promoting investment. The Ten-Year Plan for Transport envisages public and private spending in excess of £180 billion to create a modern transport network across the UK. The Secretary of State for Transport reported in December 2002 on the progress made under the plan in its first 18 months and on what it is hoped to achieve by 2006. The Department for Transport is now conducting an in-depth review of the Plan. This review will take account of the progress made so far and the challenges that have to be met in the period up to 2015 and beyond. Such long-term commitment and planning is essential to rebuild and maintain the transport infrastructure necessary for continued growth and prosperity.

Air travel provides significant economic benefits to the UK, and demand for it continues to grow. Yet UK airport capacity is fast falling behind that of other European countries, and many of the UK's largest airports are already reaching full capacity. These capacity constraints particularly affect airlines' ability to sustain 'hub' operations that allow a wide range of destinations to be served with high frequency. The Government has consulted on how best to maximise the benefits of growth in aviation, while striking the right balance between the social, economic, and environmental impact of any airport development. An

Air Transport White Paper was published at the end of 2003 in which the Government set out a strategic framework for the development of air travel in the next 30 years.

Myners Review

The Myners Review, conducted by Paul Myners, Chairman of Gartmore Investment Management, was commissioned to consider whether there were factors distorting the decision making of institutional investors. Its report (Myners 2001) was published in March 2001 and included a set of principles to codify best practice for pension fund decision-making, recommending that funds explain what they were doing to implement these. The Government endorsed these principles – after consultation – in October 2001. To assess the effectiveness of these principles in delivering change, a two-year review is being undertaken, which began in March 2003.

The qualitative research, as part of that review, was published in November 2003. The Government is committed to undertake discussions with the industry on the potential for further progress in the key areas.

The review also proposed four areas of legislative or other action:

1. *Shareholder activism*. After consultation, the Institutional Shareholders' Committee produced in October 2002 a new statement of principles, strengthening the responsibilities of institutional shareholders and agents. It recommended best practice on the part of institutional investors to promote their clients' interests through taking more active steps to engage investee companies. The Government agreed to this voluntary approach to improving shareholder activism. The impact of the principles will be reviewed after two years and provides an important opportunity to review whether a non-legislative approach can be successful in delivering behavioural change.
2. *Minimum Funding Requirement (MFR)*. The review concluded that the MFR was a flawed approach which distorted investment decisions for some schemes, without delivering the level of security which many people expected. The Government agreed to the review's recommendation that the MFR be replaced with more flexible scheme-specific funding requirements.
3. *Pension Scheme Trusts*. Pensions funds' investment decisions are of vital importance to the future security of their members and to the health of the wider economy, and the Government is committed to

requiring trustees to have the knowledge necessary for responsible investment.

4. *Brokers' commissions.* The review considered that brokers' commissions were not transparent and fund managers did not have strong incentives to minimise their costs. The FSA is consulting on proposals to 'unbundle' broking commissions into execution and research costs and to require fund managers to meet the research component.

The review also identified the constraints on institutional investment in private equity and venture capital, including perceptions of UK private equity performance, quality of performance information, cost of private equity investment and regulatory constraints. Action has been taken to reduce the regulatory hurdles identified.

Sandler Review

The Sandler Review (Sandler 2002), conducted by Ron Sandler, former Chief Executive Officer of Lloyd's of London, built on some of the recommendations of the Myners Review. The review, which reported in July 2002, examined the markets for medium- and long-term retail savings in the UK, identifying the competitive forces and incentives that drive the industries concerned, and analysing potential policy responses.

The review sets out six major recommendations which the Government and the FSA are taking forward. These recommendations are as follows:

1. A series of safer and more comprehensible 'stakeholder' investment products with capped charges, restrictions on investment profile, and the ability to exit on reasonable terms.
2. Reform of with-profits policies, including an 'ideal model' that would be transparent to support investor decisions, and clearly separate policyholders' and shareholders' interests while retaining features investors have found valuable.
3. An increased and ring-fenced consumer education budget for the FSA and better coordination of the work on financial education.
4. Reform of the market for the distribution of investment products, including specific recommendations about how remuneration arrangements of independent financial advisers are disclosed to clients.
5. A set of investment principles for providers of retail investment products, building on the approach set out by the Myners Review.

6. Simplification of the taxation system in the savings industry.

The recommendations of the Sandler Review are discussed more fully in Chapter 13.

Skills and human capital

To raise UK skill levels and increase productivity, the Government has directed policies at the improvement of both the skills of young people entering the workforce and those already in the workforce who require opportunities to acquire new skills. In July 2003, DfES published a Skills White paper (DfES 2003a) which set out measures aimed at ensuring employers have the right skills to support the success of their businesses, and individuals have the skills they need to be both employable and personally fulfilled.

Secondary education

A target has been introduced to raise standards in schools and colleges so that between 2002 and 2006, the proportion of pupils aged 16 who obtain qualifications equivalent to five GCSEs at grades A*–C should rise by two percentage points each year on average, and in all schools at least 20 per cent of pupils should achieve this standard by 2004, rising to 25 per cent by 2006. The national roll-out of the Connexions[21] service and the introduction of Education Maintenance Allowances[22] will support young people making the transition into post-16 learning to increase further participation and attainment beyond this age.

Higher education

The objective is that by 2010, 50 per cent of young people will have the chance to participate in higher education. To this end, the need is both to widen access to higher education and to improve the current funding system to ensure that universities are better able to respond to demand and to sustain teaching and research excellence. The 2002 Spending Review provided additional resources to support improvements in the UK's international research competitiveness. Increased funding per student and targeted pay incentives will allow institutions to improve teaching and to recruit and retain key staff. The significant increase in resources for science described above will also help to fund new investment in laboratories and equipment and facilitate greater leading-edge research.

The January 2003 White Paper *The Future of Higher Education* (DfES 2003b) set out a range of proposals to widen participation in higher education. These included the introduction of a new grant of up to £1,000 a year for students from lower income families from 2004, the abolition of up-front fees, and an increase in the repayment threshold to £15,000. The White Paper also proposed that universities that have drawn up Access Agreements be allowed to seek a graduate contribution of up to £3,000 per year for each course. Further, to ensure that UK universities are equipped to compete in the world economy, it allocated additional funding to reward excellence in teaching with new money for pay modernisation, rewarding good teaching and providing more fellowships for the best institutions.

Modern Apprenticeships

To widen the vocational choices available to young people and increase participation in work-focused learning, the Government has reformed, strengthened, and expanded the Modern Apprenticeships (MA)[23] scheme. The revised scheme offers young people a national framework of work-based learning and education to ensure a consistently high standard of training through key skills and sector-specific National Vocational Qualification and technical certificates. Since 1997, the number of young people enrolled in MAs has risen from 111,700 to 226,800. The expectation is that, by 2004, at least 28 per cent of young people will have enrolled in a MA.

Training

Measures are also being taken to improve training opportunities for those already in the workforce. Workforce training in the UK is inhibited by a range of market failures. Businesses may be unable to gain the full returns to investment in employer training, and many individuals face credit constraints or are poorly informed about the value of training. Evidence suggests that these market failures affect mainly low-skilled workers and those who work for small firms. An increase in the number of people participating in workplace training has been achieved through voluntary approaches. However, despite these efforts, they have not been sufficient given the scale of the problem. The Government is therefore seeking to develop policy that will generate stronger rights and responsibilities for employers, individuals and government in order to better address this problem.

The 2001 *Pre-Budget Report* announced the launch of Employer Training Pilots from September 2002 to test new measures to improve access to training. Firms that offer their low-skilled staff paid time off to train are being provided with subsidies to cover the costs involved, free training courses up to National Vocational Qualification (NVQ) level 2, and information and guidance on training.[24] Early evidence suggests that the model being tested in the pilot schemes is proving successful in engaging low-skilled individuals through their employers. To gather further evidence, these pilots were extended in the Pre-Budget Reports 2002 and 2003. The pilots also demonstrate the Government's commitment to a new relationship with employers and individuals. Government is accepting its responsibility to provide the finance for courses and to compensate employers who provide training opportunities for their low-skilled staff. Employers are delivering new training opportunities for these staff, and their employees are taking up the new training choices and opportunities on offer.

These pilot schemes build on a range of initiatives to improve adult skills. For example, the Skills for Life strategy aims to increase demand, improve supply, and raise standards in basic skills training, targeting priority groups where literacy and numeracy difficulties are known to be common. These priority groups include unemployed people, prisoners, those supervised in the community, the homeless, and those who do not speak English as their first language, as well as workers in low-skilled jobs. The programme is having an impact, and has supported some 250,000 adults in improving their basic skills by the end of 2002.

The institutional framework for further education has been substantially reorganised with the aim of making training more responsive to the needs of employers and individuals. The Learning and Skills Council was established in April 2001; operating through 47 local offices, it is responsible for funding and planning all further education and training in England. Its structure, with national oversight of the 47 local offices, is designed to ensure that it can meet local business needs. In addition, the Sector Skills Development Agency has been established to facilitate the development of a network of Sector Skills Councils. These are to be led by employers, working with trade unions and professional bodies, to identify the skills and productivity needs of their sectors and to stimulate action.

Chapter 5 sets out ways in which the specific regional dimension of the skills problem will be tackled. For example, from April 2003 pooled budgets between Regional Development Agencies and Local Learning and Skills Councils have been piloted in four regions.

Migration

Migration has always been a source of skills and labour in Britain, and over time has helped to improve productivity, raise economic growth, cover shortages in domestic skills, and provide a flexibility in times of economic uncertainty. The Government has taken steps to help employers facing skills shortages in the UK recruit from overseas, such as reforming the work permit system and ensuring that employers and individuals have access to appropriate information on UK migration routes.

The Work Permit system now provides a flexible and effective service for employers who are unable to fill positions through domestic recruitment – around 200,000 migrants a year now enter the UK through the Work Permit system and over 95 per cent of permits are processed within 24 hours.

To provide a further source of skills for the UK economy, a pilot Highly Skilled Migrant Scheme was launched in January 2002, allowing highly skilled individuals to enter the UK without a specific job offer, to work or to seek work and to make a valuable contribution to the economy. Since its introduction, the scheme has proved successful in enabling highly-skilled individuals to enter the UK – around 1,300 people entered through this route in its first year of operation, demonstrating their eligibility through educational qualifications, work experience, achievements in their field, and past income. Moreover, the overwhelming majority of candidates now applying for an extension of their permit have registered strong labour market performances over the last year, providing further evidence of the scheme's success. The scheme will be strengthened further by adjusting the threshold criteria, introducing a new category for younger applicants and taking partners' achievements into account.

Overseas students can also help to alleviate UK shortages in certain sectors which are experiencing skills shortages. In particular, there is a need to encourage students of science, technology, engineering and mathematics to utilise their skills after graduation. To this end, a new entitlement has been announced which will enable foreign students beginning or continuing courses in the UK in these subjects to work in the UK for 12 months following graduation from a UK institution.

The Government has recognised that those with high skills are not the only people who contribute to the economy; labour at all skill levels can help to fill vacancies and alleviate bottlenecks, increasing efficiency and productivity. To add to the effectiveness of the Work Permit system in alleviating employers' recruitment difficulties, the Government has implemented two new schemes for low-skilled migration in the food processing and hospitality sectors. Further work is in hand to understand the social and economic impacts of migration in the UK, particularly at the low skilled end.

Overall, evidence suggests that migrants' success in the labour market does not come at the expense of the domestic population. Recent research in the UK finds little indication of a negative impact on domestic employment and, if anything, suggests a positive impact on domestic workers' wages (Home Office 2002a). Research by the Home Office has also found that migrants made a net positive fiscal contribution of at least £2.5 billion in 1999–2000, paying more in taxes than they received in benefits (Home Office 2002b). However, the full extent of that contribution is difficult to calculate accurately, and depends on migrants' ages, economic activity, wages, skills, and how long they stay in the country.

Conclusions

As discussed in previous chapters, to raise the level of productivity the Government must tackle the market failures that occur in the labour, capital, and product markets. This can be best achieved by targeting measures at each of the five drivers of productivity: competition, enterprise, science and innovation, investment and skills.

This chapter has set out in detail the measures the Government has put in place. To enhance competition a range of reforms have been introduced including separate measures to tackle anti-competitive practices and to boost levels of competition across the United Kingdom. Anti-competitive practices in the banking sector have also been addresssed and the utility markets fully liberalised. To increase enterprise, the Government has simplified the tax system to reduce the burdens on business and investors and introduced measures to encourage enterprise in deprived areas. To encourage science and innovation the Government has increased funding for scientific research, introduced tax credits for R&D investment and put in place reforms put in place to ensure greater competition in the communications industry. The Government's macroeconomic reforms have helped set the right environment for increasing investment in capital and this is being enhanced by business tax reforms. The Government is also targeting market imperfections in the provision of investment in the UK's infrastructure through reforms to planning, transport links and air travel. It has also commissioned independent reviews addressing concerns arising over institutional investment, retail savings, and the role of non-executive directors. Finally, the Government's education policies and improved apprenticeship schemes are aimed at increasing the skills of those entering the workforce, while measures to enhance in-work training are raising the skills of the current workforce, and areas of chronic skill shortages are being addressed by measures to ease recruitment from overseas.

5
The Regional and Local Dimensions

This chapter sets out an economic analysis of regional and local variations in economic performance in the UK, and shows the steps that the Government has taken to reverse the historical disparities in regional economic performance.

Introduction

Improving the economic performance of every country[1], region and locality of the UK is an essential dimension of the Government's central economic objective of achieving high and stable levels of growth and employment. The Government has focused policy on promoting opportunity for all – every individual and business and every locality – by tackling the diverse social and market failures that have held them back. In doing so the Government's aim is to increase the productivity and realise the potential of every region, city and locality. The ambition is to raise the performance of under performing areas to that of the best and so that all, particularly disadvantaged communities, can share in rising prosperity. This new regional policy rests on two principles, as outlined in *Towards a New Regional Policy: Delivering Growth and Full Employment* (Balls and Healey 2000):

- first, strengthening long term building blocks of growth, innovation, skills and the development of enterprise by exploiting the indigenous strengths in each region and city; and
- second, a bottom up approach with national government enabling powerful regional and local initiatives to work by providing the necessary flexibility and resources.

This chapter sets the context for this policy approach, analysing the regional and local variations in economic performance in the UK, as outlined in the Treasury publications *Productivity in the UK: The Regional Dimension* and *Productivity in the UK: The Local Dimension* (HM Treasury 2001a; 2003g). It then describes in detail how policy has been shaped to improve the productivity not only of those countries, regions and localities that historically have had the highest growth but also of the least productive areas.

Regional variations in performance

This section sets out the history of the significant differences in regional levels of productivity and their corresponding impact on national growth rates. The Government's approach focuses on improving the performance of the weakest regions without constraining growth in the strongest: that is, levelling up rather than levelling down.

The ability to measure regional variations in performance is constrained by the quality of the sub-national economic data currently available in the UK. Recognising this, in March 2003 the Chancellor announced the Allsopp Review[2] to report on the regional information and statistical framework required to support the objective of promoting economic growth in all regions. The review gave an initial report at the time of the Pre-Budget Report in 2003 and is due to give a full report at the time of the Budget in 2004.

Despite the data problems, however, it is clear that the countries and regions of the UK differ significantly in their economic performance. For example, in 1999 nominal GDP per capita was nearly £7,000 lower in Northern Ireland, Wales, and the North East than it was in London, the richest region. These differences are even more striking at a sub-regional level: in the South East, for example, GDP per capita in Milton Keynes is twice that in East Sussex.

Figure 5.1 gives an illustration of the dispersion of GDP per head within regions, showing that the variation between different local areas within a region is more marked in some regions than in others, although large differences in wealth exist within all regions. Regions with levels of GDP per head above the UK average experience, in general, higher levels of absolute sub-regional dispersion.[3]

Sub-regional[4] GDP per head figures may provide a useful indication of the economic capacity and industrial structure of a particular local area. However, they do not necessarily provide a good indicator of living standards: for example, people often do not live in the locality in which

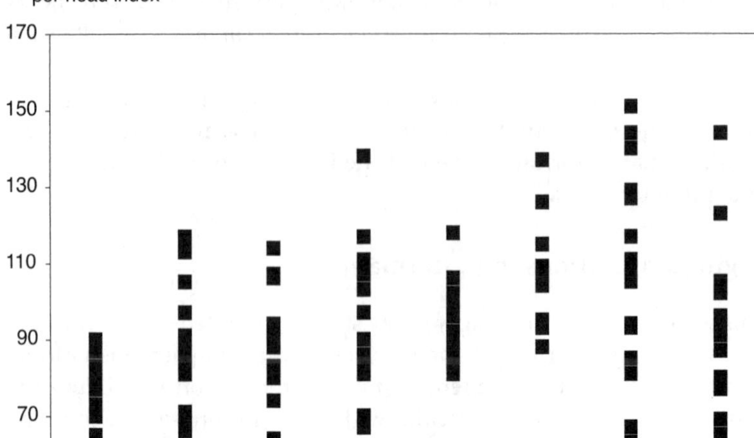

Note: Figure 5.1 shows the dispersion in GDP per head between NUTS 3 areas within a larger NUTS 2 (or Government Office Region) area. NUTS 3 areas generally refer to countries or groups of local authorities.

Source: ONS

Figure 5.1 Within-region dispersion in GDP per head (UK=100, per head index)

they work, especially around large cities such as London, Manchester and Bristol.

Comparisons of living standards using household income can be more reliable, and give a better indication of the economic welfare of individuals and families who live in the area. Once more, the divergence in sub-regional household incomes within a region is greater the higher that region's overall level of average disposable household income. So, for example, better performing regions such as London and the South East show a relatively high spread of incomes between sub-regions. Again, however, there are large differences in incomes within all of the UK's regions.

The ranking of the UK's countries and regions and the size of the differentials between them are not new. The current pattern emerged in the 1920s, when the decline of many traditional industries disproportion-

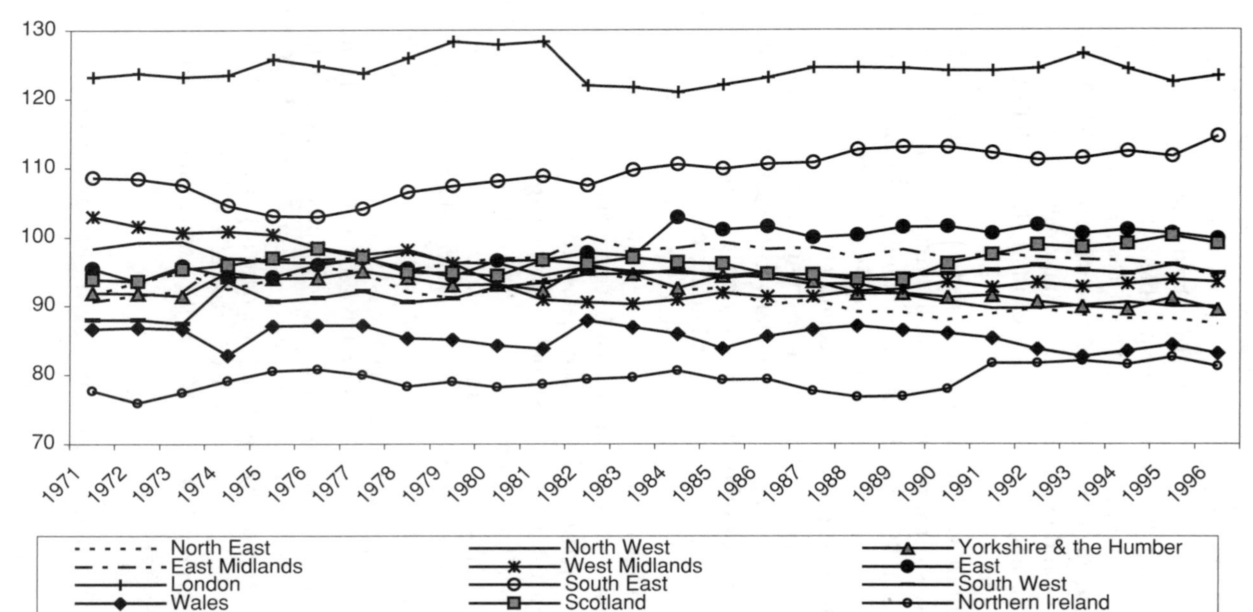

Source: ONS

Figure 5.2 Relative regional GDP per capita

ately affected northern regions. This pattern of regional differentiation has persisted over recent decades[5]. Figure 5.2 shows that between 1971–96 nominal GDP[6] per capita in London was consistently higher than it was in other regions; whereas in Northern Ireland it was consistently low.

However, there have been some notable exceptions to this pattern over the last three decades. The South East, for example, has been steadily improving its relative performance since the mid-1970s, and the East and Scotland experienced a rapid improvement in their relative position in the mid- and late 1980s. In contrast, the North East has fallen steadily behind.

The significant variation in economic performance at regional and sub-regional levels constrains the potential growth of the UK economy. Estimates for 1999 show that if the economic performance of below-average regions could be raised to the current national average, that would be enough to make everyone in the country £1,000 a year better off[7].

Government policy has therefore concentrated on raising the performance of all regions, particularly the weakest ones, and on providing the flexibility for every region to exploit its indigenous strengths rather than simply redistributing income between regions. Accordingly, there is now a new Public Service Agreement (PSA) which sets for government the aim of making a sustainable improvement in the economic performance of all English regions and, over the long term, to reduce the persistent gap in growth rates between the regions. Further details on the role of PSAs are set out in Chapter 16.

Regional flexibility would become even more important if the UK decided to join EMU. The characteristics and institutions that promote economic adjustment between UK regions would also equip the UK to thrive within EMU. Inside EMU, regions would need more flexibility as monetary policy would be set for the euro area as a whole, making interest rates less responsive to regional needs than is currently the case. The flexibility of UK and euro area product, capital, and labour markets is reviewed in the flexibility test, with an emphasis on the types of adjustment needed most inside a single currency. More details on these subjects can be found in the EMU studies *EMU and labour market flexibility*, *Prices and EMU* and *EMU and the cost of capital*. (See Annex 7.1 for further details.)

Regional productivity and employment patterns in the UK

Regional variations in GDP per capita are basically functions of variations in productivity – that is, the output of each worker, and employment patterns – which are in turn affected by the number of people of working age in an area, the proportion of those people participating in the labour market, the hours worked by those people and regional unemployment rates.

The relative importance of productivity and employment in contributing to regional GDP per capita varies by region. This is shown in Figure 5.3. Using 1999 figures, on average, productivity differentials

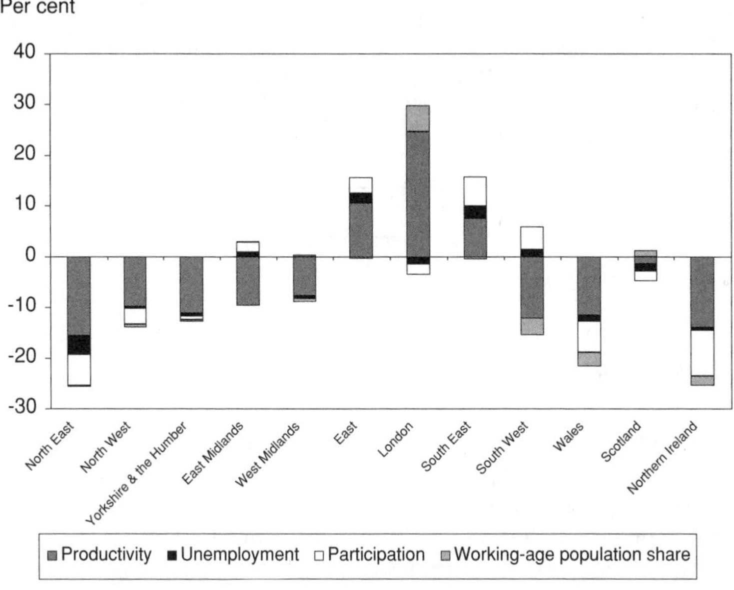

Source: ONS

Figure 5.3 Decomposition of regional GDP per capita gap with UK average (1999)

account for around 60 per cent of regional differentials and employment the remaining 40 per cent.[8]

This picture is complicated somewhat by regional variations in employment, particularly in participation and working-age population which tend to be closely correlated with productivity and hence reinforce productivity differentials. The precise reason for this is uncertain, but it is likely that highly productive regions attract more people who wish to participate in the labour market and benefit from higher wages, whereas more people leave the workforce in low-produc-

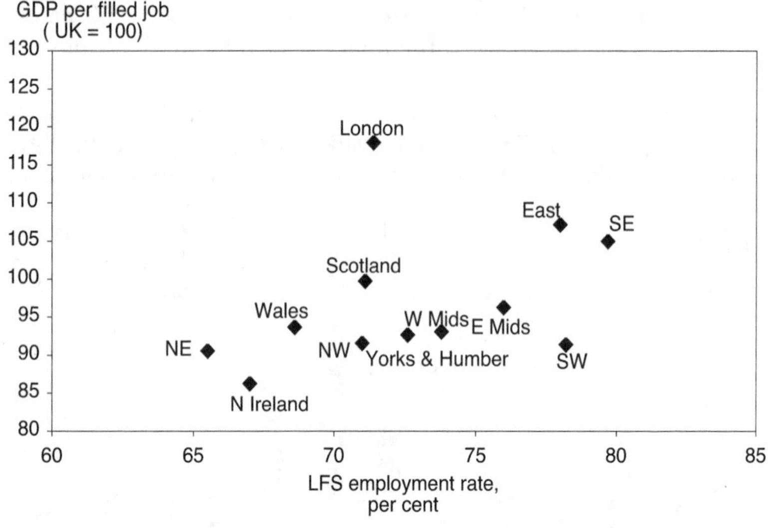

Source: ONS

Figure 5.4 Employment and productivity in UK regions

tivity and low pay regions. Figure 5.4 shows the relationship between employment rates and productivity in different UK regions.

Regional productivity differences, measured in terms of output per worker, are shown in Figure 5.5. The figure shows that, in 1999, London had the highest regional output per worker; with output per worker in the East and the South East trailing by around 10 per cent and that of other regions trailing by 15–30 per cent.

The evidence also shows that employment rates (defined as the proportion of the working-age population who are in work) vary considerably by region, although in all regions the proportion of those in employment has risen since 1997.

Unemployment rates, defined as the proportion of economically active people aged 16 and over who are unemployed, have followed a slightly different trend from employment rates. The overall pattern of regional unemployment rates has remained fairly persistent since the 1920s[7]. As Figure 5.6 shows, over the last two decades the variation in regional unemployment rates has fallen and the level of unemployment has also fallen.

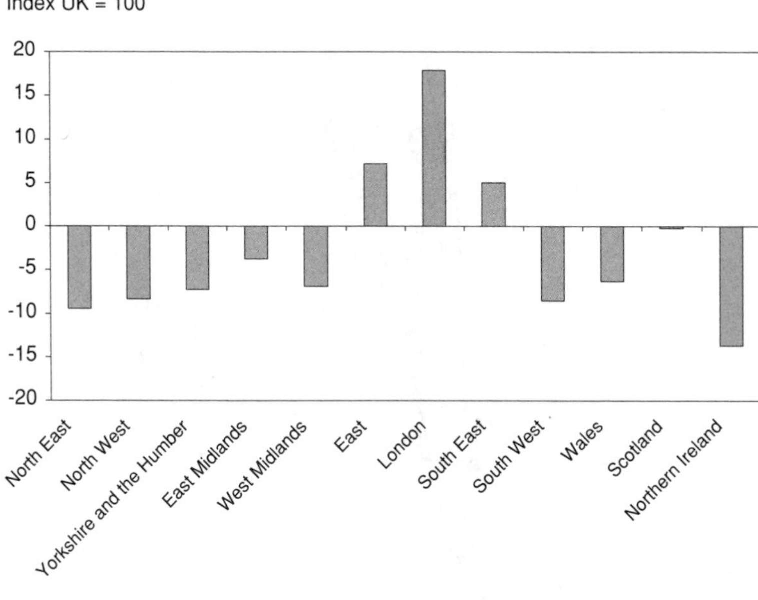

Source ONS

Figure 5.5 The regional productivity gap, 1999

In absolute terms, regional differences in unemployment rates are smaller than those in employment rates. This is because regional and sub-regional variations in inactivity are similar to those for unemployment, and therefore compound variations in employment. In October–December 2002, for example, inactivity across the UK varied from 27 per cent in the North East to 17 per cent in the South East[10].

Economic variations are also at least as significant at a sub-regional level as those at regional level. For example, while employment rates in the South West are, on average, higher than those in Wales, the employment rate in Wrexham was 81.2 per cent in May 2003 while the rate in Tewkesbury was just 67 per cent.

As with employment rates, local variations in unemployment rates remain large and significant. Indeed, within-region disparities are larger than those between regions and appear to have increased moderately over the last decade. Frequently, high levels of vacancies coexist with high levels of unemployment in the same travel-to-work areas.

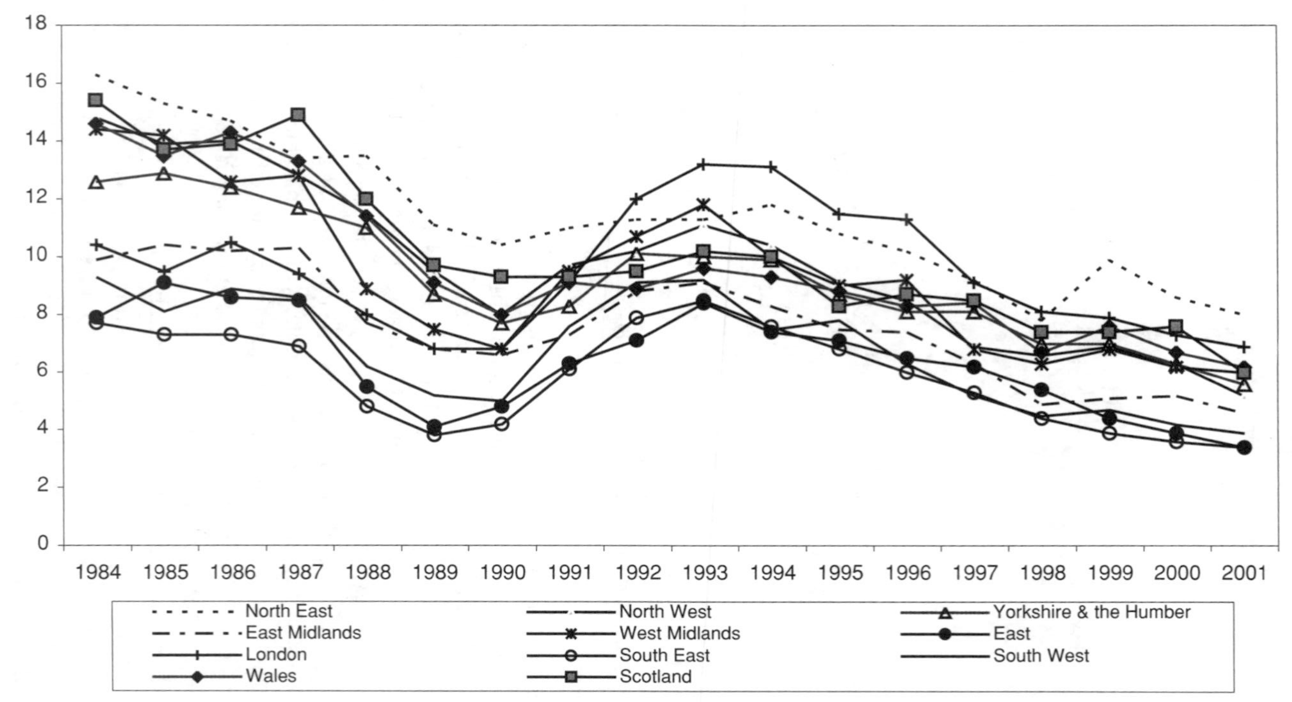

Source: ONS

Figure 5.6 ILO unemployment rate by region

Some areas of the country have also seen inactivity rates rise to very high levels; in 27 of the total 408 British local authority districts, working-age inactivity rates exceed 30 per cent. The majority of these areas are in major conurbations such as Merseyside and East London, but others are in areas that were in the past dominated by mining or heavy industry.

This evidence suggests that differences in labour market outcomes in terms of employment, unemployment and inactivity are significantly larger within than between regions. Given the local nature of many labour markets, this implies that policies delivered at a sub-regional level are likely to have a key role in driving labour market improvements. Chapter 9 sets out the specific measures the Government is putting in place to tackle unemployment at the local level.

Productivity differentials[11] also tend to vary substantially within regions. For example, in the South East of England in 1996–98, productivity levels ranged from around 20 per cent below the national average in Brighton and Hove to around 10 per cent above the national average in Surrey and Portsmouth. Similarly within the North East, where all sub-regions had productivity less than the national average, productivity ranged from 80 per cent of the national average in Sunderland and Tyneside to just under the national average in South Teeside. Any particular area's productivity is therefore a product of region-specific and locality-specific effects.

The Five Drivers of Productivity in UK Regions

Chapter 2 set out the five key factors that underlie productivity, at a whole economy level: skills, investment, innovation, enterprise and competition. This section examines how differences in performance against each of these factors help explain the variation in regional and local productivity levels.

Skills

The skills composition of the workforce varies considerably across the UK's countries and regions (see Figure 5.7). In Northern Ireland, for example, just over one-quarter of the workforce is without any academic qualifications, compared with just over one in ten in the South East. Local variations in workforce qualifications are even more pronounced.

Recent studies conclude that these variations in regions' skills composition are the major factor in explaining regional variations in productivity.[12]

The skill levels of the workforce in a region (or locality) depends on two main factors:

- generation of skills in that region through education and training; and
- movement of workers into and out of the region.

In every age group, educational attainment varies significantly between regions and localities. Figure 5.8 shows performance at school by region. The percentage of pupils in 2000/01 in their last year of compulsory schooling who achieved GCSEs at grades A*–C varies in all core subjects, from 25 per cent in the North East to 40 per cent in the Scotland. Participation rates in full-time education after compulsory schooling (age 17) in 1999/00 range from over 65 per cent in Northern Ireland to around 50 per cent in Scotland and the North East.

Regional differentials in school performance are reinforced after students graduate from university, because recent graduates are relatively mobile and are likely to relocate to regions and localities with highly paid jobs[13]. A large number of graduates move from poorer regions to wealthier regions, in particular London, the East, and the South East[14].

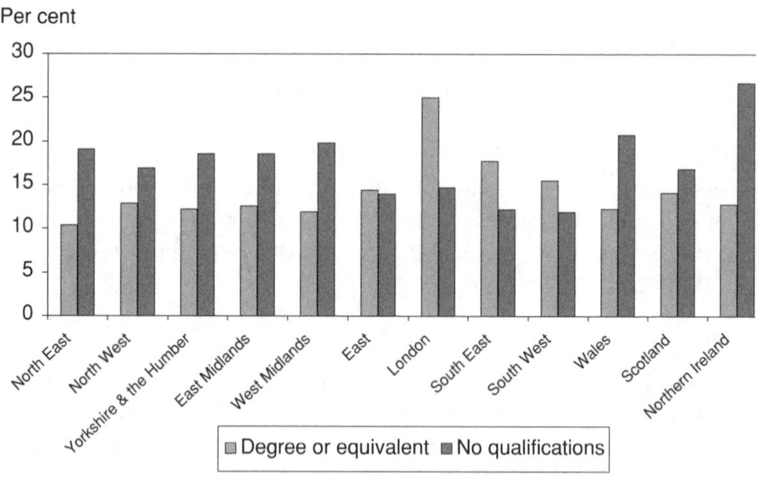

Source: *DfES*

Figure 5.7 Highest qualification (% of working age population), 2001

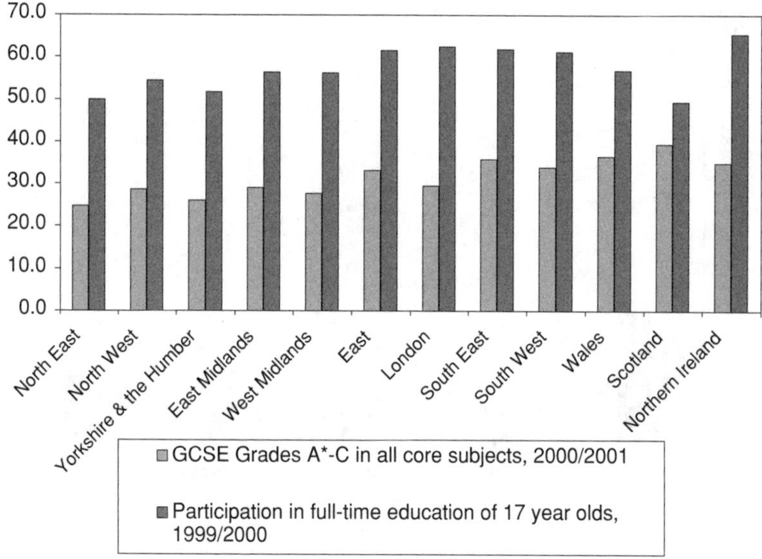

Source: DFES

Figure 5.8 Education by region

Looking at the stock of skills in the workforce in London shows that 38 per cent of the working age population have attained NVQ level 4 (equivalent to degree level) compared with 23 per cent in the East Midlands and North East.

These disparities increase further at the sub-regional level. For example, Figure 5.9, shows that, at each skill level, the disparities within the East Midlands and London regions are greater than the disparities between regions. Significant sub-regional variations exist, therefore, in both the current stock of workforce skills and the flow of skills into the labour market, leading to disparities in labour supply that must be addressed if all localities are to improve economic growth.

This analysis suggests two things. First, developing the skills of regions' and localities' workforces is essential to achieve high levels of productivity and employment. Second, measures taken to increase educational attainment in an area, while important for the UK as a whole, will not necessarily lead to improvements in the skill levels of a local workforce if high-skill workers move away. Regions can find themselves vulnerable to virtuous or vicious circles: high productivity locations can attract

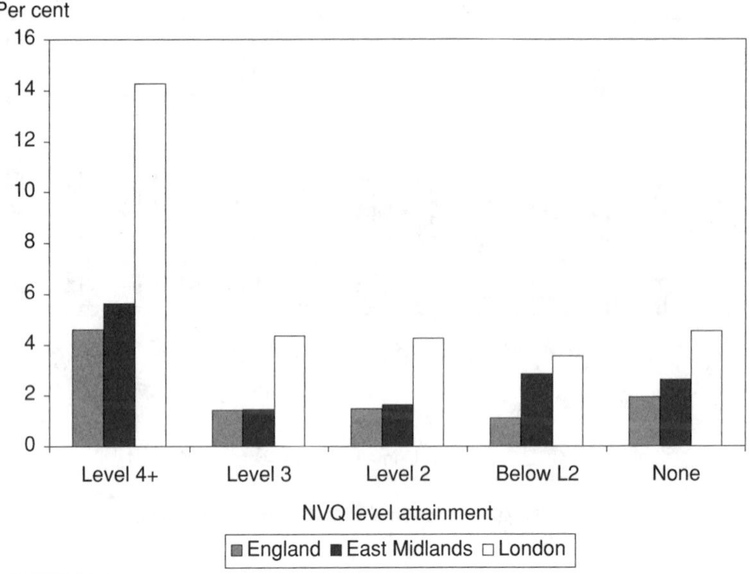

Source: DfES/HMT.

Figure 5.9 Skill levels: disparities within/between regions

skilled workers, which in turn attracts new firms; areas with low productivity firms may find it difficult to retain the highly skilled labour necessary for future development. Regions and localities need to sustain high-wage jobs to ensure that high-skilled workers remain there.

Investment

As discussed in Chapter 2, at a national level, much of the UK's productivity gap with France and Germany is due to differences in physical capital (plants and machinery) (O'Mahoney and de Boer 2001). Only limited data are available on the UK's capital stock at regional level. That which exists[15] does not suggest that there is general under-investment in physical capital in the worst-performing regions of the UK, although notable regional differences in investment patterns do exist.

Venture capital funding, for example, is significantly higher per capita in London than in any other region[16]. Foreign direct investment is also increasingly directed towards London and the South East, which attracted over 40 per cent of all investment projects in 1999/00 compared with less than one-fifth in the mid 1990s[17]. Foreign investment can be important in stimulating an area's development, since foreign-owned firms have higher average productivity levels than comparable domestic-owned firms, and provide positive spillover benefits in their areas by introducing new technologies, working practices, and competition[18].

In general, the spread of capital expenditure in manufacturing varies among regions and sub-regions. To a certain extent, differences in levels of capital expenditure (as presented in Figure 5.10) between regions may just reflect the industrial composition of different regions: the North East, for example, has relatively high levels of capital expenditure in manufacturing per worker but the manufacturing sector also accounts for a relatively high proportion of its industry.

It is also likely that some of the regional averages, and therefore the large spreads of productivity, are skewed by the presence of one sub-region where capital expenditure is especially high. In turn, this may reflect, at least in some instances, the presence of one or two firms that invest heavily in physical capital. Therefore, it is unclear whether raising investment in physical capital alone will have a substantial impact on economic growth and productivity at a local level.

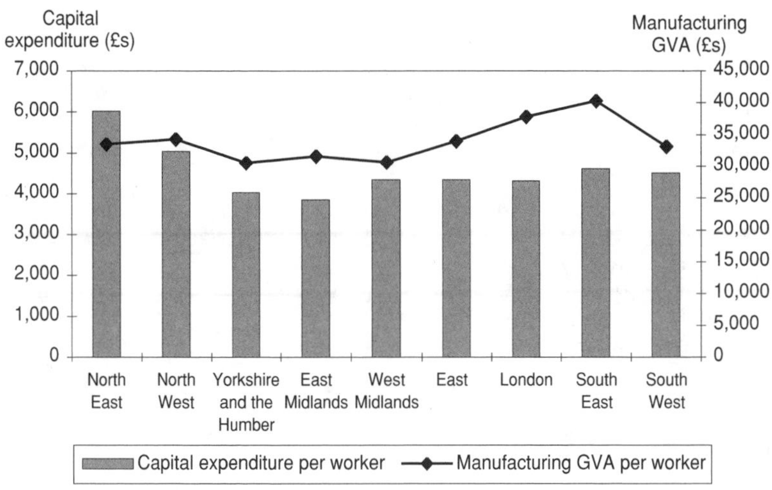

Source: ONS.

Figure 5.10 Manufacturing capital expenditure per worker and manufacturing GDP per worker, 1997

Furthermore, at sub-regional level, differences in access to capital may be important in influencing productivity. It is widely documented that people and firms in deprived communities often find it more difficult to obtain finance in order to start or develop businesses. For example, low property values can make it difficult for entrepreneurs to provide collateral to secure business loans necessary for investment[19].

Science and innovation

Measuring innovation by region is not straightforward. One indicator is expenditure on research and development (R&D), which in the UK varies considerably by region – see Figure 5.11. R&D expenditure per capita in the East and the South East in 2001, for example, totalled around £500, compared with under £100 in the North East and Yorkshire and the Humber.

Although comparable figures are not available at a sub-regional level, it is possible to get an idea of the innovative capacity of a local area by looking at the number of R&D firms. Figure 5.12 shows that the number and size of these firms vary widely within a region. However, it is

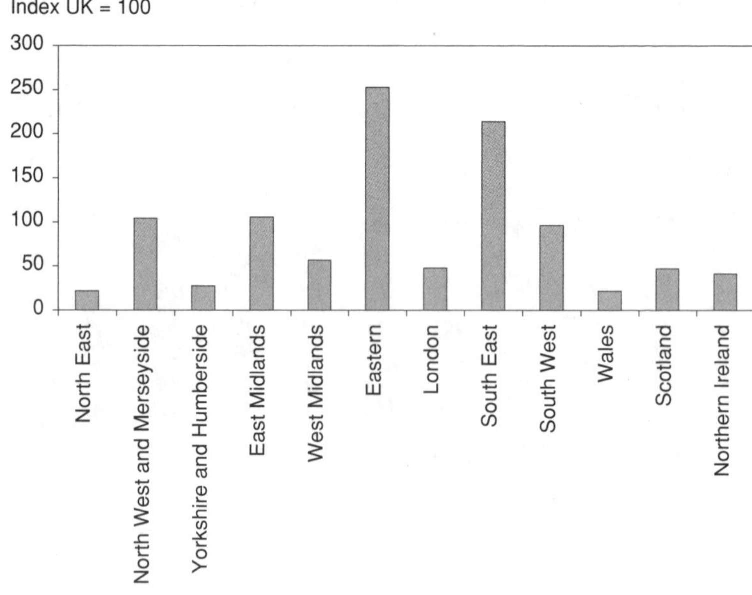

Source: ONS.

Figure 5.11 Expenditure on R&D performed in UK businesses (UK=100, 2001)

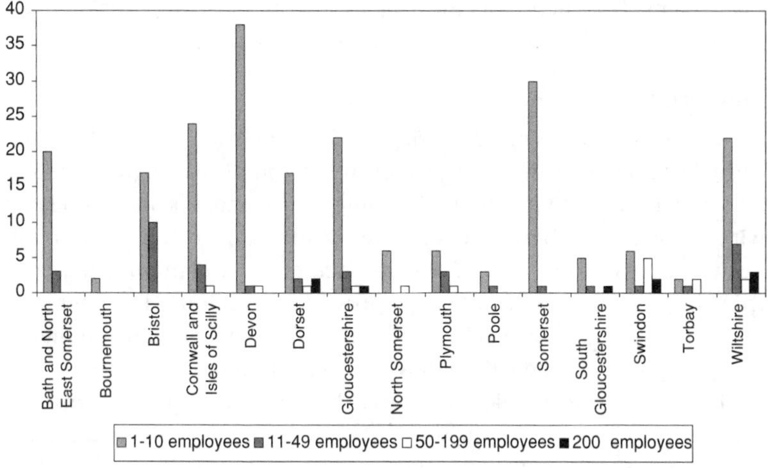

Source: ONS/ABI

Figure 5.12 Number of R&D firms in the South West by sub-region, 2001

important to treat these figures with some caution: firms that are engaged in innovative activity may not be included in these figures, and there may also be problems with the classification of firms that have plants in more than one region but whose R&D activity is centred in just one area. In addition, R&D data alone indicates little about the extent to which this research is successfully diffused and incorporated into firms' production processes.

While R&D spending is an input into the innovation process, patents are an output. There are a number of reasons why patents, looked at in isolation, may not be a good indicator of innovation.[20] Nevertheless, data suggest that there are large differences in the number of UK patents applied for in different cities across the UK and that these differences are larger within regions.

Studies have also shown that under-performing regions and localities have particular problems absorbing new technologies developed elsewhere[21]. Areas with a higher proportion of jobs in high-technology sectors tend to be more able to adopt new technologies[22]. It is therefore significant that in 2001 more than 6 per cent of jobs in London and the South East were in the high-technology sector, compared with 2 per cent or less in the North East and Yorkshire and the Humber[23].

The ability of firms to adopt innovative products and processes will depend on the other drivers of productivity, especially skills and investment. This highlights the importance of improving the skills base in all localities to help enable firms to take advantage of innovations.

Enterprise

Successful enterprises are a key driver of productivity growth. Research carried out on cities in the US, for example, found that higher levels of entrepreneurial activity are, with a time lag, strongly positively related with subsequent higher growth rates (Zoltan and Armington 2003). Businesses also form part of the bedrock of local communities, contributing to economic prosperity and social cohesion. They therefore have a key role to play in delivering sustainable regeneration and higher living standards in the UK's disadvantaged communities.

There are large regional differences in business start-up rates across the UK. People in London and the South East of England are much more likely to start a business than their counterparts in other regions of the UK. Business creation rates in 2001 ranged from 20 new VAT registrations per 10,000 resident population in the North East to 59 per 10,000 in London[24].

As Figure 5.13 shows, this is by no means a recent phenomenon but a feature of at least the last two decades. In fact, the gap in start-up levels between the regions with the highest and lowest rate of new VAT registrations has actually widened over the last 20 years.

Significant disparities are also apparent at sub-regional and local levels. Across the North East as a whole, for example, the business start-up rate is 19 VAT registrations per 10,000 of the resident adult population (Figure 5.14). However, this masks a wide variation, with Teesdale having a start-up rate of 33 registrations – over three times that of Wansbeck, at 10 per 10,000 of the resident adult population.

Competition

Competition policy is largely determined nationally or supra-nationally and, at this level, work by Nickell (1996) and Disney, Haskel and Heden (2000) finds that there is a positive relationship between competition and productivity growth.

However, while the competitive framework is set at a national level, differing levels of competitive pressures in a particular region or sub-region can have an impact on that area's economic prosperity and productivity. Firms in poorer and more remote regions may face less competition, and hence reduced incentives to cut costs and innovate. Equally, lower competitive intensity can make it less likely that business start-ups occur, affecting enterprise levels.

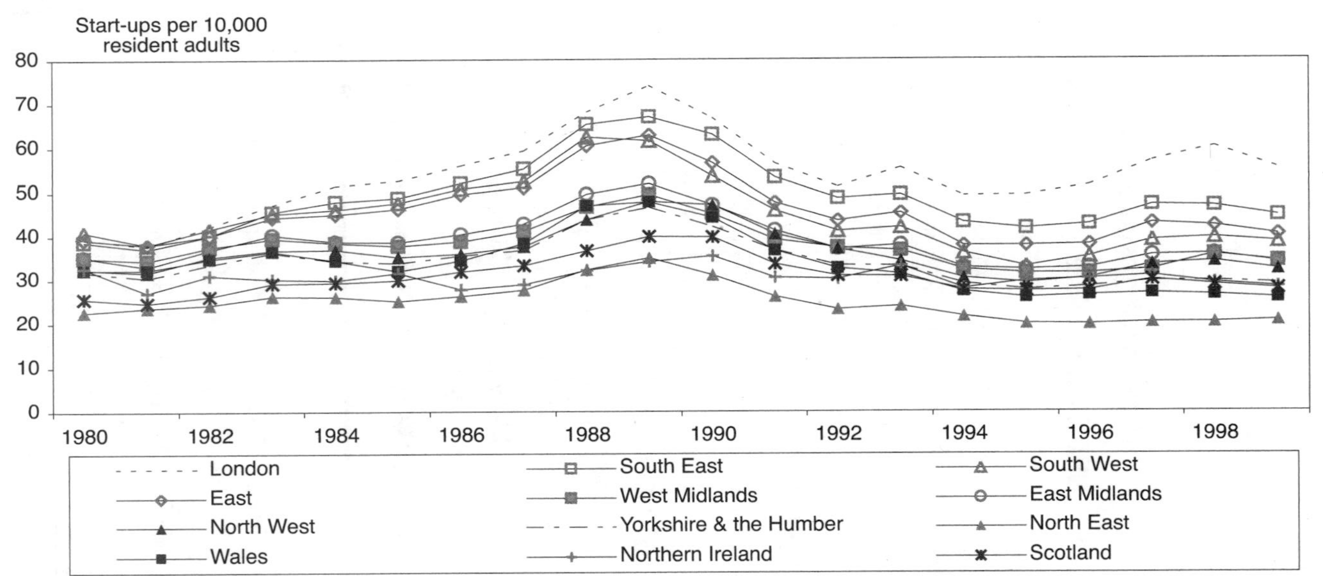

Source: Small Business Service

Figure 5.13 Business start-ups by region per 10,000 resident adults

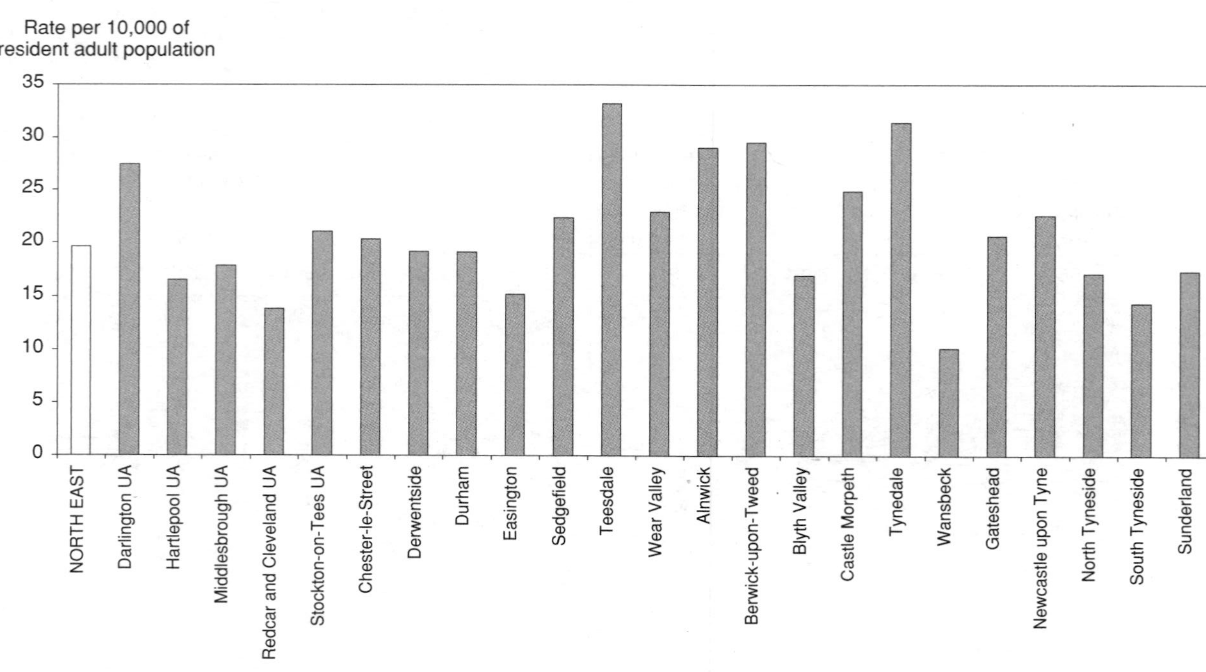

Source: SBS

Figure 5.14 Business start-ups (VAT registrations) in the North East

Since 1980, the higher start-up rates in London and the South East have increased the local business stock by more than a third, meaning more businesses per head of population and greater local competition. By contrast, the North East of England, Scotland, and Wales have seen only marginal net growth in the size of their business communities[25].

Many of the benefits of competition on efficiency, productivity and hence on economic growth originate from changes in the behaviour of firms in local areas. Competition can enhance the available information about the market, meaning that owners of firms are better able to assess the performance of their managers. This is a form of 'yardstick competition', but it holds only when firms operate in similar environments. Hence this effect is more likely to bite at a local level, where the performance and innovative activity of other firms are highly visible (Davis and Majumdar 2002). Transport links may also affect the level of competition that firms face: poorer transport links may limit the extent to which some firms are open to competition from outside their immediate vicinity.

Market failures at the regional and local level

If the economic processes driving growth worked effectively, the same patterns of economic activity would not be expected to persist. Relatively faster growth would occur in the lagging regions as new technologies and best practice spread from the leading regions and firms discovered new investment opportunities. That this has not occurred points, among other things, to market failures in the under-performing regions and localities.

Regional and local market failures, as distinct from those at the national or international level, can persist because markets are not always national in scope. Market failures can occur in:

- product markets, where a lack of competitive pressures can impact on efficiency and prices, and reduce incentives for innovation;
- capital markets, where credit rationing can result in under-investment in innovation and human and physical capital across all parts of the UK; and
- labour markets, where inflexibility, low labour mobility, and weak incentives to invest in human capital can restrict workers' and firms' ability to take advantage of new opportunities.

Location decisions of firms and workers

The extent to which productivity and employment levels converge between regions broadly depends on the location decisions of firms and workers[26].

Movements of firms and workers in smoothly functioning markets should, in theory, tend to equalise productivity and employment across the UK. This is because workers should move from depressed, low-wage regions to high-growth, high-wage regions in response to differentials in wage levels and employment opportunities. This will increase the supply of labour to high-growth areas and depress wages there and the opposite should happen in the low-wage regions. This process should lead to a convergence of regional wage levels.

Similarly, we would expect firms to move away from regions with high levels of economic activity into relatively depressed regions. They would face less competition in depressed areas, which would tend to increase their profitability; they might be able to take advantage of untapped local markets and relatively cheaper factors of production such as land and labour; and they might benefit from escaping the externalities associated with producing in high-productivity regions, such as the costs associated with pollution and congestion[27].

However, a number of factors work against convergence between regions. The following two subsections discuss in greater detail the factors that may explain the location decisions of both labour and firms and, in particular, how both decisions may be affected by the phenomenon of agglomeration or clustering.

Labour mobility

High levels of productivity and employment require efficient matching of workers and jobs at local and regional levels, as well as between regions (and even countries). Frictions in the labour market can reduce the effectiveness of labour mobility as a regional adjustment mechanism. This could result in low productivity because workers' skills and jobs are inadequately matched, and high unemployment because vacancies and workers are poorly matched. Evidence from the USA suggests that labour mobility is an important mechanism for adjusting to longer-term structural change, as discussed in the EMU study *The United States as a monetary union (see Annex 7.1 for further details).*

In fact, evidence suggests that many workers' location decisions in the UK are based on wage differentials, as theory suggests they should be[28]. But there is also evidence[29] of labour market failures which constrain labour mobility as an effective local and regional adjustment mechanism. Low-skilled workers are less likely than skilled workers to move between regions, and generally seem to look for work in local labour markets. The information costs which are borne by employers to advertise posts can also deter them from advertising low-skilled jobs very widely. These labour market failures appear less significant in the US, however, where migration rates of manual workers are slightly higher than those of non-manual workers.

The persistence of long-term unemployment in certain areas, the fact that the long-term unemployed are only marginally more likely than employed people to relocate[30] in search of work and labour market rigidities all undermine regional development. Long-term unemployment rate figures suggest that these labour-market mismatch problems are particularly pronounced in the North East, Northern Ireland, the West Midlands, London, and Wales. In contrast, the South East and the East of the UK may be constrained in their growth potential by a lack of inward migration[31].

Labour mobility is constrained in the UK by a range of factors. High levels of home ownership and regionally divergent house prices reduce the ability of workers to relocate. For example, in the North and the Midlands, over 1 million homes are afflicted by low demand and abandonment, while in other areas demand is not being met, with house building now at its lowest level since the 1920s and insufficient to meet the growth in household numbers. In addition, non-portable housing assistance schemes, such as rent controls, can reduce the ability of low-income households to move. Limited information about jobs in other areas, and the lack of informal family networks outside a region, can also act as a disincentive to move. The impact of the structure of the housing market in the UK is discussed further in the EMU study *EMU and labour market flexibility (see Annex 7.1 for further details).*

Improvements in labour migration would therefore improve skills matching in the UK. In this context, policy has been addressing the serious imbalances between supply and demand that have emerged in regional housing markets. The Government is also committed to ensuring, through intervention if necessary, that local authorities in areas of high demand deliver the housing numbers set out in Regional Planning Guidance. Funding is also being provided for new investment in housing, supporting the provision of additional affordable housing. New Regional Housing Boards have been established, bringing housing investment within a single regional pot. In Budget 2003, the Government also announced the creation of two reviews of housing to address housing issues: the Barker Review, which will review the issues affecting the supply of housing in the UK; and Professor David Miles' review of the supply- and demand-side factors limiting the development of the fixed rate mortgage market in the UK. The EMU study *Housing, consumption and EMU (see Annex 7.1 for further details)* identified housing as a key structural difference between the UK and the euro area.

However, there is a need to be cautious about the ability of inter-regional migration flows to provide a complete solution to an area's economic problems. Areas of high unemployment are frequently within travelling distance of labour markets with high levels of vacancies. If people from deprived areas are unable to compete in local markets, moving may not reduce overall unemployment rates. In addition, high mobility of skilled workers can result in an unintended negative impact on the economic performance of those workers they leave behind in more deprived areas.

Firm mobility: agglomeration effects and coordination failures

Recent work suggests that agglomerations, or clusters, of firms and skilled workers may be one of the key drivers of economic growth in localities, cities, and regions[32]. Successful clusters may be crucial to a region's success in attracting and retaining high-productivity firms and workers.

Clusters emerge in a region or a locality as firms exploit one or more of the advantages of locating near to competitors[33], such as knowledge 'spillovers' (information about local centres of research, which can be vital to innovatory firms); proximity to suppliers; and a sophisticated and skilled local labour market with an abundance of the required skills.

Agglomeration occurs because of beneficial externalities between firms and between firms and workers. But firms are not always best placed to assess the benefits of locating in different places. There may be poor information about the costs and benefits of location decisions, and there is no reason to expect different firms and workers to coordinate their location decisions optimally.

The inability of firms and workers to coordinate decisions is likely to lead to a persistence of economic differentials by preventing the economic recovery of under-performing regions and localities. First, firms may be attracted to existing successful clusters because of the benefits they bring. Second, if a region does experience a negative economic shock, perhaps caused by changes in technology or shifts in consumer demand, cluster effects can in some circumstances 'lock in' the impact. The shock will lead to a loss of jobs and a fall in GDP per capita. Where the local economy is inflexible, the region may be unable to recover. As firms go bankrupt and unemployment rises, the benefits of staying in the area decrease and firms and workers – skilled workers first –leave the area.

The situation may be further exacerbated as declining relative levels of economic activity can lead to a breakdown of public infrastructure, increasing amounts of vacant land, a rise in poverty, and a deterioration of social infrastructure. In such cases, economic recovery requires that firms and skilled workers return to the area, but this is unlikely to happen without a coordinated effort. Under-performance in a region or locality can become entrenched, as has been the experience of some northern English conurbations and former coalfield areas[34].

Clusters in the UK vary in terms of their industry, size, geographical scale, and depth. They play a key part in the success of London,[35] the South East, and the East. Clusters in these regions are more likely to consist of service-sector industries, most notably the financial services cluster in London, and R&D-intensive industries such as biotechnology and pharmaceuticals in East Anglia and ICT in the Thames Valley. Job creation in these clusters is higher than the average for these regions.

In other UK countries and regions, there are large manufacturing clusters: for example, the automotive clusters in the Midlands, metals in Yorkshire and Humber, chemicals in the North East, and shipbuilding and engineering in Scotland. However, on average these countries and regions do not seem to have the same success at exploiting the benefits of agglomeration. Cluster job-creation performance is no better than the regional average and in some cases is significantly worse.

Exploiting the benefits of agglomeration therefore requires clusters of high-productivity firms and workers. Coordination failures may have been preventing large parts of the UK from acquiring the necessary minimum threshold of economic activity to support such clusters and hence higher levels of productivity and employment. Coordination failures are likely to be a main cause of the significant and persistent economic differentials presented earlier in this chapter.

Can regions' economic performance converge?

Academic research[36] on regional convergence suggests that regional differentials can be successfully tackled, but success is by no means certain. GDP per capita is currently converging across the US states[37] and the regions of the EU[38]. But the picture is not entirely positive: over recent decades, the inequalities between regional GDP per capita in the UK have remained broadly constant from an aggregate point of view, and regional variations in productivity in the EU have proved fairly durable over time.

There are grounds for optimism. Falling transport costs and the introduction of new communication technologies could aid regional dispersal of economic activity to more peripheral regions. Call centres in the North East, North West, and Scotland are a good example. In addition, the rate of technological diffusion has increased in recent years as a result of the growing integration of capital markets, the development of communications technology, and the increase in global competition. On the other hand, other new-technology industries, especially knowledge-based industries, tend to remain highly clustered in a number of regional centres across the world, such as Silicon Valley (USA), Cambridge (UK), and Oulu (Finland).

Whether regional convergence or divergence will occur cannot therefore be taken for granted. However, over the next ten years regional disparities should be reduced by policy action to tackle the market failures and low-growth equilibria.

The role of government

Regional economic policy should not be seen as separate but rather as an integral part of the overarching policy framework for raising the rate of sustainable UK growth. However, past regional and local development policies have had mixed outcomes.[39]

In the UK and other countries, large-scale public infrastructure investments have often failed to stimulate long-term regional economic growth despite successfully stimulating demand in the short run[40]. Similarly, capital subsidies and other forms of regional support, which have often been used to cushion the effects of structural change by protecting stagnating industries, have frequently sacrificed long-term regional productivity and employment growth because they have inhibited structural change. For example, industrial coal and steel subsidies in the Ruhr Valley, in Germany, and measures to protect domestic industries in Japan have resulted in serious productivity shortfalls in the affected regions and industries[41].

In contrast, investment programmes, that have complemented and facilitated structural change, have generally been successful. The construction of international airports to support the growing tourist industry in Crete, for instance, proved critical in securing the region's economic revival. Comprehensive regional and local economic development programmes have also been successful[42].

The overall lesson is that, to be successful government intervention has to complement and promote structural development and change. Programmes to build regional economic capacity and human and social capital need to be complemented by policies to build a network of firms capable of sustaining high levels of growth, without persistent government finance.

The Framework for Regional Policy in the UK

Meeting the objective of achieving high and stable levels of growth and employment, means that every country and region of the UK needs to be able to perform to its full economic potential. Policy therefore needs to address, in every country and region, the diverse market and social failures that are holding them back.[43] The key elements of this strategy are:

- macroeconomic stability, providing a stable basis to plan and invest;
- microeconomic reforms to tackle market failures at the national, regional, and local level; and
- devolution and decentralisation so that regions and localities have the resources and flexibility to deliver locally led policies within a framework of clear accountability.

In addition, as described earlier, a target has now been set to reduce the disparities in regional growth. This is necessarily a long-term target, reflecting the degree of challenge in addressing disparities that have existed for generations. An extensive process of evidence gathering is now under way, involving engagement with local stakeholders including the Regional Development Agencies, local authorities and the business community. The aim is to reinforce the existing approach by identifying policy priorities and developing a comprehensive long-term strategy.

The Treasury publishes a series of regional pamphlets[44] setting out the impact of major policy announcements, such as the Budget, at a regional level. These will illustrate what the policy measures announced in the Budget mean for each regional area and help to link national goals with regional needs.

The Institutional Framework

As this chapter has shown, market and coordination failures can prevent regions and localities from taking advantage of new opportunities. The institutional structure will be important in tackling these issues. This section discusses the programme of constitutional and institutional reform measures taken since 1997.

Effective regional and local institutions are essential to building areas where workers want to live and where successful businesses can flourish. They can produce better-tailored and informed policies, and improved service delivery to local citizens.

In Scotland, Wales, and Northern Ireland, the Devolved Administrations have substantial autonomy over economic development functions and over key productivity drivers such as skills and innovation. In England, the Government has established eight Regional Development Agencies (RDAs) to take the lead in formulating regional economic strategies. In London, the London Development Agency under the Greater London Authority fulfils the same role. The RDAs work in partnership with local authorities, Local Learning and Skills Councils (LLSCs), the Small Business Service (SBS), and other local and regional bodies. They act as strategic leaders of economic development in their region and are responsible for carrying out a detailed analysis of the region's particular strengths, weaknesses, and needs. They have drawn up Regional Economic Strategies and are working with other regional partners to supplement these with the Regional Employment and Skills Frameworks, the Regional Transport Strategies, and the Regional Planning Strategies.

The RDAs have been given budgets rising to £2 billion in 2005–06 and unprecedented flexibility and autonomy to find the most effective way of meeting the targets which they have been set. This increased flexibility is being matched with increased accountability through both national targets and scrutiny by Regional Chambers.

Both regional and local bodies have a key role to play in driving progress towards regionally balanced growth. To this end, the Government is continuing to work closely with the LGA, local authorities, the Core Cities and the RDAs to develop the local economic growth agenda. For example, following extensive consultation the Government is introducing the Local Authority Business Growth Incentives scheme, which will give local authorities a direct financial incentive to maximise economic growth in their area – see the enterprise section below for more detail.

In England, the Government Offices and the RDAs work together to ensure that their region will get the maximum return on EU Structural Funds, the EU's main instruments for supporting social and economic restructuring across the Union. Assessing Structural Fund bids strategically across the region means that the projects supported by the funds can directly reflect the region's priority needs and directly address local weaknesses.

In order to improve enterprise and employment in deprived neighbourhoods, the Government has also set 'floor' PSA targets for public service delivery, which determine key minimum-outcome levels below which no area should fall. For example, the 2002 Spending Review included a housing target to achieve a more sustainable balance between housing availability and the demand for housing in all English regions, while protecting the countryside around towns and the sustainability of existing towns and cities. It also included a target to raise standards in schools and colleges, as discussed in Chapter 4.

The rationale behind this new approach to targeting spending in poor neighbourhoods is that much more substantial sums are spent through main departmental programmes than could ever be spent on specific area-based initiatives. The floor-target approach helps ensure that core public services take responsibility for disadvantaged areas rather than relying only on special schemes to deliver improvements in the worst-performing areas.

The National Strategy for Neighbourhood Renewal has also been established to improve outcomes at sub-regional and local levels. £525 million will be provided to the 88 most deprived local authority areas through the Neighbourhood Renewal Fund by 2005–06. In these deprived areas, new Local Strategic Partnerships (LSPs) have been established, which are responsible for drawing up strategies for tackling neighbourhood deprivation and in particular reducing isolation from the economic mainstream.

As of July 2003, Local Public Service Agreements (PSAs) have been negotiated with 92 out of 150 local authorities that have committed to deliver more ambitious outcomes in return for greater flexibilities, freedoms, and financial rewards if they succeed. As the most immediate tier of government in the localities of the UK, local authorities have a key leadership and coordinating role, bringing together local partners around the shared aims of community strategies. Government can facilitate and encourage this in two ways. First, local authorities require the legislative and administrative freedom to pursue these goals. Second, Government can provide incentives for local authorities to pursue economic growth and make policy reforms to allow local authorities to influence productivity growth at the local level. The Government can also act to promote business activity and employment in the poorest neighbourhoods.

Finally, the Government has recently published a consultation document[45] proposing reform of the EU's regional policy, based on an EU Framework for Devolved Regional Policy that would improve regional flexibility in the UK and the euro area.

Microeconomic reforms

The strategy for tackling market and coordination failures aims at increasing the long-term efficiency and flexibility of regions and localities. Although regions that are affected by large economic shocks (such as large-scale redundancies) will require assistance for a short period, it is likely that long-term dependence on such assistance would damage their long-term growth prospects by discouraging structural change.

Thus it is likely that special assistance for the most deprived areas in the UK, or those suffering large-scale economic shocks, will be effective only if it is focused on creating the foundations for higher long-term growth.

The rest of this chapter sets out how policy has addressed the five key productivity drivers at regional level. The preference is for a bottom-up approach to regional development policy, within a national framework that allows regional and local institutions to work, and improves the performance of the weakest regions without constraining growth in the strongest.

Skills

To increase the level of skills in the economy overall, funding has been provided to invest in and reform education and training in the UK. The proportion of GDP spent on education in the UK has risen from 4.7 per cent in 1996–97 to 5.4 per cent in 2004–05. Spending on education in England will show an average increase of 6 per cent a year in real terms over the next three years. These additional resources are tied to long-term goals to increase the flow of young people entering skilled employment, and increase skill levels among adults. Targets set locally for individual schools and Local Education Authorities to achieve local and national targets for 11-, 14-, and 16-year-olds will also help raise standards across each region.

Recognising the regional dimension of the skills problem, RDAs, working closely with the Learning and Skills Council at national and local levels, have been given the task of drawing up Regional Employment and Skills Frameworks. These are designed to address the skills and employment needs of employers and individuals in their region. In addition, since April 2003 four RDAs are, with local LSCs, developing approaches to joint working regionally, in particular by testing ways of pooling their budgets for adult learning and skills activities. The aim of these pilots is to increase employer demand for skills and to equip more adults with the skills, competencies, knowledge and understanding which employers need. This will allow a closer alignment of regional skills funding with Regional Employment and Skills Frameworks.

Employer Training Pilots, which were introduced in September 2002 to improve access to training, are also involving all local partners in delivering skills and training, further demonstrating the Government's commitment to the devolution of control over skills training to meet regional and sub-regional priorities and the needs of local business and employees. Chapter 4 provides more detail on these pilots and on measures to improve skills more generally.

Investment

The changes to corporation tax and tax credits, set out in Chapter 4, should encourage business investment in all regions of the UK. At a regional level, action has also been taken to reduce market failures in investment. The provision of equity capital for small, growing firms in deprived areas can be problematic. Low property values mean that firms lack the collateral with which to secure loans, and investors lack information about the viability of businesses in deprived areas. In some cases, firms' financing needs are not suited to traditional bank debt finance, but are not large enough to attract, cost-effectively, the interest of the majority of venture capital and other private equity providers.

To help tackle this 'equity gap', the Government has established Regional Venture Capital Funds (RVCFs) in each of the nine English regions. The funds will make available up to £270 million, including a government contribution of up to £80 million, for investment in early-stage businesses with growth potential. The RVCF programme aims to demonstrate the potential to make commercial returns on smaller investments, and so to encourage increased private-sector participation in the market for small-scale risk capital. The regional basis of the funds will deliver enhanced provision of risk capital across all English regions.

Innovation

The RDAs are now taking a stronger role in promoting innovation, as part of their Regional Economic Strategies. They are working with universities, industry and other regional economic agencies to develop the innovative capacity of firms and research institutions in their areas by, for example, providing local leadership through regional science and industry councils, and working to create successful clusters and promote knowledge transfer between the science base and business. The £45 million University Challenge[46] – which provided seed funding for 37 higher education institutions to help develop promising research from UK universities into projects that might attract commercial investment – is a good example of how national policy priorities can be treated flexibly, to deliver regional centres of excellence. RDAs can also play a useful role in helping shape bids to other national schemes that encourage innovation through business–university links, such as the Higher Education Innovation Fund, to play to regional strengths and contribute to regional innovation strategies.

The Department of Trade and Industry (DTI), the RDAs and the Welsh Development Agency are jointly committed to the development of a Manufacturing Advisory Service to be delivered in every region of England and Wales through Regional Centres for Manufacturing Excellence (RCMEs). The Regional Centres provide best practice guidance to manufacturing SMEs in their region. They are supported by a National Network of Centres of Expertise in Manufacturing to facilitate manufacturers' access to in-depth expertise when needed. Formal launch of the first RCMEs commenced during April 2002. They are jointly funded by DTI and the RDAs, initially for a three year period, and provide practical, 'hands-on' help for smaller manufacturing firms that want to introduce world-class manufacturing practices and technologies.

Enterprise

The range of measures described in Chapter 4 are designed to raise levels of enterprise in all regions of the UK, and the Small Business Service (SBS), which was established in 2000 to drive progress towards the aim to make the UK the best place in the world to start and grow a business, will play an important role in delivering this objective. The SBS has recently published its framework for taking forward policy for small businesses, emphasising its role in championing small businesses' needs across government.

To improve the coherence and quality of local business support, the 2002 Spending Review announced that the SBS would launch pilots in selected regions to test the regional coordination and management of business support. This included RDA management of Business Link Operators, which manage the local delivery of business support. Since April 2003, two-year pilot schemes have been under way in the East Midlands, the West Midlands and the North West (which is also conducting an adult learning and skills pilot with the local LSC). The pilots will test innovative approaches to ensuring that regional business support services are closely aligned to the needs of local businesses and are delivered effectively. The pilot evaluation will also capture lessons on joint working and new delivery models from non-pilot areas.

For the majority of small firms, the local level is where their experience of government is shaped. Local authorities enforce regulations and also help to coordinate and deliver specific business support services. Local authorities therefore have an important role to play, working with the Inland Revenue, Customs and Excise, and Business Links, as well as other local bodies, to ensure that businesses are aware of and able to access business support and advice that is relevant to their needs. More generally, local authorities play a key role in supporting economic development in their area. Recognising this, the Government has consulted extensively with RDAs and the Local Government Association (LGA) on how they can drive progress towards regionally balanced growth. The Local Authority Business Growth Incentives scheme aims to give local authorities a direct financial incentive to maximise economic growth in their area. Analysis based on historical growth rates shows that the scheme could be worth up to £1 billion to local authorities over a three-year period, by allowing them to retain a proportion of increases in local business rate revenues. The extra resources will be entirely additional to local authorities, with no ringfencing by central government. Furthermore, no business will pay more under the scheme. Local authorities can also contribute to building a positive environment for enterprise by working with RDAs on the development and implementation of the Regional Economic Strategy, and through the operation of the planning system.

The SBS is working to ensure that the most disadvantaged groups have equal opportunities to start up and become involved in business through its Phoenix Fund, which was established in 1999. By 2002, the fund had supported over 150 organisations, including business support organisations taking innovative approaches to engaging with disadvantaged communities, and Community Development Finance Institutions (CDFIs), which provide finance and support to businesses that cannot access mainstream sources of finance. The fund also provided the Government's contribution to the Bridges Community Development Venture Fund. This is a £40 million venture capital fund, made up of £20 million of public funding and £20 million of private sector investment, which makes equity investments in businesses in deprived areas that can demonstrate a meaningful interaction with the local economy. Building on its success, the 2002 Spending Review provided for the extension of the Phoenix Fund with a further £50 million over the following two years.

In addition, a Community Investment Tax Relief (CITR) has been introduced to encourage private investment in not-for-profit and profit-seeking enterprises in under-invested communities through CDFIs. Twenty CDFIs have been accredited by the SBS to offer Community Investment Tax Relief, and they plan to raise £88 million of investments over the next three years.

Furthermore, following a recommendation set out in the 1999 report of the Urban Task Force[47], an exemption from stamp duty has been available for all property transfers up to £150,000 in the UK's most disadvantaged areas. This exemption was designed to encourage both families and businesses to locate in these areas, encouraging local investment, enterprise and employment. At Budget 2003, the Government abolished stamp duty on all non-residential transfers in the qualifying areas.

Competition

To ensure the effective functioning of a single market across the UK, competition policy and enforcement is a responsibility that lies at the national level. The Enterprise Bill and the reforms to the regime for investigating cartels, outlined in Chapter 4 are designed to achieve improved levels of competition in the UK. Effective strong competition should drive improvements in productivity in every region.

Local authorities' trading standards departments have an important role in drawing competitive abuses to the attention of the Office of Fair Trading (OFT). The OFT has also run an extensive small business education programme to ensure that understanding of competition law and the benefits of competition are spread throughout the country.

Conclusion

Significant differences in the economic performance of the UK countries, regions and localities have been allowed to persist for generations. Yet the benefits to the UK if every region performed to its potential would be significant. A successful regional policy must focus on improving the economic performance of every country, region and local area by tackling the diverse social and market failures that have held them back. To address disparities in regional and local economic performance, the Government has created a new framework of regional and local institutions, focused on exploiting indigenous sources of economic strength. Working flexibly with these local and regional institutions, the Government has introduced a range of microeconomic reforms aimed at strengthening the 'five drivers', to raise productivity in each regional and locality.

6
The Environment

This chapter outlines theoretical economic approaches to the environment and the practical considerations that must be taken into account when developing policy. The chapter describes some of the measures put in place to date and discusses how progress against the Government's environmental objectives and targets can be evaluated.

Introduction

Improving the environment and delivering sustainable development is a challenge facing all governments, businesses and consumers.

Economics provides a framework for assessing the extent and nature of government action to deal with environmental issues, helping to inform judgements on how to balance environmental, economic and social impacts. In general, markets will provide the best means of allocating an economy's environmental resources. As in the areas discussed previously, the role of markets is to allocate resources efficiently and equitably. However, many markets are subject to imperfections or failures that do not price environmental costs properly. The role of government is therefore to tackle these market failures to avoid market outcomes that are damaging to the environment. The optimum level of intervention depends on the nature of the environmental problem and the extent and type of market failure. In assessing the type and scale of intervention it is necessary to take account of the dynamic nature of these markets as well as the uncertainties inherent in many environmental impacts and the scope for innovation and technological developments. This overall approach has been set out in depth in *Tax and the Environment: Using economic instruments* (HM Treasury 2002d).

This chapter sets out the economic explanations for the environmental problems experienced in the UK and the range of theoretical solutions that suggest themselves. This is followed by a discussion of how these theoretical solutions can be brought into practical effect and how policy measures should be chosen, designed and implemented. The chapter ends with a brief overview of how environmental policy can be evaluated, and assesses the progress of policy measures introduced to date.

Environmental policy-making: the framework

The framework for assessing whether and how to intervene to improve the environment is grounded in economic theory, but also takes account of good practice in policy making. There are a number of steps that need to be taken.

First, the environmental policy objective needs to be identified. The Government has strategies for each of the key environmental issues, such as tackling climate change, improving air quality, regenerating towns and cities, protecting the countryside and tackling the problems of waste. Each of these strategies sets out the issues involved and the objectives which need to be met.

Second, the rationale for government involvement in helping to achieve the objectives needs to be assessed, such as identifying and tackling specific market failures. On occasions, government may need to intervene in order to achieve specific targets or commitments.

Third, the benefits and costs of government intervention need to be appraised. The potential environmental benefits need to be compared to the costs of achieving them. In addition, the Government needs to consider the potential distributional effects and compliance costs, the impacts on the competitiveness of sectors exposed to international competition, how the intervention will be implemented in practice, and how to manage any associated risks (such as unintended consequences).

Fourth, the most efficient instruments for achieving the objectives need to be determined. The most efficient approach will be the one that provides the greatest overall economic net benefits. In practice, the instruments include taxes, spending programmes, regulation, the provision of information, voluntary agreements, and various combinations of these and other measures.

The extent to which the potential instruments have synergies or trade-offs with other economic and social objectives and the extent to which these are acceptable will also need to be factored into the choice of instrument.

Finally, the process of policy development and implementation needs to be appropriate. Given the long-term nature of many environmental problems and the significant impacts which some policy measures can have, policies to tackle the environment are generally best developed in consultation with stakeholders.

Environmental policy-making: economic theory

That, in general, markets provide the best means of allocating an economy's private sector resources is as true for environmental resources as for any others. However, markets, including environmental markets, are subject to imperfections and there is often a case for government intervention. This section looks first at the causes and effects of environmental market failure and then at the possible economic instruments that the Government could use to correct the problem.

Market failure

What causes market failure?

The most widespread market failures related specifically to the environment are externalities. Externalities can lead to the incorrect level of a good being supplied in two ways:

- *negative externalities*, where economic agents impose costs on others but do not pay these costs, and so they do not take them into account when making production or consumption decisions; or
- *positive externalities*, where actions give rise to benefits that are not reflected in the price, and so lead to under-consumption.

A market not properly reflecting its costs will implicitly contain subsidies.

Market failures can also arise as a result of:

- *information failures*, where economic agents do not make optimal decisions because they have imperfect information about the (social and private) costs and benefits of their actions, for example on energy efficiency or waste minimisation; and
- *absence of perfect competition*, where industries characterised by imperfect competition will produce inefficiently low levels of

output to maximise profits and may engage in other inefficient actions, such as price discrimination and creating and maintaining barriers to entry, in order to retain market power. Anti-competitive behaviour may have impacts on the environment, while market characteristics may also influence the way government intervenes to address environmental externalities, public goods or information failures.

Box 6.1 Example of externalities in environmental policy

Two firms, a factory and a fishery, use the same river as an input good. By using the river to dispose of waste, the factory imposes costs on the fishery and reduces its productive capacity. But the market does not reflect this cost in prices. There would be an overall gain for the economy as a whole if the amount of pollution was set such that the marginal benefit accruing to the factory from each additional unit of waste disposal was equal to the marginal cost to the fishery of each additional unit of river pollution. An efficient outcome cannot occur while the factory does not face the full costs of its activities – both its own private costs and the wider social costs.

This is illustrated in the diagram below, which shows the marginal costs and benefits faced by the factory as a function of price and quantity of output.

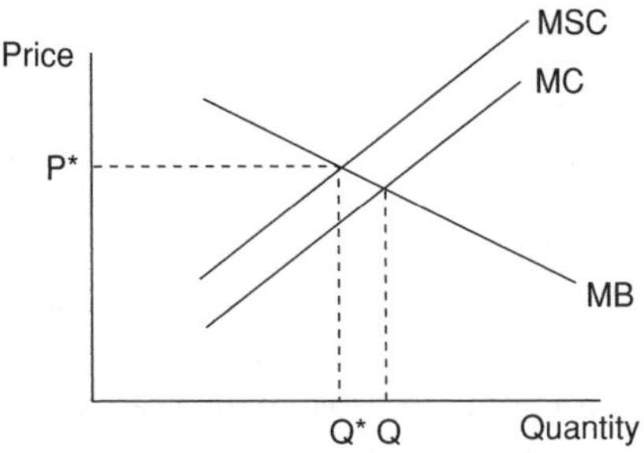

In the absence of any intervention, the factory imposes a social cost which is not reflected in price. The marginal costs to the factory (MC) are lower than the costs imposed on society. It therefore produces quantity of output Q, where the marginal benefits (MB) are equal to the marginal costs. However, the efficient outcome would arise where the factory faces the full costs of its activities, and its marginal costs are increased from MC to MSC. In this case, the quantity of output where the marginal social cost of the factory's activities (MSC) is equal to the marginal benefit (MB) is lower, at Q^*, than the original output of Q.

The effect of market failure

Market failures may have distributional effects – imposing costs on different groups. The presence of environmental externalities can lead to:

- costs for those not causing the externalities. The impacts can be:
    - local, e.g. air quality;
    - regional, e.g. river pollution;
    - national or international, e.g. sulphur emissions;
    - global, e.g. climate change; or
    - intergenerational, e.g. climate change;
- costs for those groups directly involved in the activity that are not incorporated in the price. An example is congestion, where there is no distinction between consumers who place a high value on road use and those who place a low value on it;
- differential impacts on different income groups. For example, air pollution often affects those on low incomes living in inner cities; and
- differential impacts on different sectors of the economy. For example, congestion imposes costs on sectors of business; water pollution from activities such as agriculture imposes costs on the water industry and on consumers.

Theoretical solutions

Economic theory suggests that environmental market failures where government would tend to have a role commonly arise from three main circumstances:

- when the costs of environmental damage are not appropriately reflected in the prices of goods and services;
- when environmental improvements can be achieved only by society acting collectively rather than individually; or
- when decision-makers do not have clear information about how best to reduce the costs which arise from environmental factors.

If government intervenes to correct these market failures efficiently, it will achieve better environmental outcomes alongside greater overall economic efficiency. The following paragraphs discuss the instruments, both economic and non-economic, which government may use to intervene.

Taxation

Taxation has a role to play in internalising environmental externalities in prices. They operate as incentives resulting in the absorption of environmental costs into the price structure of goods and services, thereby ensuring that those causing pollution pay the costs arising from that pollution. Taxes can also help to signal long-term structural changes required in the economy. Tax revenues can be used to reduce the level of other taxes and their distorting effects on the market. Alternatively, revenues can be taken to support the objectives of a tax via strengthening incentives for positive action or mitigating adverse impacts.

Trading schemes

Trading schemes share many of the features of environmental taxes but differ from them in two key respects.

- taxes fix the value assigned to pollution but leave the quantity undetermined, while trading schemes fix the quantum and leave the value to be determined; and
- the distributional consequences can vary depending on the way permits for a trading scheme are allocated (Cabinet Office 2002).

Regardless of how permits are allocated, a tradeable permit scheme will create the same marginal efficiencies as the correctly set efficient tax, provided that government can determine the efficient level of pollution. Such a tax will allow the market to find the cheapest way of meeting the objective.

A key issue with trading schemes is the initial allocation of permits. Approaches include:

- auctioning permits – in which case the distributional consequences will be similar to those of a tax;
- allocating or 'grandfathering' permits to existing polluters, based on their historic levels of pollution; or
- giving polluters a financial incentive to agree to a limit on pollution.

Grandfathered permits are effective in providing an efficient way of bringing pollution down to set levels. However, because firms do not pay for their initial permits, there are reduced impacts on prices and consequently on consumer behaviour. Similar arguments apply where firms obtain financial benefits for a reduction in pollution. Equity issues also arise regarding new entrants to a market that do not have a history of emissions. Additionally, grandfathered permits can act as a barrier to entry, impeding effective competition.

When deciding whether to adopt a trading scheme, it is also necessary to determine whether there is likely to be a well-functioning market to allow permit trading, and whether the potential benefits of administering the trading system are likely to outweigh the costs.

In some circumstances, combining taxes and trading schemes can achieve greater net benefits with more acceptable impacts. For example, a tax may help to reduce the regulatory burdens of a tradeable permit scheme and provide incentives for behavioural changes, ensuring that the objectives are met at lower overall cost.

Subsidies

Subsidies can be used to improve environmental performance. In principle, the same fall in pollution can be achieved from using subsidies as from using taxes or trading schemes. An efficient subsidy involves a payment equal to the marginal social benefit for each unit reduction in pollution.

Subsidies may have a role where the polluter cannot afford to reduce the pollution or where equity or distributional issues make tax or similar measures unacceptable. For example, in order to meet the goal of ending fuel poverty, significant spending programmes are now in place to improve the energy efficiency of low-income households.

Subsidies might also have a role to play where it is not possible to identify the polluter sufficiently accurately to use other measures, such as a tax or regulation, or to accelerate the response to other measures.

Subsidies can be designed to take a number of different forms:

- public spending;
- tax incentives; or
- payments by consumers.

However, subsidies have disadvantages. Where there are negative externalities, they are contrary to the polluter-pays principle. They can also have a range of distorting effects, leading to a less efficient outcome. In particular, subsidies can allow polluters to increase profits, attracting inefficiently high levels of entry into a polluting industry. If not properly designed, subsidies can therefore set up poor incentives in the long term. In addition, subsidies usually require revenue to be raised from taxes.

Regulation and voluntary agreement

There are some instances where economic instruments are not an appropriate option, particularly where local quantities of emissions are concerned or where it is essential that emissions do not exceed specified limits on any individual site. In these cases, the problem may need to be addressed through regulation or voluntary agreements. These measures may be more appropriate where there is a limited number of polluters, so the costs of setting up a scheme based on an economic instrument may outweigh the benefits.

Government can also work with other stakeholders to develop voluntary solutions. Voluntary approaches can be divided into two broad groups – formal agreements and altruistic voluntary action.

Formal voluntary agreements are usually most effective if there exists a threat of a tax or regulation. Without such a threat, 'free riders' are likely to emerge who fail to play any part in meeting the obligations agreed to. The structure of voluntary agreements may therefore be informed by game theory (Green Alliance 2001). Voluntary agreements can have the advantage of speed and a lower regulatory burden, provided the parties involved are willing to act.

Environmental policy-making: practical considerations

In practice, environmental policy-making requires assessments to be made of uncertain future environmental impacts. The most theoretically efficient instrument may not always be the most appropriate. This may be due to distributional issues, possible impacts on business competitiveness, or administrative or practical constraints. Policy-making therefore becomes a question of how to balance uncertain environmental costs against the costs of taking action, and of how to offset the various constraints that might surround particular options.

The UK Government uses an evidence-based approach to environmental policy. The discipline provided by economic analysis offers a robust framework to determine how best to appraise the costs and benefits of actions. This approach helps to identify the most efficient methods of government intervention.

In addition, since environmental policy measures involve inherent uncertainty about how individuals and businesses will respond to them, it is essential that stakeholders are consulted during the design and development of environmental policy instruments. Policy decisions need to be made clear and, following implementation, mechanisms must be put in place to evaluate their effectiveness. The following subsections examine how the principle of evidence-based policy-making is used to design and develop environmental policy.

Evidence-based policy-making

The costs and benefits involved in addressing a particular market failure need to be analysed as rigorously as possible to inform decision-making. Consequently, the efficient extent of intervention can be identified alongside the level at which action should be taken – local, national or international.

Decisions are based upon the best available scientific evidence. This can, however, prove limited. For example, impacts of climate change may have significant consequences in the longer term which is impossible to predict with any degree of certainty. The costs of not acting are rarely clear, nor are the potential risks.

Relevant environmental impacts need to be identified, quantified and valued as far as possible. Valuing environmental costs is difficult as there are often no markets for environmental goods. The UK Government's approach to valuing costs and benefits, which is also applied to determining environmental policy, is set out in detail in the revised Green Book (HM Treasury 2003b), published in January 2003. The main features of this are discussed in Chapter 17.

Government intervention will not necessarily eliminate all negative environmental impacts, nor should it. Ideally, it will reduce them to a level where the marginal (private and social) costs of the environmental impacts are equal to the marginal benefits derived from undertaking the activities which cause them. This recognition, that a *degree* of environmental impact can be economically efficient, is central to the idea of sustainable development: environmental progress is equally important to our overall quality of life as the social and economic kinds.

Policy development process

All environmental policy measures are developed in line with good practice on policy-making (Cabinet Office 2000b). Dialogue between government and other stakeholders is essential, allowing a common understanding of the objectives to be achieved and information to be shared on costs and benefits of different options. The reasoning behind any compromises will help develop an understanding and acceptance of the final policy design.

The first step in policy development is to establish the environmental objective. This will result from scientific research. Sometimes targets are set as a result of international commitments, such as the Kyoto Protocol targets, to tackle climate change. In other cases, the Government will undertake its own research to establish the environmental impacts of particular activities.

If a case for action is identified, at the same time as it undertakes its own analysis of possible policy measures, the Government will consult with stakeholders to seek the views of different groups on the most effective steps to take. Formal or informal consultation about possible policy measures can take place. In some instances, the Government has set up formal task groups to evaluate the options for action. At this stage, the choice of possible instruments will start to be apparent, and this will allow business and other affected bodies to start considering how best to respond.

The next step is usually for the Government to review the evidence gained and take a view on the most appropriate form the policy instrument should take. This will include whether it is possible to design a measure that will meet all other relevant criteria.

For example, a tax must meet the criteria set out in the 1997 Statement of Intent[1]. Similar criteria will apply to a tradeable permit scheme. Criteria can include the:

- ability to intervene directly to tackle the cause of an environmental problem;
- ability to intervene at the most appropriate geographical level – local, national or international;
- effects of a policy on the competitiveness of sectors that are subject to international competition;
- effects on competition within industry sectors;
- distributional effects of a policy on different groups within the population as a whole;
- compliance costs of implementing and administering a measure, including cost to government and to business and other groups; and
- compatibility with international legislative requirements, such as EU state aid rules.

In some cases, environmental taxes that fully internalise environmental costs may impose unacceptable costs given the current capital stock of the economy. It may therefore be necessary to introduce taxes at a rate below the economically efficient level and then increase them over time as the capital stock adjusts to future expectations. Given the life of much of the capital stock and its impact on energy use, this process of adjustment may need to take place over a considerable period of time.

Uniform tax rates do not take account of how pollution problems differ according to geography and population location. It is sometimes appropriate to use differentiated measures on a local basis to reflect environmental costs effectively. For example, the concentration of particulates is highest in urban areas, where populations and associated health risks are most dense. A differential tax rate based on location may be a more efficient way of achieving efficient standards for air quality across the county. However, this would need to be weighed against the administrative costs.

There may also be a concern about potential confusion and overlap between tax and trading schemes, particularly in the area of energy use. For example, the principal mechanism for tackling the business use of energy is the Climate Change Levy, but a voluntary emissions trading scheme has also been introduced to encourage companies to volunteer additional emissions savings. Negotiations are progressing on the proposed EU emissions trading scheme, intended to cover large energy users in industry and the electricity generation sector.

Voluntary agreements are also considered, provided they can achieve at least the same environmental improvements as the other options. Alternatively, voluntary agreements may be part of the package. Certain sectors may pay a reduced rate of tax in return for agreement to improve their environmental performance.

If the measure decided upon is revenue raising, then it will be necessary to consider how best to use the revenue. It is not feasible or desirable to design a package that ensures the outcome is revenue-neutral for every taxpayer. Such a package would lack incentives to reduce emissions or pollution and would prevent polluters from facing the full cost of their actions.

In principle, revenue can be used to:

- reduce other, more distorting taxes, such as taxes on employment;
- increase public spending or reduce borrowing; or
- more specifically, increase spending related to environmental objectives.

If there are market failures such as information failures, there may be benefits in recycling some of the revenue from a tax to tackle these. This can help to increase the response to a tax by encouraging innovation as well as to increase acceptability. There may also be a case for recycling part of the revenue by supporting investments in environmentally friendly technologies, or by supporting the development of new technologies.

Once the Government reaches a decision on which measures to adopt, it will announce its proposals. When introducing economic instruments, the Government always aims to announce them a considerable time before implementing them, so that those affected can prepare for it and begin to take action. This helps to encourage more innovatory responses, which may take longer to be developed and implemented.

Table 6.1 shows how the principles underlying the economic analysis and the policy making process have been applied to the range of economic instruments for tackling the environment.

Environmental policy-making: international considerations

The environmental problems facing the UK are increasingly international. Whilst, as with policy at the national level, international-level policy should be developed using an evidence-based approach that takes account of costs and benefits, in some instances, targets are set through a process of negotiation, such as for the climate change targets agreed under the Kyoto Protocol. This process helps to reveal the weight that society puts on the costs and benefits.

The nature of the environmental problem will determine the level at which action should be taken. This ensures efficiency in intervention and addresses any competitiveness issues in relation to transboundary problems. The UN, the OECD and the EU all have a role in ensuring the efficiency of any cross-border actions. Transboundary problems such as acid rain are best dealt with at European level. Problems that affect only the UK are best dealt with by national, regional and local measures, depending on the circumstances.

Global or transboundary problems

Where the scale of an environmental problem suggests a response at an international level, it need not be the case that regulation is the only instrument. It is now increasingly recognised that other responses may be more appropriate (EU Economic Policy Committee 2002).

By themselves, actions by individual countries will have little effect on global or transboundary problems. Tax measures addressing global problems may benefit from a common framework, with minimum rates in order to prevent objectives from being undermined. The same applies to trading schemes with the auctioning of permits – these are directly

Table 6.1 Development and implementation of economic instruments

Environmental Measure	*Climate Change Levy (CCL)*	*Aggregates Levy*	*Landfill Tax*	*Pesticides voluntary agreement*
Establishing the long-term goal	To meet Kyoto and Government climate change targets.	To tackle environmental costs of aggregate extraction including noise, dust, visual intrusion, biodiversity loss.	To internalise environmental costs of landfill eg methane emissions, nuisance, groundwater pollution; to give better price signals for alternatives to landfill; to assist in meeting waste targets in most efficient way.	DETR report in 1999 floated a possible pesticides tax. Aim to minimise pesticide use, which has impacts including water pollution and damage to biodiversity, consistent with crop protection.
Long consultation period	Advisory Committee on Business and the Environment report early 1998. Followed by Marshall task force in 1998 and consultation on tax design in 1999 to 2000.	Extensive consultation with the industry from 1998.	Tax originally introduced in 1996. Present policy based on review and consultation of tax announced in January 1998.	Consultation with the British Agrochemicals Association on possible voluntary action from 1999 to 2001.
Early signal that new or additional intervention likely to be necessary	Announcement of Marshall task force in March 1998.	Likelihood of intervention evident following research phase in 1999.	1998 review of landfill tax signalled that increases likely to be necessary.	Evident following DETR report in 1999.
Active evidence collection	Marshall task force in 1998.	Independent research and consultation with the industry followed by extensive work with the industry on design and practical implementation.	Continued evidence collection on the tax and the effects of the credit scheme.	Independent research followed by consultation with the industry.
Early signal of choice of economic instrument	CCL announced in Budget 1999 for implementation in 2001.	Levy announced in Budget 2000 for implementation in 2002.	Escalator announced in 1999 Pre-Budget Report to take effect from April 2000.	Voluntary package agreed by Budget 2001.
Recycling of revenue	Introduction of levy accompanied by a 0.3 per cent employer NICs cut and support for energy efficiency and renewables.	Introduction of levy accompanied by a 0.1per cent employer NICs cut and £35m sustainability fund.	Revenues recycled through a 0.2 per cent employers NICs cut and the landfill tax credit scheme.	Likely to be part of any tax measure (if voluntary package is not successful).

Willingness to consider a voluntary approach	Negotiated agreements with energy intensive sectors in return for reduced rate of levy.	Option of a voluntary agreement discussed with the industry but final proposal for a voluntary package was not acceptable to the Government.	All decisions taken following consultation with the industry.	Voluntary approach has been adopted rather than a tax.
Commitment to support investment in new technology to ease adjustment	Enhanced capital allowances for investments in energy saving technologies for 2,500 products and £50m per year for Carbon Trust and renewables.	£35m Sustainability Fund to reduce demand for virgin aggregates by promoting greater use of alternatives and deliver local environmental benefits.	Landfill Tax credit scheme, currently of some £135m per year, recycles funds to projects including sustainable waste management projects.	
Compensation and reliefs for hard hit groups	Revenue neutral for manufacturing as a whole, exemptions for renewable energy and CHP, 80 per cent discounts for energy intensive sectors that have entered into negotiated agreements to increase energy efficiency and reduce emissions. Levy does not apply to domestic sector given problems with fuel poverty.	Revenue recycled via a 0.1 per cent employer NICs cut. Phasing in levy in N Ireland for aggregate used in processed products.	0.2 per cent NICs cuts offsets costs to business.	
Commitment to ongoing evaluation	Rates reviewed annually as part of Budget process. Levy's impact will be evaluated by Customs and environmental outcomes will be published in Pre-Budget Reports and Budgets.	Rates reviewed annually as part of Budget process. Levy's impact will be evaluated by Customs and environmental outcomes will be published in Pre-Budget Reports and Budgets.	Rates reviewed annually as part of Budget process. Strategy Unit report on waste policy in England. Consultation on the landfill tax credit scheme.	Voluntary package overseen by a steering group involving a range of stakeholders. Reports on progress in Budgets and Pre-Budget Reports.
Commitment to future flexibility in policy	e.g. Budget 2002 announced complete exemptions for: electricity produced by CHP; coal mine methane and certain recycling processes. The world's first economy-wide greenhouse gas emissions trading scheme was launched in April 2002 including link to CCL negotiated agreements.	Government keeping the tax under review.	Budget 2002 signalled that Government anticipates a significant rise in the landfill tax in the medium term to meet sustainable waste management goals. Considering the case for a tax on incineration.	Depending on the success of the voluntary package.
Commitment to work internationally if possible	Promotion of the UK approach on tax and emissions trading at European and international level, including taking an active role in negotiation of relevant EU directives.			

linked to the achievement of a specific environmental outcome. The draft EU directives on taxation of energy products (Council of the European Union 2003) and emissions trading are both intended to address this issue.

The UK has in place comprehensive policies to tax energy use through the climate change levy and duties on oil products. If other EU countries introduced similar policies, this would help reduce greenhouse gas emissions from the EU as a whole. However, directives on tax issues cannot always be justified on competition grounds, as they would undermine the healthy tax competition between Member States.

Local or national problems

For local or national environmental problems, a different mix of instruments at the national level will achieve the optimum solution. However, there are environmental issues which do not have a transboundary effect or impact on the single market, but where the EU has nevertheless developed a large body of legislation. This is not necessarily desirable. The EU is able to add greatest value by tackling issues which have transboundary effects or which affect the single market, while Member States are best placed to deal with other issues.

Measures introduced

Since 1997, a range of policy measures has been introduced to address environmental market failures, as Table 6.2 illustrates, and which are discussed further below.

Taxation

During the period 1997–2001, the Climate Change Levy and aggregates levy (both discussed below) were introduced; landfill tax rates were increased (HM Treasury 2002d); and transport taxes such as the fuel duty, company car tax and vehicle excise duty were reformed to give greater attention to the environmental dimension. In addition, tax incentives were introduced, such as tax credits for cleaning up contaminated land and incentives for cleaner fuels (the Green Fuel Challenge), and enhanced capital allowances were made available for environmentally-friendly investments.

Climate Change Levy

The Climate Change Levy was introduced in April 2001. It is a tax on electricity, gas, coal and liquefied petroleum gas (LPG) used by the non-

Table 6.2 Examples of Government policies to address market failures

	Tax	*Trading schemes*	*Tax credits/public spending*	*Voluntary agreements*	*Publicity campaigns*	*Regulation*
Negative externalities	• Aggregates Levy • Climate Change Levy • Landfill tax • Fuel duty	• Emissions trading scheme • Landfill permits • Acid gas trading (proposed)	• Reduced rate of VAT on grant funded installation of central heating & heating appliances	• Pesticides • EU CO_2 from cars agreement		• Integrated Pollution Prevention and Control • Water quality legislation
Positive externalities or public goods			• Tax relief for cleaning up contaminated land • Public space • Agro-environment schemes			• Habitats and species protection legislation
Information failures	• Differential rates of fuel duty				• 'Are you doing your bit? • Car labelling scheme • EU eco-label scheme and energy labelling	• Environmental impact assessment directive

domestic sector, and targets the combustion of fossil fuels, the principal source of greenhouse gas emissions.

The levy is intended to encourage business to use energy more efficiently in order to help meet the UK's targets for reducing greenhouse gas emissions. It includes an exemption for most forms of renewable energy and for fuel used by good quality combined heat and power systems, to encourage these environmentally friendly energy technologies. In order to protect the competitiveness of the most energy-intensive sectors of industry, the levy includes an 80 per cent discount for these sectors, provided they enter into agreements to meet energy efficiency targets. Forty-four sectoral agreements have been entered into covering around 12,000 individual facilities.

The levy was accompanied by a 0.3 percentage point cut in employers' National Insurance Contributions (NICs) and support for energy efficiency measures and renewable sources of energy. The package entailed no net gain to government finances. The levy package continues to be kept under review.

Aggregates Levy

A levy to tackle the environmental impact of aggregate extraction was introduced by the Government in April 2002. The levy was set at a rate of £1.60 per tonne following the research to assess the environmental costs of aggregate extraction. The research had estimated these costs to be £1.80 per tonne, weighted by type of output. The levy was accompanied by a 0.1 percentage point cut in employers' NICs and a £35 million per year Sustainability Fund to promote alternatives to virgin aggregate and to reduce the environmental impact of aggregate extraction.

As the levy applies to the commercial exploitation of rock, sand or gravel in the UK, it applies to imports of aggregate as well as to aggregate extracted in the UK. Exports of aggregate are not subject to the levy. The levy on aggregate used in processed products in Northern Ireland is being phased in over a period of five years in order to allow the industry time to adapt.

Trading schemes

The UK Government launched the world's first economy-wide greenhouse gas emissions trading scheme in April 2002, which was designed to enable participants to join through three routes:

- bidding for permits in the auction held in March 2002;

- joining one of the negotiated agreements for eligible energy-intensive sectors under the arrangements for the Climate Change Levy; or
- developing approved carbon-saving 'projects' to deliver accredited emissions reductions.

Participants are thus able to find the cheapest means of making emissions reductions. The scheme has given the UK an early lead in emissions trading and will allow the City of London to become a centre for emissions trading. It is also enabling the Government to gain experience of emissions trading, which will inform negotiations on the development of international emissions trading schemes.

The proposed EU emissions trading scheme will allow the benefits of trading to be extended across EU Member States. This will help to equalise prices of emissions abatement across businesses in all Member States.

Inclusion of projects under the Kyoto Protocol's Clean Development Mechanism within trading schemes will also allow the benefits of emissions reduction projects to be extended to countries in the developing world.

Voluntary agreements

A voluntary package of measures was agreed by the pesticides sector to reduce the impact of pesticides on the environment. Other examples of voluntary measures are the agreements which the EU has entered into with European, Japanese and Korean car manufacturers. The UK played a leading role in the development of these agreements, through which car manufacturers have agreed to reduce the average carbon dioxide emissions of new cars to 140g/km by 2008/09. The average figure in 1999 was 175.9 g/km and in 2000 it was 172.0 g/km. These agreements will involve a significant improvement in environmental performance and were delivered far more quickly than would have been possible by regulation.

Information campaigns

Information schemes can overcome some of the barriers to better stewardship of the environment. Examples are the Government-run 'Are you doing your bit?' campaign aimed at householders, and schemes such as the Carbon Trust's Action Energy programme aimed at business. The EU energy-labelling scheme is an effective example of information helping to encourage environmentally friendly purchasing.

Evaluating progress

Evaluating the progress made in improving the environment and delivering sustainable development is inevitably uncertain due to the complexities involved. In recognition of this, the Government has adopted 15 headline sustainable development indicators covering economic and social dimensions in addition to environmental dimensions. The six indicators relating to the environment are set out in Box 6.3.

Figures 6.1–6.6 show the progress the Government is making against each indicator. Progress against individual measures is also evaluated. For example, the assessment of performance of the energy-intensive sectors of industry against their first milestone targets under the Climate

Box 6.3 Environmental sustainable development indicators

- emissions of greenhouse gases
- days when air pollution is moderate or high
- road traffic
- rivers of good or fair quality
- populations of wild birds
- new homes built on previously developed land

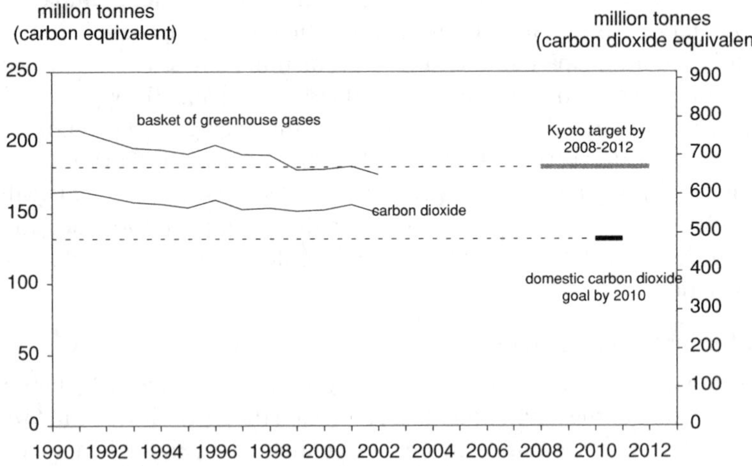

Note: Estimates for 2002 are provisional.

Source: National Environment Technology Centre

Figure 6.1 Emissions of greenhouse gases, 1990–2012

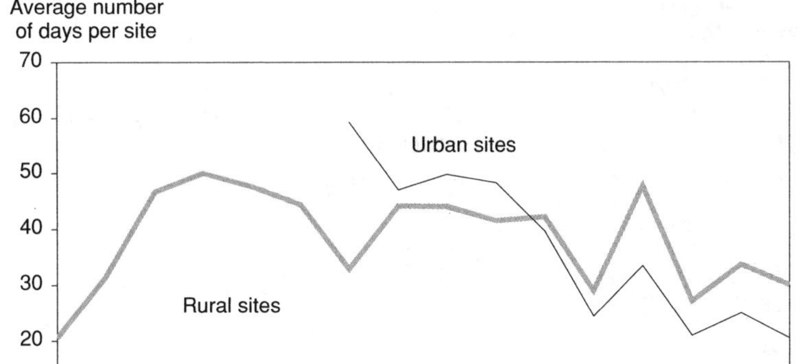

Sources: DEFRA, National Environment Technology Centre (Netcen)

Figure 6.2 Days when air pollution was moderate or higher, 1987–2002 (provisional)

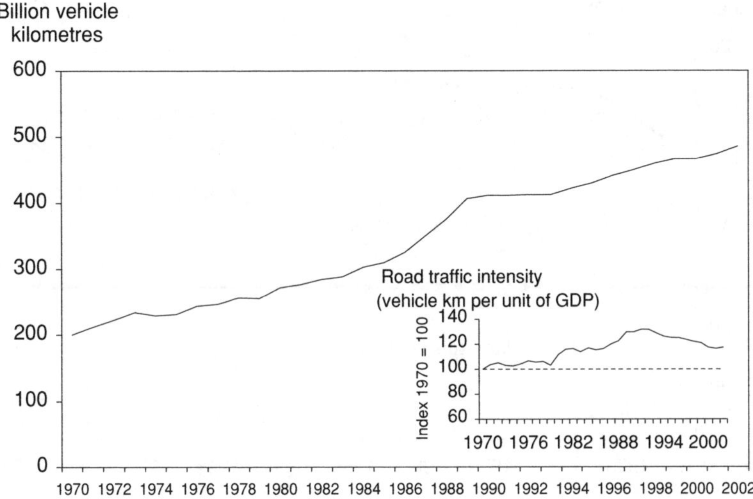

Source: Department for Transport

Figure 6.3 Total road traffic volume, 1970–2002

* *Scottish river classification network changed in 2000.*

Sources: Environmental Agency of England and Wales, Scottish Environment Protection Agency (SEPA), Environment Heritage Service (NI) (EHS)

Figure 6.4 Rivers of good or fair chemical quality, 1990–2001

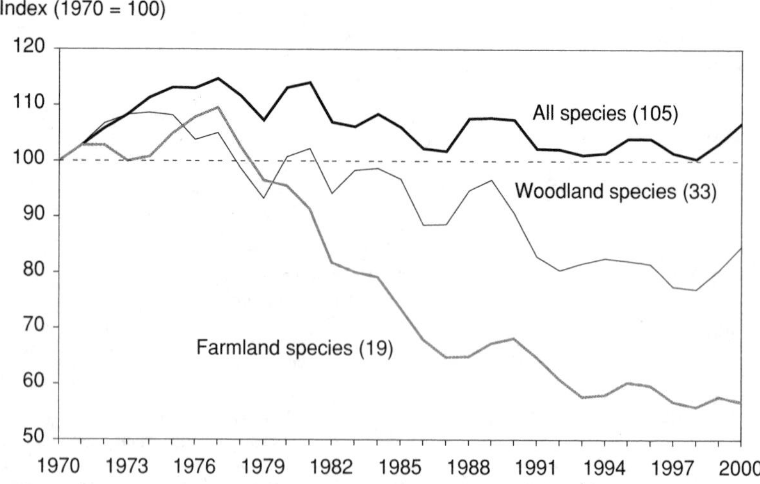

Note: Figures in brackets denote the number of species.

Sources: DEFRA, Royal Society for the Protection of Birds, British Trust for Ornithology

Figure 6.5 Population of wild birds, 1970–2000

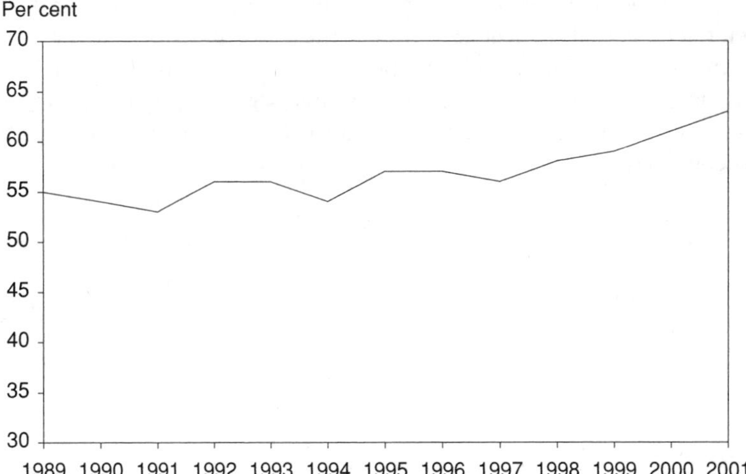

Note: Includes conversions which are estimated to add 3 percentage points.

Sources: Department for Transport, Local Government and the Regions

Figure 6.6 Percentage of new homes built on previously developed land, 1989–2001

Change Levy negotiated agreements was completed in March 2003. The results showed that the sectors covered by the agreements had reduced their emissions by 13.5 million tonnes of carbon dioxide against a 2000 baseline, almost three times above target. The performance of the energy-intensive sectors in meeting their targets was also indicated by a CBI/EEF survey in 2002 (CBI 2002) which showed that 87 per cent of firms covered by the agreements had taken action to improve energy or were planning to do so.

The indicators provide a straightforward indication of the progress that society is making in effectively protecting the environment.

Conclusion

The Government's approach to achieving environmental improvement is based on tackling market failures. Environmental taxes and other economic instruments are particularly effective in correcting market failures where there are negative externalities, for example pollution or road traffic congestion, which are not currently reflected in prices. They can improve economic efficiency, promote resource productivity, and provide incentives for protecting or improving the environment, and deter actions that damage it. Through these instruments – such as the Climate Change Levy, tradeable permits in the form of a greenhouse gas emissions trading scheme and voluntary agreements to reduce the use of pesticides – environmental goals can be achieved in the most efficient way.

7
European Economic Reform

This chapter describes the United Kingdom's approach to economic reform in the European Union, setting out key developments in the reform agenda and the UK's view on priorities for action.

Introduction

European Union (EU) heads of state and government, meeting at Lisbon in March 2000, committed themselves to a ten-year strategy of far-reaching economic reform, setting the EU the goal of creating an economy characterised by high living standards and full employment. Achieving this goal depends on increasing productivity and reforming product, labour and capital markets in all EU Member States. The previous chapters in Part 1 of this book have examined the UK approach to addressing this problem on a domestic level, and set out the framework and policies put in place to achieve these ends. The final chapter of Part 1 looks at the case for similar economic reform in the EU, based on the same principles.

The importance of implementing such economic reform has increased in recent years. The advent of the European Monetary Union (EMU) has put a premium on ongoing reform of product, labour and capital markets; employability, flexibility and stronger competition policies are crucial, if EMU is to be a sustained success. Likewise, ten new members will join the EU on 1 May 2004. This enlargement intensifies the need for reform in both new and incumbent Member States so that each are able to respond to the changes in competitive pressure and comparative advantage that a much larger Single Market will bring.

Demographic problems also need to be addressed. The EU is facing a smaller and older workforce and a rising number of retired citizens, with significant implications for growth, consumer tastes, housing needs and expenditure on pensions and health care.

Finally, on a global level, economic and political uncertainty render the creation of a more resilient and dynamic Europe all the more important. Europe must play its full role in the global economy, in particular with regard to the current World Trade Organisation (WTO) Doha Development Agenda, which includes negotiations on agriculture, services, non-agricultural goods, investment, competition and government procurement.

The chapter outlines developments in European economic reform since 1997, and then sets out the policy approach that the Government is promoting at an EU level, and describes how this complements the domestic agenda. A brief description follows of how progress is assessed and, using the metrics outlined, a snapshot view is given of the progress of the reform programme. The final section outlines the priorities for the European reform agenda over the coming years.

The recent history of European economic reform

In November 1997, EU leaders met in Luxembourg for a special 'jobs summit'. The outcome was the European Employment Strategy (EES), an annual process which involves agreement on a set of Employment Guidelines to shape priority areas for reform, with each Member State then drawing up a National Action Plan detailing progress on meeting these Guidelines. A Joint Employment Report is then drawn up by the European Commission, highlighting best practice across the EU and making (non-binding) country-specific recommendations for further action.

The EES – known as the Luxembourg Process – is based not on EU-wide regulation or legislation, but instead on benchmarking, peer pressure and the exchange of best practice; an approach known as the 'open method of coordination' (OMC). OMC has proved an important step in putting economic reform – and the need for results – on the EU agenda. The following year, the Cardiff European Council agreed that Member States should produce short annual reports on progress in product and capital market reforms, a process refined and extended under subsequent Presidencies.

The Lisbon European Council of March 2000 established OMC as a cornerstone of EU economic policy-making. EU leaders recognised that the traditional legislative and harmonising approach, which had served the EU well in the creation first of a customs union and then of the Single Market, might not always be appropriate in addressing structural reform. National reforms designed by, and tailored to fit, individual Member States were more likely to be effective. Legislation that is still required to complete, maintain, and strengthen the Single Market should be no more prescriptive than necessary. The flexible and cooperative approach to policy-making embodied in the OMC is particularly appropriate in the context of a growing, ageing and ever more diverse EU facing a wide range of microeconomic reform challenges. The Lisbon European Council concluded that the EU should aim for an economy which would, by 2010, be 'the most competitive and dynamic knowledge-based economy in the world, capable of sustainable economic growth with more and better jobs and greater social cohesion'.[1] The specific aims of the Lisbon Agenda are set out in more detail in Box 7.1.

Why economic reform is necessary

The goal set at Lisbon requires the EU to raise its performance in terms of both productivity and employment. In addition, the single currency

Box 7.1 The Lisbon Agenda

In March 2000, the Lisbon European Council set out a ten-year strategy to make the EU the world's most dynamic and competitive economy. The Lisbon Strategy has been expanded by subsequent European Councils and covers almost all of the EU's economic, social and environmental policies. As a result, the EU is committed to a number of specific targets and aims in many policy areas, not all of them quantified or time-specific. They are too numerous to list here in full, but of the agreed and quantifiable targets and objectives some of the most important include:

- raising overall employment rates to 70 per cent, female employment rates to 60 per cent and older worker employment rates to 50 per cent by 2010, with interim targets of 67 per cent for overall employment, and 57 per cent for female employment by January 2005;
- an increase of five years to the average effective retirement age by 2010;
- R&D spending of 3 per cent of GDP by 2010, of which two-thirds of the total to come from business;
- full implementation of the Risk Capital Action Plan by 2003, and of the Financial Services Action Plan by 2005;
- halving by 2010 the number of school leavers not continuing with further education; and
- visible progress on reducing greenhouse gas emissions by 2005.

places an increased premium on flexibility within the EU's economies. Flexibility allows national economies within the euro area to adjust to shocks and to realise their full productive potential. Sufficient flexibility ensures that shocks do not have long-lasting effects, and that high levels of output and employment are maintained. Such flexibility complements and supports productivity, particularly supporting the key drivers of productivity through skills, competition, enterprise and innovation[2].

This section looks, first, at the EU's current productivity and employment performance, relative both to the best in the world and to where it would like to be; and, second, at the factors that can contribute to closing this gap.

Productivity and employment in the EU

In 2002, productivity in terms of GDP per person employed is forecast to be around 19 per cent greater in the US than in the EU15. Part of this gap reflects the longer average hours worked by US employees. However, this must be set against the probability that the lower EU employment rate reduces the productivity differential somewhat by keeping less productive workers outside employment. As Figure 7.1 also shows, in terms of the proportion of its working-age population actually in work, the EU falls behind not only the US but also its own employment targets. Indeed, it is estimated that had the EU as a whole matched the US performance on both productivity and employment levels in 2000,

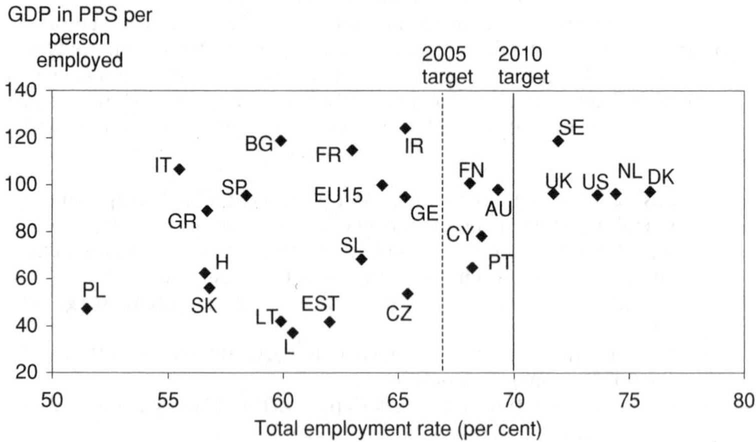

Source: GDP per employee , Eurostat; employment rates, Eurostat, except for US (OECD 2003)

Figure 7.1 GDP per person employed (EU15=100) and employment rate, 2002

its output would have been higher by the equivalent of around £5000, or €8000, per person per year.

Over the course of 2000 to 2002, the EU created almost 5.9 million jobs, resulting in an EU employment rate in 2002 of 64.3 per cent. On the basis of the prevailing working-age population, however, the 2010 target of a 70 per cent employment rate requires the creation of around 15 million additional jobs in the existing 15 Member States (the figure for 25 Member States will be 21.5 million).

Recent trends in EU employment growth highlight this challenge. According to the Commission's report 'Employment in Europe 2003', employment growth among the 25 member states is expected to be flat in 2003, rising to 0.66 per cent in 2004. Against this backdrop, employment in the enlarged Union would need to grow by an average of 1.70 per cent a year between 2005 and 2010 for the EU to meet the 70 per cent target – around 3 million a year.

As well as an overall employment target, the EU has also agreed employment goals for women and older workers. The 2000 Lisbon European Council set a 2010 target of 60 per cent for EU female employment; this was supplemented a year later with an interim 2005 target of 57 per cent. As Figure 7.2 illustrates, the EU has some way to go to reach both objectives.

Older workers (those aged 55–64 years) were not specifically targeted at the Lisbon Council, but a separate employment target of 50 per cent

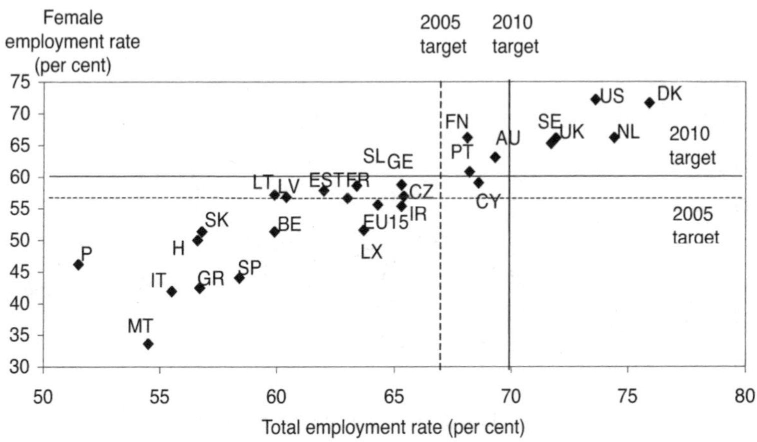

Source: Eurostat, except for US (OECD, 2003)

Figure 7.2 Total and female employment rates, 2002

by 2010 was added at the Stockholm European Council a year later. However, as Figure 7.3 illustrates, the gap to be closed remains substantial.

While the Luxembourg Process (see priority 1 later in this chapter) has undoubtedly helped to increase the strength of employment growth in its first five years, the current trajectory of employment rates, in particular for female and older workers, indicates that the 2010 targets will be very difficult to meet. Without Member States' commitment to tackling the structural barriers which remain in EU labour markets, they will be impossible to meet (Figure 7.4).

The EU's role with respect to employment is not, however, confined to the EES. It also has important responsibilities in realising the full potential of the Single Market and the free movement of people; in applying appropriate standards of health and safety; in ensuring the consistent application of competition policy; and in helping maintain the macroeconomic stability which is the precondition of economic and social success. All of this must be done in partnership with Member States, without resorting to a one-size-fits-all solution, but finding a workable compromise that benefits all, not just the majority.

That the Lisbon economic reform agenda focuses on raising employment rather than reducing unemployment does not imply that the latter is unimportant. The EU unemployment rate declined from 8.7 per cent at end-1999 to 7.4 per cent at end-2001, but moved back up to 7.6 per cent in 2002 against a background of slower growth. The choice of targets specified in terms of employment indicates, however, that a central

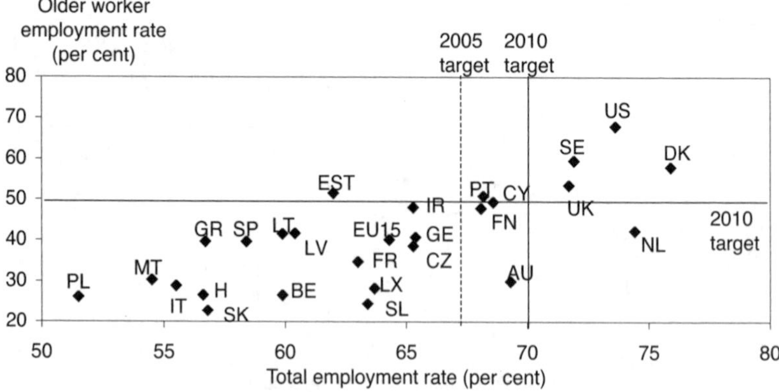

Source: Eurostat, except for US (OECD, 2003)

Figure 7.3 Total and older worker (aged 55–64) employment rates, 2002

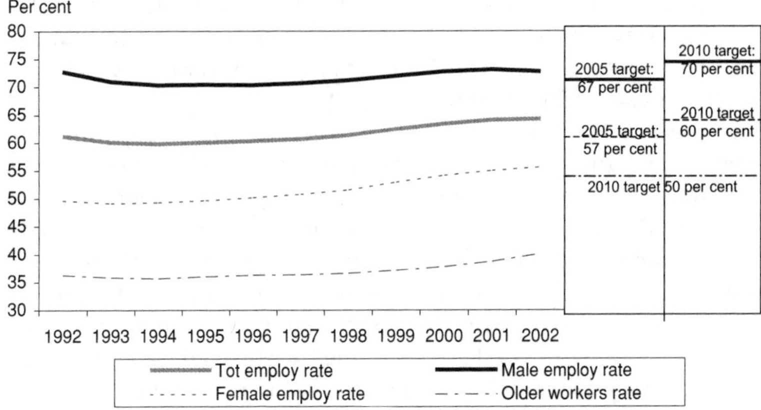

Note: 2002 employment rates in per cent – total = 64.3; female = 55.6; male = 72.8; older workers = 40.1.

Source: Eurostat

Figure 7.4 EU employment rates and the Lisbon Agenda targets

aim of economic reform is to boost participation in the labour force and employment, rather than simply to reduce one form of worklessness.

The policy approach

In order to achieve this, the Government aims to target a combination of high productivity and high employment and not just either in isolation. Realising this dual objective demands a clear focus on tackling the barriers and market failures that constrain national and regional performance. The UK has a two-pronged strategy:

- to address the five key drivers of productivity: competition; investment in physical capital; investment in skills and human capital; enterprise; and innovation. This requires a combination of reform at the national level and completion of the Single Market; and
- to boost low employment rates with appropriate reforms (of both labour and product markets) and incentives, thereby tackling a major cause of social exclusion.

The UK has also applied this strategy in the domestic sphere as the previous chapters set out. It is complemented by each Member State, including the UK, looking to see what it can learn from its partners. For example, as was discussed in Chapter 2, the UK is looking to evidence from both France and Germany for explanation as to why their productivity levels are higher than the UK.

In order to reach these objectives, the Government's approach to economic reform is based on advancing flexibility and fairness together. As Europe's policy-makers confront the challenges of the modern global economy, they must therefore eschew policies that are built on the outdated assumption of a trade off between economic efficiency and social cohesion. The UK's structural reforms have shown that by putting opportunity at the centre of the social market, economies can move beyond this old trade off. Reforms to the UK's tax and benefits system, and high quality services such as Jobcentre Plus, provide incentives and practical support to enable people to rapidly re-enter the labour market. Flexibility is the key to economic success and full employment, and full employment is the route to social justice with everyone sharing the benefits of greater prosperity.

Progress on reform

This section explains how the progress of reform is assessed and then uses the methods outlined above to measure the progress made so far towards the Lisbon Agenda.

How to monitor progress

Fulfilling the Lisbon Agenda requires a commitment by European leaders to coherent and comprehensive economic reform based upon robust evidence and complemented by rigorous monitoring of outcomes. In recognition of the importance of this, the Lisbon European Council mandated the development of a set of comprehensive 'structural indicators' to underpin analysis. The structural indicators are a database of statistics covering a wide range of economic reform issues, and published by Eurostat.[3] The indicators cover six broad areas: the general economic background, employment, innovation and research, economic reform, social cohesion, and the environment. Within each of these categories, seven indicators provide important information for policy-makers, enabling them to analyse economic reform in some detail, to benchmark progress and to identify priority areas. The structural indicators also, and importantly, encourage a focus on outcomes rather than processes – on the results of reform, and on how these are being delivered to EU citizens.[4]

Progress to date

On some important parts of the Lisbon Agenda, reform efforts have already delivered substantial success (though this does not, of course, preclude the need in most cases for considerable further effort). These areas include the following:

1. *Employment:* the EU employment rate rose from 62.5 per cent in 1999 to 63.4 per cent in 2000, 64.1 per cent in 2001 and 64.3 per cent in 2003.
2. *The regulatory environment:* the 2001 Mandelkern Report paved the way for the 2002 Commission Better Regulation Action Plan. The recent adoption of the Inter-Institutional Agreement on Better Regulation marks a step forward in entrenching better regulation principles at an EU level.
3. *Research and development*: an R&D action plan was published in April 2003. This is a very important step towards achieving the Lisbon goal of increasing EU expenditure on R&D, with the aim of approaching 3 per cent of GDP by 2010, with two thirds coming from the private sector.
4. *Innovation*: the sixth Research Framework Programme, adopted in 2002, concentrates substantial resources on integrating Community research, and transforming it into commercial success.
5. *Communications*: adoption of EC legislation comprising a new regulatory framework for electronic communications, and a new e-Europe 2005 Action Plan.
6. *Energy liberalisation*: agreement to open electricity and gas markets fully to competition by 2007.

In other areas, progress – while evident – remains less substantive. In *labour markets*, for example, while job creation overall has been strong, employment among older workers has shown little improvement; most of the employment gains have occurred in younger age groups. Unemployment, however, remains unacceptably high (at about 15 million across the EU in 2003), with long-term unemployment still of particular concern.

In *capital markets*, the Financial Services Action Plan (FSAP)[5] was adopted in 1999 with the aim of creating a single European capital market. Of the FSAP's 42 measures, 36 had been completed by the 2003 Spring Council, but much remains to be done on implementation and enforcement.

In *product markets*, the European Commission has taken welcome steps to modernise the competition rules to create common standards across the Union and to allow for a more proactive and strategic approach to enforcement. Member States have given a clear commitment to moving towards less and better state aid, which requires more effective targeting of government support to firms to address clearly identified market failures; this needs now to be followed through. Political agreement was reached on a Community Patent in March 2003; implementation is vital if EU firms are to have the correct incentives to invest and innovate. The European Charter for Small Enterprises, agreed in June 2000, calls on Member States and the Commission to create a more friendly environment for new and small businesses. Efforts to reduce the regulatory burden and improve access to risk capital continue. The Commission published a consultative Green Paper on entrepreneurship in early 2003, with an action plan to follow in 2004..

Ensuring that suppliers have access to open procurement markets is an important aspect of the Lisbon Agenda. Progress to create a Single Market has been more evident with respect to goods than to services. The Commission has identified major intra-EU barriers to trade in services; action to reduce these obstacles must now be taken. Liberalisation and normalisation of the aviation industry has been considerably furthered by agreement on the 'Single Sky' (affecting airspace and air navigation services); attention must now focus on the reform of slot allocations.

Finally, *sustainable development* – ensuring a better quality of life for everyone, now and for generations to come – is an integral part of the economic reform process. The EU Sustainable Development Strategy was adopted by the Gothenburg European Council of June 2001, and the EU's new programme of impact assessments is being introduced in 2003.

Priorities in European economic reform

The economic reform measures set out necessarily encompass a wide variety of overlapping policy areas. One of the major challenges facing the EU at any particular time is to determine its main priorities (which will, clearly, shift over the course of a ten-year reform agenda). Where and how should Europe's efforts be most usefully directed?

Ten key steps on European economic reform can be identified. These measures do not constitute an exhaustive inventory; instead they head a lengthy 'to do' list of reforms needed to enhance both productivity and employment.

1. Modern social policies that promote skills, employment and labour market flexibility, in particular among older workers

A competitive, dynamic and socially cohesive Europe needs to extend employment opportunity across all ages and groups. The Stockholm European Council of March 2001, as noted above, highlighted the importance of full employment in an ageing EU population; the Barcelona European Council, one year later, called for measures to facilitate the retention of older workers in the labour market by, for example, more flexible approaches to retirement and greater access to lifelong learning. Barcelona also called for an increase in the average effective retirement age (59.9 years in 2001) of about five years by 2010.

Encouraging more people to remain active for longer during their working lives is an EU-wide priority. It entails policies aimed not only at older workers *per se*, but also at younger workers to ensure that they retain high participation rates as they move into older age brackets. This demands a wide-ranging approach, including the removal of structural barriers to job creation, and encompassing a variety of policy areas.

Different national circumstances, strengths and weaknesses mean that there is no single EU blueprint for labour market reform. Different countries may need to take different approaches to similar problems in order to achieve similar results; hence the applicability to labour market policy of the Open Method of Coordination (within which objectives are agreed at an EU-level, but the policies to reach those objectives are set nationally).

Notwithstanding the need for tailored solutions to individual circumstances, the EU has an important part to play in boosting employment both among older workers and across all age groups. The 'Luxembourg Process' – the European Employment Strategy (EES) – has, over the past six years, provided an invaluable mechanism for monitoring, evaluation, peer review and the exchange of best practice. The newly revised and streamlined process should have job creation as its highest priority. The Employment Taskforce, which published its report in November 2003, adds further impetus to reform efforts.

The 2003 Spring Council established a European Employment Taskforce, headed by Wim Kok, to identify practical reform measures necessary in Member States to achieve 'the most direct and immediate impact on the ability of Member States to... achieve its objectives and its targets'. The Taskforce published its report on 26 November.

The report focused on the reforms necessary to promote job creation and made concrete recommendations about clear priorities where individual Member States should be reforming labour markets. The report represents a vital opportunity to reinvigorate labour market reform in the EU. It will be important for Member States to demonstrate the political will to implement the proposed changes to reach the Lisbon goals.

2. Promotion of entrepreneurship to create jobs across all ages and groups

Enterprise makes a vital contribution toward the Lisbon goal. Not only is it a key driver of productivity growth and a source of job creation, but it can also be an important means of generating prosperity and social cohesion in disadvantaged communities. Indicators suggest that the EU suffers a significant 'enterprise gap' in comparison with the US (Figure 7.5).

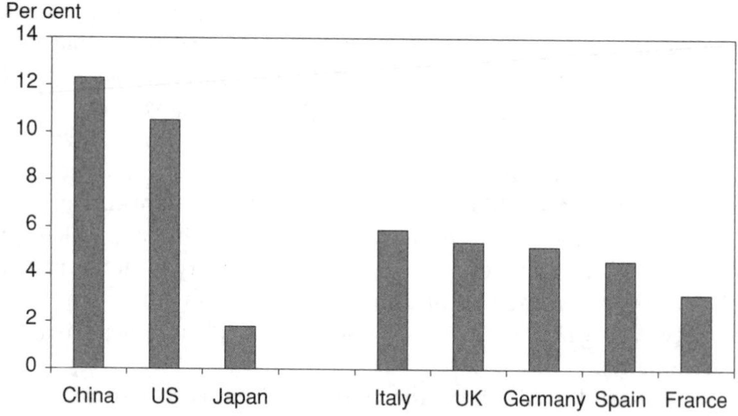

Source: Global Entrepreneurship Monitor (2002)

Figure 7.5 The 'enterprise gap', 2002; percentage of working-age population involved in starting a new business or managing a business less than 42 months old.

Barriers to entrepreneurship may be rooted in culture and attitude, or they may be of an entirely practical nature, such as access to finance or information. In an EU context, the main barriers to enterprise may include:

- the burden of administration and legislation, whether EU or national;

- cultural and social barriers, such as the fear of failure or the low status of self-employment;
- lack of access to finance, especially for disadvantaged groups, minority groups or micro-businesses seeking risk capital; and
- inappropriate education and training, despite enterprise education being available in almost two-thirds of Member States.

As explained in Chapter 4, enterprise is a key contributor to the productivity agenda, as it creates competitive pressures through entrepreneurs who start up new firms, introduce innovative practices and new technology and challenge incumbents' performance.

Success with the economic reform agenda therefore entails advancing the enterprise agenda. The European Commission published a Green Paper on Entrepreneurship in January 2003.[6] If the reform agenda is to be achieved, this consultation document needs to be followed by concrete actions, such as:

- ensuring that the potential for enterprise to lead to sustainable regeneration is reflected in the priorities of the EU Structural Funds and the European Investment Fund Start-Up facility;
- targeting EU funding towards under-represented and disadvantaged groups. Some entrepreneurs and potential entrepreneurs, in particular from disadvantaged groups, may find it more difficult to raise finance from the private sector;
- a review of bankruptcy rules to identify best practice, so that the rules maintain sanctions against the unscrupulous or dishonest but do not excessively penalise business failure;
- a coherent and thorough European Commission assessment of the effect of regulation on small firms throughout the business cycle, in the context of the Commission's Better Regulation Action Plan. The regulatory burden is likely to represent more of a burden for small firms than for large, in that the demands in terms of both time and effort for compliance are often proportionately greater;
- a commitment to a 'lighter touch' for new EU legislation as it affects small firms, perhaps even exempting them on a case-by-case basis; and
- raising awareness of enterprise among young people, ensuring that not only the skills base but also the cultural environment is such that it fosters entrepreneurship and extends choice and opportunity.

3. Boosting the knowledge-based economy via an R&D framework that better promotes innovation, especially in clean technologies

Research and development (R&D) and innovation are catalysts of productivity growth, helping to open markets and increase opportunities through the creation of new, improved products, services and processes. While innovation is broader than R&D alone, firms with high levels of investment in R&D appear also to have higher levels of productivity and innovation.

The European Commission's 2003 European Innovation Scoreboard shows that the US leads the EU on ten of the eleven performance indicators available for both; US leadership is particularly marked in the areas such as parenting, the provision of early stage venture capital and tertiary education. The Scoreboard also showed that the growth of business sector R&D continues to be slower in the EU than in the US. In June 2003, EU leaders endorsed a new Action Plan designed to support progress towards the Union's aspiration to raise expenditure on R&D to 3 per cent of GDP by 2010, with two-thirds of new investment coming from the private sector. As Figure 7.6 illustrates, this represents a considerable challenge for most Member States and for the EU as a whole. The European Action for Growth initiative, endorsed by EU leaders at the December 2003 European Council, will make an important contribution to this. Some €40 billion of European Investment Bank resources will be mobilised in order to boost investment in R&D and innovation, particularly in leading edge technologies (such as the use of hydrogen as fuel), by providing access to finance for some of Europe's most innovative firms.

Establishing conditions conducive to stimulating business investment in R&D cuts across a number of aspects of the economic reform agenda, including high levels of competition to stimulate innovation; accessible, low-cost capital markets; a supply of appropriately skilled labour; an effective intellectual property regime; and a strong two-way flow of information between business organisations and research establishments.

Fiscal incentives, including tax credits, can be a useful tool in delivering additional R&D, though it is important that the system be stable, simple, and well-understood, and that each Member State be able to adopt the policy mix most appropriate to its own economic structure and social model. There is also an important role for state aid in addressing the market failures that inhibit EU innovation, though it is questionable whether the current state aid rules for R&D adequately reflect this role. There might be merit in the Commission instigating an independent review of the role of state aid in facilitating business R&D.

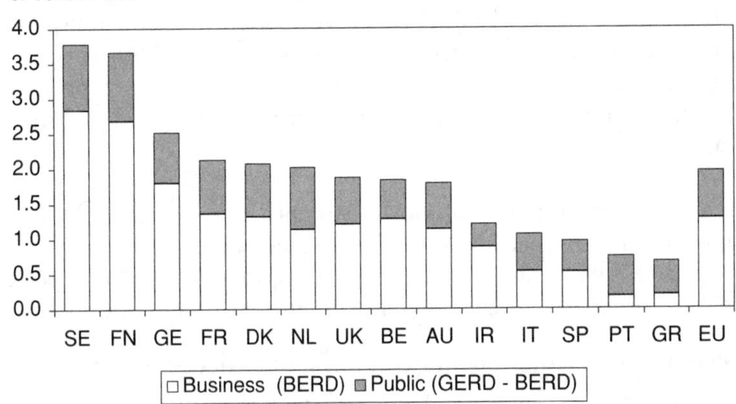

* Data for 2001 except for Denmark and France (2000); Belgium, Greece, Italy, Ireland, Netherlands, Portugal and Sweden (1999); and Austria (1998)

Note: Public R&D spending is the difference between total R&D expenditure (GERD) and business enterprise R&D expenditure (BERD). Therefore, the public measure also includes higher education R&D expenditure (HERD), government R&D expenditure (GORD) and private non-profit R&D expenditure (PNRD).

Source: European Innovation Scoreboard (2001; 2002)

Figure 7.6 R&D as per cent of GDP (latest year*)

4. Stronger and more effective competition policy

Competition drives growth, productivity and job creation, and facilitates an efficient distribution of resources between enterprises and sectors. It promotes innovation, efficiency and enterprise; and it ensures that the benefits of these improvements are passed on to consumers through lower prices, increased quality and greater choice. Empowered consumers both drive and benefit from an effective competition regime.

At an EU level, two major initiatives represent progress towards even stronger competition policy.

1. *Modernisation of the European competition rules.* Competition policy is a shared competence between the Community and Member States. The Commission's modernisation plans promise greater consistency, applying Community law in all cases affecting cross-border trade. This should lead to a 'levelling up' of competition regimes across the EU, and help promote a stronger competition culture.

2. *Changes to the mergers regime*. These include: measures to increase the transparency, predictability and accountability of decisions, with greater independent oversight; greater recognition of the benefits of efficiency improvements to consumers; and a more practical and effective process for identifying the correct level of jurisdiction in merger cases.

These changes, and the proposed strengthening of the European Commission's Competition Directorate-General's economic expertise, are consistent with the Government's own vision of competition policy as strong, proactive, independent and grounded in economic analysis.

5. Better implementation and enforcement of better regulation

Effective and well-focused regulation contributes positively to economic growth and welfare by correcting market failures, promoting fairness, ensuring public safety and contributing to a healthy environment. Unnecessary or poorly enforced regulation can, however, restrict competition, stifle innovation and reduce investment and employment. The cost to the EU of badly drafted regulation has been put at about €50 billion per year (European Commission 2001), and the burden is particularly weighty for small businesses. Strict regulation of entrepreneurial activity can dampen both the entry of new firms and the rate of expansion of successful ones. Deregulation in such circumstances can result not only in increased competition and lower mark-ups but also in higher productivity (as new entrants may be more likely to employ relatively new technologies).

At both EU and domestic levels, the Government is committed to ensuring that regulation is transparent, accountable, targeted, consistent and proportionate to the problem it is intended to solve. The use of regulatory impact assessments for new regulations, and the continuous review of existing regulation, are necessary and complementary aspects of the effort to improve the environment for entrepreneurs.

Building on the EU's Better Regulation Action Plan, the Government's priorities are:

- supporting impact assessments to lessen the negative economic effects of regulation;
- promoting ongoing review of existing legislation, to modernise and improve it; and
- making better use of non-regulatory approaches to policy, including strengthening competition.

Both product and labour market regulation affect investment and employment decisions. The OECD has found that anti-competitive product market regulations have significant negative effects on employment, while strict employment protection legislation can reduce innovation in manufacturing (though the impact differs with the industrial relations regime and the technology level of the industry concerned) (OECD 2001).

Job security and fair employment are highly desirable social aims, and additional costs for business can be justified in terms of legitimate social protection. Regulation can encourage a more efficient use of labour and improve the quality of job-matching, thereby reducing labour turnover costs and enhancing efficiency. It is important, however, to find the right balance between regulation and flexibility. Employees' rights are not best safeguarded by denying those without work access to work. Regulation must both protect and promote employability and enterprise.

6. A single market for services

In 2002, the Commission estimated that, since 1992, the Single Market had boosted EU prosperity by €877 billion, created an additional 2.5 million jobs and, by 1996, had reduced inflation by 1–1.5 per cent, compared to a situation where the Single Market had not been instituted. However services have, to date, been less exposed to the effects of the Single Market than has the goods sector. As Figure 7.7 shows, the proportion of firms reporting increased competition from elsewhere in the EU as a result of the Single Market is lower for service sector firms than for their counterparts in construction, industry or trade. This is a particularly important area for reform since services, both public and private, equate to nearly three-quarters of the EU economy – for the UK just under £600bn per annum in 2002 – but account for only a quarter of trade flows.

In 2002, the European Commission completed a comprehensive inventory of the remaining Internal Market barriers to trade in services, paving the way for steps to remedy the problem. Mutual recognition of professional qualifications (rather than harmonisation) would be one such step allowing the free provision of services under the original professional title. Another would be greater exploitation of e-commerce which, by untying the provision of some services from their location, enables transactions without a physical presence and opens up markets to trade.

The free movement of services is already guaranteed by the EU Treaty (Articles 49–55 of the Nice Treaty). That barriers persist is partly due to

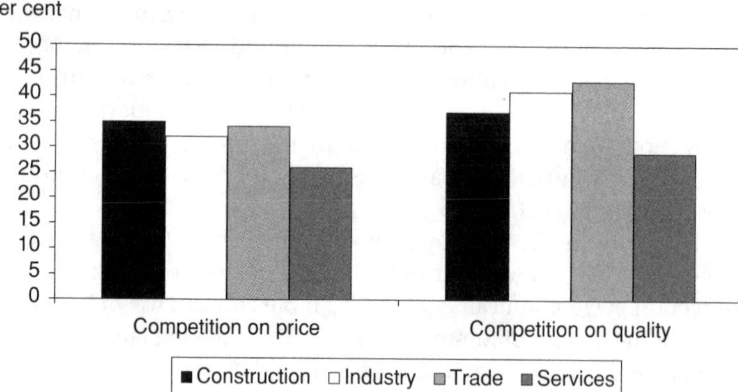

Source: European Commission (2002a)

Figure 7.7 Percentage of firms reporting increased competition from elsewhere in the EU, as a result of the Single Market

ineffective enforcement at both EU and national levels. Only if the remaining barriers are tackled and measures that have already been agreed are enforced, will consumers and business be able to realise fully the benefits of a genuinely Single Market.

7. Progress on, and implementation and enforcement of, the Financial Services Action Plan (FSAP) to deliver better access to low-cost capital, and greater choice

While 36 out of the 42 FSAP measures had been completed by end 2003, it is important to ensure that the new 'Lamfalussy arrangements' (see Box 7.2) are fully exploited, and that the measures set out in the FSAP remain the focus of legislative effort and are properly implemented. The benefits from capital market integration are substantial: the extra costs resulting from a lack of a Single Market in financial services have been estimated at around €43bn in 2000[7].

This framework is now being extended to banking and insurance, and a new Financial Policy Committee has been set up to provide political advice to the ECOFIN council (which consists of EU finance ministers) and to improve delivery of results. As the FSAP nears completion, it is important that the focus be implementation and enforcement of what has been agreed, with the European Commission taking a more proactive approach towards monitoring and assessment. The latter task requires a number of questions to be addressed: whether capital markets are more

Box 7.2 The Lamfalussy arrangements[8]

The new Lamfalussy arrangements are intended to reform the process by which European financial markets' legislation has traditionally been made. The often slow and inflexible process is an increasing problem in a globalised sector where circumstances can change with particular rapidity.

Introduced originally for securities' legislation, the proposals are aimed to improve the quality and effectiveness of EU financial services legislation by:

- committing the legislative process to greater openness and consultation;
- creating output-focused and principles-based legislation;
- supporting these principles with more detailed rules drawn up by committees of national experts enabling European law to respond more quickly to market developments; and
- requiring greater cooperation between regulatory authorities to ensure that new rules are effectively implemented.

accessible as a result of the FSAP, and the cost of accessing capital lower; whether retail markets offer customers more choice and better value; whether European actions are facilitating integration; and where future reform efforts should, in the light of this information, be focused.

8. A modernised state aid regime

Figure 7.8 illustrates that state aid, as a percentage of GDP, has fallen substantially in recent years. If this momentum is to be built on, it is important to:

- tackle effectively the market failure that holds back the productivity and employment performances of countries and regions across the EU;
- streamline state aid procedures, in particular to deal much more quickly and simply with state aid that is not economically significant; and
- focus European Commission and Member State attention on, and apply the most rigorous processes to, the most significant state aids.

State aid rules must enable governments to tackle market failures wherever they occur, to the extent that they occur, and in a proportionate way. State aid rules have become better targeted on identified market failures, but there are still some instances that are not currently

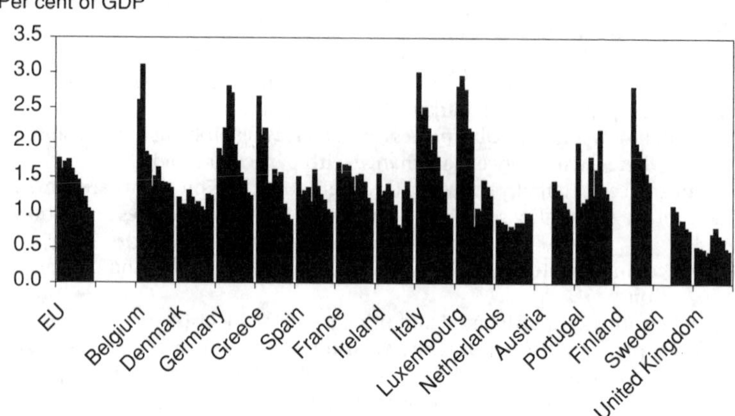

Note: Bars show data for 1991–2001, except for Austria, Finland and Sweden.

Source: European Commission, State Aid

Figure 7.8 State aid to industry by Member State, 1991–2001

covered. The UK is committed, in particular, to securing effective state aid rules to address the market failures associated with regeneration. Such reform is crucial if we are to strengthen market forces in every country and region across the EU.

Focusing community and member state attention on state aid, which is economically significant, could mean concentrating on state aid which:

- has a significant impact on trade or competition across the EU;
- exceeds certain thresholds (analogous to antitrust thresholds); or
- has significant spillovers impacting on other Member States.

Such steps would need to be complemented by a less onerous and much swifter process for dealing with aid that is not economically significant. Taken together, these reforms could embed robust economic criteria at the heart of the state aid regime, speed up the processes, and – by focusing on the information relevant to each case – reduce the compliance burden on individual Member States. This last consideration becomes particularly important in the context of an enlarged EU.

9. An effective regional policy that supports economic reform and addresses market failure

The EU can achieve its Lisbon goals – including those for social and economic cohesion – only if every region is able to reach its full potential. To ensure this, the UK Government believes that there is a need to devolve and decentralise the delivery of regional policy substantially, so that regions have the flexibility to identify and address local needs within a context of accountability, common principles and shared objectives. This will mean ensuring that the instruments of EU regional and cohesion policy – such as the Structural and Cohesion Funds (which help finance multi-annual development programmes), the state aid rules, and the European Investment Bank – allow the objectives for a flexible, modern regional policy to be met.

10. The role of external openness

External openness has an important role to play in helping to achieve the Lisbon goals of increased growth, productivity and employment. Reduced barriers to economic activity across the EU's external borders, through trade liberalisation in one form or another, are a natural counterpart to efforts to reduce barriers to economic activity within Europe. In this respect, greater external openness can be viewed as an extension of the Single Market programme and a driver of increased economic performance.

In economic terms, reducing the barriers to external trade could be considered a natural extension of the Single Market programme, with the potential to deliver important gains in growth, productivity and employment across the Union and to multiply the benefits of structural reform. EU external trade therefore offers an important route to advancing the Lisbon goals. At the same time, external openness places a higher premium on the need for structural reform to deliver greater flexibility in labour, product and capital markets.

There are strong links between trade openness and growth, and important costs associated with continued barriers to trade. The majority of cross-country studies suggest that increased openness has a positive and significant impact on national income[9]. A European Commission study[10] suggests that the ten years of the Internal Market have seen EU GDP boosted by €164.5 billion, 2.5 million jobs created, and the accumulation of extra prosperity to the value of €877 billion. Greater external openness has the potential to deliver gains of a similar magnitude: one estimate puts the cost to consumers of EU trade protection at 7 per cent of GDP, or €600-700 billion[11].

There is solid research evidence to suggest that external openness can enhance the key drivers of productivity. Exposure to wider global markets increases competitive pressure, improving business efficiency and delivering gains for EU consumers, and also increases the potential for cross-border transfers of technology and innovation. There may also be positive benefits to enterprise and to the allocation of capital within an economy.

These gains in productivity will be realised only if an economy is able to reallocate resources, especially labour, quickly and efficiently to the most productive sectors and firms. This underlines the importance of the Lisbon agenda in delivering greater flexibility in labour, product and capital markets. Dynamic and flexible markets are key to realising the potential benefits of openness and minimising the extent of any short-term costs. Where flexibility exists, studies suggest that increased competition in product markets has the potential to improve employment rates, as well as growth[12].

Conclusion

This chapter has shown that the EU – including the UK – is not living up to its potential in terms of productivity and job creation. The performance of individual Member States on either measure shows considerable variation. Taking both employment and productivity together, however, the EU is performing less well than its global competitors and is not meeting its own targets as set out at the 2000 Lisbon European Council.

The challenge for the EU is not simply to close the gap, but to do so within a framework that commands public and market credibility and that delivers the benefits of rising prosperity to all sections of society. EU Member States share common economic ambitions – high productivity and full employment – and a common commitment to social values. The Lisbon economic reform agenda explicitly recognises the multi-faceted economic, social and environmental nature of policy-making; economic gain must be combined with social justice. The importance of these reforms is enhanced by the single currency, membership of which has put a premium on ongoing reform of product, labour and capital markets.

Overall, employability, flexibility and stronger competition policies must be a priority so that EMU can be a sustained success.

Annex 7.1
The EMU Assessment: Supporting Studies

The Chancellor announced the results of the Treasury's assessment of the five economic tests for UK membership of the single currency – convergence, flexibility, investment, financial services and growth, stability and employment – to Parliament on 9 June 2003 (full details of this assessment are published on the Treasury's website[13]).

The assessment covered a wide range of microeconomic issues relevant to the subject matter in this book. In particular, the second test assesses the flexibility of labour product and capital markets. The investment test considers how EMU would affect the microeconomic attractiveness of the UK, for example by lowering transaction costs and increasing competition. The fifth test looks at how EMU membership could affect each of the five key drivers of productivity and raise output growth.

The assessment is accompanied by 18 supporting studies, which were also published on the day of the announcement, and these are summarised briefly in this Annex.

1. The EMU study by HM Treasury *The five tests framework* describes the framework for assessing whether membership of EMU is in the UK's national economic interest. It outlines the main issues that are examined in the assessment of the five economic tests and the approach taken in coming to a decision. This study can be seen as a guide to the assessment and the accompanying EMU studies.

2. The EMU study by Professor Michael Artis *Analysis of European and UK business cycles and shocks* reviews literature relevant to the convergence test based on business cycle and shock correlations, updating previous work and analysis. The study considers methods of defining and measuring the convergence of business cycles. It also discusses the ways in which UK business cycles and shocks differ from other countries, making particular comparisons between the UK and the rest of the EU and the US, and whether monetary conditions in the euro area have tended to suit the UK or not.

3. The EMU study by Professor Simon Wren-Lewis is titled *Estimates of equilibrium exchange rates for sterling against the euro.* Equilibrium exchange rates (EERs) are important in analysing possible entry into EMU. They measure the rate to which the real exchange rate (the nominal rate combined with measures of domestic and overseas prices) tends over the medium to long term. Professor Wren-Lewis examines the theories and empirical evidence on economic forces that determine EERs

and considers different methods of estimating EERs. He uses a new model to estimate new medium-term equilibrium rates for sterling-euro and euro-dollar equilibrium exchange rates.

4. The EMU study by HM Treasury *Housing, consumption and EMU* considers in detail an important structural aspect of the UK economy: the housing market. The study addresses the question of whether UK households are more sensitive to changes in interest rates than euro area households on average as a result of differences in housing market structures, and the implications of this for consumption.

5. The EMU study by HM Treasury *EMU and the monetary transmission mechanism* analyses the speed and strength of the response of the economy to changes in monetary policy in the UK and the euro area. It considers whether the UK response to changes in monetary policy is different from that of the euro area, what the effect of those differences might be and whether any differences would be likely to remain if the UK were to join EMU.

6. The EMU study by Dr Peter Westaway *Modelling the transition to EMU* is intended to inform discussion and evaluation of the possible transition costs were the UK to join EMU. The overall aim of the study is to provide a conceptual framework and tool-kit to aid policy-makers in their thinking about the transition issue, and considers how they might ideally go about implementing this type of regime change so as to minimise the transition costs. The study is based on two complementary modelling exercises, one stylised, the other empirically based, both of which utilise a simplified version of the real world. These models are employed to examine how the sterling-euro conversion rate on entry might ideally be chosen and, more generally, consider how macroeconomic policy might be set in any transition period up to and beyond entry itself.

7. The EMU study by Dr Peter Westaway *Modelling shocks and adjustment mechanisms in EMU* applies a new stylised model to analyse adjustment processes in and out of EMU, with possible UK entry in mind. Outside EMU, UK interest rates are available to respond to economic shocks and the bilateral nominal sterling-euro exchange rate is free to vary; inside EMU, UK interest rates would be determined by the European Central Bank's single monetary policy and the bilateral sterling-euro exchange rate would be irrevocably fixed. The study considers how the UK's macroeconomic costs of adjustment to economic shocks compare inside and outside of EMU.

8. The EMU study by HM Treasury *EMU and labour market flexibility* analyses the flexibility of the UK labour market and also flexibility in

existing euro area economies, particularly since 1997. Labour market flexibility is a central element in determining the overall performance of the UK economy, irrespective of whether the UK decides to join EMU, but a low level of flexibility could be more costly within EMU than outside it, since neither an independent monetary policy nor the sterling-euro exchange rate could operate as adjustment mechanisms in the face of economic shocks. The study is structured around a comprehensive and coherent framework designed to assess the efficiency of different labour market adjustment mechanisms, and constructs a new indicator of labour market flexibility that combines a variety of institutional factors in the labour market.

9. The EMU study by HM Treasury *The exchange rate and macroeconomic adjustment* considers whether nominal exchange rate flexibility aids macroeconomic adjustment, both in theory and in practice. Focusing on the role of the nominal exchange rate when the economy is away from equilibrium, the study considers how the real exchange rate responds to imbalances between aggregate supply and demand, and the part that real exchange rate movements play in enabling the economy to adjust to unexpected events or shocks. It also considers explanations for the strength of sterling since 1996.

10. The EMU study by HM Treasury *EMU and the cost of capital* considers the potential impact of EMU on the cost of capital for UK firms. The cost of capital is an important component of a firm's investment decision. The study considers the ways in which firms raise capital for investments, focusing on the implications of EMU for the cost of external finance, and what the implications for the cost of capital might be, stemming from changes in the structure of UK corporate finance prompted by EMU entry.

11. The EMU study by HM Treasury *EMU and business sectors* considers the extent to which EMU entry might help, hinder or reshape the UK's industrial performance, and the distribution of this impact across different industries and over different time periods. The study considers evidence on the extent to which potential short- to medium-term effects of EMU on business have been observed. It uses evidence on the impact of the Single Market in the EU, as well as comparisons with the United States, to consider the potential long-term effects of EMU.

12. The EMU study by HM Treasury *The location of financial activity and the euro* considers the factors that drive the location of wholesale financial activity, and examines the evidence and emerging trends in the sector. The study's main focus is on the cluster of wholesale financial services

activity in the City, and the relative impact, if any, of currency as a factor affecting the competitiveness and the location of wholesale activity.

13. The EMU study by HM Treasury *EMU and trade* focuses on the key issue of the extent to which UK trade with the euro area economies might be increased through participation in EMU. Increasing trade is desirable because both theory and empirical evidence suggest that more trade leads to higher income, and may increase the long-run growth rate of an economy. The study reviews the extensive economic literature on the impact of currency unions on trade and relates this to the potential impact EMU entry could have on UK trade, output and income over the longer term.

14. The EMU study by HM Treasury *Prices and EMU* examines a key element of the potential microeconomic gains from a currency union. The study explores the causes of price differentials in the EU at present, and assesses how far and how quickly EMU membership might encourage greater convergence between prices in the UK and the euro area. The study also explores evidence from the United States and what it suggests about how prices might converge in the euro area.

15. The EMU study by HM Treasury *The United States as a monetary union* considers how the US – a monetary union broadly similar to EMU in terms of the overall size of its market – functions as a large economy with a single currency, and how this has contributed to economic performance. The study examines the costs and benefits of monetary union in the US, assessing the degree of divergence in regional business cycles, how regions adjust to a single monetary policy and how the existence of a single currency has benefited the US in terms of both macroeconomic and microeconomic performance.

16. The EMU study by HM Treasury *Policy frameworks in the UK and EMU* examines the robustness of the frameworks for macroeconomic policy in both the UK and the euro area, and the implications for the UK in achieving the goal of macroeconomic stability inside or outside EMU. Experience has shown that effective frameworks for macroeconomic policy can make a significant contribution to prosperity and economic stability. The study considers fiscal policy, monetary policy and financial stability, as well as macroeconomic policy coordination.

17. The EMU study *Submissions on EMU from leading academics* brings together 23 submissions from leading academics who were approached by HM Treasury to update the work they had previously undertaken on the economics of monetary union. The contributions brought together in this volume have proved extremely valuable to the Treasury, and the

insights and analysis that they provide have fed extensively into the Treasury's work on the EMU studies and the assessment of the five tests.

18. The Treasury discussion paper *Fiscal stabilisation and EMU* assesses whether a greater stabilisation role could be delivered through fiscal policy, were the UK to join EMU. Were the UK to join EMU, and be subject to asymmetric shocks or common shocks that had an asymmetric impact due to different structures, monetary policy set by the European Central Bank for the euro area as a whole would not be able to react to UK circumstances alone. In such circumstances, there may be a case for an enhanced stabilisation role for fiscal policy. The paper explores a number of policy options to make discretionary fiscal policy more effective for stabilisation purposes and strengthen the automatic stabilisers, including a new symmetrical fisscal rule to trigger the Government to consider taking action and publishing a Stabilisation Report to enhance transparency.

Copies of the five test assessment and all of the studies listed above are available on the HM Treasury website[14]. Full references to each study are listed in the bibliography to this book.

Part 2

Full Employment and the Labour Market

8
Historical Performance of the UK Labour Market

This chapter sets out the changes seen in the labour market up until 1997 and describes how the incidence of worklessness varies between particular social groups, households and communities.

Introduction

The Government's policy goal, as set out earlier, is to achieve employment opportunity for all in every region. Achieving this aim means helping the two groups that make up worklessness: the unemployed and the economically inactive.

This chapter first explains the individual and social costs of worklessness. It then sets out the recent history of the UK labour market and examines the underlying changes in the decades preceding the change of administration in 1997, the reasons for these changes, and the effects they had. The progression of the labour market since 1997, including the broad scope of microeconomic reforms aimed at delivering a flexible labour market that has the ability to adjust to changing economic conditions, is discussed further in Chapters 9 and 10. In addition, the EMU study *EMU and labour market flexibility* provides a detailed analysis of the UK and euro area labour markets, including an assessment of recent labour market performance, the efficiency of the different labour market adjustment mechanisms, and the institutions that influence such adjustment (see Annex 7.1 for details).

The importance of tackling worklessness

'Worklessness' is a term which encompasses more than just those who are unemployed. It encompasses the entire inactive population – all those who are out of work and are either not actively seeking or not available for work – as well as the unemployed. To realise its goal of full employment by 2010, the Government must help and support all those without work, who want to work, whatever the reason.

Worklessness as a whole is a constraint on Britain's economic growth potential and one of the most important causes of poverty and deprivation. When prolonged, it represents an unacceptable waste of human resources, the effects of which are compounded over time. The long-term workless are at risk of becoming permanently detached from the labour market and reintegrating them into the labour market is central to increasing the effective supply of labour. Alongside measures designed to raise productivity – increasing the amount of output produced per worker – expanding the supply of labour is vital to improve the economy's long-term growth potential.

The following section gives a brief overview of developments in the UK labour market in the twenty years up to 1997.

Developments in the UK labour market pre-1997

For much of the post-war period, Britain's macroeconomic performance was poor compared with other G7 countries. The UK had one of the highest average inflation rates and, at the same time, below-average growth. This was associated with high volatility, some of it policy-induced; a scenario of macroeconomic instability which was damaging to the labour market.

The early 1980s saw large increases in the unemployment rate and large falls in the employment rate. Over time, many people drifted into long-term unemployment and some eventually into dependency on sickness and disability-related benefits. Towards the end of the 1980s, the situation reversed; employment increased and unemployment fell. By the early 1990s, however, the situation of a decade earlier had returned; employment was once again on the decline, and the unemployment rate again rose above 10 per cent.

Despite improvement through the 1990s, the number of people claiming unemployment benefits in 1997 was still over 1.6 million and unemployment on the ILO definition stood at a rate of 7.2 per cent. Over 400,000 people counted as long-term unemployed[1], and long-term youth unemployment[2] stood at more than 175,000.

While aggregate unemployment levels had fallen substantially from their early 1990s peak unemployment was only part of the picture. The 1980s and early 1990s also saw a rise in the number of people classed as

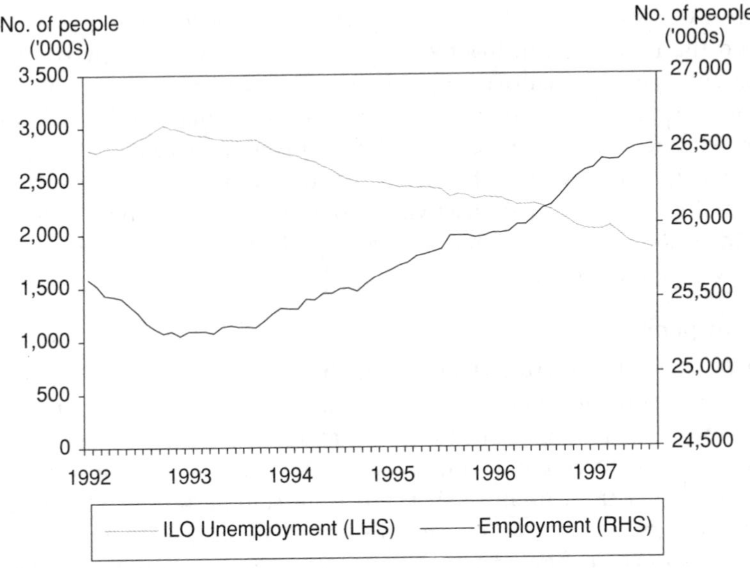

Source: ONS

Figure 8.1 Employment and ILO unemployment

inactive as many of the long-term unemployed were offered insufficient help to move back into work and so left the labour market altogether. This wider worklessness had become concentrated among certain individuals, households and communities, and was particularly high among the low-skilled and other disadvantaged groups. The number of households in which no one was in work grew from around one in ten to more than one in six. There were also pockets of persistent high unemployment in certain deprived communities. Hence, inactivity and concentrations of worklessness among disadvantaged groups and communities also presented considerable challenges.

The following section looks in greater detail at the labour market on a disaggregated basis and, in particular, at the problem of inactivity.

Inactivity

Inactivity, as noted above, implies being not only without work, but also not actively seeking or being available for work. The inactivity rate has been fairly stable over the last 20 years, at between 20 and 25 per cent. This stability masks, however, a sharp rise between the late 1970s and the mid 1990s in inactivity among certain groups such as lone parents, people aged over 50, young people, and disabled people or those with health problems. The incidence of inactivity – and of worklessness overall – has also become increasingly concentrated among particular social groups, households and communities. This section examines the problem of inactivity among each of these groups in turn, and explores also the extent to which inactivity is linked to gender, qualifications and geography.

Lone parents

Between the late 1970s and mid 1990s, the number of non-working lone parents on Income Support trebled. This was in part a reflection of a more than doubling in the number of lone parents over this period. It was also, however, a function of a decline in the employment rate for lone parents; from around 50 per cent at the start of the 1980s to 41 per cent in 1992 (during which time the employment rate for mothers in couples was increasing). Employment rates for lone parents in the 1990s were low not only in historical terms, but also relative to some other major economies; in the USA and France, for example, lone parent employment rates were over 60 per cent.

Some of this change in lone parent employment is attributable to changes in the composition of the lone parent population. Lone mothers (around 90 per cent of lone parents are women) who have never been married, or who have very young children, are much less likely to work than their counterparts who have been married or who have older children. A rising proportion of lone mothers who had never married or who had younger children, accounted for just under a third of the decline in employment.

The employment gap between lone mothers and mothers in couples[3] is particularly marked for younger mothers (in part, because older mothers will tend to have older children). Mothers in couples aged under 25 are nearly twice as likely to work as lone parents of the same age. While it is widest for younger mothers, the gap is, however, still evident across all age groups. This may reflect a variety of factors.

First, lone parents are more likely to have low qualifications; a quarter have no qualifications compared with one in eight mothers in couples, which reduces their chances of finding work. In addition, poor qualifications appear to impact more on the employment opportunities of lone parents; under a third of lone parents with no qualifications are in work, compared with nearly a half of mothers in couples with no qualifications.

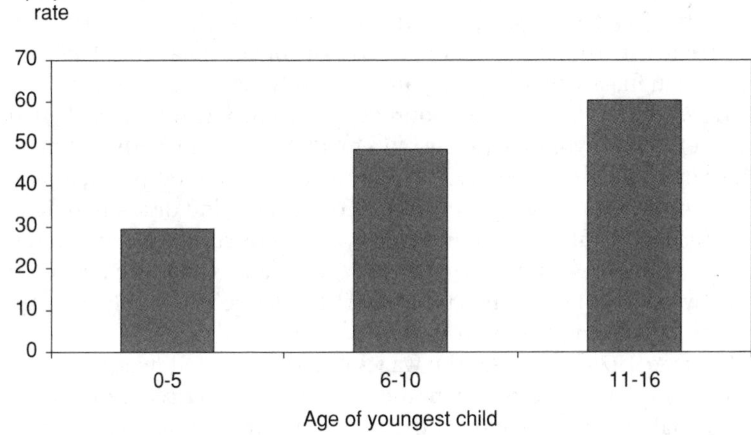

Source: Labour Force Survey, ONS

Figure 8.2 Lone parent employment rate by age of youngest child

Second, lone parents are more likely to live in areas of high unemployment and deprivation. Over half of lone parents live in social housing compared with one in six couples with children. In England, in 1996, 13 per cent of lone parent households were living in a neighbourhood offering 'poor' living conditions – twice the proportion of households overall.

During the 1990s the labour market prospects of lone parents improved. The employment rate of lone parents rose from 40.9 per cent in 1992 to 45.6 per cent in 1997 but remained well below the level of mothers in couples or of lone parents in most other OECD countries. For example, in the mid 1990s, the employment rate of lone parents was close to 70 per cent in both the USA and France.

Over-50s

Between 1979 and 1984, the inactivity rate of people aged between 50 years and the state pension age jumped from under 20 per cent to over 30 per cent. Although inactivity among this group fell slightly in the late 1980s, this fall was not sustained and quickly went into reverse in the recession of the early 1990s. The inactivity rate of older workers reached a new peak of 32 per cent in the mid 1990s.

As successive generations earn more than their predecessors, some of this increase in inactivity might be expected to be explained by increases in voluntary retirement. However, while some people did choose to retire, two key factors suggest that this is an insufficient explanation of the trends in the labour market position of older people. First, the increase in inactivity was greater among poorly educated older men than those with more education – poorly educated people were less likely to be able to afford voluntary early retirement. Second, the path that many older men take to inactivity – losing their job, a period of unemployment, moving on to long-term receipt of sickness and disability-related benefits, and finally early retirement – is not consistent with a voluntary choice to retire. A more convincing explanation is that the decline in employment and rise in inactivity among older people largely reflects a lack of labour market opportunities.

Between 1979 and 1997, the wages of older men fell relative to men in their mid-40s, at a time when older men experienced a disproportionate fall in employment. At the same time, the employment rates of older women did not rise in line with those of younger women. This suggests that fewer employment opportunities were available to older people. For example, older men were much more likely to have been working in industries which lost employment: half worked in industries whose employment fell by 12 per cent or more between 1990 and 1995, while total employment during that period fell by less than 4 per cent.

This pattern has also resulted in a fall in employment rates overall, as older people who lost their jobs were much less likely to return to work. Over the period 1990–96, around half of the men aged 45–49 who were displaced from employment returned to work, but, of those aged 55 and over, only one in nine did so. Similarly, around a third of women aged 45–49 returned to work after being displaced from work; but, of those aged 55 and over, just one in eight returned to work. One factor behind this is the higher costs of job loss for the over-50s. Data[4] reveal that people over 50 who have been displaced return to work at a weekly wage 24 per cent below that which they would have commanded had they stayed in work continuously. The equivalent figure for workers aged 25–49 was 18 per cent. Furthermore, many over-50s had access to relatively generous out-of-work benefits, such as the previous earnings-related component of Invalidity Benefit.

The decline in the employment prospects of the over-50s has been accompanied by a big rise in the number of people aged over 50 on sickness and disability-related benefits, as discussed below.

Young people

Inactivity among people aged 18–24 is bolstered by the choice of many to delay their entry into the labour market in order to continue in full-time education. This is not to downplay the serious problems caused for both individuals and society by worklessness among young people; it is simply to recognise that the data for this age group will inevitably be affected by educational choice. In spring 1997, the inactivity rate of young people aged 18–24, excluding students, was just 13.5 per cent, compared with 25.5 per cent if students were included. Partly as a result of the expansion of higher education, the inactivity rate of young people therefore rose from its most recent low of 21.9 per cent in 1993, to 25.5 per cent in 1997.

Sick and disabled people

In 1997 there were more than 2¼ million people claiming sickness and disability related benefits, more than double the level seen 15 years earlier. Sickness and disability are the most common reasons for inactivity among the over-25s. In 1998, nearly three-quarters of 'prime age' (i.e. aged 25–49) inactive men were classified as sick or disabled, as were 60 per cent of inactive men aged over 50, and 42 per cent of inactive women aged over 50. Only among prime age women were sickness and disability not the main reason for inactivity, it being superseded in this age group by caring for home and family (the primary reason for inactivity for three quarters of inactive women aged 25–49).

Sickness and disability-related benefit recipients tend to remain on benefits for much longer than do the recipients of unemployment or Income Support benefits. Only 19 per cent of the unemployed claiming Jobseeker's Allowance had, in 1997, been on benefit for more than two years; for recipients of sickness and disability-related benefits, however, the figure was 66 per cent.

The increase in sickness and disability-related inactivity has been particularly evident among those with low skill levels. Between 1979 and 1998, the proportion of men with no qualifications aged 25–54 who were inactive because of sickness or disability rose from 3 per cent to 17 per cent, and among those aged 55–64 from 9 per cent to 35 per cent. In contrast, for men with degrees the increases over this period were from just above zero to 1 per cent for those aged 25–54, and from 2 per cent to 7 per cent for those aged 55–64.

Sickness and disability-related inactivity also rose strongly among people aged between 50 and state pension age. Between 1980 and 1995 the number within this age group on sickness and disability related benefits increased from 383,000 to 1,068,000.

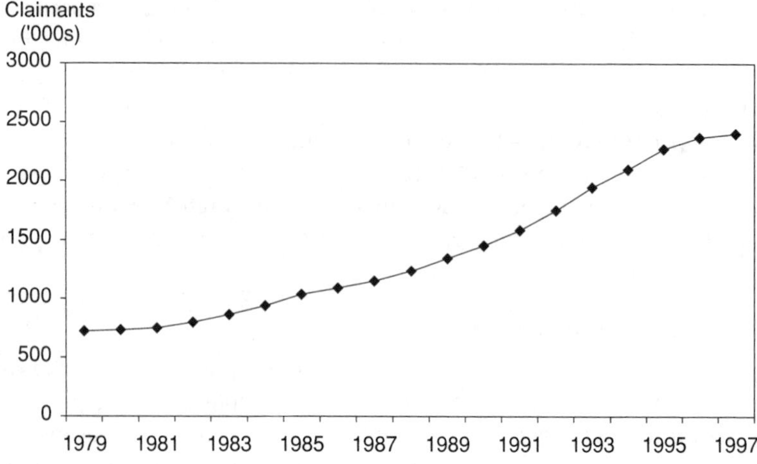

Source: DWP

Figure 8.3 Working age claimants of incapacity-related benefits (excluding IB short-term lower cases), 1979–97

Gender

The overall general stability in the inactivity rate in the 1980s and 1990s concealed distinct gender-related differences. The male inactivity rate rose from 10 per cent in 1979 to around 15 per cent by the mid 1990s; female inactivity, meanwhile, fell from just over a third of women of working age, to just over a quarter, with more women in the labour force than ever before.

The rise in male inactivity reflected in part the growth in higher and further education (i.e. more young people at university and other post-18 education or training facilities), and an increase in early retirement. Much of the growth, however, also reflected a rising number of men receiving incapacity or other benefits. Around a third of men aged between 50 and state retirement age were out of work: most had not retired voluntarily, and almost half relied on benefits for most of their income.

There is a further complication to the overall picture in that the rise in male inactivity and the fall in female inactivity have mostly taken place in different households. Many women who entered work had a partner who was already in work; many men who withdrew from the labour market either lived alone or had a non-working partner.

Economic activity has, as a consequence, become increasingly polarised into 'work-rich' and 'work-poor' households.

Households with a mix of adults both in and out of work fell from 37 per cent in 1975 to 21 per cent in 1995[5]. Over the same period, the proportion of workless households more than doubled, from 7 per cent to 19 per cent, as shown in Figure 8.4, and the chances of an inactive person living in a household with no work rose from around 20 per cent in the mid 1970s to over 50 per cent in the mid 1990s.

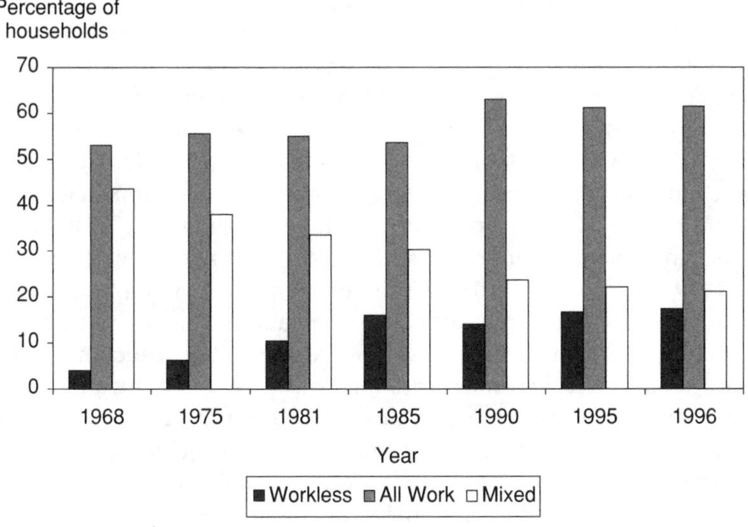

Source: LFS and FES, Gregg, Hansen and Wadsworth (1999)

Figure 8.4 Changes in the way households organise their work

The rising proportion of single adult households accounts for part of the increasing divide between work-rich and workless households. A household with just one adult cannot, by definition, contain adults both in and out of work. One study[6], however, suggests that this demographic factor accounts for only around one third of the increase in the number of workless households observed over the 30 years to the mid 1990s.

The increase in workless households has had a major impact on the extent and distribution of poverty in Britain, especially among families with children. While the living standards of workless people have often in the past been bolstered by other workers in the household, workless people during the 1980s and 1990s were increasingly likely instead to find themselves reliant on benefit payments. By the mid 1990s, around 80 per cent of children in workless families were living in low-income households.

Qualifications

Inactivity rates differ with levels of educational and professional qualifications. Across the working age population as a whole, inactivity rates rose for those with the lowest levels of qualification, and in particular among younger people with no qualifications. For both men and women, the trends in inactivity among the least qualified 25 per cent were worse than among individuals with higher levels of qualification.

This rise in inactivity partly reflects a significant decline in the demand for unskilled workers relative to skilled workers over recent decades across the developed world. In 1979, around nine out of ten men with no qualifications were in work, but by 1995 this figure had fallen to around six out of ten. The employment rate for women with no qualifications also fell over this period, although women as a whole experienced a significant rise in their employment rate, from 61 per cent in 1979 to 66 per cent in 1997. This fall in employment for unqualified women was reflected in a particularly dramatic increase in inactivity.

On top of this, there has also been a substantial reduction in the earnings prospects of workers with low skills. Over the 1980s and 1990s, the pay of people with no educational qualifications fell substantially behind the pay of those with some educational qualifications[7]. For example, in the mid 1970s men with A-level qualifications earned 22 per cent more than those without them; by the mid 1990s, this difference had more than doubled, to 46 per cent. Diminishing prospects in the labour market led to many people with low skills – encouraged by the nature of the benefit system – becoming distanced from the labour market and eventually moving into inactivity.

Arguments as to why the demand for unskilled workers has declined tend to be two-fold; first, the rapid development and diffusion of new forms of technology and organisation which better complement intermediate or high skills than low skills; and, second, to a lesser extent, increased international trade with countries that have a relatively abundant supply of low-skilled workers. (The latter effect in particular is by no means undisputed; some studies[8] find little evidence of a negative impact of globalisation on unskilled workers and point to the relatively low volume of trade between developed and less developed countries.)

The proportion of low-skilled workers has fallen as overall educational standards have risen. The general rise in educational attainment among the population reduced the share of working-age people with no qualifications from 28 per cent in 1992 to 19 per cent in 1997. However, demand for low-skilled workers fell faster than their supply and the 'penalty' for those without qualifications, in terms of lower pay and a higher chance of being out of work, increased dramatically. All too frequently insufficient help was offered to low-skilled people to facilitate their remaining in contact with the labour market. As a result, many ended up inactive, often on sickness and disability-related benefits.

Local concentrations of worklessness

By the late 1980s, worklessness was concentrated in certain areas of the country. In April 1997, the claimant count rate of unemployment across the UK varied from 0.9 per cent in Hart to 13.4 per cent in Hackney – as shown in Figure 8.5.

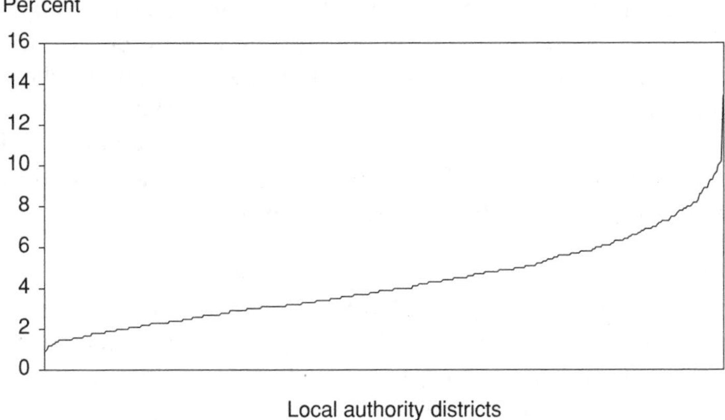

Source: NOMIS(ONS)

Figure 8.5 Claimant rate, UK regions, April 1997

This pattern of inactivity was mirrored by the geographical distribution of workless households. In 1998, a quarter or more of households in Tyne and Wear, Merseyside, and Strathclyde were workless. At the other end of the spectrum, the prevalence of workless households was around half this rate in East Anglia and the South East outside London.

The local differences in inactivity are even starker for people in disadvantaged groups. In 1999, areas with employment rates above 78 per cent had inactivity rates among less-skilled men nearly half that in areas with employment rates below 70 per cent – 15 per cent compared with

28 per cent. For less-skilled women, inactivity rates were at 39 per cent compared with 26 per cent, one-and-a-half times higher in low-employment areas than in high-employment areas.

The variation in inactivity is even greater at the local authority district level. Twenty four out of 408 British districts had inactivity rates in excess of 30 per cent. These districts tend to be in large conurbations, for example Glasgow, East London, and Merseyside, or in areas that were in the past dominated by mining or heavy industry, such as parts of the North East and the South Wales valleys, and which suffered subsequent high degrees of structural unemployment. These also tend to be areas in which a high proportion of the local populations either are on sickness and disability-related benefits or are lone parents on Income Support. The percentage of people on inactive benefits tends to be higher in areas that have higher rates of unemployment.

A further geographical factor is the concentration of inactivity among people living in social housing. In 1997, 30 per cent of men of working age living in social housing were economically inactive. In addition, the rise in male inactivity between 1984 and 1997 was faster among those living in social housing than elsewhere. Some housing estates have very high rates of inactivity. A survey of seven estates in England revealed that nearly one in three heads of household on these estates was inactive compared with one in seven for England as a whole.

Hours worked

Employment, unemployment and inactivity rates are key indicators of the health of the labour market, but are far from the only useful ones. The number of hours worked is an important labour market indicator, not least as it captures information on the intensity of labour utilisation.

Average hours worked declined from the mid 1960s to 1982. Much of this fall was probably associated with national collective agreements to moving the standard working week from 48 hours to 40. In addition, changes in the share of employment accounted for by different sectors of the economy may also have played a part. Manufacturing and agriculture tend to be characterised by longer average working hours than do services. Hence the growth in the share of services will have tended to reduce average hours.

Between the early 1980s and the mid 1990s, the trend then appears to have been broadly flat around a level of about 33¼ hours a week (see Figure 8.6). In contrast, total hours worked in the economy rose throughout the mid 1990s as the number of people in work rose.

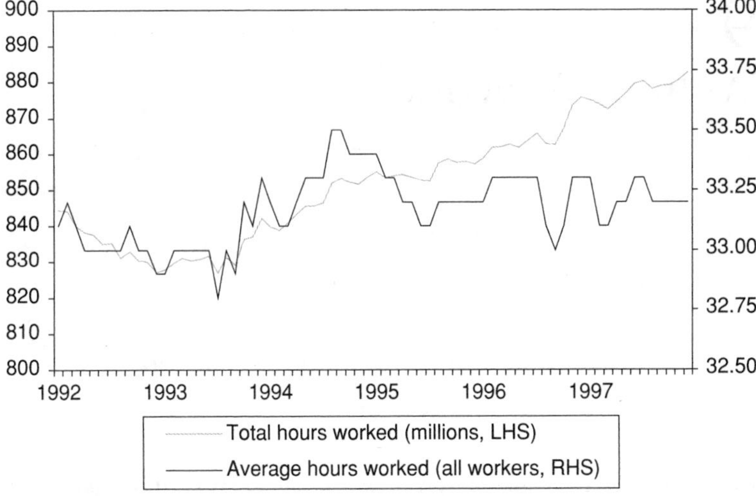

Source: ONS

Figure 8.6 Total and average hours worked 1992–97

Conclusion

Worklessness is both an economic and a social problem; a constraint on the UK's economic growth potential, and an important cause of poverty, deprivation and social exclusion. Tackling it means helping and supporting both the unemployed and the economically inactive.

The disaggregated analysis of the labour market up until 1997 set out in this chapter suggests that policy should be targeted on helping those groups and areas which are the most disadvantaged in the labour market so as to tackle effectively the concentration of worklessness among social groups, households and communities.

The following two chapters discuss the specific policy measures the Government has developed to do this and assesses the progress which has been made towards achieving the policy goal of employment opportunity for all.

9
Welfare To Work

This chapter describes how policy is aiming to deliver employment opportunity for all in the context of the structural labour market challenges described in Chapter 8. It explains how strategies have been developed around the fundamental premise that work is the best route out of poverty for those who are not in employment but are able to work.

Introduction

The Government is committed to extending employment opportunity to all – the modern definition of full employment. For the majority of individuals and their families, work is the single most effective means of avoiding poverty, both now and in the future. Government policy has therefore been directed at facilitating employment for a greater proportion of people than ever before by 2010, and full employment in every region.

Macroeconomic stability is a prerequisite for full employment, but is not of itself sufficient[1]. It also requires a labour market that is characterised by both flexibility and fairness – a flexible labour market being one that adjusts to changing economic conditions so as to maintain high employment, low unemployment, inactivity and inflation, and sustained growth in real incomes. It is essential that the ability of individuals to make genuine choices in the labour market is not constrained by barriers to employment or progression within work. Effective intervention is required to realise these goals and to enable those without work to compete effectively in the labour market. This is the aim of the Government's Welfare to Work strategy, which is based on making work pay, providing work-focused support to all those of working age, easing the transition into work, and investing in education to improve skills.

Labour market policies have traditionally tended to concentrate almost entirely on helping the unemployed to find work. The initial focus of the Welfare to Work programme itself was on tackling long-term and youth long-term unemployment, both of which are particularly damaging. However, and as set out in Chapter 8, achieving employment opportunity for all and enhancing structural flexibility in the labour market means also extending support to those who are able to work but are inactive or disadvantaged. Rapid success in reducing long-term youth unemployment enabled the Government to widen the scope of Welfare to Work policy to provide work-focused support to the entire workless population, and to tackle the causes of the concentration of worklessness among groups, households and communities.

This chapter identifies the goals and assesses the impact of active labour market policy and, in so doing, describes the breadth and depth of the Welfare to Work agenda. It concludes by outlining the challenges still ahead.

Active labour market policies

The UK has a dynamic labour market, with around 1.5 million people either moving into employment or changing jobs every quarter. This dynamism and flexibility is vital to ensuring that the labour market can adapt quickly to changes in global and domestic conditions.

However, while the prevailing degree of labour market flexibility ensures that unemployment is a short-term experience for most unemployed people, those who do not return to work rapidly are at risk of prolonged disadvantage and encounter greater difficulties finding work than do those who have been unemployed for short periods. The long-term unemployed are also more likely to move on to other benefits and drift into inactivity. Long-term youth unemployment is particularly worrying, as early spells of unemployment can have a detrimental effect on future employment prospects.

Effective support for job search is central to taking advantage of employment opportunities. The Welfare to Work programme is designed to allow the unemployed and inactive to compete more effectively for work and to smooth their reintegration into the labour market. This can enhance the flexibility of the labour market through a number of channels:

- *increasing competition in the labour market.* Long periods without work can both demotivate and cause skills to atrophy, and employers may regard a sustained period of unemployment adversely when sifting job applications. This means that the long-term unemployed are less likely to be hired and less able to compete effectively in the labour market. Employment programmes can re-skill the workless and re-engage them with the labour market, thereby increasing the effective supply of labour;
- *increasing the matching of the unemployed to job vacancies.* Programmes can help the unemployed to search for a job more intensively and effectively. This increases the speed of matching potential employees with jobs and encourages the economically inactive to return to the labour market, increasing the pool of people available to fill vacancies; and
- *reducing the mismatch between labour demand and labour supply.* Carefully targeted training programmes can reduce the potential mismatch between the skills possessed by those without work, and the skills required by employers.

Tackling unemployment

The Government is pursuing a range of active labour market policies, including in particular the New Deal, introduced to tackle long-term unemployment, particularly among young people. As this and the following section illustrate the New Deal is complemented by a range of supporting initiatives to reduce the economic and social problems caused by sustained unemployment or inactivity.

The New Deal for young and long-term unemployed people

The Government launched the New Deal for Young People (NDYP) in 1998 to tackle long-term youth unemployment, funded by the one-off Windfall Tax on the excess profits of the privatised utilities. It aims to equip young people who have been out of work for six months or more with the skills and opportunities they need to find and remain in work, and to ensure they do not become detached from the labour market while out of work.

NDYP provides a range of support for 18 to 24 year old jobseekers, including regular contact with personal advisers, help with job search activities and assistance in addressing basic skills gaps. For those who do not move into work from the initial Gateway period of intensive personalised help and support, there is a range of further options providing full-time intensive activity and a follow-through period to capitalise on employability gains. These rights are balanced with responsibilities: the New Deal ends the option for young people of remaining indefinitely on Jobseeker's Allowance.

The development of the New Deal for those aged 25 and over (ND25+) built on the success of the NDYP by providing assistance on a similar basis to people in older age groups caught up in long-term unemployment.

Macroeconomic statistics on the UK labour market provide a measure of the success of the New Deal. Against a backdrop of a prolonged period of global economic uncertainty and rising unemployment elsewhere, the UK labour market has remained remarkably resilient.

To date, NDYP has helped more than 440,000 young people into work, while. ND25+ has helped more than 150,000 into jobs. The NDYP and ND25+ have made substantial contributions to the reduction in long-term unemployment and long-term youth unemployment by more than three quarters since 1997.

Source: TES data, NOMIS (ONS)

Figure 9.1 Long-term unemployment, youth and 25+

The positive impact of the New Deal was confirmed by independent research in 2000 by the National Institute of Economic and Social Research (NIESR)[2]. NIESR found that, without NDYP, the level of long-term youth unemployment would have been twice as high as it was at that time. A study by the National Centre for Social Research[3] also concluded that NDYP had had a significant impact on the employability of young people. Separately, Van Reenan (2001)[4] estimates that unemployed young men are around 20 per cent more likely to find jobs each month as a result of NDYP. Finally, the Institute for Employment Research (2002) concluded that the re-engineered ND25+, launched in spring 2001, has had a positive impact on job entry.

The New Deal for the over-50s

As outlined in the previous chapter, the 1980s and 1990s saw a sharp increase in the levels of worklessness amongst people aged between 50 and state pension age, and a growing detachment from the labour market (with many becoming inactive rather than unemployed). A third of men aged between 50 and state retirement age are out of work and of these less than a third retired voluntarily; furthermore, many of those who have left early live on low incomes. Almost half rely on state benefits as their main source of income; and early exit in this fashion from the labour market onto benefits contributes significantly to future years in poverty.

As discussed in Chapter 8, industrial restructuring may have been one factor in this trend. Others, however, include perverse incentives in the pension regime that encouraged employees and employers to agree to early retirement, and obsolete skills exacerbated by uneven access to lifelong learning.

To help older unemployed workers, the Government introduced the voluntary New Deal for the over-50s (ND50+) throughout the country in 2000. Unlike the NDYP and ND25+, participation in ND50+ is not mandatory for the unemployed within this age group. ND50+ offers a package of personal advice, help with job search, and in-work training and support for those claiming Jobseeker's Allowance (JSA), Incapacity Benefit (IB), Severe Disablement Allowance (SDA) and Income Support (IS) for more than six months, and their dependent partners. Since its introduction, ND50+ has assisted more than 90,000 people into jobs.

A package of back-to-work help has been introduced as part of the recent Green Paper *Simplicity, security and choice: Working and saving for retirement*[5]. Measures have also been taken to tackle age discrimination via the Code of Practice on Age Diversity in Employment. Since its publication in 1999, the proportion of employers using age in recruitment has halved and two-thirds of employers now include age in their equal opportunity policies. The Government is also committed to introducing legislation to outlaw age discrimination in the labour market by 2006.

As a result of the variety of approaches towards tackling the problem of unemployment among older workers, the employment rate of those aged between 50 and pension age has risen from 65 per cent in 1997 to 70 per cent in 2003.

Employment Zones

Alongside the New Deal, Employment Zones are testing a new and innovative approach to getting long-term unemployed people aged 25 and over back into work. Currently operating in 15 areas of England, Scotland and Wales, Employment Zones allow jobseekers and their personal advisers to use funds flexibly to overcome individual barriers to work. Further steps are being taken to extend the help provided by Employment Zones more widely and to encourage innovation among providers by extending the approach to people who would otherwise return to the NDYP for a second or subsequent time. Competition is being introduced via the introduction of multiple providers in half the Zones. Employment Zones will also replace the New Deal for Lone Parents (NDLP) in the five London Zones, and for those returning for a second or subsequent work-focused interview in the other Zones from April 2004.

Tackling unemployment

Recent years have seen a substantial improvement in Britain's labour market performance, which now compares favourably with previous periods and is strong by international standards. Despite weakness in the global economy, unemployment remains at its lowest for a generation. Employment of more than 28 million means that there are more people in work than ever before. The employment rate, at 74.7 per cent in spring 2003, is close to its historic high of 75 per cent reached in spring 1990; the difference between the two periods is that in 1990 the economy was at a cyclical peak, whereas thirteen years later, growth was closer to its trend rate – indicative of a structural improvement in labour market performance.

Claimant count unemployment has fallen and has remained below 1 million since the start of 2001 – the first time this has happened since 1975. The unemployment rate on the ILO definition stood at 5.0 per cent in spring 2003, the lowest among the G7 economies for the first time since the 1950s.

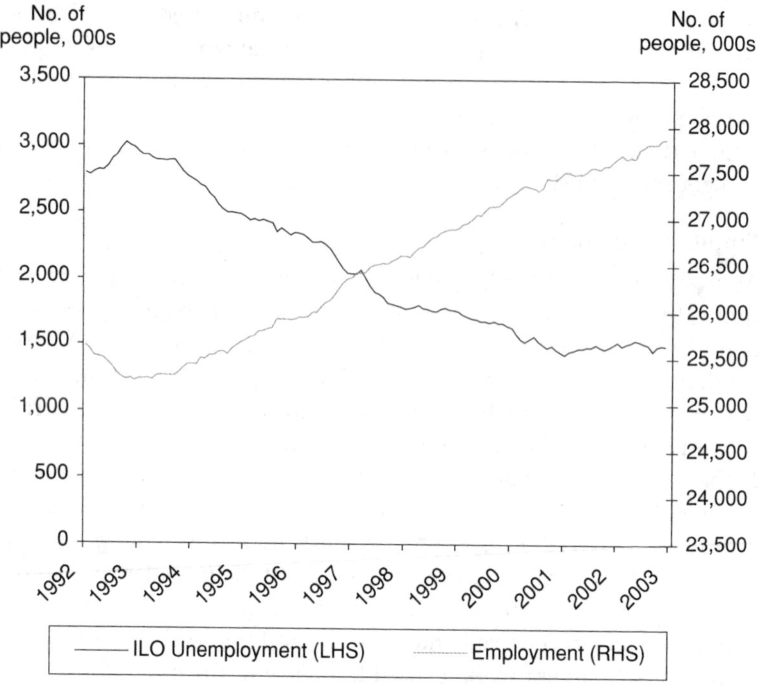

Source: ONS

Figure 9.2 Employment and ILO Unemployment

Furthermore, these falls in unemployment and rises in employment have been achieved without the acceleration in average earnings growth which accompanied similar previous improvements (Figure 9.3). This suggests both a structural improvement in the performance of the UK labour market (consistent with evidence[6] suggesting that the structural rate of unemployment has fallen in the UK in recent years) and an increase in wage flexibility.

The ILO unemployment rate has remained broadly flat at just over 5 per cent for the past couple of years, yet average earnings growth has stayed at or below the 4.5 per cent the Bank of England considered consistent with trend productivity growth and the inflation target[7]. In part, subdued average earnings growth in recent years may be a product of institutional change such as greater decentralisation of wage bargaining[8]. A more important influence may, however, have been the decision to give the Bank of England operational independence to set

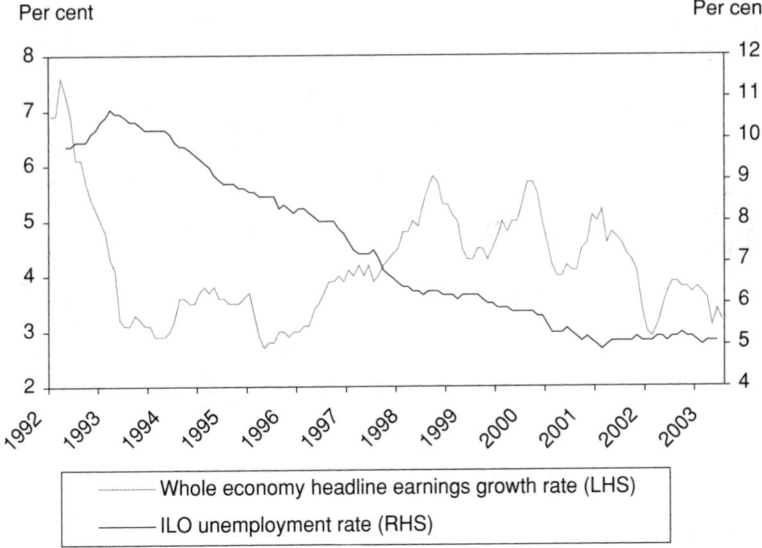

Source: ONS

Figure 9.3 Earnings and Unemployment

interest rates to meet its inflation target[9]. This appeared to 'anchor' inflation expectations around the 2.5 per cent target set for the Bank.

The reductions in unemployment seen in recent years have been largely achieved by a reduced incidence of long-term unemployment. Long-term unemployment has fallen by more than three-quarters since 1997, as has the number of young people unemployed for six months or more (Figure 9.1). Long-term ILO unemployment (lasting over 12 months) now constitutes around one fifth of total unemployment; this compares with over 30 per cent in 1997 and over 40 per cent in the early 1990s.

Hours Worked

As mentioned in the previous chapter hours worked also provides an important labour market indicator as it captures information on the intensity of labour utilisation.

Figure 9.4 shows that during the second half of the 1990s average hours continued to decline (with this decline accelerating from 1997), despite the economy moving from below trend growth to above trend.

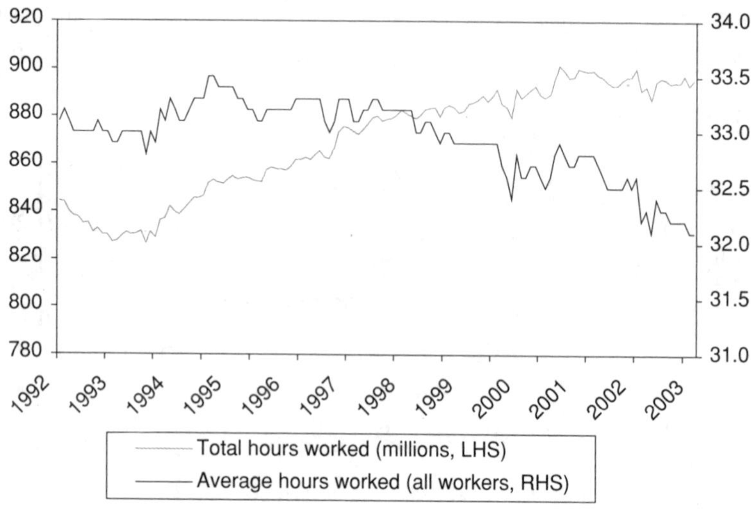

Source: ONS

Figure 9.4 Total and average hours worked

However, while average hours worked per person employed fell, total hours worked in the economy continued to rise through the latter part of the 1990s as the number of people in work rose. More recently, the total hours worked have leveled off; while employment has continued to rise, the effect of this on total hours has been offset by the decline in average hours worked.

It is not possible to explain fully why the average hours worked declined from the mid 1990s at a time when the economy was close to trend growth, though a number of factors are relevant.

The decline is not a simple story of a shift towards part-time employment; the share of part-time in total employment has been stable since 1996 at around 25 per cent. Moreover, average hours worked by part-time employees have actually risen; the fall in overall average hours worked has been driven by a fall in full-time average hours.

One possible factor in the decline could be the falling proportion of self-employed in the workforce. The self-employed tend to work longer hours than do employees; according to LFS data for 1999-2001 about 5 hours more than the average. The number of self-employed has fallen since 1997, from 12.9 per cent in 1995 to 11.3 per cent in 2001, but the share has stabilised since then. This suggests that the fall in the level of self-employment may have caused some of the fall in average hours.

Tax and benefit reforms, which have increased the returns to work, may have encouraged some people to work longer hours but may have encouraged others – because fewer hours are now needed to maintain living standards – to reduce them. Reform of employers' NICs may have increased the incentive to employ two people rather than one, for a given number of total hours worked. While the Working Time Directive introduced in April 1999 will have tended to reduce average hours at the upper end of the hours distribution, this fall was happening before 1999.

Changes in the share of employment accounted for by different sectors of the economy may also have played a part. Manufacturing and agriculture tend to be characterised by longer average working hours than do services. The growth in the share of the latter will have tended to reduce average hours, though this ongoing restructuring is by no means a new development and hence not a sole explanation of the acceleration in the decline of average hours worked seen in recent years.

Tackling wider worklessness

The rising concentration of worklessness described in Chapter 8 meant that the number of workless households had risen significantly to almost 3.5 million – more than one in six – by the mid 1990s. Most of these households lived on low incomes.

The increase in worklessness was a function more of economic inactivity than of unemployment. Many people, particularly older people, were not offered sufficient help to return to work after losing a job, and became detached from the labour market. For families with children, especially lone parents, and people on disability benefits, a lack of active help to search for jobs was compounded by poor work incentives from a tax and benefit system that did not recognise them as having the potential to return to, or begin to, work. The concentration of worklessness among households was exacerbated by the unequal geographical distribution of employment. Regional disparities in employment and unemployment rose sharply during the 1980s. Although they subsequently narrowed during the following decade as all regions experienced falling unemployment and rising employment, pockets of high worklessness and deprivation within regions persisted throughout the country such that in February 2003 the claimant count rate of unemployment across the UK varied from 0.7 per cent in North Dorset to 6.5 per cent in Tower Hamlets. These areas have not able to share fully in the rising national prosperity brought about by macroeconomic stability.

While the initial focus of the Government's Welfare to Work programme was on reducing long-term unemployment, the strategy has been extend and resources provided to give all workless benefit claimants the ability to excercise real choice in the labour market as described below.

Jobcentre Plus

Jobcentre Plus sits at the heart of the extended Welfare to Work strategy. Launched in April 2002, it brings together the Employment Service and those parts of the Benefits Agency dealing with working-age people, extending to all working-age benefit claimants the level of work-focused support already available to the unemployed.

Rather than just having their claims processed, anyone making a claim for benefit at a Jobcentre Plus office now meets a personal adviser to discuss the available opportunities for work, and can access job vacancies, advice, training and support. This both ensures that all working-age benefit claimants are aware of the support available to them so that they do not become detached from the labour market and, by increasing the effective supply of labour, expands the pool of workers available for firms looking to recruit.

Since its launch in April 2002, more than 250 new Jobcentre Plus offices have opened. The Government aims to complete the nationwide rollout of 1000 offices in 2006.

Helping lone parents

As discussed in Chapter 8, the employment rate of lone parents has consistently lagged behind that of lone parents in other countries and of couple mothers in this country. Lone parents make up fewer than one in ten of all households, and yet account for one in five of all workless households. Recognising that most want to work, and that helping them to find employment is key to reducing the number of workless households and the incidence of child poverty, in 2001 the Government set itself a target is to ensure 70 per cent of lone parents are in work by 2010.

Lone parents face particularly difficult choices when seeking to balance work and caring responsibilities, and have too often in the past lacked the help and support to look for work, the financial incentives to consider work, and the requisite help with childcare. The policy response is therefore threefold: providing work-focused support through Jobcentre Plus and the NDLP; making work pay through tax credits (see Chapter 10); and broadening access to good quality and affordable childcare through the National Childcare Strategy (see Chapter 11).

All lone parents are required to attend regular Work Focused Interviews (WFIs) at a Jobcentre Plus office to ensure that they are aware of the help and support available to them. Help for those who wish to look for work is provided through NDLP. NDLP provides a voluntary, comprehensive package of support which includes: access to a personal adviser; help with training, education and childcare; and advice on benefits, on in-work financial support and on self-employment. Since its launch in 1998, eligibility for NDLP has been extended to all lone parents who are either not working or work fewer than 16 hours a week.

Employment among lone parents has risen substantially, from 45.6 per cent in spring 1997 to 53.4 per cent in spring 2003 (Figure 9.5), while the number of lone parents claiming Income Support has fallen by almost one-fifth since 1997. NDLP has contributed significantly to this. Within 18 months of NDLP being introduced, the number of lone parents on Income Support had been reduced by 3.3 per cent; an initial impact similar to that of comparable lone parent welfare-to-work programmes

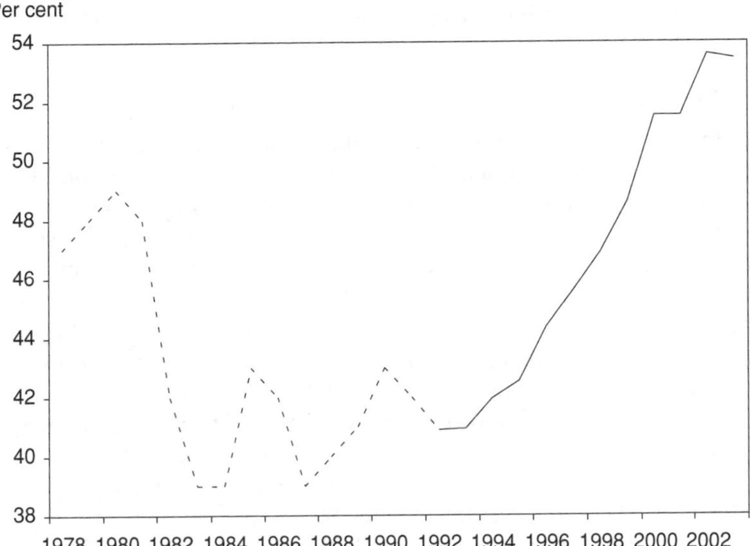

Note: Data from 1978 to 1992 refers to lone mothers and is derived from the General Households Survey. Data from 1992 onwards is from the Labour Force Survey and refers to all lone parents.

Source: General Household Survey and Labour Force Survey

Figure 9.5 Lone parent employment rate

overseas[10]. More than 200,000 lone parents have moved into work with NDLP support, and independent research[11] suggests that the programme more than doubles the employment chances of participants.

Help with childcare

Access to childcare is for many parents, and in particular, lone parents, key to participation in the labour market. Good quality, accessible and affordable childcare enables low income parents to move into paid work and to lift their families out of poverty. It also provides the opportunity for all parents to balance their work and family lives, with significant benefits for their children. The Government has introduced a range of measures to provide assistance with childcare costs to lower- and middle-income parents, initially through the Working Families' Tax Credit (WFTC), and since April 2003 the Working Tax Credit (WTC). These policies are discussed in Chapter 11.

In addition to financial support through the tax and benefit system, the Government's National Childcare Strategy, set out in Chapter 11, helps providers of childcare meet the growing demand, and has created places helping over 1 million children since 1997.

Helping partners

Help to find a job has, within a household, traditionally been focused on the main claimant of unemployment benefit. Reducing the number of workless households depends, however, on helping all those who are workless in a household, and not just the main claimant. Research shows that, when one member of a workless couple finds work, this triples the chances of their partner finding work[12]. Yet, even in the late 1990s, the benefit system continued to treat the partners of unemployed people (who were overwhelmingly women) as 'adult dependants' of the claimant (overwhelmingly men). The implicit assumption was that adult dependents could not or should not work, even if many of them might, in reality, have just as much chance of finding work as the main claimant.

To address this incongruity, the rights and responsibilities of Jobseeker's Allowance claimants are now extended to couples without children on an equal basis. Since April 2001, childless partners of the unemployed (where at least one partner was born after 1976) have also become joint Jobseeker's Allowance claimants. This was extended in October 2002 to all childless partners where at least one partner was born after 1957. Evidence[13] suggests that these steps have been very successful in terms of facilitating moves into work, largely via their effect on the female partner.

In addition, support to households in which both partners are workless is provided through the voluntary New Deal for Partners – a personal adviser service for partners of benefit claimants. Mandatory Work Focused Interviews for partners will begin in April 2004. In this way, partners of benefit claimants will have the help and support they need to prevent them becoming detached from the labour market and to look for work if they wish, as is already the case for lone parents. The Government is, however, committed to going further so as to ensure that all those who are workless have access to the help and support needed to make genuine labour market choices, regardless of the status of their partner.

Helping disabled people

Many disabled people face barriers to work. Just under half of working age people with a disability – 3.2 million in total – work; another 1.4 million people with disabilities but without a job would like to work.

Over the 1980s and for most of the 1990s, people on sickness and disability-related benefits were offered little, if any, help from the benefit system. They received neither the advice nor the access to employment programmes offered to the unemployed, and were unable to take full advantage of increasing employment opportunities. In addition, the tax and benefit system did not assist people to move from sickness and disability benefits into employment; indeed, in many cases it acted as a disincentive. They did not, therefore, have the help and support needed to make effective and informed labour market choices.

To address this, the Government introduced the New Deal for disabled people (NDDP) nationally in 2001. NDDP is a voluntary programme available to people on incapacity benefits; it provides a network of innovative Job Brokers, whose role is to help disabled people become ready for work and put them in touch with employers. To date, it has helped over 15,000 people into employment.

To be effective, support for people with disabilities needs to be available on an ongoing basis, particularly in the early stages of employment. The consultation document *Pathways to Work: Helping People into employment* (Department for Work and Pensions, 2002a) sets out a package of measures to be piloted from October 2003, offering new recipients of incapacity-related benefits greater support at an early stage in their claims. The pilots, for which £97 million of funding was made available in the 2002 Spending Review, will feature more skilled advisor support, more work-focused rehabilitation programmes and improved financial incentives.

Financial support is provided to help disabled people meet the additional costs they face when in work. In 2002, almost 40,000 people received in-work support through the Disabled Person's Tax Credit; more than double the number who received Disability Working Allowance at its peak. Since April 2003, disabled people in work receive financial support through the Working Tax Credit rather than the Disabled Person's Tax Credit, bringing workers with a disability into the mainstream system of support. The Working Tax Credit increases the guaranteed minimum income for a single disabled person working 35 hours a week, to £194 per week.

Growth in the number of people claiming sickness and disability related benefits has slowed in recent years (see Figure 9.6). Since 1995 the number of people between 50 and the state pension age on Incapacity Benefit – by far the main inactive benefit for this age group – has continued to rise but at a much slower rate. The absolute increase has reflected in part increased eligibility for National Insurance benefits among older women, and in part the growth in population size of this age cohort.

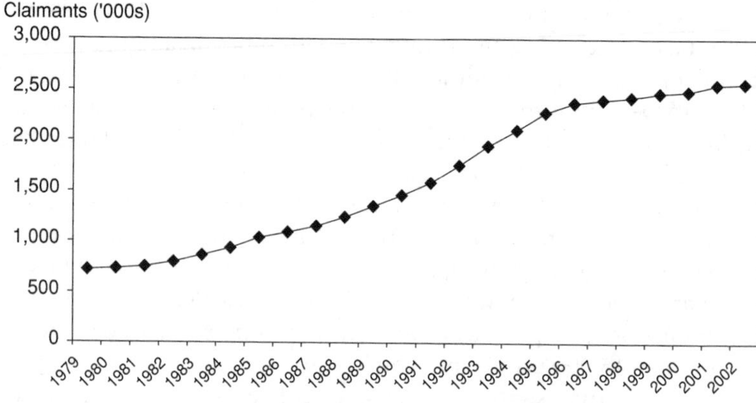

Source: ONS

Figure 9.6 Working age claimants of incapacity-related benefits (excluding IB short-termlower cases) 1979-2002

Helping people from ethnic minorities

Ethnic minorities are disadvantaged in the labour market on a broad range of measures of achievement, including employment rates, earnings levels and progression in the workplace. This hides, however, large variations between different ethnic groups. People of Indian origin, for example, have similar levels of occupational attainment (defined as the proportion in professional or managerial posts) as their white counterparts, while people of Chinese origin outperform the white population on this indicator. However, the employment rates of almost all ethnic groups are lower than those of the white population, with some groups having very low employment rates compared to both the white population and other ethnic groups. For example, the employment rate if women of Bangladeshi origin stands at 16 per cent, and, for women of Pakistani origin, at 29 per cent.

Ethnic minorities currently represent 8 per cent of the UK population and will account for nearly half of all growth in the working age population over the next decade. As well as its social implications, failure to improve labour market outcomes among these groups will have serious economic consequences for the whole economy.

There is no single cause or explanation for this pattern of labour market disadvantage. Important contributing factors, however, include:

- Education: educational underachievement is both a symptom and and important cause of labour market disadvantage. The proportion of pupils who get five or more GCSE grades at A*–C is much lower among Black, Pakistani and Bangladeshi pupils (especially boys), than among Whites (though Indian attainment at GCSE level is higher). It is, however, important to note that, even allowing for differences in educational attainment, ethnic minorities – including the 'successful' groups – are not doing as well in the labour market as their educational achievements would suggest.
- Geography: people from ethnic minority groups are heavily concentrated in London and in the big cities of the Midlands and the North. They are four times more likely than white people to live in the 44 most deprived areas of England. They are also more likely than their white counterparts – and this is particularly true of Bangladeshi and Black Caribbean groups – to occupy social housing; a characteristic generally associated with poor employment prospects.
- Discrimination: while equal opportunities legislation has had some success in combating overt discrimination and harassment, indirect discrimination (where policies or practices have the inadvertent result of systematically disadvantaging ethnic minorities) remains a problem.

Steps to address the multiplicity of difficulties faced by ethnic minorities in the labour market include the introduction of Action Teams in 63 disadvantaged areas of Britain, many of which contain large ethnic minority communities. A new outreach service was launched in April 2002 in the five urban areas which are home to three-quarters of Britain's ethnic minority population. This service aims to inform people about the employment and support services available to them, and encourage their take-up; improve links between communities and employers; and, where appropriate, provide specialist training where this may help individuals to find work.

A recent Cabinet Office Strategy Unit report[14] on steps to improve the position of ethnic minorities in the labour market has set out the future policy agenda. Building on the conclusions of the report, specialist advisers are being introduced in Jobcentre Plus districts with high ethnic minority populations and a new fund to provide Jobcentre Plus districts with the resources to develop solutions to help people from ethnic minorities back into work is also being made available.

Tackling wider worklessness

While inactivity has also fallen, the decline has been much more gradual, as Figure 9.7 demonstrates. The working-age inactivity rate stood at 21.3 per cent in spring 2003, having remained largely flat over the past decade.

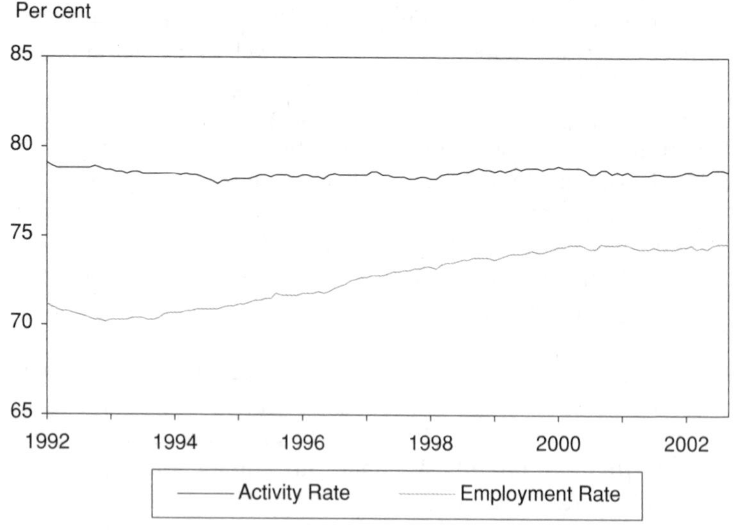

Source: ONS

Figure 9.7 Percentage activity and employment rates for population of working age (16–59/64)

A greater proportion of this inactivity now reflects increased participation by young people in higher education. In spring 2003, excluding students, the inactivity rate of young people was 14.6 per cent, compared to 25.7 per cent including students. However, the last few years have also seen reductions in the inactivity rates of lone parents and the over-50s, and increases in their employment rates. The percentage of households with children where no one is in work has also fallen, from 17.9 per cent in 1997 to 15.9 per cent in 2002; a reduction in absolute terms of more than 300,000 and a sharp contrast with the rise of more than 700,000 between 1990 and 1996.

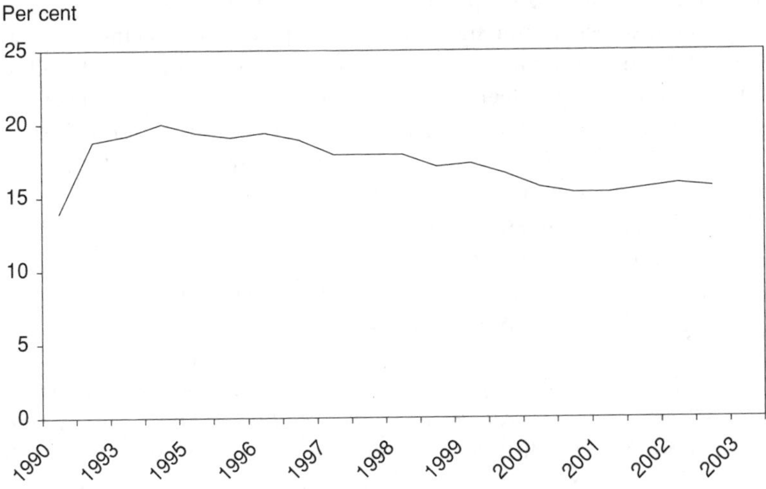

Source: ONS

Figure 9.8 Children in workless households, 1990–2002

This is not, however, to ignore the considerable challenges still ahead, and which current policies are designed to tackle. While the proportion of lone parents in work has risen from 45.6 per cent in 1997 to 53.4 per cent as at 2003, this still remains some way short of both the rates found in some other countries, and the Government's 2010 target of 70 per cent. Furthermore, although inactivity among the over-50s has fallen, it remains – at 27.8 per cent – high relative to the overall inactivity rate of 21.3 per cent in spring 2003.

The challenges ahead

Significant progress has been made in improving labour market outcomes for most groups but there is much further to go if the Government's goal of employment opportunity for all is to be realised. Unemployment has fallen to its lowest rate since the 1970s, but inactivity has declined more slowly. Employment rates have risen for all disadvantaged groups but remain lower than the overall employment rate; and, while regional disparities have narrowed significantly, pockets of high unemployment within regions persist across the country. Tackling these challenges not only a national framework of incentives and sanctions, but also regional and local flexibility.

While macroeconomic stability is a prerequisite for full employment, and while the national New Deal programmes have successfully led to higher overall employment rates, delivering employment opportunity for all depends also upon regions and localities becoming more flexible and better equipped to adapt to change. Such local flexibility will enhance the New Deal's ability to respond rapidly to changes in local or regional circumstances, delivering a more effective service to both potential employees and employers.

Improving regional and local responsiveness is therefore an important policy priority. Measures to achieve it include:

- *Allowing advisors at Jobcentre Plus offices greater flexibility to match their actions to local labour market conditions.* Local staff within Jobcentre Plus districts are often best placed to identify the needs of local labour markets, and to adapt programmes to provide local solutions to employment problems in specific areas. Giving them the scope to do this can help ensure that people move back into employment quickly and are able to change jobs in response to changing local conditions. Jobcentre Plus districts have accordingly been given greater flexibility and discretion.
- *Building on the introduction of Action Teams in the most deprived areas to develop innovative solutions to worklessness.* Action Teams, launched in the autumn of 2000, work with the long-term unemployed and inactive people in the most deprived areas to identify suitable vacancies in neighbouring areas, and bring the two together. They also provide important help in overcoming a key barrier to employment by providing funding for transport, enabling people to travel to jobs in surrounding areas. Action Teams work in partnership with employers and voluntary sector

organisations to promote employment and equality of opportunity, tapping local ideas to encourage the innovative and effective application of funding. Action Teams have helped more than 75,000 people into work, and data shows that almost half of people who found jobs through Action Teams, moved into sustained work.

- *Piloting an intensive and accelerated approach to tackling concentrations of worklessness in 12 of the most deprived neighbourhoods in the country.* Concentration of worklessness means that, in some communities, worklessness is no longer the exception but the norm. Such areas often do not simply 'lack jobs'; many combine high vacancies with low employment, or are found alongside districts characterised by high vacancies. Pilots offering intensive support to help local residents access jobs within travelling distance of their homes, will begin in 12 of the most deprived neighbourhoods in April 2004. These pilots will also offer accelerated and intensive support via the New Deal programmes, and funding will be provided to encourage the formation of local community partnerships in order that local barriers to work can more effectively be addressed.

Conclusion

Worklessness is a constraint on Britain's economic growth and one of the most important causes of poverty, deprivation and social exclusion. The strategy to reduce worklessness is based on making work pay, providing work-focused support to all, easing the transition into work, and investing in education to improve skills. The New Deal – which embodied this approach – has lead to a reduction in worklessness and has been extended from an initial focus on the long-term unemployed, to the economically inactive population as a whole. Tackling barriers to work among the inactive, as well as the unemployed, is a vital step towards the goal of employment opportunity for all. Further progress will require greater flexibility at a local level, and an active benefit system which extends the proper balance of rights and responsibilities to all workless benefit claimants. It is also important to ensure that work pays; and the complementary policies intended to ensure that this is the case, are the subject of Chapter 10.

10
Making Work Pay

This chapter describes the key policies in the Government's strategy to make work pay. It covers important reforms to income tax and National Insurance Contributions and focuses is on the two central policies in this context: the National Minimum Wage and tax credits.

Introduction

The Government's policies to make work pay are best seen as part of the wider Welfare to Work agenda. This has two complementary components. The first of these is helping jobseekers to compete effectively in the job market through active labour market policies – these policies were discussed in the previous chapter.

The second is to ensure that the gains from work are sufficient to encourage participation. These measures are discussed in depth in this chapter.

The challenge of ensuring that work pays has increased in recent years because of profound changes in the labour market and demographic trends. As discussed in Chapter 8, in recent decades labour market and demographic trends have led to weaker real wage growth for workers in lower-paying jobs; weaker labour market attachment among low-skilled and older men; and an increase in the number of households headed by a single parent, as outlined in *Employment Opportunity in a Changing Labour Market* (HM Treasury 1997c) part of the Treasury's 'Modernisation of Britain's Tax and Benefit' series. These trends together led to a sharp rise in the proportion of working-age households with no adult in work[1] and to a significant increase in the number of children in low-income households.[2]

The relative deterioration in real wages for adults with low skills is especially problematic for families with dependent children because their out-of-work income level will typically be higher than that of a household without children, due to the additional financial support for children within the social security system. As a result, the "gains to work" – the increase in net family income when an adult moves into work – may be insufficient to induce that individual to take up work. Lone parent and dual-earner households with children face an additional barrier to taking up work: the need to provide childcare during working hours.

The reforms to income tax and National Insurance Contributions (NICs), and the introduction of the National Minimum Wage (NMW) improve financial incentives to work for low-income households generally. The additional barriers to work faced by families with dependent children are the primary focus of the tax credits which have been introduced. Further, the social security system generates a reservation wage through out-of-work benefits (there is no incentive to supply labour for wages below the level of income provided through benefits). As a result the tax credits are key to combining full employment and labour market flexibility because they ensure that households face positive financial incentives to work while the labour market responds flexibly to economic shocks (in particular shocks which may depress labour demand). In addition to improving labour market performance the Government's reforms to make work pay expand choice for working age housholds. For out of work households, the decision to move into work is now supported by a guaranteed minimum income. For working households on low incomes, the reforms have tackled the poverty trap where the household's choices are distorted by the effects of the tax benefit system, which weakens the link between increased gross earnings and improved living standards.

The discussion in this chapter begins by outlining the two key problems – the unemployment trap and the poverty trap – which policy-makers face in this area. The following sections set out in depth the tax credit and minimum wage measures the Government has introduced before the final section assesses the overall success of the policies so far.

The unemployment trap and the poverty trap

The Government's strategy to make work pay is addressed towards two problems:

- *the unemployment trap*, when those without work find the difference between in-work and out-of-work income too small to provide an incentive to enter the labour market. The unemployment trap reduces labour market flexibility as people choose not to take jobs, even if vacancies are available; and

- *the poverty trap*, when those in work are discouraged from working longer hours or from taking a better-paid job because it may leave them little better-off. The poverty trap restricts functional and employment flexibility since workers see little gain from adjusting their working patterns.

The unemployment trap can be measured by the difference in income for an individual or family after taking up a job compared with the benefits they would receive out of work. This can be expressed as the gain to work – the difference in income after all taxes and benefits are taken into account – or as a Replacement Ratio, where this difference is expressed as a percentage of in-work post tax income.

The poverty trap is measured by the Marginal Deduction Rate (MDR) that a family faces. The MDR is 1 minus the increase in net income resulting from a marginal increase in gross income. This depends on the rates at which income tax and NICs are paid and the rate at which in-work benefits are withdrawn. The main benefits paid to low earning families (Housing and Council Tax Benefit and – until the reforms which brought in tax credits – Family Credit) are withdrawn as income post tax and NICs rises.

A set of reforms to income tax and NICs have complemented the introduction of the NMW and tax credits in a strategy to tackle the unemployment and poverty traps. The reforms to NICs and the introduction of tax credits were among the recommendations of the 1998 Taylor Review. Tax credits and the NMW are discussed in detail below but we begin with the reforms to income tax and NICs.

Along with income tax, the system of NICs is crucial to making work pay. Contributions are levied on earnings and before the reforms implemented in Budgets 1999, 2000 and 2001 certain aspects of the NICs system distorted the labour market and were a barrier to improving work incentives for the low paid. Firstly, employee NICs were payable at a lower earnings level than income tax reducing the gain to work in particular for low paid workers. Secondly, the system of NICs tended to distort the labour market. Higher contribution rates for employers were triggered once earnings reached certain thresholds, but the higher rate also applied to all earnings up to the thresholds, not just to marginal earnings. As a result employers faced step changes in contributions at each threshold, distorting their incentives to pay employees according to their marginal product. Further, the step increase in contributions also applied to employee NICs causing some workers to face MDRs in excess of 100 per cent – as their gross income rose their net income would actually be reduced. This was due to the 'entry fee' in NICs where once an employee earned over the Lower Earnings Limit (LEL) she or he paid NICs at a rate of 2 per cent on all earnings up to the LEL[3]. A larger entry fee also applied to employer contributions[4]. This led to a bunching of employees at the earnings level just below the LEL indicating that the 'entry fee' was having a distortionary effect on the labour market.

The NICs system therefore was a barrier to making work pay especially for those with earnings close to the LEL and it distorted the labour market through the step changes in employer contributions at different earnings levels. The reforms to the NICs system implemented in Budgets 1999, 2000 and 2001[5] addressed these problems first by raising the level of earnings at which employees and employers would begin to pay NICs to align it with the personal allowance in income tax, secondly by removing the 'entry fee' both for employers and employees and finally by replacing the 'stepped' nature of employer contributions with a flat rate. As a result of raising the level of earnings at which NICs become payable, 900,000 workers were taken out of paying NICs altogether[6].

The reforms to NICs removed one of the remaining sources of MDRs in excess of 100 per cent, improved Gains to Work for low paid workers and reduced the distortions to the labour market. In addition to these reforms, the starting rate of income tax was reduced from 20 per cent to 10 per cent, halving the marginal tax rate for around 3 million low earners since 1999. In combination with the Working Families Tax Credit, the 10p rate of income tax helped tackle the poverty trap by reducing the incidence of high MDRs.

Tax credits

This section describes the range of tax credits introduced. The economic theory underpinning tax credit policy is set out in detail in Annex 10.1.

The idea of in-work financial support for families dates back at least to the introduction of the Earned Income Tax Credit (EITC) introduced in the US in 1975 and to the Family Income Supplement in the UK which was introduced in 1971. The EITC provided a tax credit for families with a dependent child and related to earned income. It has evolved over time, becoming more generous, extending to families further up the income scale and including increased help for families with two or more children. In 1988, Family Credit was introduced in the UK, replacing the

Family Income Supplement. It provided financial assistance to families where at least one adult worked at least 16 hours per week.[7]

As part of its strategy to tackle child poverty and improve gains to work, the Government has introduced a range of tax credits, building on earlier policies in the UK and the US. These include the Working Families Tax Credit (WFTC) and two new tax credits, the Working Tax Credit outlined below and the Child Tax Credit discussed in Chapter 11.

Working Families Tax Credit

The UK personal tax and social security systems have traditionally been seen as distinct, operated by different government departments and with wholly different objectives. According to the traditional model, the main purpose of income tax is to raise revenue and it does this by assessing an individual's income. By contrast, the social security system was oriented to helping those in financial need and its unit of assessment is the household.

While each system was effective in performing its own functions, the interaction of the two led to problems particularly for families in low paid work. The Taylor Review of the interaction of the tax and benefits system[8] found that in-work financial support for families, provided by Family Credit, was perceived to be insufficient to tackle the unemployment trap and that the high rate of withdrawal of in-work benefits created a poverty trap which disincentivised low paid workers from increasing their earnings. Further, there was insufficient help with in-work costs, especially childcare, and the fact that Family Credit was a social security benefit was thought to affect willingness to take up entitlement.

Working Families Tax Credit replaced Family Credit in October 1999. The two credits had similarities – they both boosted net income for lower-paid families in work by providing a fixed six-monthly award that was a decreasing function of income. In addition, to prevent perverse outcomes where partners of rich individuals were eligible, the WFTC preserved the principle that in-work financial support for families would be based on family, not personal, income. However the WFTC brought in key changes to in-work financial support, focused on addressing the problems of inadequate work incentives for families on lower incomes.

First, the income threshold above which the tax credit award would be tapered away and the maximum credits payable for children were raised, increasing the gains to work for eligible families. Secondly, the WFTC improved help with childcare costs, especially for families on very low incomes. Family Credit operated a disregard which off-set childcare costs against net income. As a result families receiving the maximum award, who had the lowest incomes, did not receive an increased award and therefore did not get help with their childcare costs. WFTC replaced the disregard with a credit which paid families 70 per cent of the eligible childcare costs they incurred, up to certain limits.[9]

Perhaps the most important change introduced by the WFTC was the reduction in the rate at which awards were tapered away as post tax income increased – 55 per cent compared with 70 per cent in Family Credit. This had a major impact on the MDRs faced by low income working households. The effects of the Government's reforms of MDRs are discussed in the final section of this chapter.

Finally, while Family Credit was a benefit paid by the then Department of Social Security to the mother in a working family, the WFTC was administered by the Inland Revenue and was paid through the wage packet. The overlap between the income tax and social security systems meant that around 500,000 families paid income tax to the Inland Revenue while receiving Family Credit from the then DSS (see *The Working Families Tax Credit and Work Incentives* (HM Treasury 1998b) for more details). The association of the WFTC with work through payment by employer was aimed at reinforcing its role as a work incentive and increasing the acceptability of the tax credit both for claimants and taxpayers.

New tax credits

In April 2003, the Government introduced the new tax credits, the Child Tax Credit (discussed in Chapter 11) and the Working Tax Credit. They represent a further profound change in the way in which financial support to families with children and low-income working households is provided.

First, the new tax credits are much more closely integrated within the tax system. Secondly, they are also far more inclusive, with approximately nine out of ten families with children eligible for the Child Tax Credit. Thirdly, tax credit awards now take account of families' changing circumstances – for example, a reduction in income or a significant change in childcare costs. Fourthly, the Child Tax Credit provides, for the first time, financial support for children that varies with family income but is independent of the employment status of parents. Furthermore, the Working Tax Credit has been extended to people who do not have children or a disability. Lastly the new tax credits change the way financial support for working families takes account of assets.

Together these changes, which are now discussed in more detail, amount to the biggest single change in financial support for families since the Beveridge reforms of the 1940s.

The new tax credits are aligned with the tax year: awards last for the duration of the tax year and are assessed against tax year income (initial awards are based on previous year income). Unlike the WFTC, awards are based on family income before tax and NICs. The rate at which new tax credit awards are tapered away as income rises is reduced from 55 per cent under the WFTC to 37 per cent. As a result of these changes families will typically have to renew their tax award only once a year, many more dual earner couples will benefit from the new tax credits and work incentives for second earners, especially those working part-time, are significantly improved[10]. Further, unlike previous in-work financial support, new tax credits awards will not be contingent on families having financial assets below a certain value. Instead, income from capital will be assessed in a way much more akin to the treatment of capital within the tax system, improving incentives to save for families in receipt of tax credits.

In addition to closer alignment with the tax system, the two most significant changes introduced by the new tax credits are the extension of in-work financial support to households without children or a disabled adult, and the treatment of changing family circumstances. The first topic is covered in the section below on the Working Tax Credit, following a discussion of how tax credits respond to changing circumstances.

WFTC awards were fixed for their six-month duration[11] but as new tax credit awards last for a tax year, they need to be responsive to changing income and circumstances. Awards can change where (i) a couple heading a household breaks up or where people start living together as a couple or (ii) circumstances change so that the composition of the award is altered (for example due to the birth of a new child) or (iii) childcare costs change or (iv) income changes between the current and previous year.

Even excluding changes to household income triggered by the formation of new households, income for families in the new tax credit population is dynamic: analysis of the British Household Panel Survey (BHPS) shows that around one million households will experience a fall in annual income from one year to the next of £4,000 or more while around 1.2 million will see an increase of this magnitude[12]. This raises the issue of how to trade off a responsive tax credit system which will help families whose incomes fall while preserving work incentives for families whose income are rising and also minimizing the administrative burden on households. To achieve this, the new tax credits apply a disregard to the first £2,500 increase in income compared with the previous year (on which the initial award is based) but they can respond to income falls of any size. The BHPS data show that, of households experiencing an increase in income from one year to the next, around 40% see increases below £2,000[13]. The disregard will remove the burden on these families to report their change in income and will improve work incentives by ensuring that no family receiving tax credits will experience a reduction in award as a result of increasing their earnings up to the disregard level. At the same time, families whose incomes fall will be able to get extra help in-year.

Working Tax Credit

The Working Tax Credit (WTC) ensures adequate financial returns to working by boosting in-work net income. For families with dependent children and households with a disabled worker to be eligible, at least one adult must work at least 16 hours per week. The WTC is now also available to families without children or a disabled worker where at least one adult works 30 hours per week or more and is aged 25 or over.

Like the Child Tax Credit, the WTC is made up of various elements: a basic element for which all households in receipt of the WTC are eligible, an element for lone parents and couples, and additional elements for disabled workers and people aged over 50 returning to work. The WTC also includes a 30-hour element to encourage full-time working. Finally, the WTC has a childcare element which reimburses families 70 per cent of eligible childcare costs up to certain limits.[14] Like the Child Tax Credit, this is paid directly to the main carer in the family but the other elements are paid directly to the worker claiming the WTC, in the pay packet if he or she is an employee.

Extending the WTC to households without children will help to improve incentives for this group, especially for couples, and will contribute to tackling the problem of persistent low income among working people without children. Work incentives tend to be weaker for couples than for single people because out-of-work benefits reflect the presence of a second adult in the household. Further, around one million people without children live in households with an income below 60 per cent of the median and where someone is working more than 16 hours per week. Around half of this group live in households where the main earner is 25 and over and works 30 hours or more per week.

There are two key reasons why the WTC for households without children is restricted to people aged 25 and over. First, those aged under 25 are likely to have better work incentives. People in this age group are more likely to be single and therefore have better work incentives than couples without children. Further, they are less likely to face substantial housing costs because many more of them live with their parents (56 per cent of the 22–24 age group lives with their parents against 9 per cent of those 25 or over). Their gain to work is therefore much less likely to be eroded by Housing Benefit. Secondly, people under 25 are less likely to be a member of a poor household (again largely because they are so much more likely to be living with their parents). More importantly, even if they have low earnings, they are less likely to remain poor because their earnings level partly reflects relative inexperience. Data from the Labour Force Survey[15] suggest that across the age range 16–30 earnings are much higher for older workers while above this age range earnings appear to increase with age at a shallower rate.

The National Minimum Wage

The National Minimum Wage (NMW) is the second key part of the Government's strategy to make work pay. This section looks at the design, implementation and impact of the NMW. Annex 10.2 sets out in detail the economic considerations surrounding the NMW.

Aims and objectives

The policy on the NMW is to be seen in the wider context of the objectives that drive reform in the labour market and the tax and benefit system.

Increasing levels of employment and at the same time boosting earnings is the key to providing a sustainable way out of poverty. As described earlier in the chapter this means tackling the unemployment and poverty traps. The NMW and tax credits system strengthen incentives to participate in the labour market while helping to insure households against future fluctuations in their income. The minimum wage is also a crucial complement to the tax credits system because it ensures that the incentives to work provided through tax credits are not displaced by lower earnings. However, as discussed in Annex 10.2, economic theory warns of possible disemployment effects if the NMW were set at an inappropriate rate. This concern was taken into account in the design of the NMW.

Design and implementation

In order to design and implement the NMW, the Government set up the Low Pay Commission (LPC), an independent body composed of academic experts and employers' and employees' representatives, with the remit of analysing the low pay labour market and recommending the rates of the NMW. The Government accepted all recommendations in the first report from the Low Pay Commission, and the NMW was introduced in April 1999.

The adult rate of the NMW applies to workers aged 22 and above, while a lower youth and development rate applies to workers aged 18–21 and to workers undertaking accredited training in the first six months of a new job. At introduction, the adult rate and the youth and development rate were £3.60 and £3.00 per hour respectively. The lower youth and development rate aims to protect employment opportunities for less experienced workers, leaving employers the flexibility to devote resources to their training. The rates have subsequently increased following new recommendations from the Low Pay Commission, as illustrated in Table 10.1.

Table 10.1 National Minimum Wage rates since its introduction (hourly rate)

	Adult rate	Development rate	Youth rate
1 April 1999	£3.60	£3.00	£3.00
1 June 2000	£3.60	£3.20	£3.20
1 October 2000	£3.70	£3.20	£3.20
1 October 2001	£4.10	£3.50	£3.50
1 October 2002	£4.20	£3.60	£3.60
1 October 2003	£4.50	£3.80	£3.80
1 October 2004[1]	£4.85	£4.10	£4.10

[1] Subject to an assessment of the economic conditions at the time.

Source: Low Pay Commission (2003)

As Table 10.1 shows, the NMW has been regularly increased. Since it was established, the adult rate has increased by around 16.7 per cent, to October 2002 and the youth rate by 20 per cent. Average earnings have increased by 16 per cent over the same period.

International comparisons

International comparisons of the NMW require caution, because of differences between countries in the definition of the minimum wage, sectoral and age coverage, and different timings of uprating (which

Table 10.2 Comparison of levels of minimum wages across countries, end 2002

	In national currency	In UK £s Exchange rate	PPP	Date of last uprating
Australia[1]	A$10.79	3.79	5.12	May 2002
Belgium	€6.71	4.23	4.74	February 2002
Canada[2]	C$6.90	2.81	3.67	–[4]
France	€6.83	4.31	4.74	July 2002
Greece	€2.79	1.76	2.47	July 2002
Ireland	€6.35	4.00	4.12	October 2002
Japan[2]	¥664	3.53	2.66	2002
Netherlands	€7.11	4.48	5.02	July 2002
New Zealand	NZ$8.00	2.42	3.65	March 2002
Portugal [3]	€2.01	1.27	1.90	January 2002
Spain [3]	€2.55	1.61	2.14	December 2001
United Kingdom	£4.20	4.20	4.20	October 2002
United States	US$5.15	3.31	3.49	1997

Notes:
1 Federal Minimum Wage
2 Weighted average of provincial rates
3 Not including any supplementary pay of two additional months of salary
4 Date of last uprating varies between provinces

Source: Low Pay Commission (2003)

Table 10.3 Adult minimum wages as a percentage of full-time median earnings (men and women), mid 2002[1]

Country	Percentage
France	62.1
Australia[2] – LFS	58.4
– ES	54.9
New Zealand	52.9
Ireland	50.6
Netherlands	47.5
United Kingdom[3]	44.7
Canada	41.9
Portugal	40.0
Greece[4]	38.5
United States	33.9
Japan	32.3
Spain	29.6

Notes:
1 The minimum wage refers to the basic rate for adults whereas the data for median earnings include supplementary pay such as overtime and other bonuses.
2 Two estimates of median earnings are available on either the Labour Force Survey (LFS) or an enterprise survey (ES)
3 LPC calculation
4 Refers to manufacturing workers only

Source: Low Pay Commission (2003)

makes a comparison at a given point potentially misleading). To compound these difficulties, the problems of currency conversion have to be borne in mind. Table 10.2 converts minimum wage rates using both the current exchange rate and Purchasing Power Parity (PPP) for private consumption[16].

Bearing in mind the caveats above, nevertheless, a reasonable measure of the impact of the minimum wage is to compare the level of minimum wage with average earnings. Table 10.3 below shows adult minimum wages as a percentage of median earnings for a number of countries. The UK's NMW is in the middle of the countries surveyed.

Economic impact of NMW

Economic theory (see Annex 10.2) suggests that the effect of the NMW wage will depend on its level and the type of labour market job seekers face. This section looks at the effect of the introduction of the NMW in practice.

Coverage

In order to set the minimum wage at an appropriate level, it is crucial to estimate the number of people that will benefit from higher wages following the introduction of the NMW and subsequent increases. This requires analysing the earnings distribution before any change to current policy, and making some assumptions on how earnings would increase in the absence of an increase in the NMW. The most recent estimates show that the introduction of the NMW in 1999 benefited 1 to 1.2 million low-paid workers, while the increase in October 2001 benefited between 1.1 million and 1.5 million workers. The Low Pay Commission estimates (March 2003) that the increase in October 2003 will benefit 1.3 million workers, rising to 1.7 million with the October 2004 increase. Table 10.4 summarises these estimates, also showing how the percentage of workers who stood to benefit from the National Minimum Wage has increased over time.

Table 10.4 Number who stood to benefit from the introduction and subsequent increases in the NMW

	Absolute estimate	Percentage of the working population
Introduction	1.2 million	4.9
October 2001	1.3 million	5.3
October 2003	1.1–1.2 million	4.3–4.7
October 2004	1.6–1.9 million	6.2–7.6

Source: DTI, central estimates of low pay based on Labour Force Survey and New Earnings Survey

Employment

In the UK, the NMW was introduced against a background of falling unemployment and rising employment rates. Both the assessment carried out by the LPC and independent research show that the NMW did not have any appreciable negative effect on overall employment. Stewart (2002a) compares the change in employment for workers affected by the NMW with the change in employment of higher-paid workers, assumed to be unaffected, after controlling for other sectoral and regional characteristics. He concludes that the impact on employment of the introduction of the NMW is not significantly different from zero. Another study (Stewart 2002b) examines whether, because wage levels vary regionally, the NMW will have a greater impact in regions where earnings tend to be lower. It finds that employment growth was not significantly different in regions where the NMW could be expected to have had a bigger impact on earnings.

Although an overall impact of the NMW on employment in the UK is not discernible, it is arguable that the impact will be stronger in those sectors where low-paid workers are concentrated. Machin et al. (2002) focus on the impact on the residential home care sector. The study finds elasticities of employment to wages of between -0.2 and -0.4, but no evidence that the NMW led to closure of care homes. It should be noted that the study does not capture the extent to which falls in employment in the care home sector are offset by rises in employment elsewhere.

Competitiveness and productivity

The impact of the NMW on the competitiveness of the economy appears to be small. Estimating how the NMW impacts on costs for employers requires assumptions about how firms set wages for workers with different skill levels. As the NMW increases wages for lower paid workers, employers may also raise wages for those more qualified workers originally paid above the new minimum wage level, in order to restore pay differentials. Depending on the assumption about the extent of differential restoration, the Low Pay Commission estimates that the total impact on the wage bill of the uprating of the NMW in October 2001 ranges from 0.07–0.09 per cent (with no differential restoration) to 0.11 per cent (with full differential restoration).

These figures are for the economy as a whole, and therefore might underestimate the impact on those firms and sectors with a higher proportion of low paid workers. Figure 10.1 shows the Low Pay

Commission's estimates of the impact on the wage bill for seven low pay industries.

Figure 10.1 shows the additional wage costs that employers would face if nothing else changed in their business strategy. However, the NMW could also lead to increased prices, or an increase in productivity. Hence, the impact shown is an upper-bound estimate of the effect of the NMW on the wage bill. In practice, there is little evidence that the introduction of the NMW has significantly affected profit margins across low-paid sectors or led to higher prices of the goods they produce. It is likely that such impacts that may have occurred are dominated by other factors, such as the economic cycle or increased competition in certain sectors.

It is an interesting question as to the extent to which the NMW leads to increased productivity. The Low Pay Commission (2003) found anecdotal evidence that the introduction of the NMW put pressure on companies to find new, more productive techniques or organisational innovations, often switching to provision of higher-quality services with higher profit margins. Aggregate data by sector show that, for three out of seven low-pay sectors – hairdressing, textiles and security – labour productivity grew on average faster in 1998–2000 than in 1995–98, before the introduction of the NMW. However, Forth and O'Mahony (2003) find that there is no evidence of a direct link between the NMW and an increase in productivity in low-pay sectors overall.

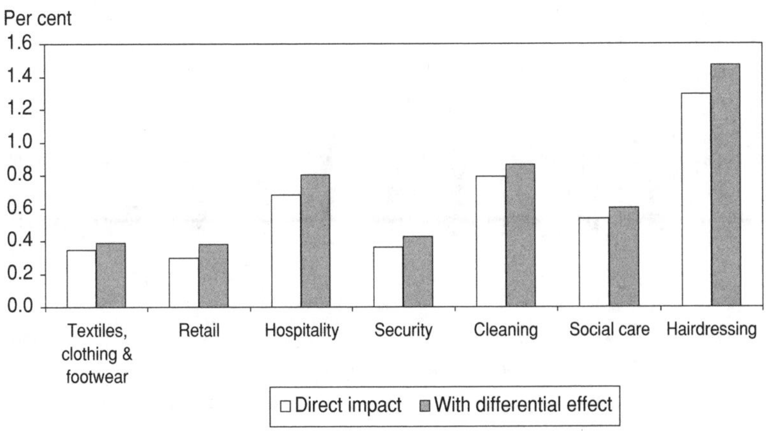

Source: Low Pay Commission (2003)

Figure 10.1 Wage bill impact in low-paying sectors of the October 2001 uprating of the NMW

In summary, as the LPC (2003) notes, 'it is difficult to assess from the aggregate data how the balance of the impact of the minimum wage has been shared between prices, profits and productivity'.

Impact on Poverty

Poverty reduction is one of the main objectives of the Government's labour market policies. It is therefore natural to ask to what extent the NMW contributes to achieving this goal.

Figure 10.2 shows the estimated average gains from the latest increase in the NMW for different household groups across the income scale.[17] It shows that, while the NMW is strongly progressive across working households, it is only moderately progressive across all working-age households because it has no impact on households with no one in work, most of which are located in the lowest income deciles.

However, the NMW has other beneficial distributional impacts, across gender and ethnicity and for disabled workers. The Low Pay Commission (2003) estimates that women, disabled people and some ethnic minorities benefit disproportionately from the NMW. Thirteen per cent of the beneficiaries of the October 2001 increase were disabled workers (compared with 8 per cent of jobs held by disabled people), and 70 per

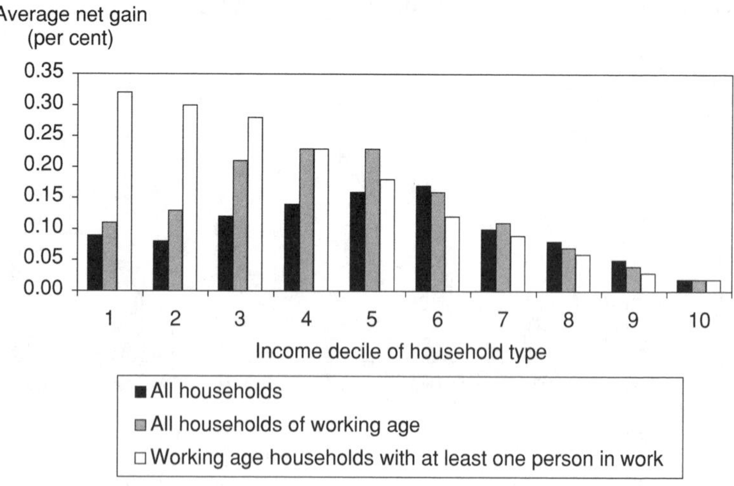

Source: Low Pay Commission

Figure 10.2 Average net gain, as a percentage of net household disposable income, from an increase in the National Minimum Wage to £4.50

cent were women. Further, following the 2001 increase, earnings of low paid Pakistani and Bangladeshi workers increased from 84.2 per cent to 93.2 per cent of earnings of low paid White workers.

Impact of the Government's reforms

To measure the overall success of policies aimed at making work pay, it is necessary to look at the combined effect of the range of policies discussed in the previous sections. Attention needs to be given to the minimum income households can expect and how this income changes as individuals move up the earnings ladder.

Together with the NMW, the introduction of the 10p band of income tax and the reforms to National Insurance Contributions, the WTC generates guaranteed minimum incomes for working households in a variety of circumstances. These incomes are net of tax and include tax credits. Table 10.5 sets out how these have increased in recent years, with rises in the NMW and greater generosity of the tax credits system.

Building on the WFTC, the new tax credits boost in-work incomes for lower-paid families – increasing their gains to work – and thereby ensuring that these families do not face an unemployment trap. This is illustrated in Figure 10.3, which shows the change in the gains to work for households with one child in the 2003/04 tax-benefit system compared with 1997/98.

The WTC has also improved work incentives for workers aged 25 and over without children. From October 2003, a couple aged 25 and over in full-time work without children or a disability will be guaranteed at least £187 per week. This implies an increase in gains to work of two and a half times compared with the gain under the tax-benefit system in 1997/98. The reforms also mean that a single person aged 25 or over without children working full-time on the National Minimum Wage will be nearly £25 a week better off from October 2003 in work compared with the previous system – an increase in the gain to work of just under 50 per cent.

While improved gains to work are tackling the unemployment trap, it is also important to ensure that workers have incentives to move up the earnings ladder. Tackling the poverty trap improves labour market flexibility by providing stronger incentives for people to respond to the opportunities generated by change – for example, by adjusting their working patterns or moving into better-paid jobs.

As described above MDRs measure the extent of the poverty trap by showing how much of each additional pound of gross earnings is lost

Table 10.5 Weekly Minimum Income Guarantees

	April 1999	October 1999	April 2002	October 2003
Family working 35 hours with one child*	£182	£200	£227	£241
Family working 16 hours with one child*	£136	£144	£167	£184
Couple 25 or over, childless, one earner working 35 hours	£117	£117	£130	£187
Single person 25 or over, childless, working 35 hours	£113	£113	£130	£158

Note: *Applies to lone parent families and couples with children alike.

Source: HM Treasury (2003j)

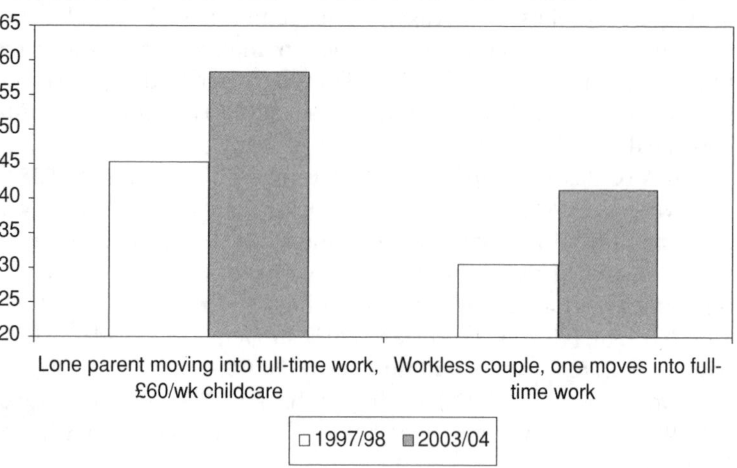

Source: HM Treasury (2003j)

Figure 10.3 Gains to work for different households with one child

through higher taxes and withdrawn benefit or tax credits. Prior to the introduction of tax credits and the other reforms to the tax and benefit system low income working families faced MDRs in the range 30 per cent to 97 per cent[18] and around 750,000 working families (around 5 per cent

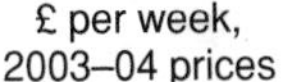

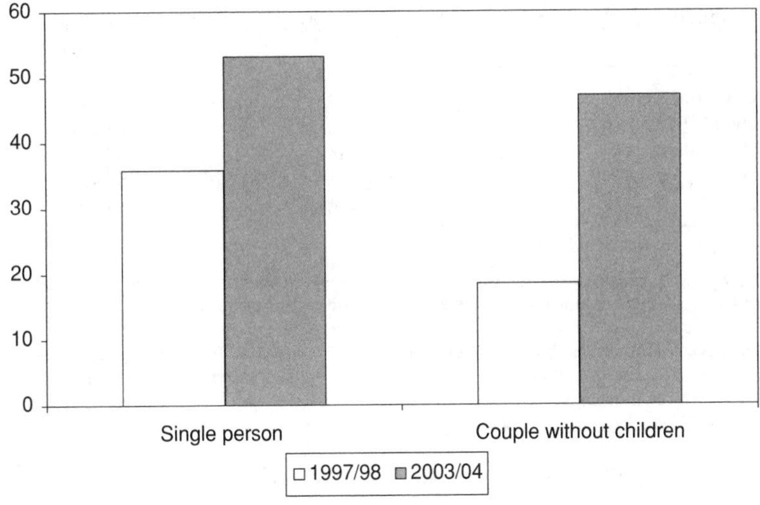

Source: HM Treasury

Figure 10.4 Gains to work for people aged 25 and over without children

of all working families) faced MDRs above 70 per cent, nearly twice the number facing MDRs at this level in the mid 1980s. The highest MDRs resulted from the interaction of financial support through Family Credit and Housing Benefit[19].

As a result of the introduction of WFTC, in combination with the reforms to NICs and the new 10 per cent starting rate of income tax, the number of working families facing MDRs in excess of 70 per cent fell to 260,000. The reforms also sharply reduced the number of working families with the highest MDRs - of over 90 per cent - from 130,000 to 20,000. In part this was due to the increased generosity of WFTC which floated around 50,000 families out of Housing Benefit altogether (HM Treasury 1998b). Following the introduction of the new tax credits, over half a million fewer low-income households now face marginal deduction rates in excess of 70 per cent than did so in April 1997. The increase in the number of households facing MDRs of between 60 and 70 per cent is primarily due to the increased generosity of tax credits, and more recently the extension of support to workers aged 25 or over without children.

Table 10.6 The effect of the Government's reforms on high marginal deduction rates

Marginal deduction rate*	Before Budget 1998	2003/04 system of tax and benefits
Over 100 per cent	5,000	0
Over 90 per cent	130,000	30,000
Over 80 per cent	300,000	135,000
Over 70 per cent	740,000	185,000
Over 60 per cent	760,000	1,490,000

Notes:
*Marginal deduction rates are for working households in receipt of income-related benefits or tax credits where at least one person works 16 hours or more a week.

Figures are cumulative. Before Budget 1998 figures are based on 1997/98 estimated caseload and take-up rates; the 2003/04 system of tax and benefits is based on 2001/02 caseload and take-up rates, and projected caseload estimates of WTC and CTC in 2003/04 based on 1999/2000 caseload and take-up rates.

Source: HM Treasury (2003j)

Labour supply

The introduction of the WFTC in the UK has stimulated a growing empirical literature. Blundell (2000) and Blundell et al. (2000) use models of household preferences, and labour market conditions, such as entry wages, to attribute probabilities to each individual of entering work at a certain number of hours, depending on their budget constraint. They find that the WFTC is responsible for a 2.2 per cent increase in employment for lone parents, only partially offset by a reduction of 0.6 per cent in employment of married women with a working partner.

Gregg, Johnson and Reed (1999) model the transition between non-employment and employment, using an estimation of the entry wages that people outside the labour market are likely to command. On the basis of these estimated entry wages, they model the probability of different household types entering work. They conclude that the introduction of the WFTC increased the probabilities for lone parents and married women with workless partners. But, consistent with the Blundell et al. (2000) results, they estimate a decrease in the probability of a move into work for married women with a working partner. The intuition behind this result can be derived from the discussion of income and substitution effects set out in Annex 10.1. Lone parents who move into work as a result of the introduction of tax credits find that the increased return to working extra hours – the substitution effect – dominates that impact of increased household income on labour supply. By contrast, women who have a partner in work may reduce their labour supply because the income effect of the tax credits boosts overall household income and because at the margin the tax credit taper reduces their financial return to working.

Conclusion

This chapter has set out the second part of the Government's strategy to increasing employment, 'making work pay'. The strategy aims to tackle the problems of the poverty trap and the unemployment trap by introducing a range of tax credits and a minimum wage, and by making reforms to income tax and National Insurance Contributions.

The impact of these policies has been to augment the income of lower-paid workers and to reduce the disincentives to employees moving up the earnings ladder.

Annex 10.1
The Economics of Tax Credits: Inactivity, Participation and Labour Supply

The theoretical model

The standard approach of labour supply theory models the individual's choice as a trade-off between higher consumption financed by increased labour income and the loss of leisure deriving from the effort of working. Typically, this is represented through a budget constraint, identifying the amount of consumption that is affordable for the individual at his wage rate and for a given quantity of labour supplied. Microeconomic theory predicts that the individual will choose to work the number of hours at which the benefits of working an extra hour are just offset by the costs. This is the point of tangency between the budget constraint and the individual's indifference curve where the slope of the budget constraint (the real hourly wage) equals the slope of the indifference curve (the marginal rate of substitution between consumption and leisure).

The tax and benefit system has an important impact on individuals' labour supply decisions because it alters the budget set. Proportional taxation of labour income changes the slope of the budget set, making

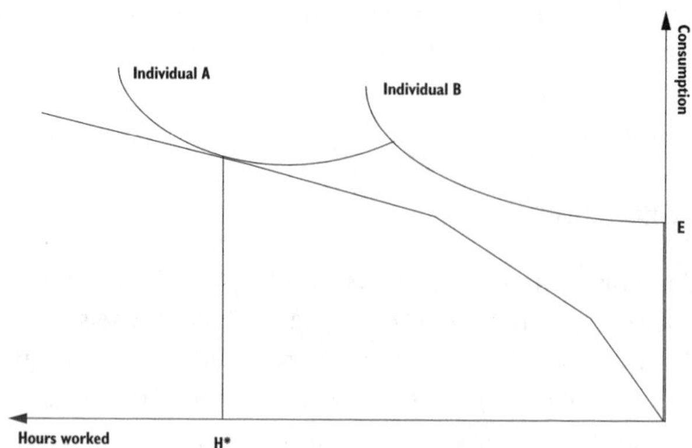

Figure 10A.1 Individual labour supply choice in the presence of a non-convex and non-linear budget set

it flatter. Further, progressive taxation introduces *non-linearities* in the budget set by creating kinks at the boundaries of tax brackets.

Budget set analysis can also be used to model the presence of fixed costs of working. The costs of transport to and from the workplace, and childcare costs for parents, constitute an 'entry fee' into the labour market. Fixed costs of working introduce non-convexities into the budget set, a further element of complication in the analysis of labour supply decisions.

Figure 10A.1 plots a budget constraint in consumption-hours space (with consumption represented along the vertical axis) in order to model the labour supply choice of an individual in the presence of a non-convex and non-linear budget set. The brackets of the UK income tax system are represented, with the first segment of the budget constraint corresponding to the personal allowance where no tax is paid, followed by the segment corresponding to the 10 per cent tax bracket, and then the 22 per cent and the 40 per cent brackets. Point E along the vertical axis models the fixed cost of working. In the presence of childcare costs, for example, when moving into work at very low hours the worker would experience a fall in consumption.[20]

Individuals A and B have different preferences, represented by the different shape of their indifference curves. Individual A will clearly choose to work H* hours, where his indifference curve is tangent to the budget constraint. Because of fixed costs of working, individual B's

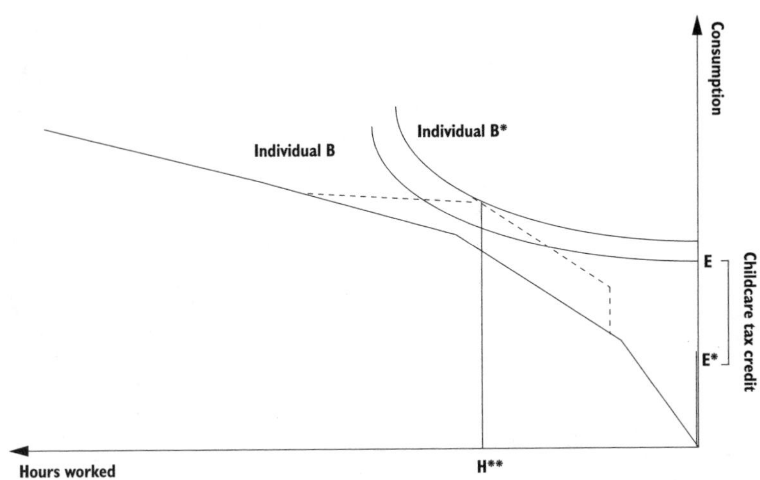

Figure 10A.2 Impact of the WTC on choice of labour supply: non worker

utility-maximising choice, given the budget set, is at point E, where no hours are worked.

What is the effect of the tax credits on individuals' participation and choice of hours?[21] The impact of the WFTC (and now the WTC) on the budget constraint is twofold. On the one hand, it shifts the budget constraint up, as it reduces the amount of tax paid by the worker and increases his net wage. The tax credits also alter the slope of the budget constraint because of the interaction of the taper with income tax. On the other hand, the childcare element reduces one of the fixed costs of working for families with dependent children, thus pushing point E down the y-axis to E*[22]. Figure 10A.2 shows the impact of the WTC on Individual B's choices.

The budget set has now shifted up vertically at the point at which the individual works a sufficient number of hours to become eligible for the Working Tax Credit. The second segment of the dashed line represents the interval in which the worker continues to receive maximum WTC as income increases. The third, flatter dashed segment kicks in at the income level where the tax credit starts to be withdrawn as income increases. As the tax credits make a larger area in the consumption/hours space affordable for the worker, he will choose to enter the labour force

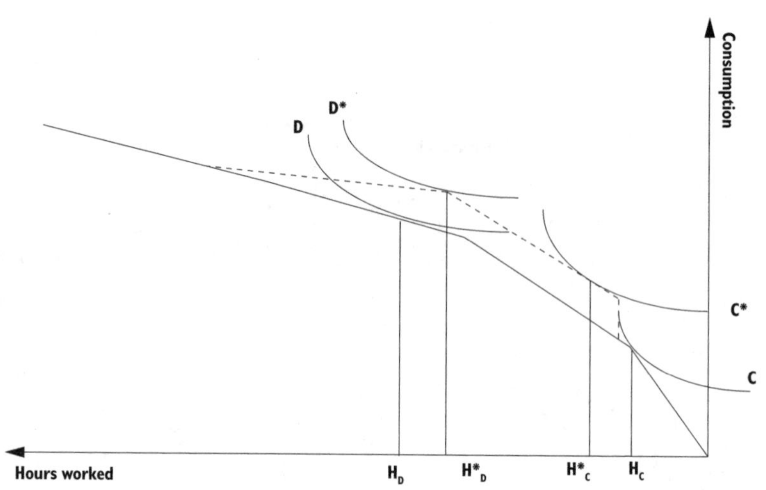

Figure 10A.3 Impact of the WTC on choice of labour supply: worker

and work H** hours and in so doing moves on to an indifference curve associated with a higher level of utility.

While the effect of the tax credit on the choice of whether to work or not is certainly positive, there might be some ambiguous effect on the choice of how many hours to work for people who are already working.

Figure 10A.3 illustrates the choice of someone who is already working before the introduction of the tax credits. (Individual C is working H_C hours before the introduction of the tax credit.) In his case, the *substitution effect* of the reform dominates *the income effect*:[23] by working more hours he will now enjoy more consumption per hour, and he is thus willing to give up more leisure, increasing his hours in work to H^*_C. By contrast, individual D, who is working H_D hours before the reform, experiences an *income* effect prevailing over the *substitution effect* following the introduction of the tax credits. With the same number of hours of work, he can enjoy more consumption and he will therefore value leisure more at the margin and reduce his hours to H_D^*.

Empirical estimates of the labour supply impact of tax credits

The section above summarised the main predictions of the impact of tax credits from the theory of labour supply. The key variable that influences the outcome is the shape of the indifference curve, that is, the preferences between consumption and leisure of each individual. This means that the actual effects of the tax credits on labour supply, or at least their magnitude, are an empirical question. This section looks at the empirical literature on the impact of financial support and begins with a brief illustration of the main methodological difficulties that need to be overcome when estimating labour supply.

Early papers in the literature studied[24] the impact of income tax cuts that took place in the US in the 1980s, using mainly time-series data and comparing different sections of the income distribution, which will be differently affected by the reforms, and cross-sectional data, using data on taxable income. This estimation strategy presents some problems. In the first place, it is difficult to isolate the effect on employment of the economic cycle, even when GDP growth controlled for, because different parts of the income distribution will be differently affected by the cycle. Second, there is a risk of overestimation of labour supply responsiveness to financial incentives because of the kinks in the budget constraint. As people increase or decrease their labour supply discontinuously, 'jumping' to one or the other side of the kink, the data could register big swings in hours worked for a relatively small change in the system.

The *natural experiment* approach uses the tax reforms as a 'before and after' divide that allows us to identify the behavioural response. The idea is to focus on a group affected by the reform (used as a 'treatment group') and compare its change in labour supply with the change in a 'control group' – a group unaffected by the reform, but similar to the control group in all other aspects (for example, because it shares the same macro-economic environment). Provided that the two groups are well chosen, the difference between the treatment and the control groups' response will represent the true effect of the reform (this is why this approach is also called 'difference-in-difference'). For the estimation to be meaningful, the control group must satisfy two assumptions:

- it must be subject to the same impacts over time effects as the treatment group; and
- the composition of the two groups must remain the same before and after the policy change.

This method was first used by Eissa (1995; 1996) and Eissa and Liebman (1996), who estimate, respectively, the labour supply response of married women to income tax cuts and the effect of the introduction of the Earned Income Tax Credit (EITC) on lone parents' labour supply. They find a strong response in the labour supply of married women to tax cuts (with elasticities between 0.6 and 1) and an equally strong response from lone parents (with the EITC being estimated to account for an increase in lone parents' employment of two percentage points).

Another interesting piece of evidence on the behavioural response to financial incentives to work comes from a randomised experiment that exploits the experimental nature of the Canadian Self Sufficiency Program (SSP). The SSP provides financial incentives to single parents working a minimum of 30 hours per week but, unlike the EITC and the WFTC, and now the Working Tax Credit in the UK, it is time-limited. The experiment consists in monitoring around 6,000 eligible households over five years of the programme, half of which receive support and constitute the treatment group while the other half do not receive support and are the control group. The experiment shows a very strong response from lone parents, with the treatment group doubling its labour supply compared with the control group.[25]

Annex 10.2
The National Minimum Wage

The economic theory of minimum wages

There are two economic models that try to explain the effect of the minimum wage on the labour market. The standard neoclassical view suggests that workers command a wage in the labour market based on their productivity. Those with a reservation wage above the market rate will not supply labour. A minimum wage implies zero demand for those workers whose productivity is below the minimum rate. Firms face an infinitely elastic labour supply schedule, and labour supply and turnover costs (the cost of hiring and training new staff once old workers have left) are extremely sensitive to the level of wage offered.

The alternative view stresses the role of frictions in the labour market such as search costs, efficiency wages or imperfect competition (union bargaining or monopsony models). Firms are faced with an upward sloping supply curve and will offer a distribution of wages. Low-paying firms will still recruit but will suffer higher turnover costs. Turnover costs (and firms' profitability) are less sensitive to wage movements.

This section analyses the assumptions underlying these two competing models and considers their implications for policy. It is based on *Myth and measurement: the new economics of the Minimum Wage* (Card and Krueger 1995).[26]

The neoclassical model

In the competitive neoclassical model, a representative firm uses labour and non-labour inputs to produce an output through a production function with decreasing returns to factors. The firm operates in perfectly competitive markets, that is, it takes the wage rate of labour and the prices of non-labour inputs and its output as given. The firm will thus maximise profits by employing an optimal number of workers, such that the marginal productivity of labour (for a given level of non-labour inputs) is equal to the wage paid.

Figure 10A.4 illustrates the effect of the minimum wage in the simplest version of the competitive model. Demand for labour from firms is represented by the marginal productivity of labour schedule, which is assumed to be a decreasing function of labour supply. Labour supply is an increasing function of wage, and the intersection of the two determines the equilibrium wage W^*, at which level L* people are employed. The introduction of a minimum wage W^M has the effect of

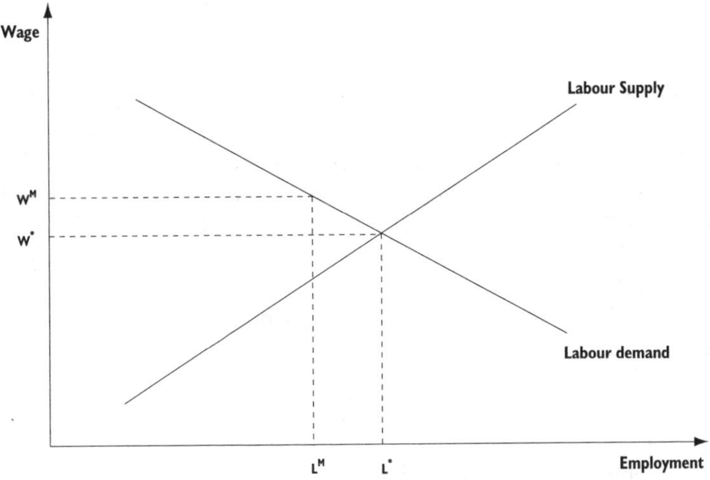

Figure 10A.4 The minimum wage in a competitive model

reducing employment to the level L^M, as firms are not willing to employ workers with a marginal productivity below W^M. There will be $L^* - L^M$ workers involuntarily unemployed.

In order to maintain the same level of output, a firm will switch from labour inputs to non-labour inputs. The flatter the labour demand curve (i.e. the higher the wage elasticity of labour demand), the bigger the disemployment effect. The empirical literature has estimated the elasticity, η, of labour demand (assuming constant output) at between –1 and 0 for most types of firms, with –0.3 being the most common estimate. This means that, in order to keep its output constant, a firm would react to a 10 per cent increase in the minimum wage with a 3 per cent reduction in labour demand.

This illustration is a simple one, and does not take into account two elements:

- the output response of firms affected by the minimum wage: the assumption so far is that companies switch from labour inputs to non-labour inputs holding output constant; and
- heterogeneity of the labour force: the assumption has been that in competitive equilibrium, all workers receive the same wage W^*. But, in reality most employers hire workers at different skill levels and wage rates.

These extensions of the model are discussed in turn.

Output effects for a competitive industry

If an industry is composed of identical companies operating in perfect competition, then an increase in the wage bill following the introduction of the minimum wage will lead to an increase in the industry selling price, proportional to labour's share of cost. The price increase will lead to a decrease in demand for the industry's output proportional to price elasticity of demand, and thus to a proportional effect on the industry's demand for labour.

Therefore, the 'unconditional' elasticity of labour demand with respect to wage η' will be:

$$\eta' = \eta + k$$

where η is the output constant elasticity of labour demand to wage as above, and k depends on labour's share of total costs and on the price elasticity of demand for output of the industry. The higher the price elasticity of demand for output and the higher labour's share of total cost, the bigger the unconditional elasticity of labour demand η' compared to the output constant elasticity η.

The competitive model therefore predicts that the introduction of a minimum wage will hit employment hardest in sectors that face a demand for output that is very responsive to prices and that employ a higher share of labour.

Heterogeneous labour

As mentioned above, different levels of skills and wages are observed in the labour force. The simplest way to model this empirical fact within the neoclassical approach is to assume that two types of labour exist: skilled and unskilled. Skilled and unskilled workers are imperfect substitutes, in the sense that skilled labour can be used to carry out unskilled tasks and vice versa, but with efficiency losses. As wages for unskilled workers are lower, a minimum wage increase will affect them more than those of skilled labour.

In this setting, employment of unskilled workers whose wage is affected by a minimum wage increase will fall. However, the decrease in unskilled employment could be partially off set by the increase in skilled employment. The size of this effect will depend positively on the degree of substitution between skilled and unskilled workers and negatively on the degree of complementarity between labour and non-labour inputs.

The monopsony model

As noted above, the neoclassical model predicts that the minimum wage decreases employment of workers who would otherwise be paid below that level. The main feature of the neoclassical model is that wages are determined in a competitive fashion, that is, firms take wages as given. This assumes that workers are fully informed about the jobs offered, are free to move across jobs, and make a decision about which one to take up. In such a market, labour supply is perfectly elastic: an employer who offered a wage just above the going market rate would immediately attract qualified applicants.

However, it is likely that labour supply is not perfectly elastic, and companies have some market power. In the extreme case, they are the only buyer of labour in a given market and have monopsony power. In such a setting, the labour supply schedule is upward sloping, and in order to attract and retain L workers companies must pay a wage:

$$w=f(L)\ .$$

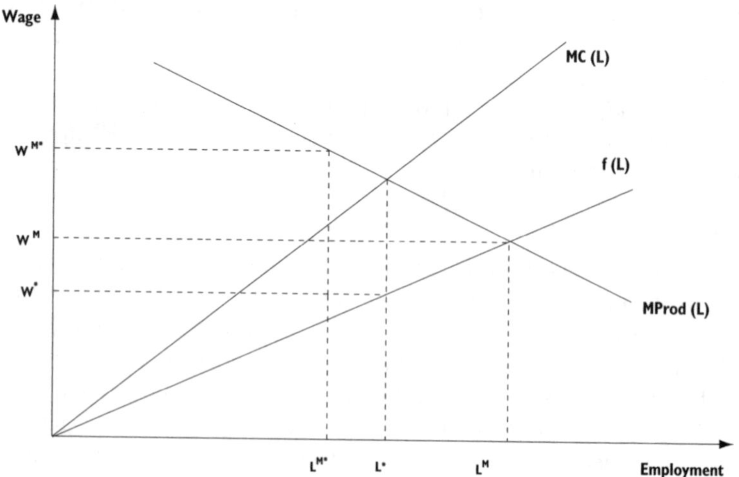

Figure 10A.5 The minimum wage in a monopsony model

In order to maximize profits, the firm will employ a number of workers such that the marginal cost of hiring an additional worker is equal to the marginal productivity of labour. Figure 10A.5 illustrates the equilibrium in this market.

Companies offer a wage W^*, which corresponds to the point on the labour supply curve (f(L)) where the level of employment equalises the marginal cost of hiring an additional worker with the marginal productivity of labour. At that wage, L^* workers are willing to supply labour. What is the effect of the minimum wage? Figure 10A.5 shows that, for a moderate level of minimum wage W^M employment can actually increase to L^M, as more workers are willing to supply labour at the new level of wage. However, this is true only for moderate increases in the minimum wage. An increase to W^{M*} would decrease employment to L^{M*}.

The intuitive explanation for this positive employment effect is that, in a monopsonistic equilibrium, companies keep a number of unfilled vacancies. The firm would ideally hire additional workers to fill these vacancies, but is not willing to increase the wage to attract more workers because it would have to pay a higher wage to the existing workers. The minimum wage increases the wage rate above the monopsonistic equilibrium and attracts new workers. However, this is true only for moderate increases. If the wage rate increases too much, employers will have to cut employment in order to raise the marginal product of labour to the minimum wage level.

How can we rationalise the presence of monopsony power in the labour market? The simplest example is a one-company town, in which there is one employer only in a given area. However, this implies that the monopsonist is a large company, but, in reality, most low-pay jobs are offered by small employers. A more plausible justification of monopsony power relies on the presence of imperfect information and costs of moving between jobs. To the extent that workers do not move immediately to the job that offers the best terms, companies are partially sheltered from competition, and can exercise some degree of monopsony power.

The presence of search costs introduces a further element in employers' choices in the case of a minimum wage increase. Assume that when a worker quits his job, his employer faces the cost of hiring and training a replacement: in other words, turnover costs. Then a higher wage carries a trade-off: on the one hand, it means that the wage bill is higher, but on the other hand, it increases job satisfaction for employees and thus reduces the probability of workers quitting and hence turnover costs. In simple terms, some employers may choose between a low wage-high turnover strategy and a high wage–low turnover strategy. An increase in the minimum wage might simply induce a low wage–high turnover employer to switch to a higher wage–low turnover strategy, with no corresponding reduction in employment.

Empirical evidence of the impact of a minimum wage

Most of the empirical evidence uses US data to look at the impact of minimum wage increases in the early 1990s, and do not seem to lead to a consensus (see Brown 1999 for an overview). Time-series analysis estimates suggest that the minimum wage had a negative employment effect for teenagers, although in many studies these estimates are not statistically significant. While there is some evidence that hours per week fell as a consequence of the introduction of the minimum wage, there is no consensus in the literature on whether the minimum wage has affected adult employment in the US.

'Cross-state' studies exploit the fact that variation in the average level of wages across states leads to variations in the impact of minimum wage increases, and thus allows a comparison between high- and low-impact states. Results from these studies typically range from a negative elasticity between 0.1 and 0.2 (i.e. a 10 per cent increase in minimum wage generates a 1 to 2 per cent decrease in employment) to effects not statistically distinguishable from zero. A negative impact on teenage employment is, however, statistically significant,[27] with one study suggesting a 7–11 per cent decrease in youth employment attributable to minimum wage increases. The importance of youth sub-minima[28] is confirmed in a study by Neumark and Wascher (1999), who provide a comparison across 16 OECD countries of the impact of the minimum wage, finding a considerable variation in effects, with smaller negative effects in those countries adopting a youth rate. Moreover, they find that policies that encourage flexible labour patterns (by removing restrictions on hours and work rules) reduce disemployment effects. Particularly relevant for the UK is the finding that countries with active labour market policies tend to exhibit smaller disemployment effects.

Part 3

Tackling Poverty and Promoting Opportunity

11
Supporting Families and Children

This chapter sets out an analysis of child poverty in the UK, and describes how policy has been shaped to give every child the best possible start in life, to be supported as they develop and to be given opportunities to achieve their full potential. The Government's strategy to tackle child poverty involves: helping people into work, supporting those who cannot work; providing excellent public services; supporting parents; and working with the voluntary and community sectors.

Introduction

This chapter describes how the Government has reformed the tax and benefit system to tackle child poverty, drawing on the paper *Supporting Children Through the Tax and Benefit System* (HM Treasury 1999d) from the 'Modernisation of Tax and Benefits' series of documents, published by the Treasury. It also considers the role of public services in breaking cycles of disadvantage. All children deserve the best possible start in life, to be supported as they develop, and to be given opportunities to achieve their full potential. Parents in turn need to be able to balance their work and family responsibilities. Tackling child poverty is not something government can achieve alone and the chapter explores the role of the voluntary and community sectors.

The chapter looks first at the extent and causes of child poverty. It then describes the Government's strategy to address the problem, and concludes with an analysis of progress to date and future plans.

Importance of tackling child poverty

The Government believes every child should have the chance to fulfil their potential, regardless of their circumstances.

Children who grow up in poverty can experience disadvantage that affects not only their own childhood, but their experience as adults and the opportunities available to their children. Poverty places strains on family life and excludes children from the everyday activities of their peers. Many children experiencing poverty have limited opportunities to play safely, live in overcrowded and inadequate housing, and eat less nutritious food, resulting in more accidents and ill health. Children growing up in low income households also have fewer opportunities to learn and, as adults, are more likely to be unemployed or earn low wages.

The Government has a role to play in both alleviating and preventing child poverty through:

- ensuring children have opportunities to develop their potential;
- providing financial security for families with children; and
- supporting parents as they fulfil their responsibilities.

The extent and effect of child poverty

Between 1979 and 1997, while the economy grew, the proportion of children living in relative low-income households more than doubled, from 14 per cent to 34 per cent.[1] The UK's experience of child poverty is not universal across industrialised countries. Bradbury and Jantti (1999) found that between 1979 and 1995 the UK experienced one of the largest increases in child poverty[2] in the industrialised world.

A substantial body of evidence[3] shows that children growing up in low-income households are more likely than their better-off peers to

- have low educational attainment;
- leave school at 16;
- have poor health;
- become teenage parents;
- come into early contact with the police;
- be unemployed as adults;
- have low expectations for the future; and
- end up earning a relatively low wage.

Box 11.1 sets out some key statistics on the health impacts of growing up in low income family.

Box 11.1 The impact of growing up poor

- The infant mortality rate in the bottom social class is double that in the top social class (8.1 per 1000 live births compared to 4) (Department of Health)
- Children in the bottom social class are five times more likely to die from an accident than those at the top (83 and 16 per 100,000 respectively) (Department of Health)
- Young men who grew up poor were found to have reduced chances of achieving A-level of higher qualifications than 'non-poor' young men (48 per cent compared to 57 per cent) (Ermisch et al 2001)
- Men who had lived in poor families were much more likely to be inactive later in life (13 per cent compared to 8 per cent). (Ermisch et al 2001).

Poverty in early life therefore not only affects children's current quality of life but also feeds through to their adulthood and on to their own children. Evidence suggests that, if anything, intergenerational effects have strengthened over time, with the correlation between a son's earnings and parental income rising between the sample of children born in 1958 in the National Child Development Survey (NCDS) and those born in 1970 in the British Cohort Survey (BCS).

Analysis from the British Youth Panel (Ermisch, Francesconi and Pevalin 2001), which looks at children born between 1983 and 1989, confirms the strong link between low family income while young and poor outcomes as adolescents. The study finds that children who experience low income are more likely to have lower self-esteem, believe that health is a matter of luck, play truant and expect to leave school at the age of 16.

Income can have a direct impact on children's outcomes, through the effect on the child's ability to participate in everyday activities of the peer group, aspirations, educational and recreational activities, nutrition and also the stress levels of the parent and the parent's ability to cope. Low income is, however, also correlated with a range of factors that are likely to lead to poorer outcomes in the future, such as housing overcrowding, deprived neighbourhoods, low educational qualification of the parent and poor parental mental health (Bradshaw 2001).

Recent evidence from American and Canadian studies of the isolated effect of income on educational outcomes suggests that programmes based on raising maternal employment without additional in-work financial support had only modest effects on family incomes and rarely had significant effects on child outcomes (Duncan, Chase-Lansdale and Lindsay 2001). However, programmes involving additional financial support generated significant effects on elementary schoolchild outcomes. The Milwaukee New Hope programme, which also supplied subsidised high quality childcare, alongside increased financial support, saw the largest gains in child test scores.

Evidence from the 1970 British Cohort Study (Blanden et al 2001) suggests that at least a third of the correlation between family income and educational attainment is due to the effect of income alone. This estimate is likely to be on the low side with an additional effect coming from the investment in the early years of a child's life. So income has an important independent role. But there are clearly factors other than income that can break or entrench the cycle of poverty and disadvantage, such as living in a disadvantaged area, experiencing poor health, lack of access to public services, financial exclusion. In many cases these factors interact and reinforce each other.

The Policy and Action Team (PAT)[4] 12 report on young people was published, by the Social Exclusion Unit, in March 2000. It identified a significant minority of young people who experience a wide range of problems and acute crises in adolescence. The scale of these problems was in many cases growing and larger than in other apparently comparable countries. The report found that problems were concentrated in, but not confined to, the most deprived neighbourhoods. The report identified an increasing body of knowledge about the risk factors that increase the likelihood of experiencing acute crises, and the protective factors that help young people overcome the odds. Some of the headline findings are summarized in Box 11.2.

Causes of child poverty

The interaction of several factors contributed to the increase in the number of children in low-income households between the late 1970s and mid 1990s:

- sharp falls in male employment combined with rising female employment, but not in the same households, leading to a concentration of worklessness in certain households combined with more dual-earner households;

Box 11.2 Policy Action Team report on young people

European comparisons

- Alongside Greece and Portugal, the UK had the lowest number of 18-year-olds in learning in the European Union (EU).
- With the exception of Portugal, the UK had the highest proportion in the EU of school leavers with no more than Level 2 qualifications. This proportion was nearly 50 per cent above the EU average.
- The rate of teenage births was twice that of Germany, three times that of France, six times that of the Netherlands.
- The UK had more 15–16-year-old drug users than any other EU country.
- England and Wales came joint top, with the Netherlands, of 11 industrialised countries for victimisation.

Trends

- The proportion of pupils with a special educational needs statement had increased by 60 per cent since the late 1980s.
- Permanent exclusions from school had risen from 4,000 per year in 1991–92 to over 12,000 in 1997–98.
- Between the mid-1980s and mid-1990s, referrals for self-harm by young people increased by a third.
- The prevalence of drug use among 12–13-year-olds had increased fivefold and, among 14–15-year-olds, eightfold since 1987.
- Overall involvement of young people as victims of crime increased by 75 per cent between the early 1980s and the mid-1990s.
- Young men were growing out of property crime later: the peak age of offending had risen from 15 in 1986 to 18 in 1994.

- a shift in the relative demand for high-skilled labour with negative impacts on the employment prospects and incomes of low-skilled workers;
- widening wage distribution with increased in-work poverty and in some cases reduced incentives to work;
- demographic change including more lone parent households whose children are at greater risk of poverty, generally because of high rates of worklessness among lone parents; and
- macro-instability leading to an increased proportion of people becoming detached from the labour market.

It has been estimated that demographic change, widening wage distribution and rising worklessness made roughly equivalent contributions to

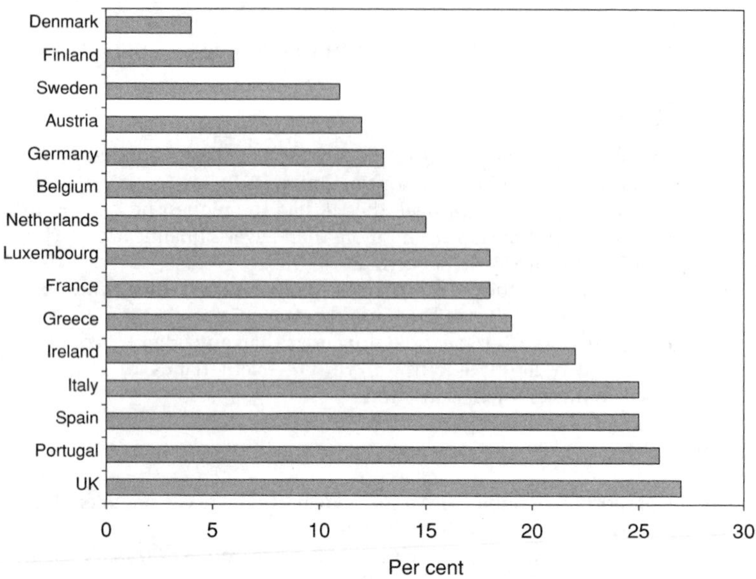

Source: European Community Household Panel 2000

Note: Children in low income are defined as aged 0–15 in households with less than 60% of contemporary median income, before housing costs.

Figure 11.1 Percentage of children in low income households in the European Union

the increases in child poverty in the 1980s and 1990s (Dickens and Ellwood 2003).

Figure 11.1 shows that in 2000 the UK had the highest proportion of children living in low-income households in the EU. In the mid 1990s (the latest date for which data are available), the UK also had the highest proportion of children in workless households. At the end of the 1970s, around 7 per cent of children lived in households with no adult in work; by 1995/96 this proportion has risen to 21 per cent.

Figure 11.2 shows that the rise in children living in low-income households since 1979 is a consequence of both rising worklessness and the rise of in-work poverty. In 2001/02, 3.8 million children were living in households with less than 60 per cent of median income (after housing costs). Around half of these children were in workless households, the majority of which were headed by a lone parent. Between 1979 and 2001/02 the number of children in lone parent households more than doubled from 1.4 million to 3.1 million.

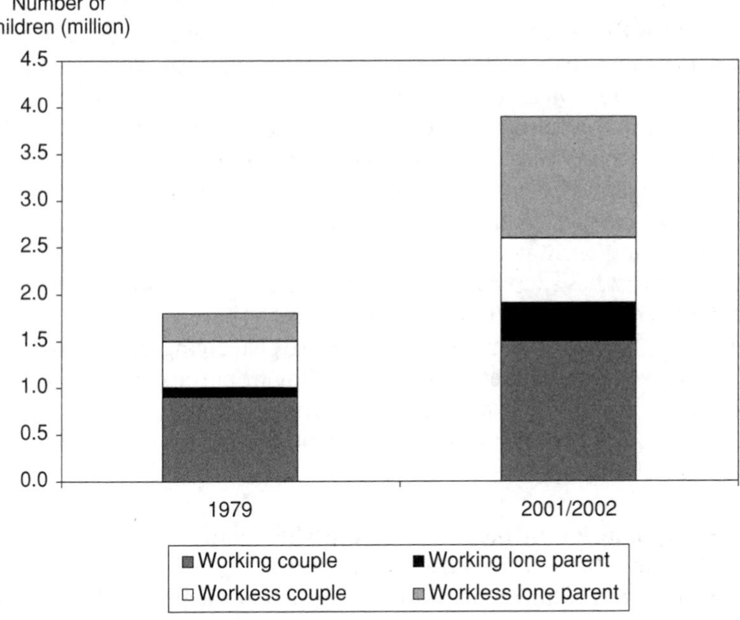

Source: 2001/02 data is taken from Households Below Average Income (DWP 2003b) which is based on the Family Resource Survey which covers GB; 1979 data is taken from the Family Expenditure Survey (FES) for GB only – the FES covers the UK but cases in Northern Ireland were excluded from this table for consistency with HBAI.

Figure 11.2 Children in low income households by family type, 1979 and 2001/02

During the 1980s, the UK witnessed a considerable widening in the wage distribution, largely as a result of the returns to high-skilled labour increasing during this period. From 1978 to 1993, wage differentials grew substantially: wages for men in the 10th percentile of hourly earnings hardly changed, the median wage increased by around 30 per cent and wages in the 90th percentile grew by over 50 per cent (Gosling, Machin and Meghir 1998).

The goal and the strategy

The Government's policy goal is to eradicate child poverty by 2020. On the way to this, it has set itself milestones to halve child poverty by 2010 and to reduce the number of children living in low-income households by a quarter by 2004/05 (from a 1998/99 base).

For the short-term 2004/05 target, low income children have been defined as those in households with less than 60 per cent of contemporary median income both before and after housing costs. This is a relative measure of low income. In addition, the Government reports annually on a range of indicators that reflect wider progress towards tackling child poverty, such as educational outcomes, health inequalities and worklessness. The Government recognises the complexity of poverty and has recently consulted on how child poverty should be measured in relation to the long-term goals. Following the consultation exercise, the Government has adopted a tiered approach to monitor progress on child poverty over the long term. This uses a set of inter-related indicators (tiers) capturing different aspects of poverty, balancing clarity and comprehensiveness while respecting the finding from the consultation that income is at the core of people's conception of poverty. Each tier has significance in its own right and the long term objective is to make progress against all indicators:

- absolute low income – to measure whether the poorest families are seeing their incomes rise in real terms;
- relative low income – to measure whether the poorest families are keeping pace with the growth of incomes in the economy as a whole; and
- material deprivation and low income combined – to provide a wider measure of people's living standards (Department for Work and Pensions 2003a).

The specific strategy to tackle child poverty now and prevent it in future has focused on:

- *ensuring a decent family income*, with work for those who can and support for those who cannot;
- *support for parents*, so that parents can provide better support for their children;
- *delivering excellent public services* for all neighbourhoods, and targeted interventions for those with additional needs; and
- *harnessing the power and expertise of the voluntary and community sectors*, providing support for innovation and good practice. (HM Treasury 2001c)

Work for those who can

Work is the best long-term route out of poverty for those who can work. Evidence suggests that around two-thirds of the movement out of low income in the early 1990s in the UK occurred because people started work or increased their earnings (HM Treasury 1999d). Work is good for the self-esteem and aspirations of the parent and the child. In work, parents may learn new skills and move up the earnings ladder. The evidence presented earlier in the chapter suggests that welfare to work programmes, combined with financial support and quality childcare, can have a significant positive effect on child outcomes and educational attainment.

The strategy for helping parents move into and remain in work includes: Welfare to Work policies to help parents move into the labour market and compete effectively for jobs (discussed in Chapter 9); policies to make work pay such as the Working Tax Credit and National Minimum Wage (see Chapter 10); a National Childcare Strategy which aims to ensure that parents can access affordable, good quality childcare and improved family-friendly employment rights (discussed later in this chapter).

Financial support for families with children

Debate about the most appropriate way to support families with children through the benefit system has tended to polarise between those who argue that support should be provided universally and those who favour a tightly targeted means test. The new welfare state puts into practice the principles of progressive universalism, supporting all families with children, but offering the greatest help to those who need it most through a light-touch income test within the tax system. The old means-test approach, which looked at a family's circumstances at a specific point, compelled families to run down any savings before they could receive significant support from the state. The result of this was that it helped only the poorest, leaving many low to middle-income families without appropriate financial support.

The Government's agenda, to modernise the welfare state so that it provides an effective way of supporting people back into work, making work pay and tackling poverty, has had a number of dimensions. Key measures have included the introduction of the 10p band in income tax, reform of National Insurance Contributions to remove the entry fee and raise the entry threshold, the introduction and subsequent increases in the National Minimum Wage, and the introduction of the Working Families Tax Credit.

The Child Tax Credit and Working Tax Credit, introduced in April 2003, were further landmarks, and are discussed further in the Modernisation of Tax and Benefit paper *Child and Working Tax Credits* (HM Treasury 2002h). Following their introduction, tax credits are now much more closely integrated within the tax system – for example, awards last for the duration of the tax year and are based on tax year income. Chapter 10 describes the system of new tax credits in more detail. The Child Tax Credit consolidated progress in reforming financial support for families with children. It is a major lever in making progress in tackling child poverty and is discussed in more detail below. The Working Tax Credit is reviewed in detail in Chapter 10.

Child Tax Credit

The Child Tax Credit provides a single, seamless system of support for families with children, payable irrespective of the work status of the adults in the household. The aim is to provide a stable and secure income bridge as families move off welfare and into work. The Child Tax Credit system builds on the definition of income used in the tax system. This extends the approach currently taken with middle and high-income families to all families. Aligning the income test for new tax credits with the income tax system means that income is looked at across the tax year as a whole. It also involves moving away from a system which excluded families with modest savings to one which, instead, takes into account only the income from that capital, thus moving from a 'means test' to an 'income test'. Under this new system of assessment the Child Tax Credit is available to families with incomes up to £58,000 a year, thereby covering nine out of ten families with children.

To ensure that more support can be directed toward those most in need, entitlement is based on the family's circumstances, and assessed against the resources available to the family. For couples, tax credits take account of the income of both partners as the natural measure of the resources the family has to meet its needs. This prevents perverse outcomes whereby partners of rich individuals are eligible for financial support while preserving the principle in personal tax that it is each individual's income which is taxable. As a result, tax credits do not need to discriminate between one- and two-earner couples.

This common framework for assessment ensures that all families are part of the same system and poorer families do not feel the stigma associated with previous forms of support. The system is also designed to be less intrusive so that those whose circumstances remain the same will only need to contact the Inland Revenue about tax credits once a year.

The Child Tax Credit is paid directly to the main carer, which, in most cases, is the mother. This allows, for the first time, all income-related payments for children to be paid directly to the main carer, in line with Child Benefit. The main carer accordingly receives a regular and secure stream of income paid either weekly or four-weekly, according to their preference. The childcare tax credit element of the Working Tax Credit is also paid direct to the main carer directly, rather than together with any wages. This has been shown to ease cash flow constraints on using paid childcare and addresses a number of other issues which arose from experience with the previous childcare tax credit component of the WFTC.

Because eligibility for the Child Tax Credit does not depend on work status, people who had previously been excluded from all but Child Benefit, such as students and student nurses, can now receive it.

The Child Tax Credit recognises that circumstances of families differ and to allow the flexibility required to meet these different circumstances it comprises a number of different elements:

- a family element paid to all eligible families, broadly replicating the Children's Tax Credit, in recognition of the responsibilities faced by families with children. A higher family element will be paid for the year following a child's birth;
- a child element for each child within the family, tapered away from families with higher incomes, as was the case with Working Families' Tax Credit, Disabled Person's Tax Credit, Income Support and income-based Jobseeker's Allowance; and
- disabled child elements for families caring for a child with a disability or a severe disability.

The Child Tax Credit is a key aspect in tackling child poverty, but there are other elements to the strategy such as the Sure Start Maternity Grant which provides a lump sum to help cover the costs of a new baby to families in receipt of Income Support, income-based Jobseekers Allowance and the per child element of the Child Tax Credit. In addition, there are further elements to the strategy to tackle child poverty that go beyond helping people into work and providing financial support. These are described below.

Figure 11.3 shows the effect by income decile of the children's tax and benefit measures introduced since 1997 on families and children.

The figure shows that, while all families have gained from the reforms, the greatest gains have been among those on the lowest incomes. Further details of progress towards the child poverty target are provided later in this chapter.

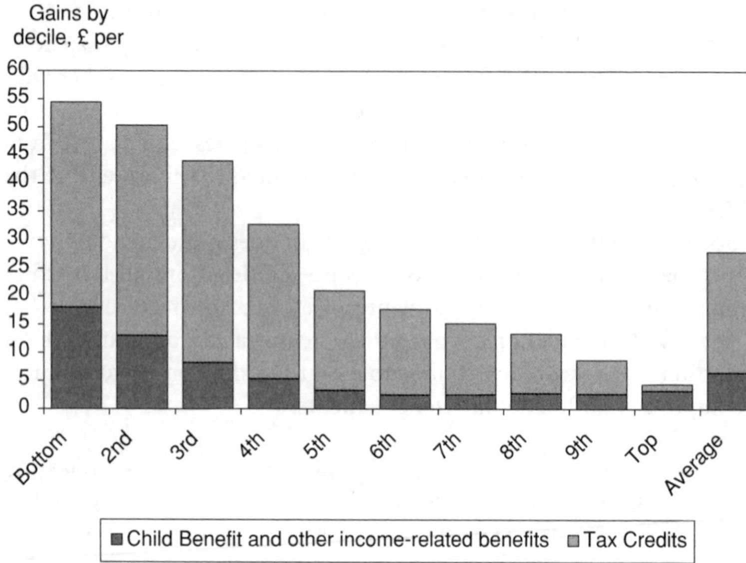

Source: HM Treasury

Figure 11.3 Gains for families with children as a result of tax credits and other children's measures between 1997 and 2004.

Supporting parents to balance work and family life

One such strand involves expanding choice for parents, helping them to fulfil their responsibility for raising children, while working alongside employers to encourage them to adopt best practice and to offer flexible working opportunities throughout the workforce. Such steps benefit employers, as well as employees, by improving recruitment and retention prospects, reducing absenteeism and staff turnover, and improving productivity and business performance.

For parents, a lack of access to childcare and flexible working can be a significant barrier to moving into work. For business, with unemployment low, attracting and retaining the skills of those with caring responsibilities has become increasingly important. Ensuring a secure family environment for children, achieving greater equality between men and women, and raising the productivity of the workforce all point to the need for public policy solutions to provide better support and choice for families.

Helping mothers and fathers to balance work and family life can, by helping them meet their parenting responsibilities, have positive impacts on their children's health, schooling and prospects in later life. Supporting low-income parents is particularly important. Low-skilled workers and their families are particularly at risk of parental and family stress, because their earnings are lower and they tend to have less choice over how they balance their work and family responsibilities.

There is now much more diversity in family structures and in the pattern of work than used to be the case. Most two-parent families are also two-earner families. There are more lone parents, more than half of whom are in work (see Chapter 9). Most women are employed – Britain now has one of the highest rates of female employment in Europe at 69 per cent. The employment rate of mothers with dependent children has risen from 57 per cent in 1990 to 65 per cent in 2000. Throughout the workforce, working hours are more diverse. Despite these changes, women still take on most caring responsibilities, with a disproportionate effect on their lifetime earnings. To help parents choose how to balance their work and family responsibilities the Government has implemented a range of policy measures that include support during the early years of a child's life, provision of childcare and working with business.

Support in early years of a child's life

In recognition of the considerable financial pressures associated with the birth of a child, the Government provides additional support to help parents through the early months of their child's life. From April 2003, new maternity, paternity and adoption leave rights[5] have improved the help available to parents seeking to balance work and caring responsibilities. To complement these reforms, parents of young children and disabled children also have a new right to request a flexible working pattern, and employers face a new duty to consider such applications seriously.

Provision of Childcare

Access to good quality, affordable childcare is a key concern for working parents and can be an important factor in helping parents, particularly lone parents, move into and progress in work. The 2002 Spending Review included a more than doubling of resources for childcare, as part of a combined budget for the new Sure Start Unit[6] that will rise to £1.5 billion by 2005–06. This will fund the development of Children's Centres – which will bring together good quality childcare, early years education, family support and health services – and will support the creation of 250,000 new childcare places.

The National Childcare Strategy will ensure the creation of childcare places to help 1.6 million children in England by March 2004. The extra resources being invested will support additional growth in childcare places, through targeted assistance to a wide range of providers, many of whom could be based within primary and secondary schools.

This investment programme will be matched by reform of delivery structures. At the centre, responsibility for Sure Start, and early years has been brought together within a single, inter-departmental unit with a minister who sits in both the Department for Education and Skills and the Department for Work and Pensions. At the local level, local authorities are being given a clearer role in supporting delivery.

The Working Tax Credit (discussed in Chapter 10) also provides an improved system of financial assistance to help families meet the costs of childcare. This includes extending eligibility for the childcare element to those who use approved childcare in their own home, benefiting, among others, parents of disabled children and those who work outside conventional hours.

Working with business

Enhancing support and choice for families requires a shift in Britain's working culture. The Government's Work-Life Balance Campaign has been set up, aimed at increasing awareness and take-up of employment policies and practices that benefit business, and to help employees enjoy a better balance between work and other demands on their lives.[7]

The campaign promotes flexible working across all businesses in the public, private and voluntary sectors. The Department of Trade and Industry is working with businesses to demonstrate the benefits of flexible working, and is at the same time providing advice on how they can develop flexible working approaches. The Work-Life Balance Campaign is not prescriptive but encourages employers to implement policies and practices over and above the legal requirements. The campaign is intended to benefit all employees, whether or not they have caring responsibilities.

Public services and mixed provision

The importance of complementing financial support with a wider strategy to improve current childhood experiences and to break the long-term cycle of poverty and deprivation was highlighted at the start of this chapter. This section considers some key public service issues that are important to the strategy to tackle child poverty.

Theoretical basis of service provision

Part 4 of this book looks at the role of public services generally. Much of government's function can be seen as establishing infrastructure in its broadest sense – educational, technological, financial, physical, environmental, and social. Government intervention, however, is no guarantee of successful service provision, as the very conditions that generate market failure can also contribute to government failure.

In terms of public sector support for families and children, state intervention can be conducted in a number of ways:

- Regulation – such as the standards for care homes and statutory obligations for child protection.
- Finance – such as direct payments to the disabled or government funding of privately provided services, such as local authorities commissioning parenting support services from the voluntary and community sector.
- Public services – public production of services, such as education and healthcare.
- Income transfers.

Many public services contribute to breaking the cycle of deprivation and disadvantage in the long run, rather than providing a short term impact. Services such as provision of basic levels of education (primary and secondary) and preventive health care services have been long been recognised as central to increasing the welfare of the poor.

Mainstream services

The framework for delivering services to tackle child poverty continues to be developed. The Pre-Budget Report 2001 document on Tackling Child Poverty (HM Treasury 2001c) recognised that mainstream services – education, health and housing – would have the biggest impacts on child outcomes and hence should receive significantly greater funding than any individual targeted programme. For such services to achieve their full impact, the public services need to fit together to benefit children and young people. A Children's Green Paper 'Every Child Matters', published in September 2003, put forward ways of making mainstream services more preventative and more responsive to the needs of children of all ages at risk of a range of adverse outcomes. It proposed reforms designed to align policy objectives, resources and incentives for delivery of services to children and outlined a strategic framework for taking forward reform of children and family services. The creation of a Minister for Children, with responsibility for children's services, childcare and provision for under-fives, family policy (including parenting support and family law) will enhance co-ordination in this area. The remainder of this section reviews the contribution to tackling child poverty made by a range of public services, early years, education, health, housing and parenting.

Investment in the early years of children's lives

The differences between advantaged and disadvantaged children are apparent from a very early age. Evidence shows that at 22 months, children whose parents are in social classes I or II are already 14 percentage points higher up the educational development distribution than children whose parents are in social classes IV or V (Feinstein 1998). The evidence also suggests that early differences in children's development continue to widen when children start school unless there is a programme of positive interventions. In response to these findings, the Sure Start programme was established in 1998.

The aim of Sure Start is to promote the physical, intellectual, emotional and social development of babies and young children – particularly those who are disadvantaged – so that they can flourish at home and when they go to school. To help achieve this, Sure Start has a number of specific targets to achieve by 2005–06:

- an increase in the proportion of young children aged 0–5 with normal levels of personal, social and emotional development for their age;
- a reduction in the proportion of mothers who continue to smoke during pregnancy;
- an increase in the proportion of children having normal levels of communication, language and literacy at the end of the Foundation Stage and an increase in the proportion of young children with satisfactory speech and language development at age 2 years; and
- a reduction in the proportion of young children living in households where no one is working.

Sure Start offers a different and radical means of organising services to tackle the causes of poverty and social exclusion. It is at the forefront of modernising Government with departments working together. Local, community-led partnerships of parents-to-be, parents and children, work together to develop services and programmes specifically to meet the local needs identified. Sure Start is different because it:

- looks at reshaping whole packages of existing services for families and children to join up services on the ground;
- fills gaps to meet real local needs; and
- focuses on earlier intervention: prevention rather than cure.

By March 2004, more than 500 programmes across the country will be reaching up to 400,000 young children most in need.

Education

Education is crucial to building a prosperous and inclusive society. Children from poorer backgrounds in general have lower attainment than those who are better-off (Gregg and Machin 2000a; 2000b). The gap grows as the child grows older. Overall, for pupils with high attainment in primary school, the difference between the median outcomes of pupils in the poorer and better-off areas was as much as 12 GCSE points in 2000 (equivalent to two B grades). The Government has therefore set targets for raising standards and narrowing the educational attainment gap in order to break the cycle of disadvantage, and to enable more equal participation in the country's prosperity. These policy objectives have been backed up by an increase in education spending in England – by an average of 6 per cent above inflation per year in the three years to 2005–06 – to 5.6 per cent of GDP by 2005–06.

Post-16 Participation

The rate of participation of young people in learning after 16 is low by international standards. By age 18, only 53 per cent of young people in the UK are in education, Turkey and Mexico are the only OECD countries with a lower proportion of the population enrolled in full-time or part-time education at age 18. The Government piloted, in one third of Local Education Authorities, Education Maintenance Allowances (EMAs) in recognition of the financial barriers which prevent some young people continuing in education, to enable young people from poorer families to pursue education beyond the age of 16. Evidence from the pilots shows that educational participation has increased, on average, by 5 percentage points among those eligible for support. Young people from the poorest families have shown the strongest results, with participation among this group increasing by 7 percentage points.

The Government is introducing Education Maintenance Allowances (EMAs) nationally from September 2004. EMAs will provide support of up to £1,500 per year depending on household income. The Government is also expanding vocational pathways into skilled work. It has set up Connexions as a universal service, but giving priority to those most at risk of underachievement and disaffection, designed to increase the proportion of young people in education, employment, or training. The aim of such services is to give more young people the opportunity to train and to gain the skills to allow them to develop a career rather than just get a job.

Health inequalities

The 2002 Spending Review found that, despite reductions in mortality over the last 20 years, inequalities in health persist. There are significant differences in life expectancy between different social classes (for example life expectancy for men in social classes I and V is 78.5 and 71.1 years respectively). Figure 11.4 shows that whilst life expectancy increased across the 20th century, for men of working age the difference in average mortality rate between social classes I and V has increased

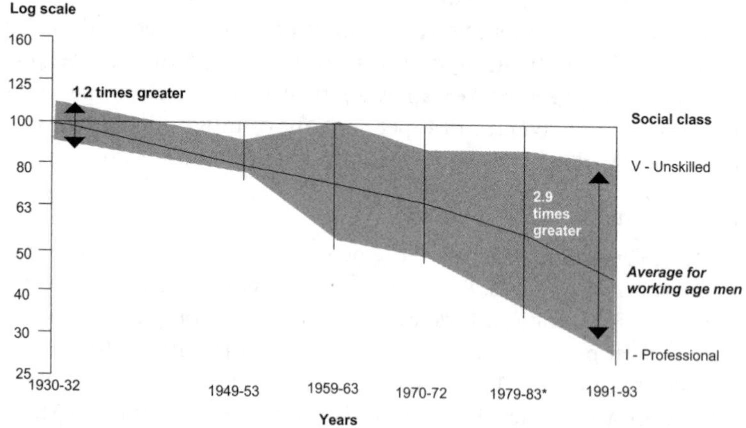

Notes: * 1979–83 excludes 1981; England and Wales; men of working age varies according to year, either aged from 15 or 20 to 64 or 65; comparisons based on social classes I and V only.

Source: ONS

Figure 11.4 The widening mortality gap between social classes

from 1.2 times greater in the early 1950s to 2.9 times greater in the early 1990s. In addition, the multiple problems of material disadvantage facing some communities have caused wide geographical variations in health. Liverpool had the lowest life expectancy in England 150 years ago and still had one of the lowest rates in 2002 (only Manchester had a worse rate). Moreover, there is strong correlation between health inequalities and deprivation that starts at birth and continues throughout life. Children born in poor families are more likely to be born prematurely, are at greater risk of infant mortality, and, as adults, have a greater likelihood of chronic disease and early death.

Based on this review, a cross-government strategy has been developed that establishes key interventions needed to break the cycle of health inequalities (poverty reduction, educational attainment and employment opportunities). It also puts in train the shorter-term action required to reduce high incidence of accidents, cancer, coronary heart disease and chronic illness among manual social classes and other vulnerable groups.

Housing

In the UK, the average investment in housing as a share of GDP has been 3.3 per cent (average 1985–98) compared with 6.7 per cent in Germany, 5.6 per cent in the Netherlands, 5 per cent in Italy, and 4.8 per cent in Ireland. This relatively low level of investment is reflected in both the supply and the condition of housing stock.

The rate of house building has fallen to around 160,000 annually, (illustrated in Figure 11.6) insufficient to replace old housing stock or meet new need. A significant feature within this has been the decline in the building of social housing by local authorities and housing associations. The Office of the Deputy Prime Minister therefore has a new Public Service Agreement (PSA) target to achieve a closer match between the numbers of households and the housing stock in all regions, through sustainable changes to the distribution, location and occupancy of housing (for details on PSAs, see Chapter 16). It aims to increase housing supply by improving the availability of land for housing development, achieving greater density in those developments, ensuring housing figures in Regional Planning Guidance are actually delivered, and by bringing forward plans for further significant future housing development in four growth areas around London and the South East.

The Government has also asked Kate Barker, formerly of the CBI and now a member of the Bank of England's Monetary Policy Committee, to conduct a review of issues affecting supply of housing in the UK and identify any further options for Government action. Her interim report

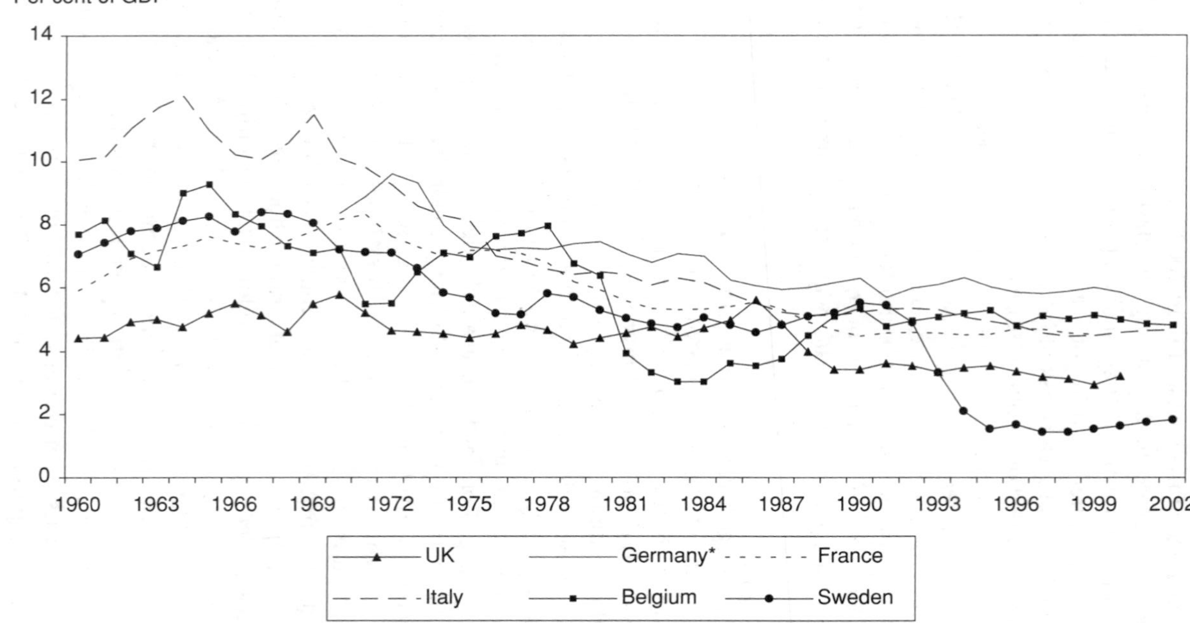

* *1970 to 1990 excludes former DDR*

Source: OECD, Deutsche Bank and HM Treasury calculations

Figure 11.5 Investment in housing as a percentage of GDP

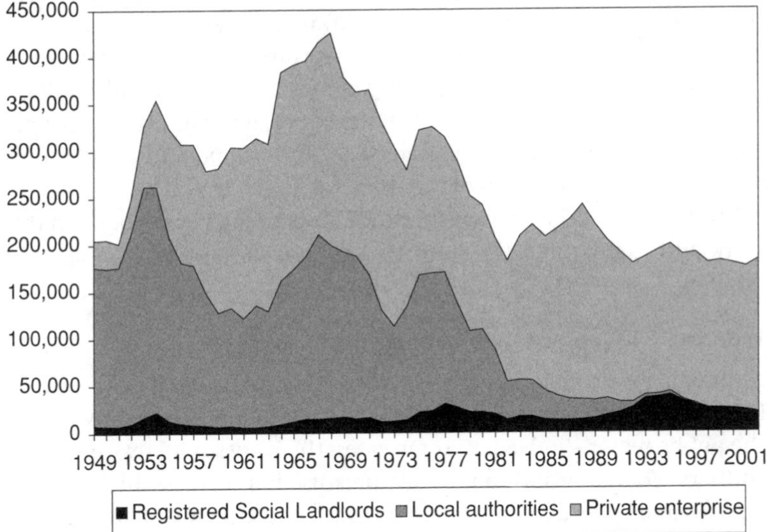

Note: Data may not be reliable for earlier years and definitions are inconsistent through series.

Source: OPDM.

Figure 11.6 Permanent dwellings completed in Great Britain, 1946–2001

was published in December 2003 and found that the underlying constraint was the supply of land, which is heavily influenced by the planning system (Barker 2003). She found that house builders' response to the volatility of the housing market and uncertainty of the planning system can further exacerbate supply and quantity problems. Her final report and recommendations will be published in spring 2004.

Parenting

The Government also recognised in the 2001 Pre-Budget Report that more needs to be done to support parents, so that parents can in turn provide better support for their children. The National Family and Parenting Institute (NFPI) in its 2001 mapping study of family support services found that there are geographical variations as well as gaps in provision of parenting support at a local level. A Parenting and Education Support Forum (PESF) survey indicated that there were particular needs among black and ethnic minority communities, lone parents, fathers and that there was relatively underdeveloped support for parents of teenage children. This is in addition to the support to help parents balance work and family life outlined earlier in this chapter.

Consequently, in addition to Sure Start, further resources have been made available to fund additional support for parents and families, including new resources to fund the roll-out of the Connexions personal adviser service and complementary services to support 13–19 year olds to stay in education and avoid truancy.

The Children at Risk review in the 2002 Spending Review built on this work and highlighted the need to improve support for parents and families.

Working with voluntary and community sectors

Although government may need to finance a particular type of service, it does not necessarily follow that the service should also be provided by the public sector – indeed, in some cases, there are sound reasons to the contrary. Voluntary and community organisations may be able to deliver services more effectively to certain groups because their structures enable them to operate in environments which the state and its agents have found difficult or impossible. These structures enable them to bring the specialist knowledge, the particular ways of involving people and the access to the wider community, often required to deliver high quality services. Mixed provision also provides a degree of contestability and innovation into service provision.

A long-term partnership with strong and independent voluntary and community sectors offers particular attractions. The aim is to create a framework so that where the voluntary and community sector is engaged in service delivery, it is able to do so effectively. Following from the Cross Cutting Review of the Role of the Voluntary and Community Sector in Service Delivery, carried out as part of the 2002 Spending Review, the Government is committed to improving funding relationships, building capacity and developing stronger partnership working with the sector.

Examples of Government working with the voluntary and community sectors include:

- a new Children's Fund, worth £100 million in 2001/02, £150 million in 2002/03 and £200 million in 2003/04, with a strong emphasis on voluntary sector delivery, to ensure that vulnerable young people make the transition safely to adulthood; and

- a Parenting Fund, worth an additional £25 million over three years, made available in the 2002 Spending Review to sponsor services designed and delivered in partnership with the voluntary and community sectors. It will offer early help to parents experiencing difficulties within the family. This approach reflects the fact that the voluntary and community sectors are often better equipped to intervene in complex situations at a family level, where formal state intervention may not be appropriate.

Progress to date and impact of policy measures

The most recent data shows that between 1998/99 and 2001/02 the number of children in low-income households fell by 0.4 million after housing costs (AHC) and by 0.5 million before housing costs (BHC), from 4.2 million and 3.1 million respectively (DWP 2003b). The Government has therefore succeeded in arresting and reversing the long-term trend of rising child poverty and is making steady progress towards the 2004/05 Public Service Agreement target. These figures do not reflect the effect of increased support from the introduction of the new tax credits in April 2003.

The reduction in the proportion of children in low-income households is particularly notable as it has been achieved during a period of high growth in household incomes. Between 1998/99 and 2001/02 average annual real median income growth was nearly 4 per cent BHC and nearly 5 per cent AHC. This income growth reflects the wider success of a range of Government economic policies, but it means that progress against a purely relative measure of poverty is particularly difficult.

This is underlined by the substantial progress made against an absolute low-income measure. Between 1998/99 and 2001/02, the number of children in absolute low-income households fell from 2.8 million to 1.6 million BHC, and from 4.0 million to 2.5 million AHC. Recent analysis has also shown that levels of severe material deprivation amongst families with children fell significantly between 1999 and 2001 (Vegeris and Perry 2003).

By 2004/05, financial support for children through tax credits, Child Benefit and other benefits will have increased by £10.4 billion in real terms from its 1997 level, a rise of 72 per cent. As a result of this investment, the Government is on track to meet or exceed its PSA target to reduce by a quarter the number of children living in low-income households by 2004/05 on a BHC basis, comparable to the European

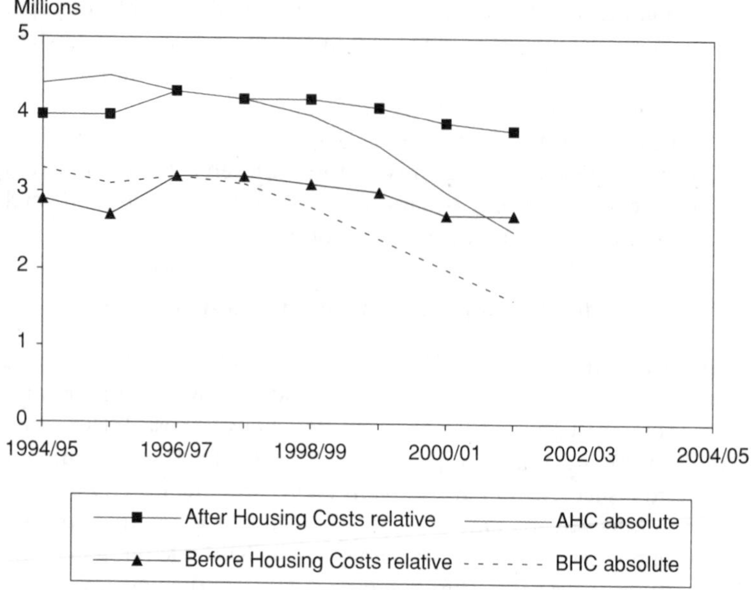

Note: Children in low-income are defined as those in households with less than 60% of median income (equivalised), the contemporary median in the case of relative low-income, and the 1996/97 median held constant in real terms in the case of absolute low-income.

Source: Data from DWP (2003b)

Figure 11.7 Children in low income households

child poverty indicator. The target is more challenging on an AHC basis. The nature of the target means that there are uncertainties either way. Analysis by the Institute of Fiscal Studies (2003) suggests the Government will make substantial progress on an AHC basis.

Eradicating child poverty is, however, a long-term agenda. The welfare system and public service provision needs to be kept under review to ensure progress is continued. A Child Poverty Review, led by the Treasury, reporting in 2004, will consider the welfare reform and public services changes needed to advance faster towards the goals of halving and eradicating child poverty.

Conclusion

Poverty remains a significant challenge within the UK. It has its greatest effect on families with children. Specific changes that have played a key role in reversing the long-term trend of a growing proportion of children living in low-income households have included:

- the integration of tax and benefit systems to reduce stigma and provide a more streamlined system;
- substantial increases in financial support for families with children;
- policies to reduce poverty and unemployment traps;
- active labour market policies to help people find work;
- support to help parents deal with the challenges of balancing work and family life;
- greater resources for parenting support; and
- new resources and radical reforms to create strong, dependable public services.

The approach is based on the premise that work for those who can is the best long-term route out of poverty. The Child Tax Credit and Working Tax Credit are a significant componentof an overall strategy designed to tailor support to families' specific circumstances, ease the transition from welfare to work and help to ensure that work pays.

It is also important to complement financial support with a wider strategy to improve childhood experiences and to break the long-term cycle of poverty and deprivation. Hence, significant reforms to public services, particularly in relation to early years and education, have already been implemented. The challenges parents face in bringing up children in today's society also need to be taken into account. A range of policies has been put in place to support parents generally, and specifically in relation to combining work and family life. The Child Poverty Review will consider what more needs to be done.

12
Promoting Saving Throughout Life

This chapter sets out the Government's strategy to extend the opportunity to save and own assets and explains why it is a necessary and complementary strand of the overall welfare strategy.

Introduction

At the macroeconomic level, savings – by the household sector, government and the corporate sector – provide the necessary funds to finance investment.[1] At the microeconomic level, savings provide a number of benefits to individuals. Savings and assets provide people with security in times of adversity, long-term independence and opportunity, and comfort in retirement. They provide the capital for people to invest in their future and help determine living standards in old age. In addition to the direct benefits of having a stock of savings, there are also indirect behavioural benefits to be gained through promoting saving. The *process* of saving can have a positive impact on individuals' self-reliance and attitude towards personal development, benefiting not only those concerned but also society as a whole.

This chapter begins by setting out the position on holdings of savings and assets across the population, then looks at the market failures which are acting as barriers to saving, before in the final section explaining the Government's strategy for encouraging saving. The next chapter looks at pensions in particular.

Holdings of savings and assets in the United Kingdom

Aggregate household saving

The aggregate household saving ratio[2] is, broadly, the ratio of the flow of household saving to household income. As Figure 12.1 shows, it has been at a relatively low level since the mid -1990s. At first sight, this suggests that, in aggregate, households may not be saving enough.

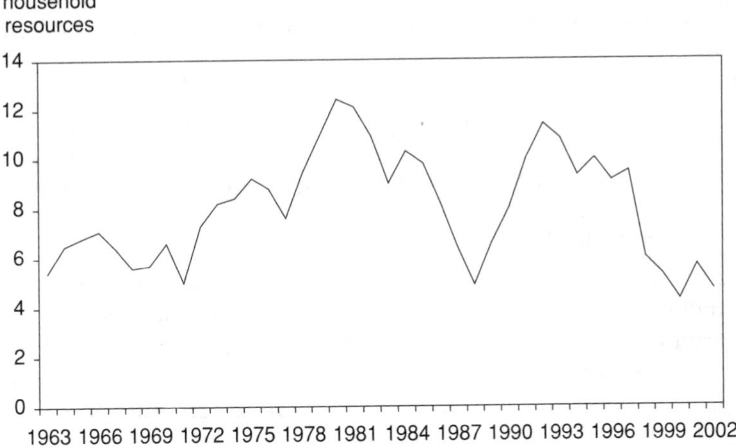

Source: ONS

Figure 12.1 Households' saving ratio, 1963–2002

However, such an interpretation should be treated with caution. The saving ratio tends to move counter-cyclically. A high saving ratio can be associated with economic weakness – households retrenching in the face of uncertainty over employment prospects or inflation. A low saving ratio may reflect greater economic stability and consumer confidence, reducing the need for households to save for precautionary purposes. The fall in the saving ratio in recent years reflects strong consumer confidence, a buoyant labour market and high levels of wealth resulting from increasing house prices. Total net household wealth rose by over 50 per cent between 1997 and 2002.

A focus on the aggregate household saving ratio also fails to take account of the complex and dynamic nature of individuals' saving behaviour. Patterns of consumption and saving will vary over an individual's lifetime, based on changing commitments, circumstances and expectations. Individuals may be saving in a variety of assets, including housing and businesses, and they may also be planning to share assets with a partner. In order to judge whether the level of saving among the UK population might be sufficient, it is therefore necessary to look at disaggregated data such as household surveys.

But, even then, the level of savings that constitutes enough is subjective. When considering the adequacy of saving for retirement for example, individuals' preferences concerning incomes in retirement will vary and many people find that their living costs are lower in later life, as they no longer face the costs of paying off a mortgage or raising children.

Disaggregated data on saving and assets

The Institute for Fiscal Studies (IFS) has carried out an analysis of the British Household Panel Survey (BHPS) to help understand the distribution of assets in the UK in 2000 (Banks, Smith, and Wakefield 2002).

Liquid financial wealth

The IFS analysis showed that holdings of liquid financial wealth (i.e. excluding pensions and housing) tends to increase with income, age and education. The data in Figure 12.2 show that the distribution of net financial wealth (savings plus investments less debt) among the population is very unequal. While mean net financial wealth is £12,363 per household, this is heavily influenced by relatively small numbers of households with very large holdings; median net financial wealth is only £600 per household.

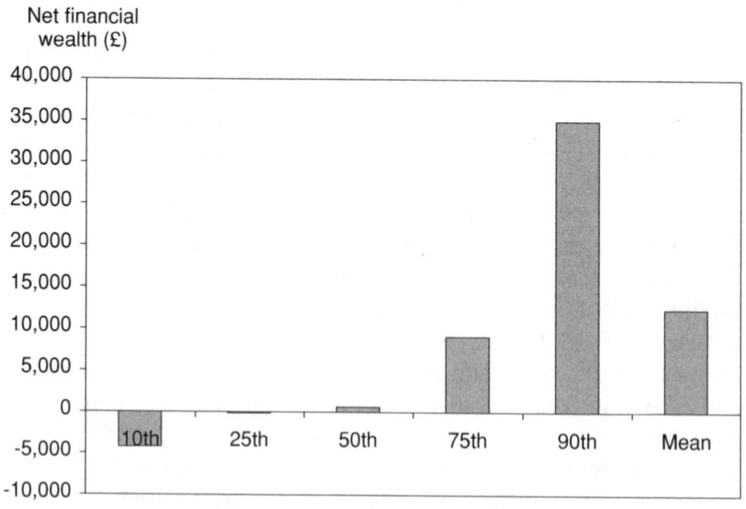

Source: IFS and British Household Panel Survey

Figure 12.2 Distribution of net financial wealth in 2000

Figure 12.2 suggests that there are likely to be many households, particularly among those on low incomes, who are under-saving for a 'rainy day' and that debt might be a problem. However, evidence of low levels of saving is not always a cause for concern . For example, it is common for those who are young to have low or negative levels of saving as they are building up commitments. In addition, the limitations of snapshot data need to be borne in mind – few people fail to save at all at some point in their life; looking at liquid financial assets in the British Household Panel Survey, Kempson and Mckay (2003) found that only 18 per cent of people had not saved at all between 1991 and 2000.

Pensions

On pension saving, the IFS (Banks et al. 2002) has analysed individuals in employment in the 2000 wave of the BHPS, and has compared the characteristics over the period 1992–2000 of those who did, and those who did not, have a private pension in 2000 (see Table 12.1). The key findings are as follows:

1. Many moderate earners (income between £10,000 and £22,000) not saving in a pension in 2000 have saved in a pension in earlier years: 56 per cent of moderate earners who did not save in 2000 had saved at some point in the period 1992–99 and they had saved for an average of four years.
2. Under-saving may therefore be more closely related to lack of persistence in saving rather than a reluctance to save at all. Those moderate earners who had pensions in 2000 had saved for an average of six of the nine years.
3. Those not saving in pensions often had interrupted work records: 48 per cent of moderate earners without a pension in 2000 had experienced a period of unemployment during 1992–99. This is twice the average of those with a pension in 2000. People with interrupted work records were more likely to have faced lower earnings and been unable to afford to save.
4. 49 per cent of low earners and 32 per cent of moderate earners not paying into a pension in 2000 had a partner who was. These couples may be planning to pool their resources in retirement.
5. People under 35 were less likely to be saving in a pension. Among moderate earners, 30 per cent of 25–34 year olds did not have a pension in 2000, whereas among 35–49 year-olds the figure was only 18 per cent.

Table 12.1 Individual characteristics from 1992 to 2000, by earnings level and pension choice in 2000, individuals aged 25 to 59 only.

Pension status in 2000	No private pension in 2000				Has private pension in 2000				
Earnings level in 2000	'Low'	'Mid'	'High'	All	'Low'	'Mid'	'High'	All	*All*
% in each earnings/pension category	14.1	10.4	2.1	26.6	10.8	36.3	26.4	73.4	*100.0*
% never a member of a private pension	68.3	43.6	26.0	55.3	0.0	0.0	0.0	0.0	*14.7*
% occasionally member of a private pension	31.7	56.4	74.0	44.7	73.7	45.6	24.8	42.2	*42.9*
% always a member of a private pension	0.0	0.0	0.0	0.0	26.3	54.4	75.2	57.8	*42.4*
Average periods with private pension	1.0	2.3	3.2	1.7	6.1	7.4	8.2	7.5	*6.0*
% experiencing a period out of employment	64.2	48.4	38.0	56.0	38.6	23.8	12.8	22.0	*31.0*
Average periods in employment	6.7	7.5	8.1	7.1	8.1	8.5	8.7	8.5	*8.1*
Median earnings when employed	£5,236	£13,017	£21,635	£9,018	£7,151	£15,341	£26,978	£17,876	*£15,378*
% occasional 'low' earner	71.6	54.8	20.0	61.0	65.6	31.7	5.2	27.2	*36.1*
% occasional 'high' earner	4.1	18.4	78.0	15.5	3.5	28.6	50.8	32.9	*28.3*
% who are owner occupiers (outright)[a] in 2000	13.0	12.0	12.0	12.1	19.3	11.6	10.3	12.2	12.2
% who are owner occupiers (mortgage)[a] in 2000	52.7	47.2	76.0	52.4	64.1	70.0	81.4	73.2	67.7
Median financial wealth[b] in 1995	£300	£300	£1,140	£400	£2,000	£1,400	£4,010	£2,028	£1,500
% with <£1,500 in financial assets[b] in 1995	65.4	64.8	52.0	64.1	46.3	50.4	33.4	43.7	49.1
Sample size	*338*	*250*	*50*	*638*	*259*	*871*	*634*	*1,764*	*2,402*

Notes: Includes individuals in paid employment or self-employment in wave 10 who were aged 25 to 59 (inclusive) and present in waves 2 to 10 of the BHPS. Care should be taken with column of 'high' earners who do not have a private pension since only 50 observations fall into this category.

[a] 'Owner occupier' applies to the individual and, where, relevant his or her partner. Earnings over time have been deflated using an average earnings index.

[b] 'Financial wealth' refers to savings and investments and excludes pension wealth and any debts held by the individual or the individual and their partner.

Source: IFS' calculations using data from the British Household Panel Survey, 1992 to 2000.

Housing

The IFS also looked at the extent to which people hold wealth through their homes. Housing wealth might provide a limited source of income in retirement, either through trading down (moving to a smaller property) or through equity release (which enables people to gain access to the equity in their home without moving). Table 12.2 shows that among moderate earners (annual earnings between £10,000 and £22,000) without pensions, 12 per cent already own their own homes outright and a further 47 per cent are owner-occupiers with mortgages. Home ownership increases with people's age; only 21 per cent of people aged 35–59 do not own their own home (either outright or via a mortgage), compared with 60 per cent of those aged under 35. The vast majority of people aged 35–59 (around 90 per cent) have a pension or some housing wealth although one cannot easily measure the extent to which housing may provide a partial substitute for pension wealth, as it depends on individual preferences.

Table 12.2 Correlation between housing wealth and pension status in 2000

		Not an owner occupier	House value <£100,000	House value >£100,000	All
Age<35	No private pension	35.4	6.7	1.4	43.5
	Has private pension	24.5	22.4	9.6	56.5
	All	*59.9*	*29.1*	*11.0*	*100.0*
Age 35–59	No private pension	9.4	7.4	3.8	20.6
	Has private pension	11.3	37.3	30.7	79.4
	All	*20.7*	*44.8*	*34.6*	*100.0*
All	No private pension	20.9	7.1	2.7	30.8
	Has private pension	17.2	30.7	21.3	69.2
	All	*38.1*	*37.8*	*24.1*	*100.0*

Source: IFS and British Household Panel Survey

Assessing the scale of under-saving

The data presented above highlight the fact that assessing levels of under-saving is complex. Account needs to be taken of alternative ways of saving and the various choices that people may make at different stages of their lives. The December 2002 Green Paper on Pensions (Department of Work and Pensions, HM Treasury, and Inland Revenue 2002) estimated that there are likely to be around 3 million people who, over time, are seriously under-providing for their retirement and that a further group of between 5 million and 10 million people may also want to consider saving more or working longer. The Green Paper also made clear that it is essential to develop good-quality data about people's saving over time, their overall assets, and the savings and assets of partners. The Office for National Statistics recently reviewed pension contribution statistics. This review highlighted a number of new data sources that are currently planned or under way, including a comprehensive survey of assets and wealth in the UK.

The barriers to saving

Empirical studies have identified individual and household characteristics such as age, income, employment status and whether there is a partner who is saving, as important explanatory variables for observed saving patterns. Qualitative surveys also point to psychological factors, such as culture and people's subjective assessment of their financial situation, as important influences on their propensity to save. These surveys also highlight a number of market failures that prevent people from making optimal saving decisions. These include:

- *Asymmetry of information.* Some people may simply lack awareness of the future benefits of saving. In other cases, people may not be aware of how much their savings are worth (particularly for pensions).
- *Barriers to entry.* Many individuals are deterred from entering the market, because they may lack even basic financial literacy skills and familiarity with financial institutions, and their trust in financial services providers may also be low.
- *Lack of transparency.* People may find it difficult to navigate their way around products offered by the financial services industry because of the complexity of products, use of technical jargon, lack of price-performance transparency and lack of access to affordable advice.
- *Lack of competition* in the financial services industry and inability of consumers to exert competitive pressure on providers (due to asymmetry of information) can lead to products that are inflexible and have high charges.
- *Distortions arising from the tax and benefits system.* The complexity of tax rules can confuse individuals and imposes burdens on providers. The treatment of capital in the benefits system can also discourage saving.

These problems disproportionately affect lower-income groups, who tend to be the least financially literate and least able to afford advice. Those who do not save are more likely to go into cycles of debt, which can be a particular problem for those on low incomes who often cannot access cheap sources of credit. Addressing market failure in provision of savings products is the central theme of the strategy to encourage personal saving.

Policy on savings

The Government's strategy is focused on:

- improving the *environment* for saving, through macroeconomic stability and an efficient and well-regulated market in financial services;
- *empowering individuals* with financial information, improved access to advice, and savings products that are simple and easy to understand;
- creating adequate *incentives* for saving by ensuring that the tax and benefit system does not unfairly penalise savers, and by assisting those on low incomes; and
- developing *saving products suitable for each stage in a person's life cycle*. As the scale of saving increases, proceeds from one product may be rolled into the next, helping people to progress up the savings ladder.

The following sections describe the measures put in place and the progress made in implementing these policies.

Improving the environment for saving

Maintaining macroeconomic stability

To make optimal savings decisions, people need a stable macroeconomic environment conducive to long-term planning. Details of the measures put in place to achieve this and the thinking which underpins them, are set out in *Reforming Britain's Economic and Financial Policy: Towards Greater Economic Stability* (Balls and O'Donnell 2002).

Ensuring a well-regulated market in financial services

To build up and maintain investor confidence, the financial services market, including the savings market, needs to be effectively regulated. The Financial Services and Markets Act 2000 replaced ten different regulators with a single regulator, the Financial Services Authority (FSA), covering the whole financial services market. The Government also introduced a single financial services ombudsman scheme to resolve consumers' complaints, a single compensation scheme and a single tribunal. The FSA has clear statutory objectives to: raise market confidence; raise consumer awareness; protect consumers; and prevent financial crime.

Establishing an efficient market: the Sandler Review

In June 2001, the Government asked Ron Sandler, a former CEO of Lloyd's of London, to conduct a review of the medium- and long-term savings industry. The review, *Medium and Long-Term Retail Savings in the UK* (Sandler 2002), was published in July 2002. It found three overriding problems:

- complexity and opacity caused by the huge range of products and product types, charging structures, complicated tax treatments, wide use of technical jargon and lack of price-performance transparency;
- problems of access such that the needs of those on low to medium income levels are not catered for sufficiently; and
- consumers who are weak in market power and unable to influence the market effectively.

The review made a range of recommendations, which are discussed in broad terms below.

The review concluded that the complexity and opacity of the market, and concerns about ensuring compliance with sales regulation, means that face-to-face selling could be costly and time-consuming. As a result, low- to middle-income consumers were finding themselves priced out of the market for retail savings, with providers and retailers reluctant to sell to them because they did not generate sufficient remuneration. The review therefore recommended the development of a suite of safer and easier to understand 'stakeholder' investment products. These would address the problems that had been identified by:

- removing unnecessary complexity in the choice between competing products;
- controlling the degree of risk exposure in the product; and
- controlling the charges and terms surrounding entry and exit.

The advantage of such products is that, by simplifying choices and controlling risk, the regulatory requirements surrounding the sales process could also be considerably simplified. In addition, by shifting the focus of regulation from the sales process to the product, the cost of selling products should be reduced. This would improve access for those on low to middle incomes without sacrificing consumer protection. The Treasury and the Department of Work and Pensions are developing the design of stakeholder products, and have commissioned independent research into how best to cap product charges. The FSA is also considering the sales regime for future stakeholder products.

Empowering individuals

The Sandler Review highlighted a lack of competition in the financial services industry, despite the presence of a number of different financial providers, caused by an asymmetry of information between consumers and providers.

Part of the solution to this problem lies in empowering individuals. By providing consumers with greater financial information, improved access to honest and straightforward advice, and simpler, easier to understand, savings products, they will be able to exert greater competitive pressure in the market and make better choices for themselves.

Clearer financial information and education

Decisions about personal finances and saving – particularly those about long-term saving for retirement – are inevitably complex. For some people, this may be enough to discourage them from saving altogether. For others, it may mean they are not making the right saving choices. Studies conducted in recent years have found that consumers have little understanding of financial services (including retail savings). This lack of comprehension is not confined to the less well-off.

For example, research for the Financial Services Consumer Panel in 2000[3] found that

- 38 per cent of people definitely agreed that they feel confident about making their own financial decisions and 33 per cent that they have a clear idea of the sorts of financial products they need;
- 50 per cent of people agreed or tended to agree that they found it difficult to understand financial leaflets and materials that they received;
- Only one-third of people regularly reviewed their finances;

- 27 per cent of people did not think investment products were straightforward; and
- 53 per cent of people thought understanding charges of investment products was difficult.

The benefits of information and education are twofold:

- they can help achieve a more competitive financial services industry since better-informed consumers are more likely to shop around; and
- they can encourage people to be more confident, understand their position and options, and, where appropriate, save.

Recognising this, the FSA has been given a statutory responsibility for financial education as part of its regulatory role – the first time a financial regulator has had such as responsibility. The FSA provides people with authoritative, independent general information and advice. For example, it has been developing stakeholder pension decision trees (described below) to guide people through decisions about saving for retirement.

Supporting the work of the FSA, government also has a role to play in promoting financial education. Financial education has been introduced into the National Curriculum from September 2000, to raise financial literacy among future savers. The Child Trust Fund (described below) will build on this foundation. Providing tailored information based on an individual's circumstances is also potentially powerful. As noted in the next chapter, this approach will be developed by increasing the number of people receiving forecasts of their own expected pension income.

Improved access to advice

Current regulations allow two mutually exclusive approaches to investment advice and sales. Tied advisers can advise on, and sell, only a single firm's products. Independent Financial Advisers have to be able to advise on, and sell, any firm's products. Both tend to be paid through sales commissions. This structure is known as 'polarisation'.

Polarisation has been widely criticised, for example by the Director General for Fair Trading, as anti-competitive; it has prevented, for instance, high street firms from being able to offer choice alongside their own products or services. Consequently, independent advice has tended to be the preserve of the better-off. Commission-driven selling has focused competition on distribution rather than on benefiting the savers ultimately buying the product. There is also some, albeit limited, FSA research evidence of bias towards the sale of high-commission products.[4]

Following wide-ranging public consultations, the FSA has decided to abolish the restrictions. The likely practical effect would be to introduce a new intermediary model. This model will allow advisers to advise on a limited range of products without having to advise on every firm's products, and should increase practical choice for the majority of consumers who currently use tied agents. The FSA also plans to reform the way commissions are disclosed, in order to make it clearer how much consumers are paying for the services of an adviser.

The FSA has also developed tools to help those who do not have access to advice to make informed choices. Decision trees (flow charts) for stakeholder pensions help consumers to decide if a stakeholder is right for them. Comparative tables allow consumers to compare products easily. The FSA is also working on an interactive generic financial advice tool to offer a 'financial health check'. In principle, such a system could be made available both over the Internet and through voluntary groups and employers.

Simpler and more accessible products

A number of simple and easy to understand products, such as Individual Savings Accounts (ISAs) and stakeholder pensions have been introduced. ISAs are the Government's primary vehicle for tax-advantaged saving outside pensions. The lack of deterrent lock-ins and ease of access to funds make ISAs more flexible than their predecessors, Tax Exempt Special Savings Accounts (TESSAs) and Personal Equity Plans (PEPs). As such, they have attracted significantly more funds, with saving spread more widely across the population. Since their launch in 1999, over 15 million investors – around one third of adults – have contributed over £120 billion (as at 5 July 2003) to ISAs. Charges, access and terms (CAT) standards introduced the idea of a good-value benchmark product, with a simple and easy-to-understand charging structure. Around half the ISA market is for CAT-standard products.

Stakeholder pensions, discussed in Chapter 13, are another example of simpler, more accessible products. The Sandler Review's proposals for simple, low-cost, and risk-controlled 'stakeholder' products (discussed above) build on the ideas behind the Stakeholder Pension. The Saving Gateway and Child Trust Fund (discussed below), will further add to the family of simple and accessible savings products.

Improving accessibility to savings products is part of a wider Government agenda to reduce financial exclusion. For example, by not having a bank account, individuals miss out on the convenience and potential cost savings associated with direct debits and, in the longer term, they may not gain access to opportunities for saving. All the high street banks now offer basic bank accounts that are free to open and run. Universal Banking Services, which was introduced in April 2003, ensures that access to basic bank accounts will be available over Post Office counters.

Creating adequate incentives for saving and assisting those on low incomes

Reducing tax-generated distortions

The Sandler Review recommended removing distortions and reducing complexity in the savings industry caused by taxation. The aim is to minimise tax-generated distortions and create a more level tax playing field. The new pension regime discussed in Chapter 13 is a good example of how the tax regime is being simplified.

The Government is currently considering the Sandler Review's proposals to simplify the tax regime relating to life-assurance policies. This will be done within a wider framework that takes account of ongoing regulatory change and other developments such as corporation tax reform.

Treatment of capital in the tax and benefit system

Reforming the treatment of capital in the tax and benefit systems is a further element of the approach to generating the right incentives to work and save.

The present system of support allows people to hold some liquid financial savings without their entitlement to benefits being affected. The Government will keep under review the treatment of capital in income-related working age benefits so that it strikes a sensible balance between providing state support and not unfairly penalising those who have acted responsibly by saving. The New Tax Credits (discussed in Chapters 9 and 10) have no capital limits as such: instead, they take into account the taxable income derived from savings. In addition, as explained in Chapter 13, the capital rules for pensioners have been reformed to remove the saving disincentives present in the previous system.

Targeted incentives for saving

By saving in a pension, individuals are committed to using the funds for a secure income in retirement in the form of an annuity. This long-term commitment is recognised by the more generous tax treatment that pensions enjoy in comparison to other forms of saving.

The Saving Gateway and Child Trust Fund

The Saving Gateway is an account being piloted and targeted at individuals from low-income groups. It aims to increase incentives to save through a publicly-funded match of all money saved, up to a limit. Consumer research suggests that matched contribution schemes may be more effective than tax relief in encouraging saving by low and moderate earners. Tailored financial information and education are provided alongside Saving Gateway accounts to help individuals make informed saving choices (see Box 12.1).

Box 12.1 The Saving Gateway: piloting a new approach

The Government launched a number of Saving Gateway pilot projects in August 2002. The pilots are being run in conjunction with the Community Finance and Learning Initiative, led by the Department for Education and Skills. The Halifax plc is providing branch, staff and account management services in the pilot areas.

Operating in Cambridgeshire, Cumbria, Gorton (Manchester), Hull and Tower Hamlets (London), the pilots involve around 1,500 participants in total. The Saving Gateway account will last for 18 months and each pound saved by participants will be matched with a pound from government. Participants will be able to save a maximum £25 per month up to an overall account limit of £375 of savings, £750 with matching funds.

The pilots have been designed to provide a regular stream of information and data, and will be evaluated to assess their effect on saving behaviour. The final evaluation report is expected in February 2005. Further development of the Saving Gateway, including the appropriate level of the match rate and the criteria to be used to determine eligibility, will follow in light of evaluation evidence.

By way of encouraging future generations to save, Budget 2003 introduced the Child Trust Fund (CTF), with entitlement backdated to include children born from September 2002 (to align payments with the school year). The CTF will provide an endowment for every child at birth, with those from the poorest families receiving the largest amounts. The CTF is intended to reinforce financial education delivered through the national curriculum, promote positive attitudes towards saving and progress towards a position where all young people start their adult lives with access to a stock of financial assets.

Following consultation, the key features of the CTF are:

- an initial Government endowment of £250. This will rise to £500 for children from low-income families – around one-third of all children;
- additional contributions can be made by parents, other family members or friends up to an annual limit of £1,200;
- access to assets in the fund, including any additional contributions, will be permissible only upon account maturity at the age of 18. There will be no restriction on the use of assets at maturity; and
- provision of CTF accounts, expected to be available by 2005, will be by open market competition – any authorised provider will be able to enter the market, subject to meeting the conditions of the CTF.

Developing suitable savings products for each stage in life

Another key strand of the Government's strategy has involved developing and providing a series of saving products suitable for each stage in a person's life cycle. As the scale of saving increases, proceeds from one product may then be rolled into the next, helping people to progress up the savings ladder.

The Child Trust Fund, the Saving Gateway, and then ISAs and/or stakeholder pensions (discussed in Chapter 13) could all form part of a life stage sequence for a wide range of citizens.

Conclusion

Savings and assets play an important role in providing individuals with security, independence and opportunity, and comfort in retirement. However, market failures in the financial products markets are likely to have militated against this and some individuals and households may make poor saving decisions. The strategy for saving has been designed to address these market failures, particularly for those which affect people on low incomes. The strategy is designed to empower individuals, provide adequate incentives and help provide products that meet individuals' saving needs throughout the life cycle. The next chapter loos at pensions in particular.

13
Security and Independence in Retirement

This chapter describes the measures taken over the past six years both to provide security for today's pensioners, and to enable and encourage those of working age – tomorrow's pensioners – to plan and provide for their own retirement.

Introduction

The Government's priority on taking office was to tackle pensioner poverty by increasing the minimum level below which no pensioner's income need fall, and ensuring that the poorest pensioners shared in the rising prosperity of the nation. The Government's reforms are based on the principle of 'progressive universalism' – providing help for all pensioners, but ensuring that more support goes to those who need it most. On this basis reforms to the State System have improved significantly the incomes of the poorest, and they have also strengthened the foundation provided to all pensioners. Pensioners across the income distribution have gained since 1997. In addition to this, and because of the introduction of Pension Credit in October 2003, most pensioners on low and modest incomes will also be rewarded for the savings they made during their working lives. The major reforms to the State System since 1997 are set out in the first half of this chapter.

Along with most other developed countries, the UK faces a number of challenges posed by an ageing population, but is significantly better placed than most to address these. Unlike many other countries the UK's

State Pension system has no problem of fiscal sustainability in the long-term. As people look forward to longer and healthier lives, it is all the more important that they plan their work and saving patterns so that they can attain their desired standard of living in retirement. The Government promoted savings for future pensioners across the income distribution. Working longer is as important an option as saving in terms of building up retirement income. The Government is acting, in conjunction with employers and the financial services industry, to enable individuals and households to make informed choices about their retirement. These choices relate to the how and when they save, and how long they work for. This is the essence of the Government's 'voluntarist' approach, as set out in the Green Paper *Simplicity, security and choice: working and saving for retirement* (DWP, HM Treasury, Inland Revenue 2002). The Government also announced the establishment of a Pensions Commission to monitor and keep under review how effectively this system is working.

Government reforms to the regulatory environment will ensure that suitable savings products are available to all, including those without access to an employer-provided pension. The Government's proposals for simplification of the tax treatment of pensions and of occupational pension regulations should make it easier for employers to run good pensions for their employees, and as a consequence make it easier for these employees to save for retirement. In order to plan in confidence for their retirement individuals need adequate protection. For this reason the Government is introducing a Pension Protection Fund for members of defined-benefit occupational pension schemes.

The second part of this chapter concludes with a summary of reforms that aim to make this a genuine choice for older workers.

Pensioner incomes in 1997

The UK pension system has historically been based on a partnership between government, individuals, employers and the financial services industry, with the government providing a foundation of support for retirement. Until 1997 the principal elements of this were the basic State Pension, the additional State Pension (at that time known as the State Earnings Related Pension Scheme or SERPS), and Income Support for the very poorest. Any income in addition to this resulted from private provision.

By 1997 this system was failing to meet the needs of a large proportion of pensioners and, if uncorrected, the situation was expected to worsen.

While average pensioner incomes had risen over the previous decades, primarily due to the maturing of SERPS and the growth of occupational pensions, improvements in incomes had not been evenly distributed. Between 1979 and 1996/97 the real median incomes of the richest fifth of pensioner couples had risen by 80 per cent. In contrast, the poorest fifth of pensioner couples had seen an increase of just 34 per cent. The story was similar for single pensioners.

These poorer pensioners, many of them older and with gaps in their work histories, had missed out on the growth of occupational pensions and had not benefited from SERPS. The very poorest were entitled to only £68.80 a week (for single pensioners) in Income Support, equivalent to about £79 a week in 2003/04 prices. In the absence of regular increases in benefits linking Income Support to the rise in average earnings, the incomes of the poorest pensioners were falling behind.

Creating fairness and security for pensioners

The immediate priority for the Government in 1997 was therefore to help those pensioners in greatest need and enable them to share in the rising national prosperity. It was for this reason that the Government introduced the Minimum Income Guarantee (MIG). Compared to alternative policy of linking the basic State Pension to earnings, the Government's approach has delivered far more to the poorest pensioners. By reforming SERPS the Government also acted to ensure that those unable to save, for instance those on low incomes and those who had unpaid caring responsibilities, were able to build up decent pension incomes though the National Insurance system. However, following the principle of 'progressive universalism' it is not just the poorest of today's and tomorrow's pensioners who have gained from reforms since 1997. Above-inflation increases in the basic State Pension and the introduction of measures such as the winter fuel payments help pensioners across the income distribution. As a consequence, nearly all pensioners have gained from the policies of this Government.

Policy measures

Minimum Income Guarantee

The Government has introduced a range of targeted policy measures to address the concerns discussed above. Income Support for pensioners was reformed, in April 1999, with the introduction of the Minimum Income Guarantee.

The MIG provided a substantially higher rate of income-related support for individuals aged 60 and over. After its first year, it has been raised in line with average earnings or more to ensure recipients' relative standards of living did not deteriorate. In April 2001 the three age-related MIG rates were aligned at the highest rate for singles and couples. The Government is committed to increasing the MIG – replaced from October 2003 by the Pension Credit guarantee – in line with average earnings, for the remainder of the current Parliament. In 2003/04, the rate is £102.10 a week for single pensioners and £155.80 for couples – real increases of over a third since 1997 for the poorest pensioners.

The State Second Pension

The State Earnings-Related Pension Scheme (SERPS) was first introduced in 1978. SERPS entitlement, like the basic State Pension, is based on National Insurance contributions. As SERPS entitlement was linked to actual earnings, those on low incomes might not accrue rights to an adequate pension. In addition, those without earnings for a period of time, including individuals becoming ill after a period of work and those with caring responsibilities, were excluded from accruing rights. Such a position was inequitable.

To address this problem, the 1998 Green Paper announced a reform of SERPS. From April 2002, the State Second Pension increases the pension rights of low and moderate earners and brings in groups of non-workers for the first time. The accrual structure of the State Second Pension is compared with that of SERPS in Figure 13.1. Under the State Second Pension, around 5 million low earners (earning between £4,004 and £11,200 in 2003/04) will be treated as if they had earned £11,200 and will build up a pension worth at least twice what SERPS would have provided. Around 2.5 million people with substantial caring responsibilities – including those caring for children below school age – and an additional 2.5 million people who become ill after a period of work will, for the first time, build up the same substantial rights as low earners. Altogether, around 20 million people have benefited from the introduction of the State Second Pension.

The basic State Pension

In addition to targeting support at those who need it most, the Government is also committed to providing a foundation of support to all pensioners throughout their retirement. The basic State Pension is usually increased each April in line with the Retail Prices Index (RPI) for the preceding September. However, due to greater than inflation

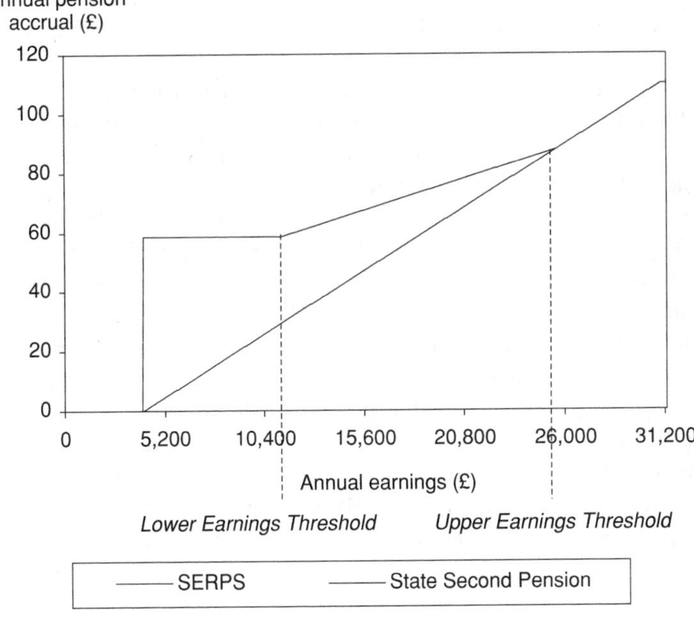

Source: DWP

Figure 13.1 State Second Pension accrual rates, compared to SERPS

increases in each of the last three years, prior to the introduction of the Pension Credit, the basic State Pension has grown by 7 per cent in real terms since 1997, to stand at £77.45 a week for single pensioners in 2003/04. For the rest of this Parliament, the Government has announced that the basic State Pension will increase by the greater of 2.5 per cent or the previous September's RPI, providing more support to virtually all pensioners. These policies have delivered and will continue to deliver real gains to all pensioners.

From April 2003, pensioners remaining in hospital for up to 52 weeks have no longer had certain benefits, including the state retirement pension, reduced. Previously, benefits entitlement was reduced after six weeks. This provides additional security for some of the most vulnerable pensioners.

Payments to meet specific needs

Irrespective of their income many pensioners have specific needs as a result of their age. Since 1997, the Government has introduced a variety of payments to meet these needs. This further demonstrates the Government's commitment to advancing the cause of 'progressive universalism'.

The Winter Fuel Payment was first introduced for the winter of 1997/98. Since then, its coverage and amount have been increased. Nearly all households with someone over the age of 60 – around 11 million individuals – will receive a tax-free payment, set at £200 throughout this Parliament. From this year, households with someone aged 80 or over will receive an additional £100 payment. Nearly 4 million households also benefit from a free television licence, given to those aged 75 and over, while those over 60 are also entitled to free prescriptions, free eye tests and concessionary bus fares. Many pensioners will also benefit from increased age-related personal tax allowances. From April 2003 these ensure that no pensioner with an income of less than £127 per week pays tax. These allowances will be raised at least in line with earnings, rather than prices, for the rest of this Parliament. In addition to the introduction of the 10p income tax band in the 2001 Budget, these reforms to the tax system benefit pensioners across the income spectrum.

The Pension Credit

In addition to these measures the Government has since undertaken a fundamental reform of the welfare system for pensioners: in October 2003 it introduced the Pension Credit. For the first time, the pension system rewards pensioners aged 65 and over on low and modest incomes if they have incomes above the level of the basic State Pension, up to a limit. This income might be the result of their efforts in building up savings prior to retirement or from the decision to carry on working after the state pension age.

Up to October 2003, pensioner households receiving the MIG were no better off for each additional pound of income they had. This was equivalent to a marginal tax rate of 100 per cent. In addition, many also saw their benefit reduced, or were excluded from help altogether, simply because they had small amounts of capital.

The Pension Credit replaces the MIG, but retaining the principle that pensioners have a guaranteed minimum entitlement. As with the MIG, this minimum will grow in line with average earnings throughout this Parliament. But the Pension Credit addresses the problems of the MIG by rewarding pensioners whose savings, second pensions, or earnings give them incomes of up to £139 a week for single pensioners in 2003/04 and nearly £204 a week for couples. Pensioners now receive 60p for every £1 of income between the level of the basic State Pension and the guarantee. This savings reward (a maximum of £14.79 a week for single pensioners, £19.20 for couples) is then tapered away at a rate of 40p for every £1 above the guarantee. Figure 13.2 illustrates the effect of Pension Credit on pensioners' final, or post-credit, income.

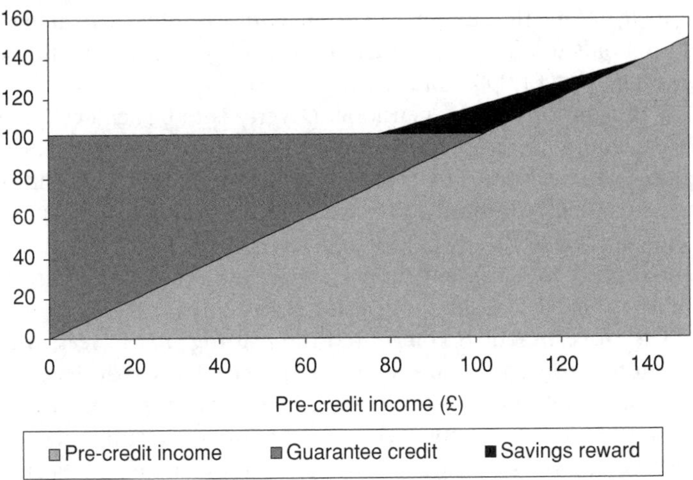

Source: DWP

Figure 13.2 The Pension Credit

For example, until October 2003, a single pensioner who had a full basic state pension of £77.45 a week and an occupational pension of £20.00 a week would have an income of £97.45 topped up by £4.65 a week with the MIG. However, following the introduction of the Pension Credit in October 2003, they now receive not only the top-up to take their income to £102.10 a week but also a savings reward of £12.00 a week. This takes their total, post-credit, income to £114.10 per week.

The Government has also acted to ensure that pensioners who have built up capital in vehicles other than a pension are treated fairly. Before April 2001 an individual's entitlement to MIG was reduced if savings were above £3,000, and households were disqualified from any support if they had more than £8,000 in capital. These thresholds were raised to £6,000 and £12,000 in April 2001. The capital rules have been further reformed under the Pension Credit to reward rather than penalise saving. The £6,000 MIG disregard has been retained, but the upper limit of £12,000 has now been abolished. Assumed income from capital above £6,000 will be halved from £1 per week for each £250 under the MIG to £1 for every £500 with Pension Credit. Housing Benefit and Council Tax Benefit rules have also been altered to ensure that pensioners receiving additional support do not see it reduced as a result of extra income provided by the Pension Credit.

In aggregate, the Pension Credit will entitle nearly half of all pensioner households to an average of £400 more a year, with some households gaining up to £1,000 more a year.

If the aim of tackling pensioner poverty is to be achieved, then it is important to maximise the level of take-up of the Pension Credit among those who are entitled to it. The introduction of Pension Credit is being accompanied by intensified efforts to improve take-up further. Publicity campaigns have already helped to reduce the stigma sometimes attached to receiving Government support, while administrative changes have helped to make it easier for pensioners to apply for their entitlement.

The Government is committed to ensuring that at least 3 million pensioner households are receiving the Pension Credit by 2006. The Pension Credit has abolished the weekly means test for the vast majority of pensioners. Most now need to apply only once and then not again for five years if their circumstances do not change significantly; the amount of Pension Credit will be uprated automatically, taking account of changes in pension income, although pensioners will be able to reapply if their circumstances change significantly. Pensioners are able to apply for the Pension Credit via a freephone number, and pensioners are now asked some brief questions when they claim their State Pension to ascertain likely eligibility to the Pension Credit. The Pension Service's local service is working with voluntary organisations and local authorities to increase take-up among those pensioners identified as the hardest to help.

The Pension Service, launched in April 2002, marks a step-change in the level of service for current pensioners, and those of working age needing information about their own retirement provision. It comprises a network of modern processing centres, using advanced telephony to deal with a wide range of benefits for pensioners. The 26 pension centres are backed up by a local service, working in the community, meeting its customers in places they prefer to visit such as libraries and community centres. The Pension Service will work closely with partner organisations in the voluntary and private sectors to encourage coordination of take-up activity. By 2006, the Pension Service will be accessible to customers and available at convenient times, to encourage the take-up of the service and entitlement, while providing tailored support to reflect different customer needs and focus resources effectively on the most vulnerable customer groups. Modern technology will improve efficiency, accuracy and customer service and enable benefits, information needs and links with other services to be managed in a single transaction. The first major challenge for the Pension Service is the successful delivery of the new Pension Credit.

Effect of pensioner policies

By 2004/05, following the introduction of the Pension Credit, additional spending on pensioners as a result of measures introduced since 1997 will be around £9.2 billion in 2004/05, more in real terms than it would have been otherwise, of which £4.3 billion will be on the poorest third of pensioners – over five times as much as an earnings link in the basic State Pension would have given them. The total expenditure is £5.7 billion more than had the basic State Pension been linked to earnings since 1998; virtually all pensioner households are better off as a result of pursuing the policies described here.

Figure 13.3 shows the distributional impact, in 2003/04 prices, of the Government's pensioner policies. Compared with the 1997 system, as a result of the Government's measures including the Pension Credit, on average, from October 2003, pensioner households will be £1,250 a year better-off in real terms. The poorest third of pensioner households will have gained £1,600 a year in real terms.

As well as delivering gains to nearly all pensioners, the Government's reforms have achieved the aim of ensuring that the State System is fiscally sustainable in the long-term. This reflects the Government's commitment to proceed on a prudent and sustainable basis with respect to public finances. An alternative policy regime based around increasing the basic State Pension by earnings would have undermined this position. Spending on State pensions currently accounts for around 5 per cent of GDP in the UK. Under the current policy regime, it is projected to remain at broadly this level between now and 2050 despite substantial demographic change (the nature of the UK's ageing population is set out below), while on average, public spending on pensions in the EU is projected to rise towards 15 per cent of GDP by 2050. Therefore, the UK is in a strong position relative to other countries to face the challenges ahead. This fiscal sustainability contrasts with the position in many other countries.

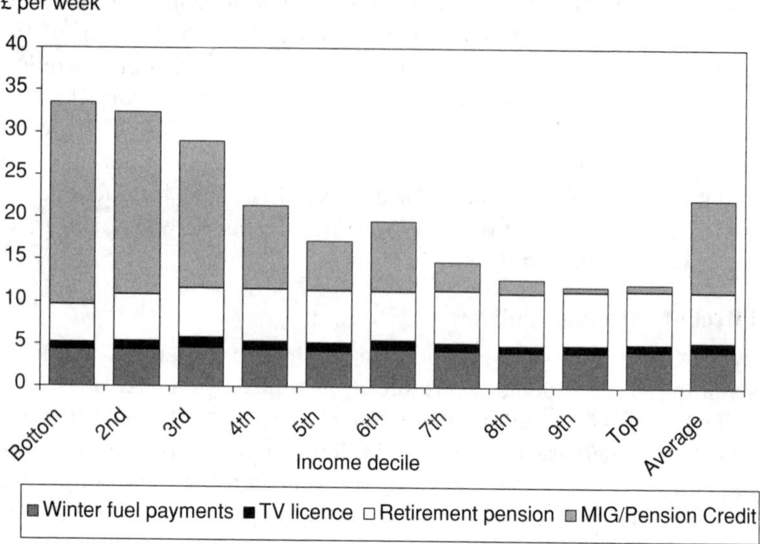

Source: DWP

Figure 13.3 Overall gains for pensioner families from pensioner policies since 1997, by income decile

Working and saving for retirement

The UK pension system has historically been based on a partnership between the Government, individuals, employers and the financial services industry – as of 2000, there were £750 billion of assets held in UK occupational pension schemes alone. This combination leaves the UK well placed to meet the demographic challenge. However, the continued success of the UK approach to pension provision relies on the renewal of this partnership between the government, individuals, employers, and the financial services industry.

Demographic context

In the UK, people can look forward to a longer retirement that ever before. The average number of years spent in retirement has increased significantly: in 1960, a man aged 65 could expect to live for another 12 years. Today, he could expect to live for another 16 years, and by 2050 it is projected that this figure will increase to around 19 years. Similar increases apply to women. Increasing longevity, coupled with lower birth rates, means that countries across the developed world are faced with ageing populations. The ageing of the population is less marked in the UK than in Japan and most EU countries. Over the next 50 years, EU countries as a whole are expected to see almost a doubling in the old-age dependency ratio (people aged 65 and over as a percentage of those aged 15–64) to nearly 53 per cent. Japan is likely to experience an even greater increase. By contrast, the old-age dependency ratio in the UK will rise by a relatively modest 14 percentage points to over 40 per cent between now and 2050.

The trend towards rising life expectancy is compounded by a tendency towards early retirement across the industrialised world. In the UK, employment rates for men and women start to decline quite sharply after age 55. By State Pension age (currently 60 for women and 65 for men), around two-thirds of men and half of women have left the labour market. In total, a third of people between 50 and State Pension age – almost 3 million people – are outside the labour market.

It is clear that, if those currently of working age are to enjoy similar standards of living in retirement as current pensioners, relative to the rest of the population, many may need to consider a combination of saving more privately and working longer in order to provide for their retirement.

Helping individuals and households make informed choices

The Government believes that, given information and the right opportunities, people will plan ahead sensibly. If informed and empowered, many would choose to start saving for retirement, save more, or work longer. At the moment, however, there remain significant barriers to making an informed decision.

Among these barriers are low levels of financial literacy and the lack of a general understanding of the importance of saving. The Financial Services Authority is taking the lead in developing a national strategy for financial literacy. This will bring together those in Government, the financial services sector, employers, consumer organisations and the media, to consolidate and build upon the many good initiatives aimed at increasing financial literacy. One of these initiatives is the inclusion of financial education in the National Curriculum.

Initiatives such as the Child Trust Fund and Savings Gateway, which encourage the habit of saving across the population, should also bring about a long-term change in culture, as more people understand the importance of financial planning. The effect of these initiatives will be reinforced by a DWP pensions awareness campaign.

The Government is working with employers and the financial services industry to provide more tailored information to individuals, giving people details of their specific circumstances. A range of forecasting tools, some delivered through the workplace, are being developed to give individuals information about the state pension rights they have accrued as well as the potential value of any occupational or personal pensions they may hold. The Government is also keen that individuals should understand the impact on their retirement income of saving more or working longer, and is developing an on-line Retirement Planner to facilitate this.

Appropriate savings vehicles

If the private pensions market is to work effectively and people are to make savings decisions that are right for them then they need access to products, which are both accessible and easy to understand. It is with this aim in mind that the Government introduced Individual Savings Accounts (ISAs), CAT standards and stakeholder pensions.

ISAs are the Government's primary vehicle for tax-advantaged saving outside pensions. The lack of deterrent lock-ins and ease of access to funds make ISAs more flexible than their predecessors, Tax Exempt Special Savings Accounts (TESSAs) and Personal Equity Plans (PEPs). As such, they have attracted significantly more funds, with saving spread more widely across the population. Since their launch in 1999, more than 14 million investors – around 30 per cent of adults – have contributed over £105 billion (as at end of April 2003) to ISAs. Charges, access and terms (CAT) standards introduced the idea of a good-value benchmark product, with a simple and easy-to-understand charging structure. Around half the ISA market is for CAT-standard products.

Personal pensions provide a retirement savings option for those who do not belong to occupational pension schemes, including the self-employed. They can be expensive, however, with high charges up front that deter people who may not be able to make substantial contributions or sustain them over a long period of time. The Government responded to these issues in the 1998 Green Paper by announcing legislation for a low charge, simple new product. Stakeholder pensions were introduced in April 2001 and are now available through the workplace to the majority of employees who currently to do not have access to an employer-sponsored pension, as well as to the self-employed and non-earners. Stakeholder pension charges are transparent and low. This allows individuals to contribute intermittently, if they cannot maintain regular contributions, without fear that the bulk of their investment will be lost in charges. By the end of the third quarter of 2003 over 1.5 million stakeholder pensions had been taken out. One effect of the introduction of Stakeholder pensions has been a fall in the level of charges across other personal pension products.

The Sandler Review of *Medium and Long-term Retail Savings in the UK* (Sandler 2002) considered further the market for personal pensions and other personal investments. The Review recommended a wider range of simple, more transparent investment products, which could be sold through a less rigorous sales process than is required under the Financial Services Authority's current rules. Stakeholder pensions will be one of the products in this suite.

A simpler pensions tax regime

The Government provides generous tax incentives in order to encourage people to save for a secure income in retirement. These reliefs – a critical component of the pensions framework – were worth around £20 billion to private pensions in 2002/03. Even when income tax paid on pensions in payment is taken into account, tax reliefs are worth around £13 billion net in the same year. To be fully effective in encouraging saving the tax treatment of pensions should not be unduly complex.

There are currently eight different tax regimes for pensions. Within these regimes, there are different rules concerning the levels of contributions and the levels of benefits. This proliferation of regimes and rules creates complexity, which makes pensions difficult to understand and explain, constrains people's choices about when and how to save, and imposes unnecessary administrative burdens on employers, individuals and pension providers.

The need is therefore to simplify the pensions tax regime. The Government's proposals to replace the existing regimes by a single regime with a lifetime allowance on the amount of tax-privileged pension saving are set out in *Simplifying the Taxation of Pensions: the Government's Proposals* (HM Treasury, Inland Revenue 2003). This would increase individual choice and flexibility, helping people make informed decisions. The vast majority of people would be able save more in a pension than existing rules allow, and many will gain from being able to take larger tax-free lump sums.

Pensions and the workplace

Employers have a crucial role in the pensions partnership, as providers of, and contributors to, occupational pension schemes, and as a source of information about retirement options. The workplace is an effective place for people to save – administration is relatively efficient and there are financial incentives in the form of relief on employers' National Insurance contributions. Employers gain from the benefits of recruitment, retention and staff motivation that good pension provision brings. The Government is keen both to strengthen the commitment of employers and to ensure the value of good employer provision is recognised by employees. The initiatives to help individuals to make informed choices about retirement that were described above should help realise this latter objective.

Employers will find that the proposals to simplify the tax treatment of pensions will bring administrative gains. Proposals in the 2002 Green Paper and the 2003 Green Paper Response *Action on Occupational Pensions* (Department for Work and Pensions 2003c) will also make it easier for employers to set up and run good pension schemes. These proposals drew on *A Simpler Way to Better Pensions – An Independent Report*, by Alan Pickering (Department for Work and Pensions 2002b). They include the radical simplification of pensions legislation and a reduction in costs on pension schemes through the replacing of the Minimum Funding Requirement with scheme-specific funding arrangements, changes to the contracting-out arrangements, and relaxation of the requirement on firms to provide compulsory indexation. This will simplify administration and allow greater flexibility.

Protection

Simplification needs to be accompanied by adequate supervisory arrangements. Regulation of the financial services market, including pensions, has been strengthened through the creation of the Financial Services Authority (FSA). The FSA replaced ten different regulators, covers the whole of the financial services market and has clear statutory objectives. The UK is the first major nation to adopt the 'one regulator, one body of law' approach.

The FSA provides clarity in authorisation, regulation and discipline, ensuring that financial providers operating in the same market have similar rules. It also provides better protection for consumers with a single financial services ombudsman to resolve consumers' complaints, and a single financial services compensation scheme. The FSA has worked to reform the structure of the market for advice on, and sales of, investments, to reform the way commissions paid to advisers are disclosed and to develop tools to help those who do not have access to advice to make informed choices.

More specifically, the 2002 Green Paper Response included a number of measures aimed at safeguarding the rights of members of occupational schemes. The Government will establish a new Pensions Protection Fund, a compensation scheme run by statutory body, to protect private sector defined benefit pension scheme members whose firm becomes insolvent with liabilities in their pension schemes that are not fully funded. A new full buy out requirement will also ensure that where a solvent employer chooses to wind up a scheme there are sufficient funds in the scheme to meet the full costs of the rights accrued by scheme members. The priority order on wind-ups is also being revised to ensure that, where there are insufficient assets to meet all liabilities, they are shared out as fairly as possible between active and pensioner scheme members. Finally, a new Pensions Regulator will target activity on badly run and high-risk schemes, putting consumers first and ensuring secure schemes continue without unnecessary regulatory burden.

Measures such as these are important not just in protecting individuals who would otherwise lose out but also, more generally, in maintaining wider public confidence in retirement saving. It was for both these reasons that the Government acted to address the problem of pensions mis-selling it had inherited. From 1988, many individuals were wrongly advised to transfer their occupational pensions into newly introduced personal pensions. Although the problems came to light in 1994, by 1997 less than 2 per cent of priority personal pension mis-selling cases had been satisfactorily resolved. Ensuring justice for the victims of personal pension mis-selling was an essential precondition for the restoration of trust and confidence in financial services needed to encourage people to make their own provision for retirement. The Government accelerated the process of compensation, 'naming and shaming' the worst performing insurance companies. By the end of 2003 over 99 per cent of consumers with mis-selling claims will have been compensated, receiving over £11 billion in redress.

Extending opportunities for older workers

The previous sections have detailed the range of Government initiatives and reforms undertaken to promote saving. In planning for retirement, working longer will be at least as large a part of the solution for many individuals. Extending their working lives can make a huge difference to the income individuals can expect in retirement. It simultaneously increases the opportunity to build up savings and reduces the length of time over which these savings provide an income. The Informed Choice initiatives should promote awareness of this. The Government is also acting to ensure that options to work longer are genuine.

The 2002 Green Paper set out proposals to provide extra back-to-work help for those aged 50 and over, such as enhancing New Deal 50+, treating men and women aged between 60 and 64 as active labour market participants, and raising the eligible age for MIG as women's State Pension age rises towards 65 between 2010 and 2020.

The Government will implement by December 2006 age legislation covering employment and vocational training, in which compulsory retirement ages are likely to be unlawful unless employers can show that they are objectively justified. The Green Paper also announced plans to allow individuals to continue working for the sponsoring employer while drawing their occupational pension and consulting on best practice to ensure that occupational pension rules do not discourage flexible retirement, with the Minimum Pension Age to be increased from 50 to 55 by 2010. For public service pension schemes, the Government intends to raise the age at which an unreduced pension is payable from 60 to 65, initially for new members. Currently, those individuals who work in retirement have a weekly income on average around twice that of those who do not work. All of the measures described here will enable people to choose to work for longer, simultaneously increasing the opportunity they have to save for retirement, while reducing the length of time in economic inactivity that will need to be funded.

State Pension age, currently 65 for men and 60 for women, is not a retirement age. There is no longer any requirement to stop working as a condition of receiving the State Pension, but individuals can defer taking their pension, currently for up to five years, and receive a higher entitlement when they finally start to draw their pension. The Green Paper announced that the Government will ensure that pensioners who defer their State Pension receive a fair deal, extending the choice available to them. The Government has not proposed a further increase in State Pension age, beyond equalisation at age 65, as it would disproportionately affect lower-income people who rely more on state benefits in retirement. The same people tend to have lower life expectancies and so, with fewer years in retirement, they would see a disproportionate reduction in their income. Instead, the Government is concentrating on helping people work up to age 65, and beyond where they wish to.

Conclusion

As a result of the reforms to state pensions much progress has been made in tackling pensioner poverty. Policies such as the Minimum Income Guarantee and Pension Credit have significantly increased the incomes available to the poorest pensioners. By strengthening the foundation provided by the National Insurance system and delivering other payments designed to meet specific needs, it is also true that pensioners across the income distribution have gained since 1997.

However, these gains have not been brought at the expense of creating a state system fiscally unsustainable in the long-term. This is the danger given the backdrop of an ageing population. Instead, the Government is working to enable future pensioners to build up secure incomes for themselves in retirement, incomes that result from saving more or working longer. It has therefore set up a Pensions Commission to monitor the effectiveness of the voluntarist approach, and make recommendations to the Secretary of State for Work and Pensions on the case for moving beyond this current approach. Its first report is due to be completed in 2005.

14
Tackling Poverty: A Global New Deal

This chapter provides an overview of the key principles underpinning the Government's approach to tackling poverty. It is drawn mainly from and updates speeches by the Rt. Hon. Gordon Brown MP, Chancellor of the Exchequer, to the New York Federal Reserve and the Press Club, Washington DC.

Introduction

At the start of the new Millennium, one in five of the world's population – 1.2 billion people – lives in abject poverty, without adequate food, water, sanitation, healthcare or education for their children. And yet this is a time of a growing abundance of knowledge, technology and capital, which is generating growing wealth and material plenty. It is now completely possible to remove extreme poverty from the human condition. It is no longer a dream to be achieved in the distant future; it is achievable in our generation if we can generate the political will. To do that, in developing country governments, the UN system, the international financial institutions and the OECD countries, we need to focus on systematic poverty reduction.

The moral case for a greater effort is clear. Current levels of poverty and inequality in the world are the biggest moral challenge humanity faces. But we live at a time when the moral challenge and our self-interest coincide. If we do not do better in reducing that inequality, it will lead to growing conflict, refugee movements, environmental degradation, disease and natural disasters. This will bring instability and danger to future generations, wherever they live. Thus, we have a clear self-interest in combining together systematically to reduce and then eliminate abject poverty from the human condition.

In September 2000, the largest ever gathering of heads of state took place at the Millennium Summit. Arising from this, the UN Millennium Declaration committed countries to doing all they can to eradicate poverty and achieve equality, peace and democracy. Arising from this, the Millennium Development Goals embody the commitment of the international community to reduce the proportion of people living in poverty by half, and to ensure that every child is in primary education, that infant, child and maternal mortality are reduced, that reproductive health services are provided for all, and that the loss of environmental resources is reversed – all by 2015. This means 1 billion people moving up out of extreme poverty between 1995 and 2015.

Globalisation is creating an unprecedented new opportunity to achieve the Millennium Development Goals – but also a new risk that the poor will be left further behind. Globalisation is not a new phenomenon. But the pace of change we see now, driven by technological innovation, increased mobility of capital and reductions in the barriers to trade and the costs of international transactions, is unprecedented.

The scale and rapidity of this change can seem alarming. But the lesson of history is clear: open societies that learn from, and trade with, others are enriched materially and culturally. In recent decades, it is those countries which have had a sufficiently enabling environment to allow them to seize the opportunity offered by more open world markets to increase exports and attract inward investment that have made the greatest strides in reducing poverty. If the poorest countries can be drawn into the global economy and increase their access to modern knowledge and technology, as part of their development plan, the world could make massive progress towards the eradication of global poverty. If they are not, we will see growing poverty, marginalisation, conflict and environmental degradation.

In the Government's view, the question has now moved beyond whether we should be for or against globalisation to how to ensure it is managed to benefit all the world's people. Managed wisely, globalisation avoids marginalisation and can lift millions out of poverty and is the best route to a just and inclusive global economy. The Government's broad objective is therefore to increase global prosperity while protecting the most vulnerable.

This chapter first sets out the current position by outlining the challenges that globalisation poses, the approach adopted by the UK Government and the goals set by the international community. It then details the international framework that needs to be put in place if global poverty is to be successfully tackled before looking in detail at the three key components of any poverty reduction programme: investment, trade and international aid.

The challenge of globalisation

Many benefits have already been secured from globalisation. Since 1970, life expectancy in developing countries has increased by nearly ten years. Child mortality and the proportion of illiterate people have almost halved. Since 1992, the number of people living in extreme poverty, i.e. people living on less than one US dollar a day, has declined by nearly 140 million.

However, millions of people are still excluded from the benefits of globalisation. Half the world's people live on less than two dollars a day and around 1 billion do not have access to safe drinking water. One child in five never goes to school and almost 1 billion adults cannot read or write. Preventable illnesses like malaria and tuberculosis kill 10 million children every year. In the worst affected countries such as Swaziland and Botswana, one in four people are infected. It is estimated that in Sub Saharan Africa as a whole growth rates could be cut by between 0.3 and 1.5 percentage points per year between now and 2015.

The Government's policy approach

In developing policy on globalisation, the Government has rejected two opposite approaches: first, outdated protectionism and isolationism that would deprive developing countries of what they need most, namely, development itself, and second, the old *laissez-faire* doctrine that says there is nothing that governments can do.

Neither of these approaches works. In the last 50 years, no country has lifted itself out of poverty without participating in the global economy. Instead, the Government believes that the better approach is to help the poor by strengthening cooperation, modernising international rules, and reforming the institutions of economic cooperation to meet these new challenges.

The last few years have seen increasing agreement about how to take globalisation forward. There is broad acknowledgement that, in order to make global economic development work in the interests of the excluded, the following are important:

- the pursuit of competition and not just privatisation;

- private capital, private companies and private investments are crucial; and
- the need for proper financial supervision as well as liberalisation, including a route map which will sequence the necessary steps in liberalising capital markets in a way that can benefit and not harm.
- public investment in the human physical and social infrastructure, which are the essential counterparts to private investment, both to attract this investment and to ensure that it furthers the goal of poverty reduction.

Stability is also seen as an essential precondition for global prosperity and growth, although it is clear that low inflation and fiscal stability are necessary *but not sufficient* conditions for securing prosperity for all. The principles behind the Government's approach to the challenges of globalisation are set out in the 2000 White Paper *Eliminating World Poverty: Making Globalisation Work for the Poor*[1] and summarised in Box 14.1.

Box 14.1 The challenge of globalisation: the UK Government's approach

The key principles underlying the Government's approach to globalisation are as follows:

- economic stability, through international economic cooperation and a new framework for a more stable global economy based on clear codes and standards, enhanced transparency, and improved crisis prevention and resolution mechanisms;
- partnership between governments and the private sector to remove barriers to investment and to adopt sound principles of corporate practice;
- widening and deepening trade to boost the economic growth central to eradicating poverty. The international community must ensure that all countries are able to share in the benefits of liberalisation in particular through investment in the infrastructure capacity; and
- substantial additional development resources so that no country genuinely committed to economic development, poverty reduction and to the genuine good governance standards should be denied the chance to make progress because of lack of investment.

The Millennium Development Goals

A strategy for prosperity entails combining policies for economic success and for social justice to tackle the causes of poverty. This strategy has led countries, international organisations, and non-governmental organisations (NGOs) to subscribe to the historic shared task of setting and meeting the eight Millennium Development Goals (MDGs) set out in Box 14.2.

Box 14.2 The Millennium Development Goals

The United Nations (UN), International Monetary Fund (IMF), World Bank, OECD, G7, G20, and all major developed and developing countries have agreed to the Millennium Development Goals, which include:

- eradicating extreme poverty and hunger by halving, between 1990 and 2015, the proportion of people whose income is less than one dollar a day and the proportion of people who suffer from hunger;
- achieving universal primary education by ensuring that, by 2015, children everywhere, boys and girls alike, will be able to complete a full course of primary schooling;
- promoting gender equality and empowering women by eliminating gender disparity in primary and secondary education, preferably by 2005, and in all levels of education by no later than 2015;
- reducing by two-thirds, between 1990 and 2015, the under-five mortality rate;
- improving maternal health by reducing by three-quarters, between 1990 and 2015, the maternal mortality ratio;
- combating HIV/AIDS, malaria, and other diseases;
- ensuring environmental sustainability, including halving by 2015 the proportion of people without sustainable access to safe drinking water, and by 2020 achieving a significant improvement in the lives of at least 100 million slum dwellers; and
- developing a global partnership for development.

The Government has introduced a new approach to tackling these issues. Grounded in the context of a global economy, but following the same principles as the domestic reform agenda, it provides new opportunities for developed and developing countries alike and in return requires them to accept new responsibilities. The aim is to build economic foundations for debt relief, poverty reduction, and sustainable development that will ensure that the world's poor can earn a fair share of the benefits of global prosperity.

The new approach consists of four essential building blocks:

1. A substantial increase in global aid flows, which the Government has proposed in the near term should be done through an International

Finance Facility (IFF), coupled with further improvements in aid effectiveness.

2. The sequenced adoption of an improved regime for trade that allows developing countries to benefit from and participate on fair terms in the world economy (see below for further details).
3. The creation in developing countries of the right domestic conditions for business investment and adoption of high corporate standards by the international business community for engagement as reliable partners in the development process.
4. A new rules based system for global economic growth and stability under which all countries can prosper, with all countries pursuing agreed codes and standards of fiscal and monetary policy transparency.

Establishing the framework

The Government believes that tackling global poverty requires new economic leadership based on a comprehensive plan that goes beyond temporary relief to wholesale economic and social development. This means, for the richest countries, new responsibilities – to open up markets, reform international institutions, and transfer resources to developing countries to help reduce poverty – but also new opportunities – from increased trade and globalisation that works in the public interest. For the poorest countries, it means new responsibilities – to pursue transparent, corruption-free policies for stability and attracting private investment – and new opportunities too – with access to increased trade and investment, supported by a transfer of resources from rich to poor.

There are a number of essential elements of establishing the framework within which countries need to do business to allow even the poorest countries to participate in the global economy. These elements are: providing codes and standards of transparency in all financial dealings and the making of economic decisions; ensuring that appropriate surveillance is in place as effective early warning procedures; improving the mechanisms for resolving crises; and establishing effective international institutions.

The first building block is improving the terms on which the poorest countries participate in the global economy and actively increasing their capacity to do so. Developing countries that most need finance are, at the same time, the most vulnerable to the judgements and instabilities of global markets. Capital is most likely to move to environments which are stable, and least likely to stay in environments which are, or become, unstable.

Macroeconomic stability is not optional but an essential precondition of economic success and the fight against poverty. Part of that stability is provided by establishing clear rules, proper transparent procedures for economic decision-making, and well-understood systems of accountability.

Codes and standards of transparency

The adoption of clear and transparent procedures in economic decisions (for example, presenting a full factual picture of the country's debt position and the health of the financial sectors) and a willingness for them to be monitored brings benefits for all countries developed and developing. It improves stability, deters corruption, provides markets with a flow of specific country-by-country information to engender greater investor confidence, and reduces the problem of contagion. These standards also support countries in the liberalisation of their capital markets, helping them to avoid destabilising and speculative inflows. This approach is a better guarantee of both an investment-friendly environment and long-term stability.

Meeting these international codes and standards is an important signal that countries are seriously committed to building good governance. Transparent, responsible, and professional institutions and processes, along with the rule of law, are essential preconditions for sustained development.

The World Bank has identified corruption as the 'single greatest obstacle to economic and social development' in the poorest countries. Corruption diverts resources away from activities that are vital for poverty reduction, deters private investors, and may even erode public support for development assistance. Fighting corruption at all levels is therefore a key priority for development; and international institutions are already taking positive action in this area, including working with developing countries to diagnose the causes of weak governance and to implement programmes to address them.

The adoption of codes and standards is a route to fairness, reducing the likelihood of crises and helping to secure growth and prosperity. However, implementing these codes means radical changes in the way governments and financial markets operate. The international community needs to offer direct assistance and transitional help to support their early implementation. The UK Department for International Development is working with the IMF and the World Bank to support technical assistance in this area to provide help for the poorest countries, which may lack the necessary expertise.

Surveillance

Crisis prevention is enhanced, not just by the operation of codes and standards and the offer of proportionate help to countries who adopt them, but also by rigorous surveillance, effective early-warning procedures, and a more consistent engagement by the private sector.

The IMF's Article IV consultation process – central to its bilateral surveillance and featuring reviews of economic and monetary developments in each of its 183 member countries on a broadly annual basis – is an invaluable tool in crisis prevention. To be fully effective, the surveillance process must be transparent, authoritative, and independent. Over recent years, there has been greater openness in publishing Article IV assessments and their press notices, and the Article IV process remains at the centre of the monitoring of codes and standards. An independent evaluation office has also been established to provide independent evaluation of the IMF's work. The evaluation office is committed to consulting extensively with internal and external stakeholders on their work programme and publishing completed reports.

Enhancing the IMF's role in surveillance of the world economy – making it more transparent, independent, and authoritative – would contribute to greater stability and ensure it is seen to be providing impartial advice independent of the inter-governmental decision-making process[2].

Financial crises can set back development for years. There have been over 50 banking crises since 1970. Yet many could have been foreseen, and some avoided, by proper national regulation and international cooperation. Domestic financial supervision matters in a way not previously understood in models of development, which concentrated on raw materials and capital. To tackle financial sector problems that have international repercussions, the Government has proposed that the Financial Stability Forum – which brings together the combined expertise of the IMF and key regulatory authorities – should evolve effective early-warning systems.

Improving crisis resolution mechanisms

Delivering an international financial system that is less prone to crises, and better able to withstand them when they do occur, will require new responsibilities to be adopted, not just by governments but also by all those involved in the system. A key component of the reform effort is the development of a new framework of partnership between the private and public sectors for preventing and managing crises, such that all parties play their part in maintaining stability.

Uncertainty over processes and outcomes across the spectrum of financial difficulties through to cases of default can protract proceedings and result in higher costs for all. Establishing internationally accepted principles and practices could clarify the roles of the official and private sectors at times of crisis resolution. As the official sector cannot and should not provide large-scale bail-outs as a standard response to crises, creditors and debtors need to find their own market-oriented solutions to payments problems. For example, the more widespread adoption of collective action clauses could facilitate creditor coordination during debt restructuring and prevent minority hold-outs from disrupting proceedings, and the establishment of well-run investor-relations programmes could aid proactive debt management and the expedition of debt workouts.

There also needs to be a clear willingness, once other reasonable options have been exhausted, to support a country that must impose temporary capital controls or a moratorium on its debt servicing as part of an orderly process of restoring sustainability, conducted in good faith.

Effective international institutions

In recent years, under the leadership of Jim Wolfensohn and Michel Camdessus and now Horst Köhler, the IMF and the World Bank have reformed to become more effective, transparent, and accountable. The World Bank publishes more documents and meeting records than it ever has before, and the IMF has set up an Independent Evaluation Office (IEO) which provides objective and independent evaluation of IMF issues. In addition, Horst Köhler has appeared in front of the UK Parliament to give evidence to the Treasury Select Committee.

In broad policy terms, the International Financial Institutions are moving away from an emphasis on the old structural adjustment policies towards a new approach in which sustainable development and anti-poverty policies are implemented at a national level, with developing countries now leading national processes to develop poverty reduction strategies. This includes consulting widely with civil society and producing a Poverty Reduction Strategy Paper (PRSP) as a framework for IMF, World Bank, and other donor support.

The poverty reduction strategies set out an individual Government's approach and its key priorities in the fight against poverty. They provide a budgetary framework to allocate government revenue, aid, and debt relief so that the impact on poverty reduction is maximised. The strategies are clearly linked to the Millennium Development Goals, with measurable indicators to monitor progress. So that the citizens of developing countries understand and engage with their Government's strategies for reducing poverty, civil society groups in the poorest countries are required to engage in, and own, their country's poverty strategies. This is intended to ensure that anti-poverty strategies are not just country-driven but community-driven – developed transparently with the broad participation of civil society, key donors, and regional institutions.[3]

The Government is committed to encouraging not only the early implementation of poverty reduction plans but to providing technical and other assistance to help the implementation of these strategies.

Developing countries are thus more able to design pro-poor budgets and policies which direct government spending towards their social sectors, basic infrastructure, and other activities that contribute to reducing poverty effectively. Along with the implementation of the Heavily Indebted Poor Countries (HIPC) Initiative,[4] cooperation between the institutions on financial sector reform and the establishment of the financial sector assessment programme, this is a good example of the World Bank and the IMF collaborating effectively to achieve their shared goals.

Investment

The Government believes that open, transparent, and accountable national policies, internationally monitored, are the foundation for macroeconomic stability and provide the framework that will enable domestic growth and development. Raising investment can help ensure this growth and development is achieved. Investment can be raised, both domestically and from foreign sources, and through public and private sectors working together.

In the last decade, foreign direct investment flows across national boundaries – including to, and between, developing countries – have increased fourfold.[5] Evidence shows that such investment is an important driver for growth and development generating higher productivity, employment, and wealth, and transferring knowledge, skills, and technology. For example, one study (Dobson and Hufbauer 2001) found, in a calculation of emerging countries' access to global capital, that, by 2000, developing countries were gaining $387 billion a year in additional GDP from foreign direct investment expansion, compared with $358 billion from trade expansion. Their GDP levels were 5 per cent higher than they otherwise would be. Another study (Borensztein et. al. 1998) examines the impact of average foreign direct investment inflows (as a percentage of GDP) on average real per capita GDP growth in 69 developing countries during 1970–89. A one percentage point increase in the average foreign direct investment inflow was associated with an increase in the average per capita annual GDP growth rate of 0.66 per cent.

However, the poorest and least developed countries suffer a double handicap. Foreign direct investment is too low, with investment per head in developing countries just $35 compared with $805 in the higher-income countries. In sub-Saharan Africa, foreign direct investment is even lower at $12 per person. In addition, domestically generated savings and investment are low, with savings that do exist often leaving the country.

Building a more favourable business environment

To encourage greater foreign and domestic investment, developing countries are working to establish a more favourable business environment. The country-owned poverty reduction strategies which replaced the old structural adjustment policies are correctly focused on creating the right domestic conditions for investment and highlight the importance of investment in infrastructure, sound legal processes that deter corruption, and the creation of an educated and healthy workforce. In Mozambique, for example, a country that has undertaken such reform, there has been a sixfold increase in foreign direct investment since 1994.

Many of the factors required to attract investment are also key to enhancing its benefits for the poor, including good governance, the appropriate institutional environment, and public investment in basic infrastructure (including to support small, medium and micro-enterprises and the agriculture sector) and human capital (particularly primary education and basic healthcare). Of particular importance is the need to support the growth of micro, small and medium enterprises, including in the agricultural sector. These are the key for job creation and poverty reduction.

As good practice emerges, the lessons learned from country-by-country experiences of development can be applied, region by region. At the G8 Summit in June 2002, the UK and other Members endorsed approach of the New Partnership for Africa's Development (NEPAD), and agreed that we must do more within the world's poorest regions to facilitate cross-border trade, creating domestic markets large enough to encourage the private sector to invest.

The NEPAD proposes a new relationship between Africa and the rest of the world, centred on African ownership and management of policies to eradicate poverty and promote sustainable growth and development. Industrialised countries, particularly the G8, must play their part by supporting improved trade access, increased investment, further debt relief, greater aid flows, and support to education and health. NEPAD proposals, endorsed by the whole of Africa at the Lusaka Organisation of African Unity Summit in July 2001, are set out in Box 14.3.

Box 14.3 The New Partnership for Africa's Development (NEPAD) proposals

The NEPAD proposals cover the following areas:

- strengthening mechanisms for conflict prevention, management, and resolution;
- promoting democracy, human rights, and public accountability;
- building the capacity of African states to set and enforce the legal framework, including maintaining law and order;
- restoring and maintaining macroeconomic stability, developing appropriate standards and targets for fiscal and monetary policies;
- instituting transparent legal and regulatory frameworks for financial markets and the private sector;
- promoting the development of infrastructure, agriculture, and diversification into agro-industries and manufacturing;
- extending education, technical training, and health services, with a high priority given to HIV/AIDS, malaria, and other communicable diseases; and
- promoting the role of women in all spheres, including reinforcing their participation in political and economic spheres.

Multinational companies and cross-border corporate accountability

One concern of those who campaign against globalisation is that in developing countries lax regulation results in a downward spiral of poor labour, environmental, and regulatory standards.

Companies and Governments must recognise the distinction between a strong market achieved by competition and a distorted market resulting from anti-competitive behaviour. For citizens to accept and welcome the presence of multinationals, there must be clear benefits for those citizens either as consumers or as employees. This requires functioning, competitive, markets and fair working practices, with multinationals operating in a socially responsible way. Beyond a focus on corporate philanthropy, they need to look at how they do business; how they operate on the ground, how they treat their employees, how they manage their supply chains, and how they engage in national policy dialogue. These factors have a direct influence on the pro-poor nature of their activities. Where multinationals are unaccountable across borders, companies and Governments need to do more to restore the right balance, increase stakeholder awareness, and achieve cross-border corporate accountability.

A range of initiatives have been established to support socially responsible business, such as the OECD Guidelines for Multinational Enterprises, the Global Reporting Initiative (GRI), the UN Global Compact, the Ethical Trading Initiative (ETI) and, most recently, the Extractive Industries Transparency Initiative (EITI), launched on 17 June 2003 by the Prime Minister.

It is essential that these continue to be reviewed to examine how they are being implemented and how they are impacting on developing countries.

Widening and deepening trade

In the last 40 years, those developing countries which have been more open and which trade more in the world economy have seen faster growth rates than those which have remained closed. Research by Dollar & Kraay (2001) found that from the early 1970s to the early 1990s, developing countries (for example China or Bangladesh) that were able to pursue growth through trade grew at least twice as fast as those that kept their tariffs high and their doors closed to imports and competition. The Government believes that all countries should have the opportunity to reap these benefits.

Research by the World Bank (2002) also suggests that full trade liberalisation could lift at least 300 million more people out of poverty by 2015 than could be achieved simply by the projected growth rates of the developing country. The World bank's findings are based on mutually reinforcing policy moves in four linked areas:

1. A pro-development trade round – where developed countries offer meaningful market access in key sectors like agriculture, textiles & clothing, and also liberalise restrictions on temporary movement of

workers; and with developing countries liberalising services and lowering barriers to import competition

2. Global collective action to promote trade – including "aid for trade" (development assistance to promote trade infrastructure), adoption of best practice standards and rules and a good investment climate
3. Unilateral action by rich countries – particularly unilateral opening of markets to poor countries, outside global trade negotiations, and bilateral "aid for trade", to complement multilateral initiatives.
4. Trade reform in developing countries – focused on improving competitiveness through lowering restrictive barriers. Economic analysis shows this would deliver large gains. Reforms reinforced by improvements in governance and the domestic investment climate can raise productivity and incomes even if done unilaterally.

Even diminishing protection by 50 per cent in agriculture and in industrial goods and services would increase the world's yearly income by nearly $400 billion: a boost to growth of 1.4 per cent. All countries and regions stand to benefit, with developing countries gaining an estimated $150 billion a year and higher than average increases in GDP growth.

International organisations also have a key role to play in taking the agenda for world poverty forward, particularly in increasing the incidence and depth of world trade.

Doha and a new 'Development Round'

The World Trade Organisation (WTO) agreement in Doha launched a new trade round with a development agenda – a package of commitments to progress in areas that will lead to major gains for developing countries and the poorest people in these countries. WTO member countries committed themselves to take development needs into account both in the policies they pursue and in offering technical assistance.

Although the September 2003 WTO Ministerial meetings in Cancun failed to reach an agreement, some important milestones have been achieved. Just ahead of Cancun, WTO members were able to reach political agreement on the issue of intellectual property rights (TRIPS) and access to medicines. This will enable poor countries with no, or insufficient, manufacturing capacity in the pharmaceutical sector to import generic versions of patented medicines in situations of public health crisis. This new flexibility provides a useful bargaining tool for governments negotiating prices with suppliers of patented medicines. While success on access to medicines requires progress on a number of other critical fronts, this agreement should help ensure poor countries are not at a disadvantage when patent law changes come into effect in developing countries from 2005

At Cancun a more transparent process combined with the emergence of the G20 and the G90 groups made it easier for developing countries to interact with the negotiations and have a stronger voice. Before Cancun it was also agreed to review the rules concerning the use of antidumping measures so that they are improved and clarified and take into account the needs of developing and least developed countries.

In addition, there was agreement at Doha on steps to address developing countries' concerns over their ability to implement existing WTO agreements. The WTO's dispute-settlement procedure has been criticised as punitive and unfair to poorer countries, which do not have resources to prosecute cases. Although the system is intended as a last resort, it was agreed that it should be improved and clarified. The UK also provides financial support to the Advisory Centre on WTO Law, which offers developing country members subsidised legal support in dispute settlement cases.

Taking the agenda forward

Despite the lack of agreement at Cancun potential benefits from the round of talks are still available. However, for this to happen the negotiations must focus on the core issues of interest to developing countries in particular open markets and fair access and the reduction of trade-distorting subsidies in all areas, notably in agriculture. With three-quarters of the world's poor living in rural areas, reforms to agriculture offers the best and quickest route for reducing poverty. An example of these are subsidies to agriculture in the OECD which run at 1 billion dollars a day – six times the amount spent by these countries on development assistance. The UK Government, remains a proponent of the commitments made in the Doha mandate and will continue to work with partners in the EU to reduce, with a view to phasing out, all forms of export subsidies and substantial reductions in trade distorting domestic support.

In addition to creating a fairer trading system, there was recognition at Doha of the importance of building countries' capacity to participate effectively in the system and the need for this to be an integral part of the new negotiations. Accordingly the UK has committed £160 million to Trade Related Capacity Building since 1998, more than treble the pledge in the 2000 White Paper, *Eliminating World Poverty: Making Globalisation Work for the Poor.*

However, as Cancun showed, the benefits of further liberalisation will not be equally shared. As such while it is essential that we continue to advocate the benefits of liberalisation, we must also ensure that the right incentives are in place to encourage developing countries to increase their engagement in the global trading system. This will require working with international organisations, such as the IMF and World Bank, to ensure that developing countries have the support they need to deal with a more open world trading system.

Consistent with its goal of growth and prosperity, the Government is committed to doing everything it can to discourage the diversion of resources into military expenditure and to diminish the subsidies for the arms trade with developing countries. The UK has banned export credit guarantees for unproductive expenditure to 63 of the poorest countries, making clear its desire to support only productive enterprise that assists social and economic development.

Financing for development

In addition to building a global framework, raising investment and increasing trade, a fourth reform is essential: a substantial increase in development aid to nations most in need and a willingness to focus on the fight against poverty. There are a number of aspects to this, including the provision of debt relief, raising the resources necessary to tackle poverty reduction effectively, improving the effectiveness of how aid is targeted, making better use of the funds which are raised, and finding new sources of finance.

Debt relief

The Government has been at the forefront of the international debate on debt relief. The Heavily Indebted Poor Countries (HIPC) process is now lifting the burden of unpayable debt from 27 of the most highly indebted countries, cancelling over $70 billion in debt and helping to build a new circle of debt relief, poverty reduction, and sustainable development. If all eligible countries – including countries in conflict – became part of HIPC, $100 billion of debt could be cancelled.

The HIPC Initiative, releasing finance directly into Governments' budgets, has helped increase social expenditures in countries receiving HIPC debt relief by $4 billion since 1999 equivalent to 2.7 per cent of GDP. On average, health and education spending accounts for 65 per cent of the use of HIPC debt relief.

But there are significant gains still to be made. Speedy, effective, and full implementation of the enhanced HIPC Initiative is critical. HIPC countries yet to benefit from debt relief should adopt the country-specific poverty reduction measures necessary to become eligible for the initiative in order to demonstrate that the proceeds of the debt relief subsequently provided will be used effectively to reduce poverty. The UK is also encouraging the IMF and the World Bank to improve access to financing for post-conflict countries coping with the double burden of debt and reconstruction of their ravaged economies. The Government has committed £2.5 million to a fund providing concessional financing to post-conflict countries to help ensure no country is left behind.

The Government continues to work to ensure a sustainable exit from debt for HIPC countries, with agreement being reached at the Annual Meetings of the World Bank and IMF in September 2002, on the need for additional funds, of up to $1 billion, to ensure that the HIPC Initiative guarantees a robust exit from unsustainable debt. Furthermore, at the 2003 Annual Meetings, Members confirmed their commitment to providing additional relief, on a case by case basis, to countries at completion point to ensure they exit the Initiative with sustainable debt levels.

The Government continues to encourage those HIPC countries that have yet to benefit from HIPC debt relief to continue working towards conditions that will secure access to such relief and ensure its effective use for poverty reduction. The UK is holding debt service payments from those countries that have yet to benefit from debt relief, which will be returned when they are able to use resources to tackle poverty. The UK will continue to work to persuade other creditors to follow this lead.

Avoiding future debt

The global approach to tackling poverty is founded on the premise that there must be a commitment never to return to a situation where countries build up unsustainable burdens of debt. The very poorest and most vulnerable countries should receive investment help primarily in the form of grants to partner their soft International Development Association (IDA) loans and grants; and all other low-income countries should be offered interest-free loans. (IDA is the concessional lending wing of the World Bank.) Some beneficiaries will be countries with millions of poor but today classified as middle-income countries. In these cases, assistance should be given through interest-reduced loans conditional upon implementing the agreed poverty reduction strategies and engaging civil society.

Financing for development

Debt relief by itself is not enough. The challenge facing the international community is to create a virtuous circle in which debt relief is followed by poverty reduction and sustainable development. The international community is therefore committed to meeting the Millenium Development Goals by 2015, set out earlier in this chapter. The additional funding needed for this programme is, however, substantial. The World Bank's most recent assessment[6] supports the $50 billion a year estimate made in Ernesto Zedillo's (2001) report to the UN Secretary General in the lead up to the UN Financing for Development Conference, held in Monterrey, Mexico, in March 2002[7].

Although the Monterrey Consensus marked a reversal of the 20-year decline in aid levels, with the EU and US agreeing to provide an additional $16 billion a year in increased aid from 2006, the international community acknowledges that a very significant financing gap remains. This is why the UK has proposed an International Finance Facility (IFF) to raise the estimated $50 billion a year needed to meet the MDGs[8]. The IFF represents a clear commitment to the principle that no country genuinely committed to economic development, poverty reduction and to the genuine good governance standards should be denied the chance to make progress because of lack of investment.

The 2003 Annual Meetings of the IMF and World Bank, in Dubai, agreed that the Fund and Bank should do further work on financing for development. As well as examining the merits of various policy options and financing mechanisms, such as an international financing facility, the IMF and World Bank will work on aid effectiveness, absorptive capacity, and results-based measurement. The Fund and Bank have been mandated to report back in 2004.

Effectiveness of targeting aid

At present, aid is not being used as efficiently as possible. It is therefore important that donor aid effectiveness is improved and international institutions strengthened to ensure better management of international funds.

Financial assistance must be targeted more effectively to low-income countries with sound economic management and where there are large numbers of poor people. Current patterns of aid provide $10 per poor person in South Asia but $950 per poor person in the Middle East and North Africa.

Aid needs to focus on creating and transmitting knowledge and capacity – supporting institutional and policy changes that stimulate growth, ensuring poverty reduction, promoting private sector activity, and improving public service delivery. That is why, where possible, aid should be:

- disassociated from procurement tied to suppliers in the donor countries, increasing its effectiveness in value-for-money terms by up to 20 per cent;
- pooled to achieve economies of scale and therefore greater effectiveness, as well as avoiding wasteful duplication, inconsistency, and ineffectiveness;
- ultimately distributed directly to budgets, reducing bureaucracy and allowing Governments to implement long-term programmes of poverty reduction; and
- concentrated on those countries with large numbers in extreme poverty but where policies are sound and effectively implemented.

Overall, better allocation, coordination, and untying by bilateral donors and international institutions could make aid twice as effective.

The Government is also working with its partners in the European Union to apply the lessons learned about improving the effectiveness and targeting of aid. The EU has already taken positive steps in adopting a clear development policy focused strongly on poverty reduction. This can be taken further. In middle-income countries, the EU should focus on loans backed up by technical assistance to support policy reform, trade access, and improved governance delivering sound administration and protecting human rights. In poorer countries, the EU should invest the significant grant resources needed to build the social and physical infrastructure essential for growth. The EU should also promote the trade access and better governance that are so often lacking. The EU is working to improve the disbursal rates of its development aid; but much remains to be done to ensure that aid is delivered as speedily as possible. Administrative reforms, closer cooperation with other donors, and untying aid are key elements in achieving this greater efficiency.

Better use of funds received

Development aid must be seen as an investment to tackle the causes of underdevelopment. This involves shifting the focus from providing short-term aid just to compensate for the effects of poverty to an approach where aid is a long-term investment in tackling the causes of poverty by promoting growth, prosperity, and participation in the world economy.

Countries themselves must be able to show that the funds they receive are properly and effectively used. They must end corruption, meet their obligations to pursue stability and create the conditions for new investment. To help this, countries may use some of the additional aid in supporting their efforts to strengthen national accountability processes and institutions, such as national audit offices. Recipient countries must also realise their commitment to community ownership of their poverty reduction strategies, and ensure that resources go effectively and efficiently to fighting poverty, including to education and health.

Many countries, including the UK, have made great advances in improving the effectiveness of aid. Experience shows that development assistance works best when it supports a strategy designed and led by the national Government in consultation with its civil society.

In return for aid-receiving countries treating aid as investment, making it more cost-effective, managing it better, and focusing on priorities, donor countries should match their commitment to the 2015 Millennium Development Goals with the resources necessary to achieve them. Increased development assistance is essential to match gains from liberalising trade, raising private investment, and entrenching stability.

UK approach to international development

Since 1997, the UK has taken a new approach to international development:

- raising the UK's aid commitments to £4.9 billion by 2005/06, a 93 per cent increase in real terms, and representing the largest-ever increase in UK aid. UK aid to developing countries will rise from 0.32 per cent of national income in 2002/03 to 0.4 per cent by 2005/06, exceeding the EU target of 0.39 per cent and underlining the Government's commitment to the United Nations' target for aid of 0.7 per cent of GDP;
- untying all UK aid allocated after April 2001 and by 2005/06 targeting 90 per cent of bi-lateral country aid on low income countries; introducing a more joined-up approach to conflict prevention, bringing together diplomatic, military, and development assistance, and banning export credits for unproductive expenditure, including arms;
- committing £1.5 billion to strengthening health systems in developing countries and implementing tax incentives to encourage

pharmaceutical companies to increase their investment in medical research so that new treatments can be found for the diseases which kill and debilitate people living in developing countries;
- playing a leading role in establishing the Global Fund to fight HIV/AIDS, TB and Malaria by providing resources for bulk purchase of medicines by developing countries. The Government's bilateral expenditure on HIV/AIDS programmes has risen from £38 million in 1997 to over £270 million in 2003. Total financial commitments to the Global Health Fund already exceed $4.6 billion, of which the UK has pledged $280 million up to 2008; and
- committing over £700 million to support universal primary education in developing countries. In 2002, the UK launched a new fund to support the achievement of universal primary education in the Commonwealth.

New sources of finance: the International Finance Facility

To meet the challenges of raising the additional $50 billion a year set out in the Zedillo Report, a broad package of measures is needed and this is subject to ongoing debate in the G7/8, IMF, the World Bank, and the United Nations. A series of innovative proposals have been put forward to help raise the funding needed, including a Tobin Tax and by Arms Tax, and by issuing Special Drawing Rights (SDRs). The IMF board proposed that developed countries could use their share of the allocation of SDRs agreed in 1997, as well as future allocations, for international development.

Other proposals for additional resources involve the richest countries making a substantial additional commitment of resources to 2015 and beyond. This will require unprecedented action by donors. To bridge the gap between what has been pledged and what is required, the UK Government has proposed a new International Finance Facility (IFF) to finance the investment needed – a doubling of current aid flows from $50 billion a year today to $100 billion a year up to 2015. This facility would capitalise on long-term commitments from donors, and leverage additional financing through the issue of bonds on international capital markets. Additional aid could then be disbursed principally in the form of grants to developing countries.

By locking in the long-term commitments from developed countries, the IFF can provide a predictable and stable flow of aid over the medium term, avoiding the short-term volatility that is so damaging to investment planning and development spending. Crucially, developing countries would be able to budget for substantially higher aid flows over the medium term to tackle poverty. An IFF would also promote a balanced distribution of resources and coordination between donors.

Donors' pledges to the IFF would be conditional upon recipient countries meeting high-level financing conditions. One condition could be prolonged arrears to the IMF. Donor payments to the IFF in respect of a particular country would be suspended if that country breached these high-level financing conditions.

Existing effective mechanisms for aid disbursement, such as the World Bank and the development agencies of donor countries, would be used to disburse the additional funding raised by the IFF. The facility would be built on principles of sound aid effectiveness to which donor countries would be expected to sign up. Examples could be that aid is not tied to specific contracts in donor countries or that it must support developing country-owned poverty reduction strategies.

There is good evidence that poor countries can successfully absorb higher levels of aid. Early evidence shows that countries implementing poverty reduction strategies have increased poverty reduction spending by 20 per cent. For example, in Uganda, extreme poverty has been reduced by 20 per cent since 1992 – with aid contributing over 50 per cent of the budget. The IFF model would also encourage increased coherence and alignment of aid flows behind strong country-driven poverty reduction strategies.

If successful, the scheme should help secure a step change in the quality of the partnership between donors and poor countries. Aid would be better managed as the provision of more predictable, long-term financing would enable countries to plan their investments effectively. Hence, no country genuinely committed to economic development, poverty reduction, and transparency and proper standards would be denied the chance to make progress because of a lack of investment.

An action plan for the global new deal

In the past, the world has set targets like the Millennium Development Goals and failed to meet them. To avoid this happening again, it is essential that responsibility for the task be shared and that the practical steps which each country must take are clearly set out and agreed. Developed and developing countries, international institutions, the private sector, and non-governmental organisations and faith groups all need to work within their powers and responsibilities to ensure a greater effort is made to guarantee the success of this global approach to poverty reduction. However, it is important that this joint responsibility reinforces, not diminishes, accountability for the outcome.

The final section of this chapter sets out the future actions required by each of the key stakeholders if poverty reduction is to be achieved.

Developed countries

The developed countries must work together to:

- move forward on debt relief, in particular to urge all official and commercial creditors to participate in the HIPC initiative;
- maximise bilateral debt relief, including through encouraging all developed countries to cancel 100 per cent of bilateral debt owed by HIPCs; and
- create a fairer trade system for developing countries.
  - (a) in agriculture, negotiating substantial improvements in market access, along with reductions in agriculture export subsidies with a view to phasing them out;
  - (b) in trade those developed countries which have not yet done so granting duty- and quota-free access to least developed countries for all exports except arms; and secondly, financing capacity building in developing countries so they can participate fully and effectively in the ongoing negotiations and continue to integrate with the world trading system;
  - (c) in improving aid effectiveness through untying and better coordination and a greater focus on poorest and best-performing countries; and
- significantly increase the overall aid effort, considering a broad package of measures to achieve this, including support for a $50 billion increase in investment aid.

Developing countries

A sound domestic environment is the foundation of poverty reduction and sustained economic growth, enabling countries to make effective use of aid and harness private sector finance in development. Developing countries need to:

- adopt new codes and standards for transparent management of fiscal and monetary systems;
- strengthen the accountability of their public financial management systems so as to eliminate corruption;
- develop, strengthen, and implement fully comprehensive and costed national poverty reduction strategies; and

- establish business environments to facilitate growth in private investment.

International institutions

The United Nations and other international institutions have a central role to play in bringing countries' efforts together and supporting developing countries. The UN, the IMF, the World Bank and the WTO need to:

- offer coordinated support for the implementation of codes and standards and draw up national route maps for capital liberalisation in stable conditions;
- strengthen surveillance by providing an early warning system for crises through the Financial Stability Forum and by exploring options for providing impartial advice independent of inter-governmental decision-making processes;
- explore options for better procedures for crisis resolution, in particular to resolve the legal obstacles to effective debt rescheduling;
- focus support on the achievement of the Millennium Development Goals, assist developing countries to measure progress against them, and publish a report annually;
- fully implement the agreed new key features of the IMF's Poverty Reduction and Growth Facility;
- continue to enhance the participation of all developing countries in decision-making processes, thereby strengthening the international dialogue and the work of the international institutions as they address the development needs and concerns of these countries; and
- strengthen cooperation between the UN and other multilateral financial, trade, and development institutions to support economic growth, poverty eradication, and sustainable development worldwide.

The private sector

Long-term investment is critical for growth and development. There needs to be a new engagement by business as reliable and long-term partners in economic development. The private sector needs to:

- work with developing countries to increase the quantity and quality of foreign and domestic investment, in particular through

participation in national and regional investment forums to share best practice, examine current barriers, and seek to build consensus for necessary actions; and
- increase stakeholder awareness to achieve cross-border accountability, in particular by applying agreed international standards of best practice for multinational companies and by assessing and reporting on their economic, environmental and social impact through such initiatives as the Global Compact, the Global Reporting Initiative and the OECD Guidelines on Multinational Enterprises.

Non-governmental organisations and faith groups

NGOs and faith groups around the world campaign to end poverty and injustice, and their support for the Millennium Development Goals is vital. The NGOs and churches need to:

- ensure that developed and developing countries, businesses, and international organisations are held accountable for progress towards the Millennium Development Goals;
- raise public awareness and campaign regarding the outrage of child poverty and the need for urgent action on the Millennium Development Goals, including progress on poverty, debt, trade, and social justice; and
- assist developing countries in designing and implementing community-driven national poverty reduction strategies.

Conclusion

The challenge of world poverty is immense but the answer is not to retreat from globalisation. Instead, there is a need to advance social justice on a global scale, to the benefit of all – and to do so with more global cooperation and stronger international institutions. Development aid must be refocused and treated as investment for the future.

The UK Government's vision of the way forward is one in which, in an increasingly interdependent world, all can benefit if each agent fulfils agreed obligations for change. This global new deal can ensure that the world's poor can share fairly in the benefits of prosperity throughout the world.

All this is grounded in the belief that the UK Government has responsibilities beyond our national boundaries.

Part 4

World Class Public Services

15 Public Services Productivity: An Analysis

This chapter discusses the importance of improving public sector productivity and assesses how it can be measured[1]. It explains the market failures and equity considerations that can justify government involvement in the funding and provision of key services and the problems which must be overcome to increase public sector productivity.

Introduction

As noted in Parts 1–3, the Government's central economic objective is to achieve high and stable levels of growth and employment. This requires progress on two fronts: a larger, more skilled workforce; and higher productivity in both the public and private sectors. Raising the productivity of public services is also the means to extend opportunity and security for all and to ensure taxpayers receive value for money.

Part 2 discussed the range of policies designed to improve the employability and quality of the workforce. Part 1 set out the Government's strategy for improving productivity in the private sector. This section examines the productivity of public services.

This chapter looks, first, at how to define public services before discussing why public sector productivity matters and how it can be measured. The subsequent section analyses the market failure and equity considerations that can justify government involvement in the funding and provision of public services. The final section looks at the generic problems that must be overcome to increase productivity in the public sector.

An overview of public services

Public services have traditionally been defined as those services that are directly provided by the public sector. However, this traditional conception of a public service confuses one particular method of delivering public services with their essential characteristics. Economists, such as Besley (2003), argue public services are best defined as those where social returns exceed private returns: that is, the benefits to the public as a whole exceed the benefits received directly by individuals using these services. The focus in this definition is therefore on the consumer rather than the producer – on the service provided, not the mode of provision.

Besley identifies three circumstances where, under his definition, services are truly public. These are:

- where society also benefits from an individual's consumption of a service – such as medical treatment for a contagious disease;
- where society has strongly held beliefs about the minimum standards of service that every citizen has a right to expect – such as universal access to education or decent housing; and
- where individual consumers lack true knowledge about the benefits of consuming a particular service – for instance, children are typically unaware of the full range of opportunities that will result from their education.

Public services are direct determinants of economic prosperity and personal welfare, not only for those people who use them but also for their families, communities and employers. For example, families gain from the education of their children and from health and social services' provision for the sick and elderly. The UK's most disadvantaged communities also benefit significantly from services such as policing that effectively tackle crime and other causes of social exclusion.

High-quality public services also contribute to creating the conditions that enable private businesses to grow and realise their full potential, thereby raising the productivity and prosperity of the economy as a whole. Strong health and education systems, plus an integrated transport network, are necessary in order to deliver an environment in which enterprise can flourish, not least by promoting a healthy, skilled and mobile labour force.

Why does productivity performance m

The productivity performance of public
reasons. In the UK, government expenditu
represents approximately 23 per cent of GDP.[2]
the public services will therefore contribute signifi
ductivity within the economy as a whole, as a direct
well as via the indirect effects on the rest of economy disc

Taxpayers expect value for money from the public serv
finance. People are willing to fund public services that promot
public interest by advancing opportunity and security, but they are n
inclined to pay taxes that finance wasteful expenditure.

Improving public services' productivity is hence an important element of any strategy for raising the rate of sustainable growth, tackling poverty and social exclusion and improving quality of life. This means the resources provided to public services should be used as efficiently as possible. Individual service providers, for example schools and hospitals, must use the resources they receive as efficiently as possible in delivering more and better *outputs* such as medical treatments and school lessons. It also means that the *outcomes* of public services, and their beneficial impacts on society more generally, such as better health and literacy, need to be maximised.

Measuring public services' productivity

Although public services are of critical importance, their productivity is notoriously difficult to measure. This is for a number of reasons, all related to the measurement of outputs and outcomes.

The value of services provided by a private company is determined by the price at which they are sold in the market. Since public services are not normally traded in a market, the outputs of public service providers cannot be quantified in this way. A further characteristic of public services is the distinction between outputs and outcomes. Public services performance is ideally measured in terms of outcomes (such as better public health), since these are the primary concern of citizens, but it is often hard to identify the extent to which these outcomes are caused by the services' outputs rather than other external factors. Additionally, the time lag that can often exist between improvements in the quantity and quality of outputs and the better outcomes they achieve creates an added difficulty in measuring productivity in the public services.

As a result of these difficulties, the measurement of productivity in public services has historically tended to ignore outcomes and outputs, focus instead on the magnitude of inputs. Both in statistical ations and in general debate, increased expenditure on public ces was regarded as equivalent to an identical increase in output. h an assumption is no longer tenable, if it ever was, and efforts are eing made to produce more meaningful estimates of public sector productivity, including the Atkinson Review, undertaken by Sir Tony Atkinson, at the ONS, which is due to present preliminary findings by July 2004 and a final report by January 2005.

The next section looks at ways in which aspects of public service performance are evaluated internationally; across local areas in the UK; and between different service providers.

International comparisons

Few public service outputs or outcomes are measured in the same way across countries, so comparisons must be treated with caution. Nevertheless, when used carefully, international comparisons can give a helpful perspective on UK public services performance, highlighting the countries where best practice can be learnt, or where the UK has strengths worth preserving.

An example of such research comes from the World Health Organisation (2001), which compares the performance of health systems across the world using a number of indicators. Figure 15.1 depicts the UK's performance against its main competitors on one of these

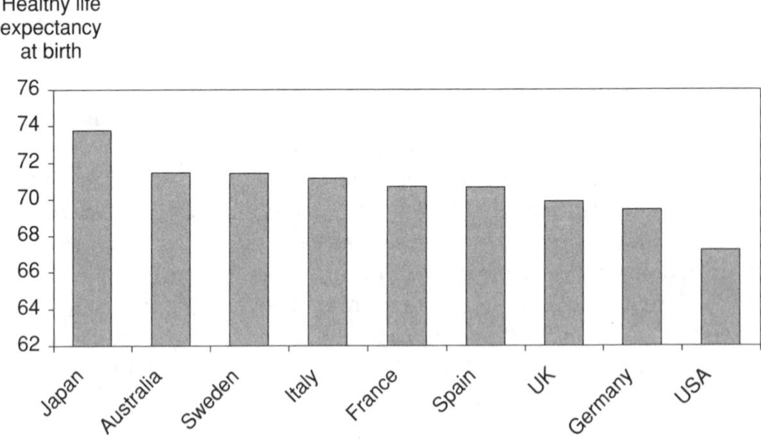

Source: World Health Organisation (2001)

Figure 15.1 Healthy life expectancy within the UK's main competitors

indicators, average life expectancy, adjusted to take into account levels of disability and ill-health.

Life expectancy is affected by many factors other than the efficiency and expenditure of the health service, including the quality of the environment, the state of housing and sanitation facilities, and general cultural attitudes to diet and exercise. Nevertheless, the World Health Organisation found a wide variation in performance in life expectancy and other indicators, even among countries with similar levels of income and health expenditure. Overall, the UK was ranked much higher than many countries, at 19th out of 191, but still below other comparable developed countries.

Increased expenditure on health care is an essential precondition for achieving improved health outcomes, but by itself is not sufficient, as Figure 15.2 illustrates. For example, despite devoting 13 per cent of its GDP to health care, life expectancy in the US is lower than in many other developed nations. Maintaining and enhancing the productivity that allows the UK to produce better results than the US at lower cost is, therefore, an equally important goal.

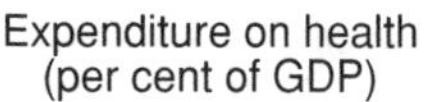

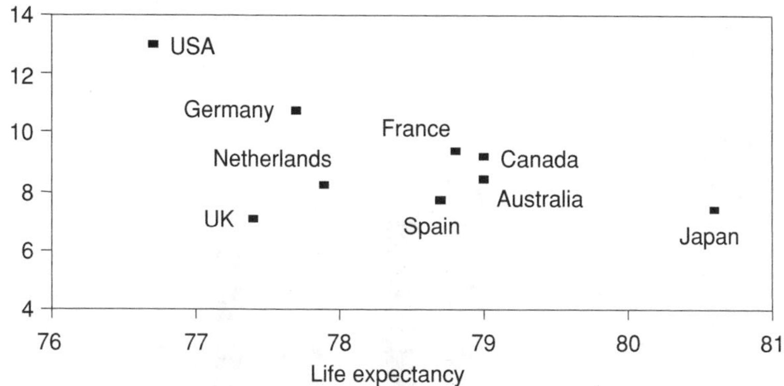

Source: OECD (2002b)

Figure 15.2 Health expenditure and life expectancy

Local variations in performance

In addition to international comparisons of public services' productivity, there is much to be gained from assessing variations across areas within the UK. Robust performance data by area, where they exist, can act to energise commitment to improvement. A notable form of this is the local authority Comprehensive Performance Assessment, developed by the Audit Commission and applied in 2002 to all single-tier and

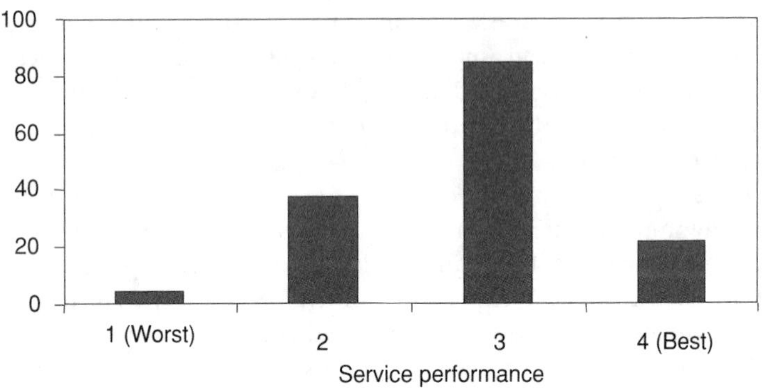

Source: Audit Commission (2002a)

Figure 15.3 Distribution of service performance across local authorities

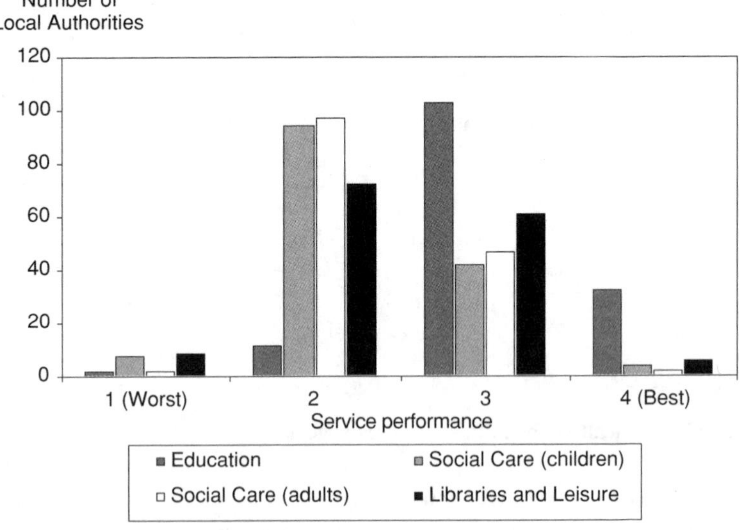

Source: Audit Commission (2002a)

Figure 15.4 Distribution of service performance by service area

county councils in England (Audit Commission 2002a). Using information on the quality of education, housing, social care, environmental and other services provided by each local authority, the Audit Commission was able to make an overall assessment of their quality of service. Figures 15.3 and 15.4 summarise these findings, and show that a large majority of councils are achieving good performance, though a significant number of local authorities have scope for improvement, particularly in social care.

The Comprehensive Performance Assessment also includes a judgement on how well different authorities manage their resources and direct them at priorities. The results show that a local authority's ability to use resources is closely correlated with its overall performance. As Figure 15.5 shows, all councils providing excellent services to the public make good use of their resources, while all councils with poor service scores make poor use of their resources.

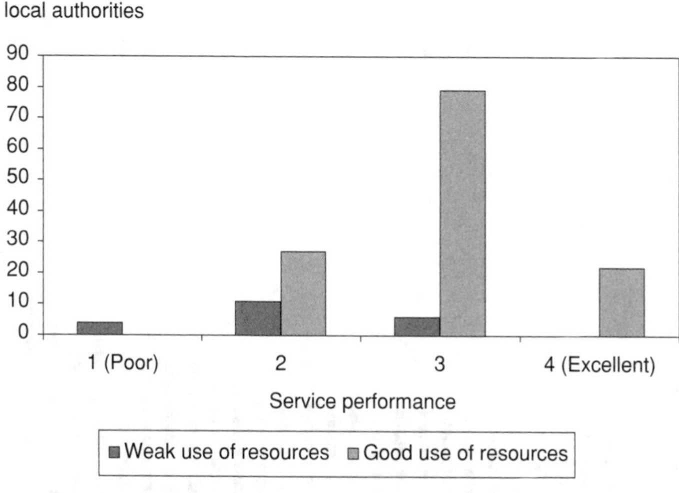

Source: *Audit Commission (2002a)*

Figure 15.5 Local authorities' use of resources and their services' performance

Individual service providers

As well as international and local comparisons, public services productivity also needs to be assessed at the level of the individual service provider. If efficient institutions can be identified, other institutions can be encouraged to improve their performance towards that achieved by

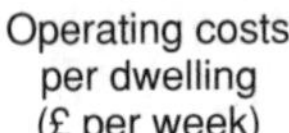

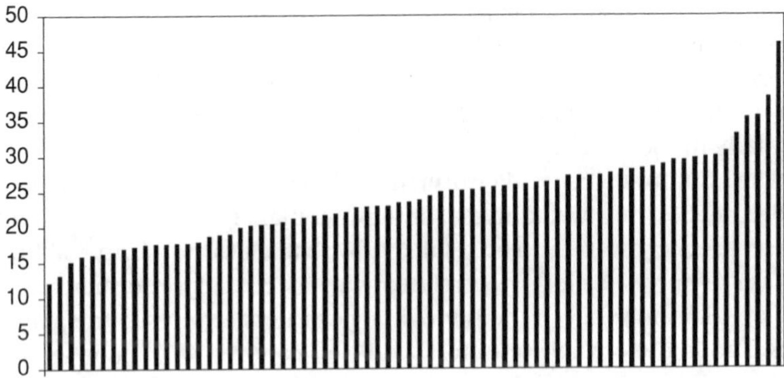

Source: Housing Corporation

Figure 15.6 Operating costs for major Registered Social Landlords in England, 2002

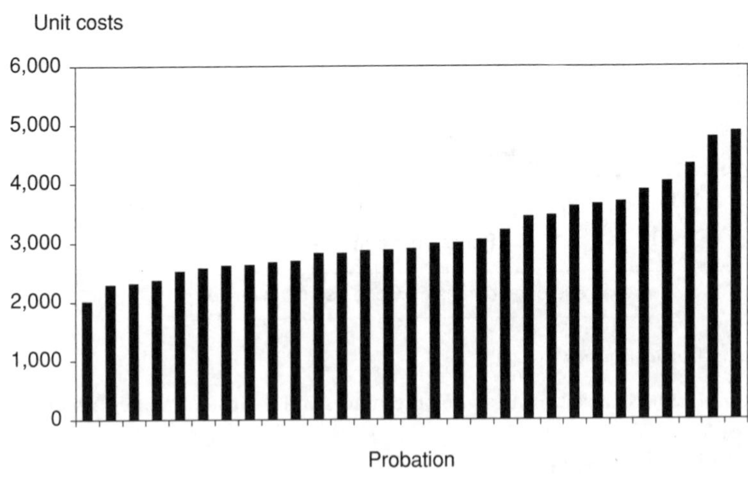

Source: Chartered Institute of Public Finance and Accountancy

Figure 15.7 Unit costs by probation area, 2001–02

the best. As a result, the performance of public services as a whole would significantly improve. This approach, known as benchmarking, is increasingly being applied across the public services.

For example, Figure 15.6 compares the operating costs of different institutions in the area of social housing. It shows a threefold variation in operating costs among major Registered Social Landlords (RSLs) in England. Similar variations occur in many other services. Figure 15.7, for instance, compares the unit costs of probation services in different areas and indicates that they experience a similar order of variation in the cost of punishing and rehabilitating new criminals.

These results suggest room for improvement, but it is important to put them in context. For example, higher costs may be justified where a higher quality of service is being provided. Furthermore, even where quality of service is the same, variations in cost may well be a function of factors outside managers' control, such as the location of dwellings or the types of tenants in the case of social housing.

To summarise, a number of possible methods – comparisons of performance internationally, across local areas in the UK and between different service providers – are available to evaluate public sector performance. Such comparisons show that, while the UK performs reasonably well on an international basis, there are significant variations in performance both across regions and by service provider. This suggests that there is room for improvement in the country's public sector productivity.

The following sections examines the problems that have to be faced in raising public sector productivity and sets out the basis for approach which is being followed.

Efficiency, equity and public services

Part 1 explained how enabling markets to function efficiently is a key part of raising private sector productivity. This is because, in many circumstances, markets are the most effective means of delivering efficient, customer-focused goods and services. In these cases, which include, for example, the markets for services such as electricity and gas, the key role for government has been to strengthen the drivers of efficiency through competition policy.

The special characteristics of public services mean, however, that the wholesale introduction of markets for their delivery would be neither efficient nor equitable. Markets failures can arise in the provision of certain public services, putting efficient customer-focused outcomes at risk. Markets also distribute goods and services solely on the basis of ability to pay, and therefore do not take account of considerations of equity or social justice. Equity is a particularly important factor in public services, given the need to ensure that key services such as health care are provided on the basis of need, and not ability to pay. Just as importantly, in some circumstances, inherent in parts of the public services, market failure are endemic, putting a limit on the potential use of market mechanisms.

The approach for raising public services productivity therefore has to respect the two critical considerations of efficiency and equity. This section describes more fully the market failures and equity considerations associated with public services, and the justification that efficiency and equity provide for government involvement in public service provision.

Efficiency

Turning, first, to efficiency, economic theory suggests that profit-maximising private firms operating in well-functioning markets can be expected to provide efficient, customer-focused services.

However, market mechanisms can be expected to produce desirable outcomes only when certain conditions are met. In particular:

- consumers must possess good information about their needs and the quality of service available from alternative suppliers. In such circumstances, they can use their income to purchase a mix of services that will maximise their welfare;
- firms are operating in a competitive environment (i.e. many suppliers and few barriers to potential new entrants), forcing them to provide high-quality products at least cost to generate custom and stay profitable;
- there are no externalities, so that the production and use of a good or service affects no one other than the firm that provides it and the individual who directly chooses to consume it; and
- the product is not a public good, so that firms are able to identify the individuals who use the service they provide, and able to quantify their consumption of it.

When these conditions are met, there is no efficiency justification for government intervention in markets. But should any of these four conditions not be met, markets may fail to produce efficient outcomes. These market failures can lead to consumers facing excessively high prices, inadequate levels of provision and other inefficiencies.

Importantly, many of these market failures would arise if private providers were given unrestricted freedom to deliver key public services.[3] For instance:

- consumers of public services often lack sufficient information to make an accurate assessment of their needs and of the quality and value for money of alternative suppliers' services. This could lead them to purchase services not appropriate to their needs, and would allow inefficient, low-quality suppliers to remain in the marketplace. Information problems are particularly severe in health care, where patients typically lack sufficient knowledge to judge accurately their medical needs, the range of alternative treatments available or the quality of care they ultimately receive;
- effective competition between different suppliers is not always present. Often public services have natural monopoly characteristics, meaning that only a single firm, or very few firms, could engage in least-cost production. Left unchecked, these firms would wield market power, enabling them to charge excessive prices and restrict their output in order to make excessive profits. Major transport networks typically exhibit natural monopoly characteristics, as do many services supplied to particular localities, such as neighbourhood refuse collection, hospital A&E departments, and schools in sparsely populated areas (Domberger and Jensen 1998);
- Spillovers, or externalities, arise when consumption of a service affects the wider community in addition to those people who directly use it. Individuals making their own personal choices are unlikely to consider the wider social effects when deciding how much of a service to consume, which would lead to an inefficient level of consumption from the perspective of society as a whole. Examples of externalities include medical treatment for a contagious disease, or an individual's education that raises the productivity not only of that individual but also of those people working with that individual; and
- if there are no limits on the number of people who can simultaneously use a service and if it is hard to prevent people benefiting from it, then the service fulfils the non-rival and non-excludable characteristics of a public good. These services will be under supplied by the market, since every individual will have an incentive to free ride on the provision funded by other users. Defence and the criminal justice system are two services that fulfil

the characteristics of a public good, since it would be difficult for a private supplier to calculate or charge individuals a price that accurately reflected their use of a service.

As described above, public services generally exhibit various market failures that would lead to inefficient levels of price and output if they were bought and sold in unfettered markets. Government intervention or financing in such circumstances may make markets work more efficiently, by addressing the market failures but, in many cases, this will not be feasible. A further option for government is then to provide the service itself, instead of relying on markets. The circumstances where public provision represents the most efficient policy option are discussed more fully below. Before that, the second key objective for the public services – equity – is considered.

Equity

In addition to the need to tackle market failures, the pursuit of equity provides a second justification for public sector involvement in the provision of certain services.

Private firms, operating in markets, provide goods and services on the basis of consumers' ability to pay. But using ability to pay as the criterion for the distribution of services, such as medical treatment or education that meet basic human needs does not take equity into consideration. It is more natural that these services should be distributed in an equitable way, using criteria that reflect need. It is equally important that public services are of a sufficiently high quality to meet these needs satisfactorily. These considerations translate into specific equity objectives for the key public services, such as a comprehensive, high quality, National Health Service available on the basis of clinical need.

Equity objectives such as these can be used to justify varying kinds of public sector involvement in public services delivery. Ensuring that access is based on need alone requires government to fund all or part of the costs incurred by those supplying public services. It can do so by negotiating contracts with private providers, or by giving individual consumers the resources they require to purchase services for themselves. An important third option is for the public sector to both fund and provide a public service, as with the NHS. The circumstances where equity as well as efficiency considerations require public funding to be accompanied by public provision are described below.

The limits of markets

The above subsections explained why, for every public service, a central question is whether the public interest can best be advanced by government intervening to make markets work better, or by directly providing the service itself. It is therefore important to recognise the limits of markets. Those circumstances where it can be both more efficient and more equitable for the public sector to fund and provide a public service include:

- when there are severe market failures or important equity considerations that would require extensive intervention by government in the conduct of private service providers to avoid inefficient outcomes. A regulator of private health care provision, for instance, would be required to undertake extensive and detailed monitoring of service providers, which would be both difficult and expensive. In such circumstances, the high regulatory costs associated with regulating private markets mean that public provision represents a more cost-effective method of delivering efficient and equitable services (Bailey 2002);
- where services suffer from multiple market failures, Lipsey and Lancaster (1956) suggest that government intervention, which is able to remedy only some of the distortions they create, can actually lead to more inefficient 'third best' outcomes. Public provision, which bypasses these market failures altogether, will be more effective at raising efficiency in these circumstances;
- when it would be extremely difficult for government to write and enforce effectively a contract with a private-sector service provider. This situation can arise, for example, if for reasons of equity the government is trying to ensure users will receive a certain quality of service that cannot be accurately specified in a contract. In this situation of non-contractible quality, profit-maximising private suppliers would have an incentive to reduce quality if it could not be observed or measured by government.[4] Public provision, in contrast, can ensure that quality of service is put ahead of the need to make profits. Public servants can, in turn, put duty, obligation and service before profit or personal reward. This *public service ethos* is discussed more fully in Box 15.1; and
- where contracts may leave private suppliers insufficiently responsive to unforeseeable changes in requirements for the provision of certain public services. This situation arises if

Box 15.1 The public service ethos

The public sector employs around 5 million people, of whom the largest groups work in the key public services of education and health. Understanding the motivations of this workforce is important in designing incentive systems that are appropriate and effective in encouraging performance. Deci and Ryan (1985), for instance, describe how solely financial incentives or crude threats of punishment can actually impair performance, by driving out the so-called *intrinsic* motivations that encourage people to undertake activities 'for their own sake'. It is equally important to recognise any special attributes required of those who provide certain public services when making a judgement between public and private modes of provision.

A recent Audit Commission (2002b) report on recruitment and retention in the public services found that for 42 per cent 'making a positive difference' was the first or second most important reason for pursuing a career in the public services. Thirty-nine per cent also cited the opportunity to serve people – especially children – as a significant motivating factor. It can be argued that these responses reflect a wider set of values that have traditionally been held by public sector employees. Known as the 'public service ethos', it includes:

- *a commitment to furthering social welfare*, rather than maximising personal gain;
- *a dedication to meeting the needs of service users*, irrespective of their ability to pay;
- *recognition of a duty to use professional expertise responsibly*, building a relationship with service users based on trust – such as that which exists between doctors and their patients; and
- *valuing cooperation rather than competition* between different providers of the same service, such as teachers.

appropriate objectives for the service frequently change, due to uncertainties about the exact specifications of the service required, even in the short term. Public sector provision, therefore, gives assurance that services, such as the armed forces, are able to respond rapidly to unforeseeable demands.

As an example, Box 15.2 shows how these considerations provide a strong argument for a publicly funded, publicly provided National Health Service. Similar considerations also hold for the public financing and provision of other key public services, notably school education, defence and the criminal justice system.

Box 15.2 Efficiency, equity and the National Health Service

A number of deeply entrenched market failures, plus the equity concern that access to health care should be based on clinical need and not ability to pay, are reflected in the design of the NHS.

People are typically unable to predict their future health care needs, and are naturally concerned about its potentially high cost. In these circumstances, private insurance, which pools clients' risks, might appear to be a means of funding health care. However, market failures exist in private insurance markets for health care, such as asymmetric information, moral hazard and adverse selection, that can lead to inefficient and inequitable outcomes. For example:

- insurers may fail to cover some people or conditions at all;
- insurers may set excessively high premiums or simply refuse to cover 'bad risk' clients, such as those suffering from chronic or terminal medical conditions;
- incentives are created for people to under-insure to demonstrate that they are low risk clients; and
- high premiums arise from the transaction costs incurred when insurers conduct risk profiling and attempt to manage uncertainty.

Social insurance can avoid most of these problems but creates efficiency losses by loading all the costs of health care onto one subset of the tax base – employers and their employees. Additional administrative costs are also created under social insurance schemes because they duplicate the existing tax system. Together, these factors create a strong case for tax-funded health care.

The case for public provision of health care, meanwhile, rests on the presence of extensive market failures on both the demand and supply side that could not be effectively or efficiently resolved by government regulation alone:

- *price signals do not always work*: consumers may lack sufficient information to make optimal choices about their health care needs;
- *the consumer is not sovereign*: asymmetries of information between consumers and health care providers can create a risk of supplier-induced demand;
- *there is a potential abuse of monopoly power*: economies of scale (especially in emergency and specialist care) create local monopolies, and high barriers to entry, and self-accreditation can lead to professional monopolies;
- *it is hard to write and enforce contracts*: the non-standardised, patient-specific nature of medicine makes it hard to judge or contract for specific outcomes; and
- *it is difficult to let failing hospitals close*: individuals are entitled to expect continuous, high-quality, health care wherever they may live.

However, these arguments for a publicly funded, publicly provided NHS do not constitute a reason for not making such a service as efficient as possible.

Nevertheless, even when a market is inappropriate, policy design must avoid the trap of simply replacing market failure with state failure and, applying the public interest test, achieve equity and efficiency, diversity and choice. Choice and equity in the provision of public services is discussed further in Box 15.3.

Box 15.3 Individual choice in public services

The Government is committed to ensuring that public services achieve outcomes that enable citizens to lead fulfilling and productive lives. To this end it is committed to achieving and maintaining world-class standards in public services that are accessible to all on the basis of need. It is also committing to responsive and diverse public services that can address the diversity of need and circumstances among citizens and localities. Increasing choice is a key way in which public services can be more tailored to individual and local need.

The NHS, for example, has sought to increase choices available to patients, as a means to improve patient and user experience, by offering a choice of hospital for patients waiting over six months for elective surgery, and from December 2005 a choice of hospital to every patient at the point of referral from their GP. The Government is also extending choice in education, by enabling more pupils and parents to have a wider choice of schooling by working directly with LEAs, poor-performing schools and the local community to address weak leadership and raise standards. The enterprise pilots, which started in September 2003 following the Davies Review of enterprise and education, also provides a good example of different learning experiences and skills that can widen meaningful choice options in line with particular pupils' needs. In social housing, there is now greater choice in letting for tenants who can make their own trade-offs between availability and desirability rather than simply being allocated housing by the landlord. In social services, direct payments are empowering 5,000 disabled people so they can purchase the mix of social care support that suits them best, increasing independences and improving satisfaction.

The scope for markets

While there are limits in what the markets can deliver in some public services, there are some cases where private sector suppliers and market mechanisms can deliver the best diverse outcomes for public services. For example, the expertise of private sector contractors to deliver cost-effective high-quality investment in the infrastructure supporting a range of public services can be, and has been, used to good effect (see Box 15.3). This use of the private sector to deliver public services is termed 'Public Private Partnership' (PPP).

Box 15.3 Examples of Public Private Partnerships

Private sector investment through PPP contracts typically makes up between 10 and 15 per cent of total investment in any one year. By 2005, the Government expects that contracts worth at least £12 billion will have been signed, with many other deals in procurement. PPPs are already being utilised to deliver successful projects, including:

- *delivering new hospitals*. Since 1997, Private Finance Initiatives (PFIs) have provided 34 new hospitals with more in construction or procurement. Successful projects to date include the new Dartford and Gravesham hospital – an acute general hospital on the Darent Valley site, which consolidates services from three hospitals into a single modern, flexible accommodation. The hospital was open in just 44 months – far faster than would have been the case under a conventional public procurement. In addition to PFIs, the NHS is also taking advantage of spare capacity in the private sector to secure faster treatment for patients requiring routine procedures, without jeopardising efficiency or equity;
- *funding of the Ten-Year Transport Plan*. Around £56 billion is expected to be funded through private sector finance, including PPPs. Successful projects to date include the extension of the Docklands Light Railway, which was completed in 1999. This project had a capital value of £200 million, and was delivered within budget and two months early; and
- *improving schools*. 96 PFI projects, with a total value of £1.3 billion, and covering over 560 schools, have been signed. Successful projects to date include the Barnhill Community School in Middlesex, a new school providing state-of-the-art facilities to educate 1,450 children.

Public Private Partnerships bring public and private sectors together in long term partnership for mutual benefit. The PPP label covers a wide range of different types of partnership including the Private Finance Initiative (PFI), where the public sector contracts to purchase quality services on a long-term basis so as to take advantage of private sector management skills incentivised by having private finance at risk.

PPP contracts are pursued only where they represent the best value for money option. Where this is the case, they offer a number of important benefits. Well-designed incentive structures are a crucial part of this. They can, for example, be used to move the companies involved to deliver high levels of service over the long term, or ensure that public assets are delivered on time and to budget. Moreover, by focusing attention on the outcome that a service should deliver, PPPs allow new scope for private sector innovation in the way those outcomes are delivered.

Raising productivity in publicly funded, publicly provided services

For those public services that, on grounds of efficiency and equity, are most effectively provided by the public sector, the task is to find means for them to achieve higher productivity and satisfy the needs and choices of a diverse range of consumers of public services. Several studies, discussed below, have highlighted a number of generic issues.

Evidence suggests that public service providers are helped to achieve high productivity if they have a clear understanding of the objectives they are expected to be pursuing. For instance, the Audit Commission (2001a) has found that those local service providers that have identified a small number of core goals have been most successful in achieving large and durable improvements in performance. A National Audit Office (2001a) report on value for money within the public sector also found that a failure to specify the required outputs properly in advance was the root cause of cost overruns in many information technology-related projects.

Another Audit Commission (2001b) study identified inadequate prioritisation as a further factor that compromises service delivery. This analysis, which was based on 600 inspection reports on local authorities, found that prioritisation presented a special challenge for those charged with delivering public services, since they were often trying to achieve a number of different objectives at the same time. This finding is supported by academic research. Dixit (2000), for instance, lists the multiple goals of education as imparting basic skills to children; preparing them for work; instilling ideals of citizenship; and fostering emotional growth. Although they are not contradictory, these goals compete for resources and for the attention of teachers.[5] Clear prioritisation in such circumstances is crucial.

Public service providers also frequently encounter information problems. Complex health services, for instance, can be provided only if those managing and delivering the services have access to reliable, well-structured and timely information. The Commission for Health Improvement (2002), drawing on its reviews of clinical governance in 175 NHS Trusts found, however, that doctors and nurses sometimes lack ready access to the information they need to treat patients effectively.

Robust accountability structures, with clarity about roles and responsibilities, are also essential to the delivery of high-quality public services. A recent Public Services Productivity Panel (2002) report found that the absence of well-designed accountability structures in the public services

– which frequently have a national, regional and local dimension – has often undermined efforts to achieve high performance.

There is also an issue about customer focus and what users of public services want from the services they receive. A possible explanation for this can be found in the results of the Public Services Productivity Panel (2001) report on 'Customer-Focused Government', which found that there is often considerable ambiguity within the public services concerning who their main customers actually were.

Private sector firms generally face a similar set of managerial issues, but the market environment in which they operate usually forces them to adopt behaviours that mitigate the associated problems. In particular:

- firms are subject to an objective of maximising profits for their owners and shareholders that, at least in part, influences their behaviour. The system of corporate ownership and control means that effective pressure can be brought to bear at all levels of the delivery chain to serve this objective; and
- consumers' freedom to purchase any products they can afford (consumer sovereignty) and the presence of competitors, both create incentives for individual firms to keep their prices low and produce goods and services that satisfy consumers' needs. Offering value for money and maintaining customer focus is therefore crucial to a firm's survival.

Clearly, not all firms fit this stylised textbook model, but when these factors are present and working well they provide clarity and focus. Specifically:

1. *Objectives* – which are determined by market forces, and managers ensure that the whole firm pursues them.
2. *Prioritisation* – priorities are similarly determined. Firms concentrate on producing those products that sell best in the market and are likely to earn them the highest profits.
3. *Information* – competitive markets enable customers to signal the value they put on goods and services through the prices they are prepared to pay. Strong focus on profit maximisation ensures that firms have a good reason to monitor their costs closely.
4. *Accountability* – it is in shareholders' interests that they hold managers fully to account, to ensure that managers are fully devoting their efforts to the goal of profit maximisation.
5. *Customer focus* – maintaining close attention to customers' needs and preferences is essential if firms are to produce goods and services that will earn them a profit.

Accordingly, a key part of the strategy to improve public services productivity has to be to find ways of providing the same clarity and focus, in the absence of market mechanisms to do this. The Government's approach towards this is set out in the next chapter 'Public Service Reform'.

Conclusion

This chapter has explained why raising the productivity of public services is an important part of any strategy to achieve high and stable levels of growth and employment. Public services not only account for a significant proportion of national output in their own right, but also help create the conditions in which private enterprise can flourish, thereby raising productivity across the whole economy. Achieving higher productivity in the public services will produce additional benefits, including offering taxpayers better value for money and delivering higher quality services for consumers.

Comparisons of public services' expenditure and outcomes across countries, and between areas and providers within the UK, demonstrate that it is not just the level of resources that matters in generating improved outcomes for the public, but also the way those resources are used. In addition to tackling areas of under-investment, therefore, the task has been to identify the underlying problems that constrain public services' productivity and devise an effective strategy to overcome them.

As the analysis presented in this chapter has shown, the special characteristics of public services mean that the wholesale introduction of markets for their delivery would be neither efficient nor equitable. Markets distribute goods and services solely on the basis of ability to pay, not in terms of equity. Markets can also fail, and efficient, customer-focused outcomes are then put at risk.

The challenge, therefore, is to design a framework for raising the productivity of those key public services, such as health care, where public finance and provision best serve the public interest. As discussed, issues such as clarity of objectives, prioritisation, availability of information, accountability and customer focus are all important to this. The framework needs to deal adequately with the challenges they present, in the absence of a market environment. Chapter 16 sets out the Government approach being taken to meet this challenge.

16
Public Service Reform

This chapter sets out the Government's framework being employed for improving public service performance; including a focus on outcomes, constrained discretion by service providers and improved governance of public services. It shows how the framework has underpinned the policies towards the key public services and gives examples to demonstrate a range of reforms in public services.

Introduction

The previous chapter explained why the productivity of public services is an important part of any strategy to achieve high and stable levels of growth and employment. It identified some of the fundamental problems faced by public service organisations in improving performance and explained why they arise.

This chapter sets out the framework for raising the performance of public services. The first section describes the three key policy building blocks (a focus on outcomes, constrained discretion by service providers and improved governance of public services) and how they together form a single framework for raising public services productivity. The following section examines how this framework has underpinned the Government's policies towards the key public services. Finally, examples are used to demonstrate the range of reforms in the public services that this framework has engendered.

The building blocks of policy

The framework for meeting the public service productivity challenge is constructed from three 'building blocks':

1. *A focus on outcomes*, placing improvements in public services' outcomes as the central aim of policy rather than focusing solely on inputs.
2. *Constrained discretion for local service providers*, increasing their operational freedoms and flexibilities, subject to appropriate minimum standards and regular performance monitoring.
3. *Improved governance of public services*, reforming institutions to reflect the importance of clear objectives, appropriate incentives and good performance information in the achievement of higher productivity.

A focus on outcomes

At the heart of the Government's approach to improving public services' productivity is the proposition that the performance of public services should be judged on the basis of the outcomes achieved by these services. For example, the performance of the health service should be assessed in terms of the results achieved in improving the nations' health, not in terms of the numbers of hospital staff or operating theatres. This outcomes-focused approach means that choices between different methods of delivering public services should be based solely on an assessment of which option is most likely to deliver improved outcomes (for example, better health for the nation), and not be tied to a particular set of inputs (for example, the number of nurses), type of output (number of operations or amount of medication prescribed) or mode of provision (public or private).

A constrained discretion model for local service providers

For many years, UK public services were characterised by a 'command and control' framework, in which central planners imposed uniform solutions on the providers of public services to suit all circumstances. But this approach has limitations, making it unsuitable for many key public services[1] as:

- local initiative is suppressed, which may constrain innovation and undermine employees' morale; and
- local needs and circumstances are ignored, potentially leading to the delivery of one-size-fits-all, poor-quality services to diverse communities.

The weaknesses of the command and control approach arise because it detaches those responsible for the design and delivery of public services from the customers and local communities they serve. A more productive approach to the management of many public services is to grant more responsibility for operational decisions to those individuals best placed to understand customers' needs and issues involved in satisfying those needs.

A growing literature,[2] which has become known as the 'new localism' school, argues that these individuals may often be at the local service level, since:

- empowered local service providers have the flexibility to tailor services to reflect the needs, preferences and circumstances of the communities they serve;
- greater discretion over the use of their funds enables local providers to develop innovative approaches to service delivery;
- increased responsibility for the services they deliver can generate a greater commitment among local providers to achieving improved outcomes in their area; and
- a number of autonomous local service providers can improve the ability to monitor performance, by allowing comparisons to be made between the achievements of different providers operating in similar circumstances.

These arguments have force, and suggest that a move away from centralised, top-down, decision-making in the public services offers potential benefits.

However, increased local flexibility in delivery also risks creating local variations in the quality of public services. Additional discretion for local service providers must therefore be constrained by appropriate accountability mechanisms that define acceptable service standards and effectively monitor service providers' performance.

It is this constrained discretion which forms the second building block of the strategy for raising public services' productivity. Box 16.1 describes the central role the concept of constrained discretion has in the new framework for monetary policy.

Improved governance of public services

Robust and well-functioning accountability arrangements are at the heart of the constrained discretion model. More generally, the outcomes achieved by public service providers will be enhanced if the governance structures they are subject to are well designed to deal with issues such as clarity of objectives, prioritisation and information, set out in the previous chapter.

Box 16.1 Constrained discretion and the monetary policy framework

The concept of constrained discretion underpins the Government's framework for monetary policy, which was introduced shortly after it entered office in May 1997, and is detailed further in Balls and O'Donnell (2002).

The Bank of England was granted operational independence to set interest rates, but has to exercise this power to meet an inflation target set by the Government. The framework recognises that the economy can be subject to unexpected events which can cause inflation to depart from its desired level, but the onus is on the Bank's Monetary Policy Committee (MPC) to explain how it proposes to return inflation back to target. Should inflation deviate by more than one percentage point below or above the target, the Governor of the Bank of England is required to write an Open Letter to the Chancellor of the Exchequer, explaining why the divergence has occurred, the action being taken to deal with it, the period within which inflation is expected to return to target, and how this approach is consistent with the Government's objectives for growth and employment.

Under this new framework, the Bank of England is *constrained* by the Government's inflation target and the requirement for the MPC to account for its actions, but the Bank is also granted new *discretion* to respond flexibly to changing economic conditions. The strategy for raising public services' productivity offers similarly constrained discretion to front-line service providers, by enabling them to exercise greater operational autonomy but subject to constraints such as minimum service standards and regular performance monitoring.

Economic theory offers an established body of thought, known as principal-agent theory, which addresses the issue of organisational governance.[3] The theory offers three key insights into the characteristics of effective governance structures that have informed the framework for raising public services' productivity. In particular:

- objectives must be specified to ensure that service providers are clear about their strategic direction and can identify their priorities correctly. They also provide a benchmark for performance assessment;
- incentives for public service providers are necessary to ensure they pursue their objectives. Well-designed incentive systems recognise the ethos that motivates public service employees, reward success and expose poor performance so that it can be addressed; and
- information is required for objectives to be established and for incentive systems to be designed. Performance also needs to be monitored so that service providers can be rewarded or sanctioned

accordingly, while local communities are entitled to clear information about the performance of their public services.

It follows that public services should have governance structures which support the setting of clear objectives, the design of appropriate incentives and the effective utilisation of information. A particular question is to what degree should they be held to account nationally, regionally or locally?

Central government may be well suited to governing certain public services, especially where nationwide objectives and standards are required to:

- ensure consistently high quality of service wherever people may live;
- provide clear standards by which services are judged, allowing incentives to be offered on the basis of performance against targets; and
- provide a clear focus for public service providers, and inject an ambition and urgency for improved performance.

But national governance structures also have their weaknesses. While centralised objective setting and performance management may be appropriate for services such as national defence, in other areas it can lead to excessive central control over the objectives and conduct of public services, which fails to reflect the priorities or circumstances of the communities they actually serve.

The Government's task is therefore to identify those public services whose performance could be improved by devolving more responsibility for their governance to democratic institutions at the regional or local level. In particular, strengthened regional or local governance offers the prospect of:

- improved objective setting for public service providers, to reflect more accurately the needs and priorities of those they serve;
- more appropriate incentive schemes for service providers, for instance by taking account of local labour market conditions;
- better monitoring of public services' performance, by creating greater opportunities for service users and other stakeholders to provide feedback on service quality;
- more effective coordination of numerous local service providers to meet each community's full range of needs;

- better coordination of monitoring and inspection regimes to reduce the burdens on local public service providers; and
- greater citizen participation in the management of local public services, encouraging greater social cohesion and community identity.[4]

But the potential benefits of governance being based on greater local accountability must be weighed against its potential problems, including the creation of unacceptable variations in the quality of services across the country, and the loss of administrative economies. It would also be important that regional or local bodies, granted new responsibilities for the governance of public services, had sufficient powers, expertise and information to perform their new role effectively. Success would also depend on the active and informed participation of the communities they represent.

The framework for raising public services productivity

The building blocks set out above represent the basis of the Government's strategy for raising productivity within the public services. They translate into a clear framework to guide those designing and implementing policy.

1. *Clear long-term goals, expressed as desired outcomes.* Clear objectives provide a comprehensive statement of priorities and sense of direction for all those involved in the delivery of public services.
2. *Greater discretion for local service providers, constrained by effective governance structures.* By allowing greater discretion, service providers will have more opportunities to innovate, design and develop services around the needs and priorities of their communities. Decentralisation of the governance of public services may not be desirable or practical in all circumstances, but many public services will be more effectively governed by regional or local bodies, with better knowledge about providers' performance and the needs of the communities they serve. Greater local discretion for providers must, however, be constrained by effective governance structures to ensure accountability and value for money
3. *Improved information about performance.* High-quality, reliable information about the performance of public services is vital if sustained pressure for improvement is to be created. Independent and effective arrangements for audit and inspection, for instance, are

an important means of ensuring that the performance of departments and agencies is closely monitored and reported. Those who govern and use public services therefore need to receive regular, externally validated, information on their performance.

4. *Better incentives for service providers to meet users' needs.* The incentive structure needs to be based around greater operational flexibility and extra funding, and to be designed to reward the most successful public services' providers and support continuous improvement in standards. Where public service providers are not meeting required standards, the Government needs to intervene to ensure that action is taken to improve performance.

Table 16.1 sets out how this framework has informed the Government's policy reforms in four key public service areas: health, education, criminal justice, and transport.

Public service reforms

Resourcing of public service reforms

Sound public finances lay the foundations for economic stability and for investment in public services. Building on the macroeconomic framework detailed in *Reforming Britain's Economic and Financial Policy: Towards Greater Economic Stability* (Balls and O'Donnell 2002), and the firm fiscal rules which are part of that framework, fixed three-year Departmental Expenditure Limits (DELs), with separate budgets for capital and current spending, give departments certainty to plan over the medium term. Departments are now also able to carry any underspend in one year forward to the next, through end-year flexibility, removing the incentives towards wasteful end-of-year spending. Resource accounts and budgets that reflect full economic costs have also been introduced, giving departments new incentives to maximise benefits from their assets and manage liabilities more effectively.

Working within these spending rules, resources going into the public services have increased significantly since 1997. Between 1997/98 and 2002/03, average real terms growth in spending on health was 6.3 per cent a year; and on education 5.1 per cent a year. In addition to this, the 2002 Spending Review (SR2002), which sets the spending plans for 2003/04–2005/06, made a further £61 billion available for the public services, with the greatest increases targeted on the priority services of health, education and transport.

Table 16.1 Major public service reforms since 1997

	Health	Education	Criminal Justice	Transport
Clear long-term goals, expressed as desired outcomes	Ten-Year Plan with objectives for increased resources. Target to reduce inequalities in health outcomes by 10% as measured by infant mortality and life expectancy.	National targets for attainment. Floor targets for every school and Local Education Authority. Streamlined National Curriculum.	Five-year crime reduction targets. New target to reduce the gap between the best and worst performing Crime and Disorder Reduction Partnership areas.	Ten-Year Plan with targets to be delivered by 2010, and a review ongoing to roll it forward to 2016. Minimum service standards for train operating companies and London Underground.
Greater discretion for local service providers, constrained by effective governance structures	Primary Care Trusts introduced in April 1999. Foundation Trust proposals announced in December 2002.	Greater local flexibility on pay and recruitment in schools and less ring-fencing of budgets. Increase in School Standards Grant paid to each head teacher.	More funding to be allocated to the front line through police Basic Command Units (BCUs) to address local priorities.	Local transport plans introduced. Local transport public service agreements (PSAs).
Improved information about performance	NHS hospital cost and quality benchmarking. New independent Commission for Healthcare Audit and Inspection announced in 2002. Publication of star ratings for all NHS organisations.	National league tables of school performance. Increased frequency of Ofsted inspections for weaker schools and new inspection framework from 2003.	Police Best Value Regime. Publication of police performance monitors. Consolidating and developing the role of the new Police Standards Unit.	Local congestion benchmarks. Strategic Rail Authority established, publishing performance data (e.g. punctuality) on the Train Operating Companies.
Better incentives for service providers to meet users' needs	High performing hospitals rewarded with greater autonomy, less monitoring; automatic access to discretionary capital funds. New hospital funding arrangements will sharpen incentives, support patient choice, encourage contestability and improve value for money.	Head teachers can earn more autonomy in return for strong performance. Leadership Incentive Grant. Top-performing Further Education colleges to be given higher funding, and receive lighter inspection.	Police force and BCU funding to be linked to performance against PSA target. New management for failing prisons through contracting out.	Local delivery incentives through local transport plans give greater long-term focus and stability.

However, providing adequate resources is a necessary but not sufficient condition for improving public services. For this to be achieved, and for resources to be translated into outcomes, a programme of reform, following the framework set out in the previous section, has been put in place to match the additional investment.

Clear long-term goals, expressed as desired outcomes

Public Service Agreements

The approach to clarifying public services' objectives and setting firm standards is based on a series of agreements. These agreements are known as Public Service Agreements (PSAs) and are a means of linking objectives, outcomes and funding. PSAs are negotiated between the Treasury and spending departments at each Spending Review (every two years or so), and are structured so that a statement of aims is broken down into a series of objectives. Objectives are then matched by targets stating the outcomes and outputs that spending departments agree to deliver in return for funding.

PSAs represent a new approach. They replace a system where goals were imprecise and funding was tied only loosely, if at all, to delivery. PSAs create a powerful framework for translating high-level aims into practical policies for change, and provide a judicious constraint on the behaviour of service providers. The potential benefits of PSAs include:

- providing direction and focus to service providers efforts, by clearly setting out the Government's objectives;
- nurturing ambition within the public services, by setting challenging targets and raising expectations;
- increasing public services' accountability, by tying resources to the pursuit of specific objectives; and
- enhancing equity, by setting national service standards that users can expect, and establishing floor targets for every provider to exceed.

As part of SR2002, new PSA performance targets were agreed for all of the public services for 2003–06. Key examples are described in Box 16.2. PSA targets have played a key role in achieving change, for example in relation to literacy and numeracy in schools and waiting times in hospitals.

Box 16.2 New Public Service Agreements for 2003–06

New PSAs were published as an integral part of the Government's spending plans in SR2002. New or revised PSA targets include the following:

- *Education* – to raise standards in schools and colleges so the proportion of those aged 16 who get qualifications equivalent to five GCSEs at Grade A*–C rises by two percentage points a year, and in all schools at least 20 per cent of pupils achieve this standard by 2004, rising to 25 per cent by 2006.
- *Health* – to reduce the maximum waiting time for an outpatient appointment to three months, and the maximum waiting time for an inpatient treatment to six months by the end of 2005; and to achieve further reductions with the aim of reducing the maximum inpatient and day-case waiting time to three months by 2008.
- *Crime* – to reduce crime and the fear of crime; improve performance overall, including reducing vehicle crime by 30 per cent between 1998/99 and 2004; domestic burglary by 25 per cent between 1998/99 and 2005; and for robbery in the ten Street Crime Initiative areas by 14 per cent between 1999/2000 and 2005.
- *Housing* – by 2010, to bring all social housing into decent condition, with most of this improvement taking place in deprived areas, and to increase the proportion of private housing in decent condition occupied by vulnerable groups.

Extending PSAs

PSAs are most successful where:

- they focus on outcomes rather than process, thus empowering providers to develop their own approach to service delivery;
- they are stretching but achievable;
- they are used judiciously and genuinely focus on the strategic outcomes wanted – the trend in successive spending reviews has been towards fewer rather than more targets;
- they are part of a coherent package of mechanisms to drive up performance – targets complement but cannot substitute for good management; and
- front-line service providers are fully involved at the target setting stage, maximising ownership and minimising perverse incentives.

Local Public Service Agreements are also being extended and strengthened. Local PSAs involve local authorities agreeing with central government a number of targets, some determined by central government and others by local priorities, with freedom and flexibilities and reward money if targets are met.

As PSA targets begin to be achieved and national standards established, consideration is being given to how the role of local communities can be further strengthened. The new approach to this, as detailed in the Devolved Decision Making Review[5] on targets and local performance management, allows for fewer nationally set targets and a greater focus on locally determined outcomes, developing a stronger local performance management capacity. In addition, the approach looks for ways to eliminate unnecessary bureaucracy and introduce more transparent and regular reporting of data, to encourage greater local pressure for improvement.

An important extension of PSAs are the Government's longer term frameworks, which help to clarify the objectives for specific public services and particular localities. The ten-year NHS plan, for example, was published in July 2000 and set out a series of objectives to be delivered with the significant, sustained increases in resources that the NHS is receiving.

Other policy initiatives, such as the streamlined national curriculum for schools, can be seen as national reforms that make their operational impact at a more local level. Fixing the target at school level locates the performance issue where the service is actually delivered and where failure to deliver can do most damage. This approach avoids the problem of average area targets, which may conceal a long tail of under achievement. As a result, an objective has been set for each relevant public service to improve its average level of performance by raising standards among the worst performers towards those of the best. For example, in SR2002, new 'floor targets' were set for each school with the aim of guaranteeing that minimum standards are met in every school in every area. A similar rationale lies behind the target of reducing the gap between the best and worst performing Crime and Disorder Reduction Partnership areas[6].

Greater discretion for local service providers, constrained by effective governance structures

The programme of public service reform focuses on giving local service providers more freedom and flexibility to take forward delivery of agreed PSA targets. This constrained discretion is designed to give service providers the freedom to innovate and improve the services they provide, within governance structures that enforce high standards.

Local authorities have a key role in delivering more than 40 of the Government's PSAs, either as the lead front-line agency or as a principal partner of other agencies. As already discussed, Local PSAs are being negotiated between central government and individual unitary and county councils. Each council commits to achieving 'stretched' performance across about a dozen targets that reflect a balance of central government PSAs and local priorities. As a result, every Local PSA is different. Typically, Local PSAs include targets on educational attainment, employment, social services, health, housing, waste, transport, and crime reduction. Bespoke negotiation means they can be focused on those areas most in need of improvement.

Local PSA targets are outcome-focused, and how they are achieved is a matter for the local authority. Central government may, however, agree to provide specified freedoms and flexibilities in order to facilitate delivery. A substantial reward grant is payable for achieving targets, along with pump-priming funds to kick-start the process.

The first round of Local PSAs was piloted from April 2001. In SR2002, the Government announced that it was committed to a second round of local PSAs. Building on local government's enthusiastic response to the first round, central government is working with local authorities and the Local Government Association in developing the shape of the second round.

Major changes in the structure and funding of the NHS have been made in order to shift resources and decision-making closer to local people. The establishment of Primary Care Trusts (PCTs) is a key component in the plans for decentralising and devolving power in the NHS to local communities. These trusts have been introduced in phases since April 1999 and, with the establishment of 138 new PCTs in April 2002, there are now just over 300. PCTs are run by GPs, nurses and other health and social care professionals, together with representatives of patients and the community.

PCTs are responsible for determining the health needs of local people and commissioning the right mix of services to meet these, including: hospitals, dentists, mental health care, walk-in centres, NHS Direct, patient transport (including accident and emergency), population screening, pharmacies and opticians. In addition, they are responsible for integrating health and social care so that the two systems work together for service users.

Through reforms such as the expansion of the School Standards Grant, which gives money directly to head teachers, the Government has devolved flexibility and responsibility in education to the front line. This enables head teachers to become increasingly responsible for managing the balance of teachers, school assistants and other educational inputs to maximise the effectiveness of their school.

Improved information about performance

High-quality, reliable information on public services' outputs is vital if those who govern and use services are to be able to assess performance and continue to exert pressure for improvement.

Between 1997 and 2002, benchmarking systems were deployed for a number of key public services, including schools, housing, prisons and local transport. This allowed the outcomes achieved by particular public service providers to be compared against the best performers in their field. Benchmarking increases the information available to those monitoring public services' performance and holding them to account.

In education, schools that were failing or facing particularly challenging circumstances have been made subject to more frequent inspection by Ofsted. This has enabled action to reduce the number of failing schools by more than one half since 1997.

In health care, the aim is to provide comprehensive but easy-to-understand information on the performance of local health services. An important step towards this was taken in September 2001 when, for the first time, information was published on the relative performance of all NHS trusts providing acute hospital services. This information was updated in July 2002 and again in July 2003. There is a considerable programme of work under way to expand and improve the range of performance information available which will be reflected in future annual publications of NHS performance ratings. In tandem with the increase in performance information, as Box 16.3 outlines, the National Institute for Clinical Excellence (NICE) was established in April 1999 to

Box 16.3 The National Institute for Clinical Excellence

The National Institute for Clinical Excellence (NICE) was established in April 1999 in response to concerns that there was a 'postcode lottery' in patients' access to medical treatments and drugs. Its role is to provide patients and health professionals with authoritative and reliable guidance on current best practice. It encourages the faster uptake by the NHS of clinically and cost-effective new treatments and promotes more equitable access to these.

Since its establishment, NICE has issued guidance on over 100 new drugs and treatments. It has also quickly gained an international reputation for assessing the effectiveness of these, and its guidance is used by many health services around the world.

provide patients and health professionals with authoritative and reliable guidance on current best practice.

League tables for schools and the police performance monitors have also improved the quality of information available to service users. The Home Office, in collaboration with police forces, police authorities and other key stakeholders, is constructing the Police Performance Assessment Framework that will measure performance to ensure national delivery of a consistent first-class service. Police forces also participate in Best Value reviews, designed to challenge the way they deliver their services, and present their conclusions to their local Police Authority and the public.

The development of value-added league tables for schools is enhancing the information available on schools' performance and facilitating the spread of best practice. Schools have now implemented a consistent method of financial reporting, supported by investment in new management information systems. This enables the benchmarking of schools' costs and outcomes, so that since 2002 every school can now compare its expenditure on inputs and pupils' attainment with those achieved by other schools with similar local circumstances.

Better incentives for service providers to meet users' needs

A number of policies aim to reward success and increase the incentives for public service providers to achieve good performance and to innovate.

For example, SR2002 announced three years of funding – £175 million in 2003/04 – for a new Leadership Incentive Grant to back good leadership and help schools in the most challenging areas. A partnership between all schools in a locality will be developed, with funding for the strongest made conditional on their contribution to improved leadership in weaker schools in the locality.

The Department of Health is now able to reward high performing hospitals across the country with greater autonomy, less monitoring, and automatic access to discretionary capital funds. NHS Foundation Trusts will replace central control with greater local public ownership and accountability, so removing central government from day-to-day performance management and allowing services to be more responsive to local needs.

Well-motivated public sector workers are critical in ensuring that public services are improved. It is therefore essential to ensure that every public service has sufficient numbers of motivated employees with the right skills, in the right place. Box 16.4 below describes the steps the Government is taking to secure a well-skilled, responsibly paid workforce.

Box 16.4 Pay and workforce strategies

Achieving real improvements in the performance of public services means having sufficient numbers of motivated employees with the right skills in the right place. This needs proper planning, not least because public service providers are competing with the private sector and other public service providers in a tight labour market. Accordingly, departments have been asked to prepare pay and workforce strategies. These strategies set out:

- the staffing needed, in terms of both numbers of people and skills, to enable the department to meet its key service delivery priorities;
- the plan to reach this staffing level, including recruitment, retention, training and workforce development strategies;
- the risks involved, and how these will be managed; and
- a timetable and set of milestones against which progress can be measured.

Pay is clearly one item that will be addressed in these strategies, as it is a key lever in recruiting, retaining and motivating workers. To ensure stability and value for money in public services, public sector pay rises, just as in the private sector, must be set at a sustainable rate and be justified by productivity. Public sector pay represents a significant element of spending on public services. The need is to ensure that these resources are used effectively and that pay frameworks supports reform and delivery of public services. Wherever possible, pay responsibility should be delegated as close as possible to the point of delivery, to ensure it is responsive and appropriate to prevailing local conditions.

The introduction of the Comprehensive Performance Assessment scheme for local authorities, meanwhile, allows successful councils to be identified and high performance rewarded (see Box 16.5).

Assessing performance

In order to ensure transparency and accountability of performance towards key goals, departments publish assessments of progress towards their PSA targets twice a year: in departmental reports each spring and, since 2002, in annual autumn performance reports.

In April 2003, the Government also launched the PSA performance website[7], which contains the latest performance information for all the most recent (SR2002) targets, in a single place. This allows the public to assess how the Government is delivering across all areas of government and public services, and is regularly updated to reflect new data published by departments.

Box 16.5 The Comprehensive Performance Assessment

The Comprehensive Performance Assessment (CPA) is a key element of the agenda for raising the performance of local government. The CPA will support improvement in planning by local authorities; lead to co-ordinated and proportionate audit and inspection; and increase freedoms and flexibilities for local government.

The Audit Commission has formed a judgement on the performance and proven corporate capacity of every unitary authority and county council in England. Published in December 2002, these CPAs provide the public with a rounded assessment of the quality of local services delivered by every council; whether they will improve; and how well the council is run. The CPA provides for the first time a scorecard showing a council's overall result (excellent, good, fair, weak or poor), and separate results for key local services.

The Audit Commission is working with central government departments, the Local Government Association (LGA), the Improvement and Development Agency (IDeA) and other inspectorates to develop the CPA for district councils and refresh the first round scores.

In November 2002, the Government announced a range of freedoms to allow local authorities to focus their attention on delivery. Some of these will be available to all authorities, while others will depend on their CPA. The best authorities will be freed almost entirely from ring-fenced grants, requirements to submit plans for government approval and annual inspections, in order to release their abilities, energy and commitment to deliver better public services in innovative ways.

Linking the CPA and local PSAs is the new Innovation Forum, will bring together 'excellent' authorities and senior Government representatives. It will help central and local government explore ways of eliminating bureaucratic barriers to local innovation and excellence.

In addition to regular public reporting of key performance data, departments use various other types of information in order to understand delivery problems; to develop policy which is based on evidence of what works; and to ensure the delivery of the key public service improvements that are wanted.

Conclusion

This chapter has set out the framework that the Government has built to raise public sector performance and productivity.

The framework has four elements:

- clear long-term goals, expressed as desired outcomes;

- greater discretion for local service providers, constrained by effective governance structures;
- improved information about performance; and
- better incentives for service providers to meet users' needs.

This framework has engendered major reforms across all the key public services. Innovations such as Public Service Agreements (PSAs), independent inspection and school league tables provide good examples of public service reforms, which are improving delivery and raising productivity.

The challenge ahead will be to build on these reforms to ensure that sustained improvements in the performance of public services are achieved.

17
Public Investment and Capital Appraisal

This chapter continues the theme of public service delivery. It sets out the Government's strategy of increasing investment in the country's infrastructure and explains how the extra resources being invested in public services are being matched with reforms to ensure that the quality of investment is raised.

Introduction

The previous two chapters of Part 4 have looked at how the public sector can be made more productive and how the delivery of public services can be improved. This final chapter in Part 4 looks at the policy towards investment and utilisation of public sector assets.

There are two principal reasons for having public assets and spending public resources to enhance them. First, investment in the asset base matters because of its impact on productivity growth. Increasing the sustainable rate of productivity, as discussed in Chapter 2, is central to the Government's objective of achieving high and stable levels of growth and employment. Improving infrastructure in transport and housing, and developing educational and research facilities to improve skills, make an important contribution to this aim.

Second, successful delivery of public services depends on providers having the right capital – hospitals, schools, military equipment and so on – to be able to do so. Moreover, improved infrastructure can also play a key role in improving the cost and quality of public services, for example by providing the infrastructure to support the delivery of services in different ways.

Substantial sums of public capital are tied up in the asset base. This capital needs to be used to best effect. The public sector must have the right kind of assets, maintain them to the required standards, use them as effectively as possible, and redeploy capital from assets that are no longer needed.

This chapter sets out the historical investment problems that have had to be faced and the strategy being used to address these problems. It then discusses resources devoted to public sector investment and the related reforms to the budgeting framework that have been put in place to ensure these additional resources are being spent in the most efficient way. Subsequent sections discuss the role of the private sector in public sector investment, how public sector projects are appraised and the organisational changes put in place to ensure best practice across the public sector.

Investment in the public sector

The public sector asset base

The public sector owns about an eighth of the total asset base of the United Kingdom: by the end of 2001/2, this was valued at £612 billion against the national balance sheet total of nearly £5,000 billion. Figure 17.1 shows how the asset base was divided between sectors at March 2002. The majority of the asset base is held outside central government, with local government owning 58 per cent of the total and public corporations a further 14 per cent. The majority of assets are commercial and industrial

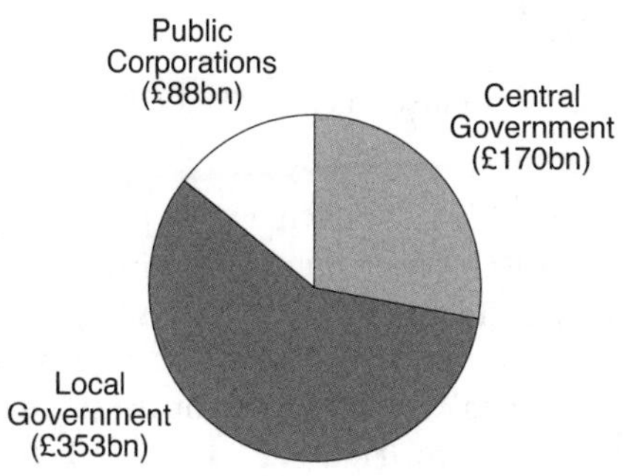

Source: ONS (2003)

Figure 17.1 Distribution of public sector assets, March 2002

buildings and engineering works, with the remainder being made up of residential buildings, machinery, vehicles and other minor categories.

Historic trends in investment

Figure 17.2 shows the level of Public Sector Net Investment (PSNI) from 1975 onwards. PSNI is gross investment less depreciation on existing assets, and therefore measures the amount by which the public sector capital stock is increasing or decreasing. PSNI fell from over £30 billion in real terms in 1975/76 to just over £6 billion by 1997/98. This represented a reduction from 5.5 per cent of GDP in 1975 to just 0.7 per cent of GDP in 1997. Between 1991/92 and 1996/97, PSNI fell by an average of more than 14 per cent in real terms each year.

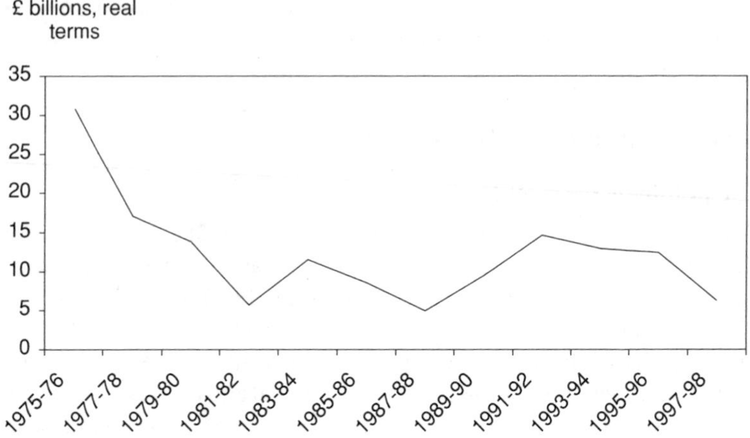

Source: HM Treasury (2003l)

Figure 17.2 Public sector net investment, 1975–1998

The fall in public sector investment is partly explained by the decisions of successive Governments to move away from certain activities previously delivered by the public sector. This included the former nationalised industries and most local authority provision of housing. However, the fall in public sector investment was not fully explained by these changes. Figure 17.3 sets out gross fixed capital formation, the acquisition (minus disposal) of fixed assets, by government sector. These figures show not only the decline that might be expected from the change in the size of the public sector over the

1970s and 1980s, but also the marked decline in general government spend – central plus local government – since the start of the 1990s.

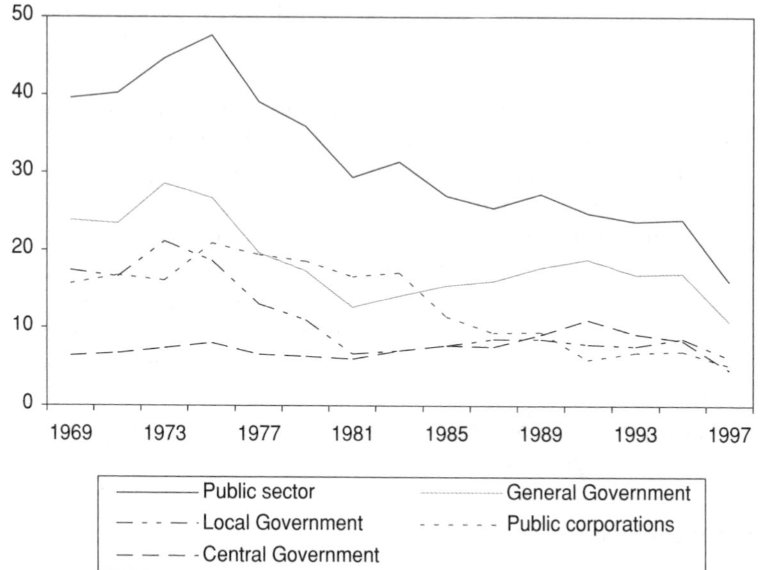

Source: HM Treasury (2002g)

Figure 17.3 Gross fixed capital formation, by government sector, 1969–1997

This low investment led to a marked deterioration in the quality of the assets used to deliver public services. By 1997, there were maintenance backlogs estimated by relevant departments at over £7 billion in schools; over £3 billion for NHS buildings; up to £6.75 billion on local authority roads; and £10 billion on council housing.

Part of the explanation was the budgeting system, which had an in-built bias against capital investment. In particular, there was no separation between capital and current budgets and capital investment tended to be sacrificed in favour of current spending. Budgets were revisited annually, which militated against capital investment programmes that frequently took more than a year to deliver, and encouraged wasteful end-year spending as unspent resources were usually returned to the Treasury at the end of the year. In addition, there was no coherent investment strategy to deliver the assets needed to support public services.

Objectives to underpin investment

A new strategy has been developed to address the problems set out above. It has five key objectives:

1. Improving the nation's infrastructure – improving the facilities that allow productivity and competitiveness in the economy;
2. Modernising public services – funding the asset base necessary to underpin improvement in public service delivery;
3. Focusing on the long term – extending planning horizons from the previous annual cycles, to fixed three-year spending plans, and longer-term plans for key programmes, such as transport and health;
4. Tying resources to results – linking the allocation of resources to defined outcome-related targets, as described in the previous chapter; and
5. Making the most of the assets – so that public assets are used as productively as possible.

Future investment plans

Between 1997/98 and 2001/02, PSNI grew by an average of 12 per cent a year in real terms – from just over £6 billion to nearly £10 billion.

By 2005/06, the Government plans to increase net investment in public services to over £25 billion – over £17 billion higher in real terms than in 1997 – and an increase from 0.7 per cent to 2 per cent of GDP. Total investment, which includes investment gross of depreciation, reinvesting proceeds from asset sales and investment from the private sector through Public Private Partnerships and the Private Finance Initiative, is set to increase to over £48 billion.

This level of investment is nevertheless consistent with maintaining sustainable public finances and meets the sustainable investment rule, according to which public sector debt as a proportion of GDP will be held over the economic cycle at a stable and prudent level[1]. The Government has stated that net debt will be maintained below 40 per cent of GDP over the economic cycle. As Figure 17.4 shows, this rule has been met in every year since 1998 and is projected to continue to do so up to and including 2009.

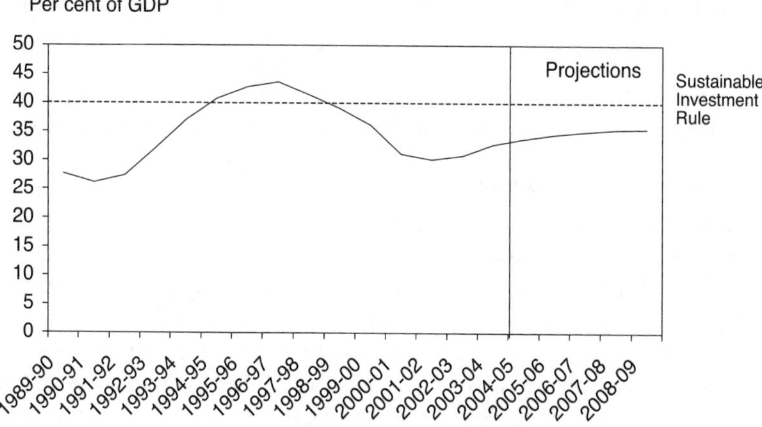

Source: HM Treasury (2003l)

Figure 17.4 The sustainable investment rule, 1989–2009

Within the increased level of resources devoted to investment, the focus has been on four priority areas: education, transport, health and housing. Figure 17.5 shows how public investment in each of these areas will increase from 1997 through to 2006.

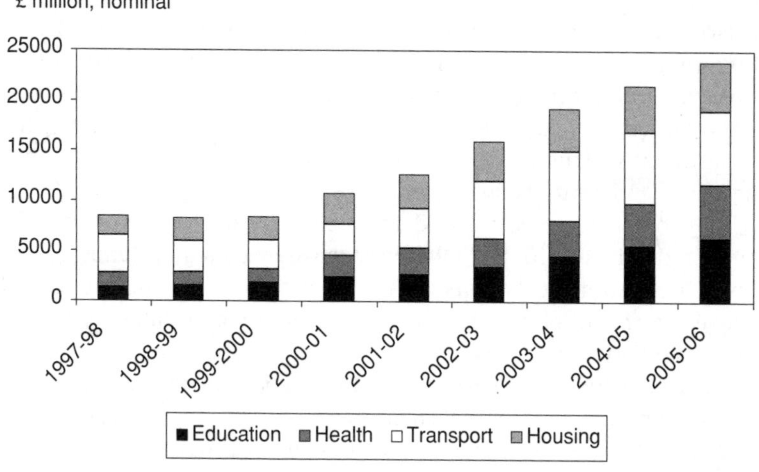

Source: HM Treasury (2002g)

Figure 17.5 Public investment in public services, 1997–2006

Matching resources with reforms to the budget framework

The increased level of resources has been matched with a number of reforms to the budgeting framework to ensure that the extra public money is being spent cost-effectively and to achieve the intended outcomes.

Planning for the long term

Changes have been made to deal with the inherent biases against capital spending discussed earlier.

Under the new framework, fixed three-year budgets are set for each department, which are reviewed every two years. Capital and current budgets are set separately. This enables planning of investment programmes over a sensible time frame. In addition, with the new system of End Year Flexibility, departments can carry over unspent funds from one year to the next, protecting planned investment programmes and again providing incentives to plan complex programmes realistically.

For some programmes, for example health and transport, a longer time frame is necessary for planning, because of the size and complexity of the investment required. In those cases, longer-term budgets have been set. The ten-year plan for the NHS, for example, has been strengthened by the announcement in Budget 2002 of a fixed five-year budget for health, which gives health managers certainty to plan for the future.

Setting the strategy

Historically, there was also a lack of a coherent strategy linking investment to improved delivery of public services. Departmental Investment Strategies (DISs) were introduced in 1998 to meet this gap. DISs, which are published by each main department, set out the department's plans to deliver the scale and quality of capital stock needed to underpin its objectives.

DISs cover a three-year period and are reviewed every two years. The aim of the DIS is to set out how each department intends to use investment to meet its objectives, how it chooses to allocate capital between different objectives, and how it will it secure value for money from its investments.

The DIS includes information about the department's existing capital stock and future plans for that stock, as well as plans for new investment and sales of assets no longer being used. It also sets out the systems that the department has in place to ensure that it delivers its capital programmes effectively. The most recent set of DISs, published in 2002, also report on progress against the plans set out in previous strategies.

Improving asset management

The Government's investment strategy includes not just plans for new investment, but also better management of existing assets. This means having a thorough knowledge of the size and condition of the asset base and comparing that to the infrastructure needed to deliver objectives. It also involves using assets to their maximum potential. A range of initiatives has been introduced to promote this aim.

National Asset Register (NAR)

The first NAR was published in 1997. It included a comprehensive list of assets owned by every government department and their sponsored bodies. The NAR was an international landmark in transparency and accountability. For the first time, anywhere in the world, Government and the public had a complete picture of the country's assets.

An updated version of the NAR was published in 2001. The NAR now includes the value of every major asset, and each department's entry includes a comprehensive description of all significant changes since 1997.

The NAR is an important part of the drive to improve efficiency in the public sector, enabling more informed decisions about the holding, acquisition and disposal of assets. It complements the DIS by helping to ensure that resources are allocated to where they can be used most productively.

Resource accounting and budgeting

A further development has been the introduction of full resource accounting and budgeting. The United Kingdom is one of the few countries in the world in which the Government has a statutory requirement to report its assets, liabilities and all other key financial information in the same way as private sector companies are expected to report.

In 2000, the Government introduced new legislation that requires departmental accounts to follow generally accepted accounting practices (UK GAAP), adapted as necessary for the public sector context. In line with these statutory requirements, individual departments now produce full resource accounts, which includes full disclosure of all actual and contingent liabilities.

This has also been extended to departmental budgets, which in the 2002 Spending Review were set on a full resource basis. Resource budgets provide a better measure of the costs of running services because they capture the full cost of the activity. From 2003/04, Departmental Expenditure Limits include charges for economic costs such as using and holding capital and future liabilities (for example, the future costs of cleaning up contaminated sites).

Under resource budgeting, departments pay capital charges on each of their assets. The charge incorporates depreciation and a cost of capital charge, set at 3.5 per cent of the value of the asset (for a fuller discussion of the cost of capital charge/discount rate see the section on Capital Appraisal below). The cost of capital charge represents the opportunity cost of tying capital into a particular asset. Enabling departments to recognise the full cost of holding assets within their budgets allows them to make more informed choices about whether they should be making more use of those assets, or disposing of them to free up resources for other priorities. Resource accounts also provide departments with a wealth of other management information, including the age profile of their assets and their likely time scale for replacement.

Asset utilisation and disposal

The majority of departments have targets for improved asset utilisation and the new reforms on asset management are helping to deliver on these targets. As a result, assets are now being used more productively to secure a wider range of public service objectives and efficiency savings. For example, the Lord Chancellor's Department set a target to reduce courtroom over-capacity by 10 per cent by March 2002, using a common measure of annual courtroom capacity. The target was achieved by

Table 17.1 Proceeds of sales of fixed assets, 1991/92–2002/03

Year	£ billion
1991/92	2.9
1992/93	2.9
1993/94	4.1
1994/95	3.4
1995/96	3.3
1996/97	4.4
1997/98	4.1
1998/99	4.1
1999/00	4.6
2000/01	4.6
2001/02	4.3
2002/03	4.7

Source: HM Treasury (2003l)

allowing courtrooms to be used for other purposes, such as asylum appeals and inquests, and rationalisation by co-locating courts in one building and disposing of surplus space.

Where assets are no longer required, it is important that they be disposed of to release resources for other priorities. As an incentive, departments can now retain receipts from asset sales for further investment rather than having to hand them back to be reallocated centrally. Table 17.1 shows receipts received by central and local government since 1991, which shows a general improvement in asset sales receipts.

The role of the private sector in delivering public sector investment

So far, this chapter has explained the budgeting framework that has been put in place to underpin the Government's investment strategy. One of the key objectives is to secure the most cost-effective infrastructure for public services. To achieve that objective, the public sector needs to be as comprehensive as possible in considering delivery channels that secure best value for money. This includes harnessing the expertise and experience of the private sector where it can be appropriately used, particularly in the delivery of major capital infrastructure projects. This section explains the reforms that have been introduced to allow private sector involvement in the delivery of public investment, focused on the areas where it can be most effective.

One way the Government is seeking to deliver investment in public services more effectively is through the Private Finance Initiative (PFI). PFI is one form of Public Private Partnership (PPP), structures designed to bring the best of the public and private sector to bear on service delivery. Where the PFI can be appropriately used, it can help bring private sector skills and management to public investment, with performance incentivised by having private money at risk. PFI is used where it can offer the best value for money to government, based on a rigorous evaluation and options appraisal following the methodology set out in the Green Book, as discussed below, and in accordance with the Government's committment to equity, efficiency and accountability.

In PFI private consortia sign long-term contracts with the public sector to build and manage major investment projects. While private sector expertise and experience has always been used in public sector procurement, PFI contracts bind the private sector into a long-term relationship, ensuring that they take responsibility for the quality of the work they do. Whereas with the public procurement of the past private companies built and then walked away, PFI requires the companies involved to compete to deliver a clear level of service, locked-in over the long term and at a fixed price, and with substantial levels of private capital at risk to performance. This link between payment and performance helps ensure that public investment is used efficiently and effectively. Furthermore, PFI encourages the public sector to make investment choices that represent the best value for money over the whole life of an asset. This prevents false economies in construction or maintenance leading to higher costs later on, or resulting in run-down, sub-standard assets. So, under PFI, the public sector can benefit from the efficiency that can come from contestability and the private sector in pursuit of better-quality public services and, throughout, retains control of the services it runs, enabling these services to be comprehensive, efficient, universal, and, where it is the Government's public policy decision, free.

Where PFI is effectively utilised, it offers a number of advantages in delivering public sector infrastructure. These advantages stem from the sharing of project risks within a structure which puts the private sector's own capital at risk to delivery and performance. This helps ensure:

- *investment is likely to be delivered on time* – as the private contractor is not paid until the facility is operational. The record of traditional procurement is poor in this respect, with frequent delays;
- *delivery on budget* – as the public sector only pays for the service it has contracted for, at the price it has contracted for;
- *desired service standards are maintained* – as private capital at risk provides a strong incentive to ensure high and reliable standards throughout contract life;
- *the incentive to invest in high quality assets* – designed and built to be cost-effective in the long term, as the private sector bears operating and maintenance costs over the whole life of the project; and
- *new ways of working and approaches to the delivery of the service* – the public sector defines the service to be delivered, but the private sector partner determines how to deliver it, drawing on its own innovation and experience. This provides the private sector requirements, and allows the public sector to harness the efficiency that can come from contestability.

PFI currently plays a limited but important part in public sector capital investment. So far, investment worth around £35.5 billion has been undertaken through PFI, with further investment made in public services through other kinds of PPPs like National Air Traffic Service (NATS). Investment through PFI and PPP has historically amounted to between 10 and 15 per cent of total investment in public services in a single year. Investment in public services has increased significantly since 1997, and PFI investment has expanded in proportion.

PFI investment has so far delivered extensive new public infrastructure, with a record of on time and on budget delivery that greatly improves on that of traditional procurement methods. Over 450 PFI projects have now delivered operational facilities, including 34 hospitals and over 200 new and refurbished schools. Furthermore, the record shows that 88 per cent of PFI projects have been delivered on time and all within public sector budgets, compared with traditional procurement methods which saw around 70 per cent of projects coming in late and over 70 per cent over budget.[2]

A number of improvements to the PFI process have been made both to improve the efficiency of the use of PFI, and to protect the rights of public sector employees more fully. In May 1997, universal testing of public investment for the potential application of PFI was ended, allowing departments to dedicate skilled resources to those areas most likely to produce effective PFI projects. Since then, a series of measures to improve public sector procurement skills and reduce delays in the procurement process have ben taken, including the establishment of the Office of Government Commerce and Partnerships UK (described in more detail below) to provide expert procurement support to public sector clients, and the introduction of standard PFI contracts to reduce legal fees and other costs, and time involved in negotiation with bidders. Measures have also been taken to ensure fair and reasonable treatment of the workforce in PFI projects. This has included the introduction of the Fair Deal for Staff Pensions in 1999 to improve protection for transferring staff. This was augmented in 2001 with the Cabinet Office Statement of Practice (COSOP), to extend protection beyond central government and ensure that TUPE regulations (Transfer of Undertakings Protection of Employment regulations) were followed by the public sector for all PFI, PPP and outsourcing contracts.

In July 2003, the Treasury published *PFI: Meeting the Investment Challenge, an Assessment of the PFI Programme* (HM Treasury 2003f), which contains proposals for a number of further improvements. These included reform of the value for money appraisal process to help ensure that there is no inherent bias between different procurement options, and a reassessment of the role of PFI in delivering IT projects and projects with a low capital value. In these areas, the evidence suggested that PFI can offer poor value for money overall. In individually procured small projects, high pre-contract costs relative to overall project value threatened value for money, while in the IT sector structural characteristics, such as the fast pace of technological change and the difficulty in effectively transferring business risk were at odds with the principal benefits of PFI. PFI in these sectors is being replaced with more appropriate procurement options.

Departments are also encouraged to make better use of their assets by engaging in commercial services where appropriate. This applies to both physical and non-physical assets, such as databases, skills and intellectual property. Such public sector commercial activity can generate additional receipts to be recycled into public services. As an incentive, departments are allowed to keep such receipts to be reinvested in other areas. Examples include the Royal Parks Agency, which, through a partnership company, has developed an extensive range of commercial activities based on the Royal Parks in London, such as concerts, sponsorship and publishing opportunities; and the Ministry of Defence, which engages in a range of wider markets activities, including the marketing of spare training capacity and the provision of maintenance and repair services to commercial sector customers.

Capital appraisal

The previous sections in this chapter have described the overall investment strategy and the budgeting framework put in place to support it, including appropriate involvement of the private sector. The strategy and framework need to be backed up by effective appraisal arrangements to ensure that the right decisions are made about individual projects and programmes.

Government departments and executive agencies appraise proposed public investment projects before taking any decision to go ahead. Appraisal is essential to ensure that the right projects are taken forward in the way that represents best value for money, including deciding on the nature of private sector involvement, if any, as explained in the previous section. Full appraisal takes a rigorous approach to measuring the costs and benefits of individual policies and projects. Similarly, evaluation throughout and at the end of a project enables its success to be assessed and lessons to be learned more widely. This section gives an overview of how such appraisals and evaluations are undertaken.

The Green Book

The Treasury's recommended approach to public sector appraisal and evaluation has for many years been contained in guidance known as the 'Green Book'. The principal technique outlined in the guidance is option appraisal, combined with cost benefit analysis. A brief summary of the process for appraising and subsequently evaluating government action is as follows:

- before taking action, reasons for any form of intervention need to be provided (such as the need to address a market failure or meet an equity issue);
- objectives for government intervention – be it a new policy, programme or project – should be set;
- options to meet those objectives should be created, and assessed by analysing their costs and benefits;
- the best option should be selected, using net present value as the main decision criterion, and refined into an affordable, viable solution; and
- finally, once implemented, the results should be evaluated and compared against the objectives set, to consider whether the government intervention was successful (such as whether or not the market failure was tackled, or the equity concern addressed, as envisaged).

A new version of the Green Book was published in January 2003[3], following a public consultation, to encourage a more thorough, long-term and analytically robust approach to appraisal and evaluation. There were a number of key changes in the new edition.

First, the Government's 'discount rate', which is used to convert all expected future costs and benefits into a present day value to enable comparison, was changed from 6 per cent to 3.5 percent in real terms. The new discount rate is based solely on an estimate of society's preference to receive goods and services sooner rather than later, and to defer costs to future generations. The new lower rate, based on this 'social time preference', discounts the future much less than before, thus greatly encouraging decision makers to take more account of the long-term effects of their proposals. Proposals that deliver long-term benefits, or long-term cost-savings, will therefore be given a higher ranking than under the old rate.

Secondly, a greater emphasis is placed on clearly identifying and valuing the benefits of proposals, and subsequently ensuring that they are delivered to time and budget; so that proposals should only be accepted if it is clear that their benefits outweigh the costs, and that there is a viable, affordable, implementation plan.

Thirdly, appraisers will now have to recognise and adjust explicitly for the widespread tendency to be over-optimistic when preparing forecasts. The previous 6 per cent discount rate was too high to be justified purely on the basis of social time preference, and implicitly, but imperfectly, offset elements of optimism bias. As a result of the change in the basis of the discount rate, optimism bias must be allowed for explicitly and separately. This will help decision makers understand earlier the likely true cost of spending proposals, and encourage good practice in procurement and project management.

Finally, appraisers must now consider explicitly the distributional impacts of different options (the effects they have on different sections in society). Proposals might have differential impacts on individuals, amongst other aspects, according to their income, gender, ethnic group, age, geographical location or disability. It is important that these distributional issues are assessed.

The guidance is more accessible, explaining to senior managers more clearly what specialist techniques are appropriate, and when they should be used – thus helping them to act as more informed critics and clients. It encourages better communication between those who commission the appraisal work, those who perform and review it, and those who take decisions on its results.

Gateway reviews

The prescribed appraisal process set out in the Green Book is only one part, albeit a crucial one, of the way in which projects are tested, managed and evaluated throughout their development. Launched in February 2001, Gateway reviews are designed to ensure that government projects are subject to rigorous tests through a series of procurement gates. Over 500 projects, covering proposed spending in excess of £40 billion, have been reviewed to date. They involve a thorough examination of the project, including its management structures, at initiation and then at key decision points in its development. Gateway reviews are led by the Office of Government Commerce (OGC), whose role is explained in more detail in the next section.

Promoting best practice

The previous sections have set out the budgeting and appraisal frameworks that have been put in place to ensure that the extra investment results in improved productivity and improved public service outcomes. However, these frameworks will be successful only if those making investment decisions implement them effectively. A failing of the previous system was that there was no way of passing on or promoting lessons learned, and best practice, in procurement and investment across the public sector. Filling this gap raises the quality of investment by building on the expertise and experience gained from previous projects.

The Government has created a number of organisations to promote best practice across the public sector, as follows:

1. The Office of Government Commerce, created in 2000, to improve the efficiency and effectiveness of public sector procurement. It achieves this by working across central civil government to promote improved procurement and management techniques, and by operating the Gateway process (described in the previous section). The OGC was set a target to achieve £1 billion value for money improvements in central civil government procurement between 2000/01 and 2002/03 through its work with departments. At the end of this period, value for money gains of over £1.6 billion have been achieved in total. The target has now been extended and increased to achieving £3 billion of gains across the period 2003/04 to 2005/06.
2. Partnerships UK (PUK), created in 2001, was formed to help the public sector meet the challenges that arise from Public Private Partnerships. PUK acts as a PPP developer working in partnership with public bodies to assist with the creation of fast, efficient, value-for-money PPPs. PUK also has an important role in spreading best practice and developing standardised contractual arrangements. PUK is itself a PPP, with the public sector owning a minority interest and the private sector the majority interest. This governance structure has been designed to match private sector disciplines with PUK's public sector mission.

Conclusion

This chapter has shown how increased investment in recent years has reversed a declining trend in net public sector investment, and how it is underpinned by a reformed budgeting and appraisal framework that provides incentives to improve the quality of investment decisions and to promote improved management of the existing asset base.

In addition, the chapter has discussed why, to ensure the most cost-effective infrastructure for public services, the need is to be as creative as possible in considering delivery channels that secure best value for money. This includes harnessing the expertise and experience of the private sector, where it can be most effective.

Finally, it has emphasised the importance of backing up the investment strategy with effective appraisal arrangements (as set out in the Green Book) – which ensures the right decisions are made about individual projects and programmes, and with the creation of new organisations to promote best practice across the public sector.

Taken together, these policies am to ensure that the extra resources being invested in the public services are matched by an increase in the quality of investment.

18
In Conclusion

This chapter summarises the policy discussion of the previous chapters and highlights the common themes and principles which run through the Government's approach to both modern macroeconomic and microeconomic policymaking.

The Government has set five long-term economic goals of:

- maintaining economic stability;
- meeting the productivity challenge;
- increasing employment opportunity for all;
- building a fairer society; and
- establishing world class public services.

The companion volume to this book, *Reforming Britain's Economic and Financial Policy: Towards Greater Economic Stability* (Balls and O'Donnell 2002), set out the macroeconomic and financial reforms implemented to achieve the first of these goals. This book provides a guide to the microeconomic reforms implemented to achieve the four remaining goals.

Part 1 of the book described the productivity challenge faced by the UK, set out the Government's approach to raising the sustainable level of productivity and economic growth in both the UK and in Europe, and assessed performance thus far in achieving this ambitious goal. Part 2 looked at recent trends in the UK labour market and discussed the reforms which the Government has implemented in order to achieve its goal of employment opportunity for all, the modern definition of full employment. Part 3 looked at measures introduced to secure fairness, expand individual choice and ensure social justice at home, and to tackle poverty in the UK and overseas. Finally, Part 4 focused on policies to improve productivity in the UK's public services, set out the new framework for public expenditure and explained how the extra resources being invested in public services are being matched with reforms to ensure high standards of delivery.

These reforms have been built upon a foundation of greater macroeconomic and financial stability established by the Government's comprehensive reforms to the frameworks for monetary policy, fiscal policy and financial regulation described in the earlier companion volume. These reforms were necessary but not in themselves sufficient to achieving the goals of higher productivity, full employment, fairness and social justice. A commitment to stability is being combined with a comprehensive programme of microeconomic reform to target the key market failures that had to be overcome to deliver, with resources, the Government's long-term objectives. These microeconomic reforms have not only brought the Government closer to achieving these long-run goals, but also helped lock in the macroeconomic stability established by the Government's fiscal, monetary and financial reforms. For, in a modern global economy, macroeconomic and financial stability cannot be secured and sustained without rising productivity, flexible and responsive labour markets, a modern welfare state that provides security without undermining individual incentives, and high quality public services.

The first volume explored the challenges of delivering macroeconomic stability in a modern global marketplace. Recognising the power and potential of markets - especially global capital markets - this book considered how to establish credibility and pre-commitment in the face of key market failures including information asymmetries and imperfect adjustment of wages and prices.

This second volume also starts from an appreciation of the role and power of markets. But it also recognises, that in some areas, markets can fail to deliver socially optimal outcomes requiring intervention to make markets work in the public interest. And it discusses how in other areas pervasive market failures or concerns about equity can justify government replacing markets altogether in the provision of key services.

This central theme of recognising the role of markets, enhancing their performance where possible and responding to their limitations where necessary runs through the discussion of productivity, environment, employment and skills, welfare support, savings policy and public service reform. The common principles that have guided the Government's microeconomic intervention are those of:

- constrained discretion in institutional design;
- looking over the lifecycle in the design of policy;
- matching new rights with commensurate responsibilities; and
- remaining vigilant to the risk of government failure,

and each of these are discussed in greater detail below.

Constrained discretion

The previous volume established the principle of *constrained discretion* as a key principle for policy making in a modern open economy. Constrained discretion means that policymakers are committed through institutional arrangements to the delivery of long-run goals but are given the maximum operational flexibility that is consistent with achieving that goal. Constrained discretion is established through institutional arrangements that deliver:

- *credibility* – through the alignment of agents' incentives with long-term objectives;
- *flexibility* – through the devolution of operational responsibility to front-line agents; and
- *transparency* – through clear, precise and publicly-stated objectives, and through regular reporting of agents' performance against their objectives.

This model of constrained discretion formed the basis of the Government's reforms to:

- monetary policy through granting operational independence to the Bank of England, establishing a symmetric inflation target and providing greater transparency about Monetary Policy Committee decisions;
- fiscal policy through the establishment of firm fiscal rules which are symmetric over the cycle, enhancing accountability through the Code for Fiscal Sustainability, and increasing transparency through more comprehensive auditing of economic assumptions;
- financial regulation through the creation of the Financial Services Agency as an independent financial regulator with clear statutory objectives and transparent principles as to how to go about achieving them; and

- debt management through the creation of the Debt Management Office, that manages the government's domestic borrowing programme and cash management in a transparent manner separate from monetary policy and operations.

This volume draws upon the constrained discretion model to explain the basis for many of the Government's key microeconomic policy reforms.

In order to raise the UK's rate of productivity, the Government has granted competition authorities full operational independence, constrained by transparent objectives and more robust reporting requirements. In regional policy, the Government has devolved power to Regional Development Agencies, empowered to act as strategic leaders in their regions and given full flexibility in the use of their resources through the single pot. In employment policy, through the creation of Jobcentre Plus, the Government has strengthened the focus on the employment-first principle by combining all forms of working age support through one agency. The performance of each Jobcentre Plus district is monitored on a quarterly basis against a range of performance objectives for each key client group. And as national levels of unemployment have fallen, the Government has given individual Jobcentre managers and advisers greater discretion to tackle the remaining employment challenges facing particular client groups and regions.

In the delivery of public services, the Government has used constrained discretion to improve performance, encourage innovation, and focus resources and activity on national and local priorities. At the centre of the Government's approach to improving public service delivery has been a need to engender a greater focus on outcomes rather than inputs as the central aim of policy. In health, for example, the PSA target on waiting times for operations has helped deliver a 42 per cent reduction in the number of patients waiting six months for an operation and the virtual elimination of waits of longer than 12 months. But within this framework of outcome-based targets, providers are given greater freedom to innovate and adapt the services they provide to local needs. For example, in local government, the Local Government Act 2003 has introduced new freedoms and flexibilities for local authorities including new powers to borrow for capital investment and trade to adapt service delivery to local needs. However, this flexibility is constrained by effective governance structures and regular evaluation of performance against PSA targets to ensure maximum transparency and accountability. From April 2003, departmental performance against PSA targets has been regularly updated through web-based reporting.

Facilitating choices over the lifecycle

A second important theme of the Government's microeconomic reforms has been the importance of tailoring policy to the lifecycles of individuals and firms and of facilitating choice throughout their lifecycle so that everyone is able to reach their full potential. This theme runs through the Government's approach to encouraging enterprise, providing employment opportunity for all, encouraging saving and providing security for pensioners, and improving public service delivery.

The Government's productivity agenda facilitates choices at each stage of an enterprise development. First, the Government has helped to improve the environment for the creation of new enterprise by reducing the starting rate of corporation tax, promoting enterprise education in schools, improving the availability of venture capital and encouraging enterprise in disadvantaged areas. Second, the Government has removed regulatory, tax and knowledge barriers to the growth of those enterprises through enhancements to the Capital Gains Tax regime, simplification of the planning regime, and measures aimed at enhancing workforce skills. Finally, the Government has helped those firms to move to and remain at the cutting edge in a competitive global market place through unprecedented investment in scientific research, improved incentives for firm-level innovation and a strengthened competition regime.

The Government's welfare-to-work strategy has sought to enhance employment opportunities at different stages of people's careers. First, for those groups traditionally disadvantaged in the labour market, such as lone parents, partners and those on incapacity benefits, the New Deals offer a comprehensive package of individually tailored advice, training, rehabilitation, advice on benefits and in-work financial support, and work-search assistance to help those who can work to find suitable employment. Second, for those actively seeking work, the Government has reformed the Jobseekers' Allowance regime to allow individual jobseekers, working with their personal adviser, to develop tailored worksearch strategies to suit their individual needs and circumstances. Third, for those in employment and seeking to increase their hours or progress in work, the Government's reforms to the tax and benefit systems have helped to remove the poverty traps that once acted as a disincentive for those on low incomes to move up the income scale. And the Government's reforms to promote workforce training have helped employees to develop their skills and achieve their potential. Fourth, for those looking to find a better balance between work and family lives, increases in statutory maternity pay, support for childcare provided through tax credits and employer incentives, and the expansion of Sure

Start programmes have helped to expand the range of choices for working parents. Finally, for older workers looking to extend their working lives, proposals to enhance the benefits of state pension deferral, abolish mandatory retirement ages and allow individuals to carry on working while they draw their pension, have given older workers a genuine choice about when and how to retire.

In the area of savings and pensions, the Government has developed a suite of savings products tailored to each stage in a person's life-cycle. The Child Trust Fund will strengthen the savings habit of future generations by ensuring that every child born from September 2002 will start their lives with a stock of assets and a stake in the wealth of the nation. The Savings Gateway helps those, typically at the start of their working lives, who would otherwise have difficulty starting on the savings ladder. To help make saving and the benefits of saving easier to understand, the Government introduced Individual Savings Accounts (ISAs) as the primary vehicle for tax-advantaged savings. The simplicity, flexibility and security that ISAs provide allows individuals to accumulate savings for key stages in their life-cycle – for example, providing a deposit on a house. For those looking to diversify their savings, the suite of "Stakeholder Products" being developed based on the recommendations of the Sandler Review will provide a range of safe, easy to understand options suited to different types of investors. Finally, as people look toward retirement, the Government has sought to simplify the pensions landscape through its proposals for tax and regulatory simplification and, through the introduction of the Stakeholder Pension, to extend to previously excluded groups the opportunity to save toward retirement. Over an individual's lifecycle, the design of each of these products ensures that as the scale of individual savings increases, the proceeds from one product may be rolled into the next, so helping people to progress up the savings ladder.

A similar life-cycle approach has been taken to improvements in the quality of and access to public services. In the case of education, the Government has sought to facilitate individual choice and expand educational opportunities from childhood through to adulthood. For young children, unprecedented investment in Sure Start and early years education has extended the opportunities of free early years education to 1.1 million 3 and 4 year olds. For children of school age, plans for personalised learning will encourage schools to become more responsive to individual pupils' needs, supported where appropriate by workforce reform, curriculum flexibility, extended schools and better links to children's and other local services. Expansion of access to higher education and improvements to the quality and availability of further education have helped to give young people a more flexible range of choices about post-18 education. Finally, for those already in the workforce, the Government's investment in workforce training through the expansion of Modern Apprenticeships, roll-out of Employer Training Pilots and reforms to further education have helped to expand the employment opportunities of hundreds of thousands of low skilled adults.

Combining rights and responsibilities

A third theme has been the importance of combining enhanced rights and opportunities with increased individual responsibility. In employment policy, the Government's welfare-to-work strategy is rooted in an implicit contract between government and the jobseeker, balancing the responsibility of the jobseeker to actively seek work with a commitment from the Government to provide the jobseeker with the skills, guidance and opportunities they need to find suitable employment. But, in addition, to help enhance UK productivity, the Government's Employer Training pilots combine a new right of individuals to acquire level 2 skills; of employers to deliver new training opportunities to their low skilled staff; and of training providers to provide flexible training methods that suit the needs of individual employers. To help working parents find the right work-life balance, the Government has combined increased support for childcare costs with improved maternity, paternity and adoption leave, along with an obligation on employers to consider parents' requests for flexible working. Finally, in pensions policy, the Government provides a solid foundation for income in retirement though the State Retirement Pension and Pension Credit while encouraging individuals to take responsibility for their retirement provision above this foundation through a framework of tax incentives, common-sense advice and, simple and safe products.

Progressive universalism

A fourth theme has been progressive universalism in the delivery of government support – the principle of support for all but the most support for those that need it most. This principle has underpinned the Government's modernisation of the welfare state and integration of tax and benefit systems. Built on the foundation of universal benefits such as Child Benefit and the Basic State Pension, the system of tax credits and the Pension Credit have improved levels of support offered to the most vulnerable while providing a more responsive and flexible system of support for those further up the income scale. But the Government's strategies for promoting enterprise and improving the nation's public services reflects a similar approach to the allocation of scarce resources. In productivity policy, the Government has simplified tax and regulation for all corporations but focused the most intensive support on small and medium enterprises which suffer the most pervasive market failures. In public services, the Government's framework of PSA targets has helped to focus resources on the nation's priorities and to improve outcomes across the board. At the same time, the use of floor targets in key areas such as health inequalities and school performance has helped to ensure that no families or communities are left behind by the drive to raise standards.

Remaining vigilant to government failure

A final theme has been the importance, when attempting to overcome market failure through government intervention, of remaining vigilant to the risk of government failure. Specifically the temptation on the part of public service providers:

- to rely excessively on regulation of activity where less prescriptive measures may be sufficient: to tackle this, all new policy proposals with an impact on business, charities or the voluntary sector must now have a Regulatory Impact Assessment (RIA) to determine the costs and benefits of the proposals; and the Government has established a rolling Regulatory Reform Action Plan which has so far identified over 650 measures for removing or reforming regulatory burdens;
- to focus on easily quantifiable inputs and processes rather than outputs and results: the public spending framework has addressed this through PSA targets clearly expressed in terms of measurable outcomes;
- to attempt to run policy from the centre with one-size-fits-all solutions that do not take into account the needs of diverse regions, localities and communities: to ensure that policy is informed by the local needs, the Government has devolved power and resources to a range of regional and local institutions including the Regional Development Agencies, local authorities, Jobcentre districts and local Learning and Skills Councils;
- to focus on annual and incremental spending decisions at the expense of long-term investment in improving public services: by setting government departments three-year fixed budgets with separate budgets for current and capital spending the public

spending framework has helped to reverse the legacy of short-termism and under-investment in Britiain's public services;

- to be constrained by departmental boundaries at the expense of consumer needs: through the use of pooled budgets for cross-government priorities and cross-cutting reviews into issues such as the role of the voluntary sector, caring for children at risk and childcare, the Government has broken down the organisational barriers that have prevented departments from offering a customer-focused service; and
- to pay insufficient attention the consistency of service offered to different clients – resulting in "post code lotteries" that fail to meet public expectations: through the setting of floor targets for the performance of every school and LEA, and targets for the reduction of inequalities in areas such as health, crime and regional development, the Government has looked to reduce disparities in service provision and inequalities in key outcomes.

In summary

The Government has undertaken an extensive programme of micro-economic reforms since 1997 to realise the goals of a stronger, more enterprising economy and a fairer society.

These reforms respond to the challenge of the modern global economy and, recognising the role and limits of markets, follow a model for British economic policy based on devolution of operational power and responsibilities to those best placed to make expert and managerial decisions, clear and measurable long-term goals, and transparent mechanisms for accountability. The same underlying model underpins monetary policy and fiscal policy, financial service regulation, competition and regional policy, employment policy and the new regime for public service delivery. At the same time, the reform strategies described in this book have reflected the Government's overarching microeconomic principles of facilitating choices over the lifecycle, matching rights with responsibilities, combining universal standards of support with targeted intervention for those most in need while driving efficiency and delivery in public service provision.

Notes

Introduction

1. See speech to Social Market Foundation (Chancellor of the Exchequer 2003).

Chapter 2

1. This measure captures both the employment rate and the population of working age.
2. The ILO unemployment rate measures people without a job who were available to start work in the two weeks following their Labour Force Survey interview, and who had either looked for work in the four weeks prior to interview or were waiting to start a job they had already obtained. The rate is expressed as a percentage of the economically active population, including people in employment or looking for work, and excluding people such as students and those on incapacity benefits.
3. Calculations are based on OECD average annual hours worked per person in employment figures (OECD 2002a). The data may not be entirely consistent with other data in this publication as different sources may apply dissimilar measurement methods. Figures are intended for comparison of trends over time rather than levels for a given year.
4. Physical capital has been regarded as an essential ingredient of growth since the development of the Solow-Swan growth model. Numerous empirical studies have looked at the relationship between physical capital and growth; an influential, albeit controversial, study is by DeLong and Summers (1991). See also Rowthorn (1999) on the role of physical capital in growth.
5. Measuring the capital physical stock is difficult. The current capital stock consists of a large number of different vintages run at different utilisation rates. The recent boom in computer investment has made the task even harder, with computers rapidly depreciating and computer power increasing greatly. Nonetheless, using similar methods across different countries allows comparison.
6. This is partly because the actual cost of capital varies from project to project according to the method of financing used and the degree of associated risk
7. The importance of human capital growth has been suggested in the endogenous growth literature, for example in Lucas (1988), a finding confirmed by empirical studies of growth, for example Benhabib and Spiegel (1994) and Mankiw, Romer and Weil (1992). However, many cross-country empirical studies have been affected by problems in the basic data set measuring human capital.
8. Griffith, Redding and Van Reenen (2000) and Cohen and Levinthal (1989).
9. HM Treasury (2001a)

10. Comparable data for France are not available.
11. It should be noted that comparative skill levels across countries are difficult to measure, making it difficult to provide a full comparison between countries. The classifications used are at a high level of aggregation and mask substantial differences in the education systems of countries.
12. See, for example, Griliches (1992; 1994); Griffith, Redding and Van Reenan (2000); and Haskel and Criscuolo (2002).
13. Measured as output per hour worked.
14. O'Mahony and De Boer (2001).
15. Business investment (measured using constant prices) was 17% higher in 2002 than 1997, and has increased over 50% in the last decade 2002–1992. See also Godden, D. (2001), Head of the Economic Policy and Enterprise Group, Confederation of British Industry (CBI).
16. See Bartelsman and Doms (2000) for an overview of the literature on plant-level evidence. For UK evidence see Haskel and Martin (2002).
17. Crisculol, Chiara and Ralf Martin (2002).
18. Haskel and Martin (2002).
19. Oulton (1996).
20. Bartelsman and Dhrymes (1998); Bullock, Cosh and Hughes (2000); and Haskel and Martin (2002).
21. Haskel and Pereira (2002).
22. Innovators are defined as firms that have introduced an innovation during the previous two years.
23. Johnson and Winterton (1999).
24. Storey, Watson and Wynarczyk (1989); Jones (1991); and Dunkelberg and Cooper (1982), as quoted in Storey (1994) and Cosh and Hughes (2000).
25. Lichtenberg (1992) and McGuckin and Nguyen (1995).
26. Baily, Hulten and Campbell (1992).
27. Oulton (2000).
28. Lichtenberg and Siegel (1991) and McGuckin, Streitweiser and Doms (1998).
29. Cosh and Hughes (2000).
30. Doms, Dunne and Troske (1997) and Nickell and Nicolitsas (2000).
31. Nickell and Nicolitsas (2000) and Zvi Griliches (1994).
32. See Blundell, Griffith and Van Reenan (1995); Nickell (1996); and Disney, Haskel, J., and Heden, Y., (2003).
33. Studies by Blundell, Griffith and Van Reenan (1995) and Nickell (1996).
34. London Business School (1999).
35. Baumol, Willig and Panzer (1982) and Porter (1985)
36. Disney, Haskel, J., and Heden, Y., (2003), .
37. Global Entrepreneurship Monitor (2002).
38. Griliches, Z. (1994).
39. See for example, Cameron, G. (1998).
40. See for example, Griffith, R., (2000).
41. A number of academic studies have also found a relationship between stability and growth. For example, Ramey and Ramey (1995) find evidence that instability in output has an adverse effect on growth in a sample of OECD countries.
42. See HM Treasury (1997a; 1998a; 2000a).

43. See the Chancellor of the Exchequer's speech at the Royal Economic Society Conference 2000.
44. Balls (1998).

Chapter 3

1. For a detailed discussion of the UK's macroeconomic reform agenda, see Balls and O'Donnell (2002).
2. This is due to the workings of 'automatic stabilisers', which are defined as features of the spending and taxation system that automatically reduce public borrowing when the economy is in the above trend phase of the cycle and increase it when the economy is operating below trend.
3. Over the 1987–89 period, the output gap averaged at 3.2% of the trend output, and the public sector surpluses averaged over £3.5 billion per annum. Consequently, the public sector net debt fell to 27.7% of GDP in 1990.
4. For more detail, see Wickens (1995).
5. For more detail, see Hodrick and Prescott (1980).
6. Gross value added in 1995 prices, excluding oil and gas.
7. Described in more detail in HM Treasury (1999a).
8. The combined contribution to trend growth of average hours, the employment rate and the population of working age can be described as the contribution from the growth in trend employment, as distinct from the contribution from trend labour productivity.
9. The 'new to average worker productivity ratio' was estimated in 2001 with an econometric model using output per worker, employment and the output gap data from the period 1986–97.
10. The features of the UK's macroeconomic framework are set out in Balls and O'Donnell (2002).
11. The ratio of average unemployment benefits to average earnings.

Chapter 4

1. Barclays, Royal Bank of Scotland, Lloyds TSB and HSBC
2. The climate change levy is a tax on the business use of electricity and fossil fuels other than mineral oils, which was introduced in 2001 to encourage all sectors of business to improve energy efficiency and to reduce emissions of carbon dioxide, the main greenhouse gas.
3. Department of Trade and Industry (2002).
4. For more information see the HM Treasury (2002a).
5. See, for example Cosh, A. and Hughes, A. (2003) and Council for Excellence in Management and Leadership (2002).
6. The seven cores strategies are: building an enterprise culture; encouraging a more dynamic start-up market; building the capability for small business growth; improving access to finance; encouraging more enterprise in disadvantaged communities and under-represented groups; improving small businesses' experience of government services; and developing better regulation and policy. For more information see Small Business Service (2002).

7. Taper relief reduces the amount of a gain that is charged to tax.
8. Mason and Harrison (1999).
9. Higgs, D. (2003).
10. The revised code can be found on the FRC's website, www.frc.org.uk
11. In June 1998, the London Stock Exchange published the *Principles of Good Governance and Code of Best Practice* ('the Combined Code'), which embraces the work of the Cadbury, Greenbury and Hampel Committees and became effective in respect of accounting periods ending on or after 31 December 1998. The Combined Code established 14 Principles of Good Governance and 45 Best Practice provisions, with which companies are required to state their compliance throughout their accounting period.
12. Smaller listed companies are required instead to have at least two independent non-executive directors.
13. http://www.london.edu/tysonreport/
14. Full details of the Government's strategy for supporting science are published in *Investing in Innovation* (HM Treasury 2002b), which drew on the Roberts' Review (Roberts 2002).
15. There is evidence showing that tax credits are effective in raising the level of R&D expenditure. See for example Hall and van Reenen (1999).
16. Eurostat, http://europa.eu.int/comm/eurostat/
17. www.ukonlineforbusiness.gov.uk/benchmarking2003
18. For further information see Cave (2002) and the Government's response, www.spectrumreview.radio.gov.uk
19. Empirical studies examining the relationship between physical capital and growth include DeLong and Summers (1991).
20. The Regional Spatial Strategy will be a statutory document, prepared by the Regional Planning Body, which sets out the Government's planning policies for the region. It is intended to guide local planning authorities as to the broad pattern of development in their region.
21. Connexions is a personal advice service which offers information, advice and practical help for people aged between 13–19, e.g. on future career options, aspects of school life or family life.
22. The Education Maintenance Allowance (EMA) offers weekly payments to young people in order to encourage participation, retention and achievement in further education.
23. Modern Apprenticeships (MAs) offer people aged over 16 the chance of paid employment linked with the opportunity to train for jobs at craft, technician and management level.
24. Further details were published alongside the Budget 2002 in HM Treasury and DfES (2002).

Chapter 5

1. 'Country' is used throughout to refer to England and the devolved administrations of Scotland, Northern Ireland, and Wales.
2. For more information on the Allsopp Review, including its terms of reference, see the HM Treasury website http://www.hm-treasury.gov.uk/consultations_and_legislation/allsopp_review/consult_allsopp.

3. GDP per capita in central London is much higher than that in the rest of the UK, largely reflecting the location of industry and commuting patterns, rather than the living standards of the people who live in the local area. For these reasons, London has not been included in this figure.
4. 'Sub-regional' refers to a geographical area, which is smaller than a 'region'. Exact definitions vary but include areas such as counties and local or district authorities.
5. Feinstein, Matthews and Odling-Smee (1982).
6. The longest time series available is based in the old Standard Statistical Regions (SSRs) for which data is only available up until 1996. This data gives an indication of the patterns of growth over time. Data using the Government Office Regions (GORs) and the ESA95 accounting convention are available from 1989, and this data is used to give up-to-date estimates of levels.
7. HM Treasury (2001a).
8. This measure captures total factor productivity and statistical discrepancies in the productivity component of the decomposition of GDP per capita. The productivity figures given here may not be consistent with the ONS figures, which are calculated on a different basis.
9. Feinstein, Matthews and Odling-Smee (1982).
10. ONS (2002).
11. The sub-regional administrative units at which productivity levels can be calculated are individual counties and unitary authorities. The official description for these sub-regional administrative units is NUTS 2 areas (see HM Treasury (2001a) for further details); there are 93 such areas in England.
12. Blackaby and Murphy (1991; 1995); Harris and Trainor (1997); and Campbell, Chapman and Hutchinson (2000).
13. McCormick (1997) and Braunerhjelm et al (2000).
14. DfES.
15. ONS.
16. Global Entrepreneurship Monitor (2001).
17. Invest.UK.
18. Girma, Greenaway and Wakelin (1999); Outlon (2000); and Girma and Wakelin (2000).
19. Black et al. (1996); HM Treasury (1999c); and Bank of England (2000).
20. Problems with patents as an indicator of innovation include the following: they refer specifically to technological as opposed to more general definitions of innovative behaviour; they use the patent applicant's address as the location of innovative activity, which may not always tally with where the innovation actually took place; and they do not include patents that UK firms apply for in other countries.
21. Girma and Wakelin (2000) and Rodriguez-Pose (2001).
22. Atkinson and Stiglitz (1980); Acemoglu and Zilibotti (2001); and Caselli and Coleman (2000).
23. Trends Business Research.
24. ONS (2001a).
25. Small Business Service.
26. Braunerhjelm et al (2000).
27. Fujita, Krugman and Venables (1999) and Ottaviano and Puga (1997).

28. HM Treasury (2001a); Martin (2000); McCormick (1997); and Braunerhjelm et al (2000).
29. McCormick (1997) and Braunerhjelm et al (2000).
30. McCormick (1997).
31. ONS.
32. Porter and Ketals (2003); Braunerhjelm et al (2000); Midelfart-Knarvick et al (2000); Haaland et al (2000); Amiti (1997); and Audretsch (1998).
33. Fujita, Krugman and Venables (1999) and Ottaviano and Puga (1997).
34. Armstrong and Taylor (2000) and McCormick and Redding (2001).
35. The financial services cluster in the City is examined in the EMU study *The location of financial activity and the euro*, see Annex 7.1.
36. Hurst, Thisse and Vanhoudt (2000).
37. Barri and Sala-i-Martin (1995) and Braunerhjelm et al (2000).
38. Moucque (2000).
39. See for example Hurst, Thisse and Vanhoudt (2000) and Moucque (2000).
40. Vanhoudt, Matha and Smid (2000).
41. Baily and Gersbach (1995).
42. Regional Studies Association (1983); Hurst, Thisse and Vanhoudt (2000); Rodriguez-Pose (2000); Armstrong and Taylor (2000); Helg, Peri and Viesti (2000); and Braunerhjelm et al (2000).
43. This new strategy for regional development is set out in HM Treasury (2001a).
44. Leaflets are available on the Treasury website on the impact of Budget 2001 on 12 different regions of the United Kingdom.
45. HM Treasury (2003k).
46. The recipients of the University Challenge, run jointly by the Government, Wellcome Trust and Gatsby Foundation, were announced on 10 March 1999.
47. Urban Task Force (1999).

Chapter 6

1. The Treasury published a Statement of Intent on environmental taxation, in the 1997 Budget, setting out the role that the tax system can play in delivering environmental objectives.

Chapter 7

1. The full text of the March 2000 Lisbon European Council conclusions is available at http://ue.eu.int/Newsroom/LoadDoc.asp?BID=76&DID=60917&from=&LANG=1. The quote refers to paragraph five.
2. HM Treasury (2003a; 2003h).
3. Statistical Office of the European Commission http://europa.eu.int/comm/eurostat/.
4. The full list of structural indicators are available at: http://europa.eu.int/comm/eurostat/Public/datashop/print-product/EN?catalogue=Eurostat&product=1-structur-EN&mode=download.
5. for more information on the FSAP see the Commission's strategy for the single financial services market and summary of legislation at: http://europa.eu.int/scadplus/leg/en/s08000.htm.

6. The full text of the Green Paper is available at http://europa.eu.int/comm/enterprise/entrepreneurship/green_paper.
7. HM Treasury (2003e).
8. Final report of the Committee of Wise Men on the Regulation of European Securities Markets (February 2001).
9. See, for example, Frankel and Romer (1996) and Frankel and Rose (2000).
10. European Commission (2002c).
11. See Messerlin, P. (2001) 'The Real Cost of European Protectionism', Paris: Institut d'Etudes Politiques de Paris.
12. Nicoletti et al (2001).
13. http://www.hm-treasury.gov.uk/documents/the_euro/euro_index_index.cfm.
14. All 18 studies are available at http://www.hm-treasury.gov.uk/documents/the_euro/assessment/studies/euro_assess03_studindex.cfm.

Chapter 8

1. Defined as aged 25 and over, unemployed for more than 18 months.
2. Defined as aged 18-24, unemployed for more than 6 months.
3. The overall increase in the female employment rate between the mid 1970s and 1998 has been demonstrated to have been almost entirely attributable to woman with working partners; see Desai, T. Gregg, P. Steer, J. and Wadsworth, J. (1999).
4. Gregg, P. Knight, G. and Wadsworth, J. (1999).
5. See Gregg, P. and Wadsworth, J. (1999).
6. Gregg, P. Knight, G. and Wadsworth, J. (1999).
7. Nickell, S. (2003).
8. See Francois, J. and Nelson, D. (2003).

Chapter 9

1. The policy framework introduced to deliver macroeconomic stability is discussed in full in Balls and O'Donnell (2002).
2. National Institute for Economic and Social Research (2000a).
3. National Institute for Economic and Social Research (2000b).
4. Van Reenan, J. (2001).
5. Department for Work and Pensions, HM Treasury and Inland Revenue (2002).
6. See OECD (2002a); McMorrow, K. and Roger, W. (2002); and Turner, D. Booner, L, Giorno, C. Meacci, M. Rae, D. and Richardson, P. (2001).
7. As noted in the Bank of England's inflation report from August 1997.
8. Turner, D. Richardson, P. and Rauffet, S. (1996), for example, suggests that structural reforms have increased real wage flexibility in recent years.
9. Pissarides (2002) and Sargent (2002).
10. Hasluck, C. Elias, P. and McKnight, A. (2000).
11. Iacovou and Berthoud (2000).
12. Joint claims for JSA – quantitative evaluation of labour market effects, ESR117, PSI, July 2002.
13. Cabinet Office (2003).
14. Department for Work and Pensions and University of Bath (2003).

Chapter 10

1. From 1968 to 1998 the proportion of working age households with no adult in work increased from 4 per cent to 17.9 per cent.
2. 'Low-income' is defined as a household whose equivalised income is below 60 per cent of the median.
3. A second cause was the interaction of the 20 hour premium in Family Credit with Housing Benefit.
4. In 1998/99 the increase in weekly earnings from £63.99 to £64 triggered an NIC charge for employees of £1.28 and £1.92 for employers.
5. HM Treasury (1998e; 1999e).
6. The level of earnings at which employee NICs were payable was raised from £64 per week in 1998/99 to £87 per week in 2001/02, a real terms increase of 25 per cent.
7. On its introduction, the minimum working hours in Family Credit was 24 per week. This was reduced to 16 in 1992 with the intention of encouraging adults in households where no one was in work to work part-time.
8. HM Treasury (1998e).
9. At the time of the WFTC's introduction, the upper limits for eligible childcare costs were £100 for one child and £150 for two children. These have since increased to £135 and £200 respectively.
10. For example, where the first earner in a couple is on £14,100 and the non-working partner moves into work part-time at typical entry wages under the new tax credits the weekly gain to work will have risen by £14 per week, an increase of over a third.
11. With the exception that the award could be revisited if the family had a new child.
12. See HM Treasury (2002h).
13. *Ibid.*
14. The limits are the same as for the WFTC - £135 for one child and £200 for two or more children.
15. Data on hourly earnings by age averaged over the four quarters, March to May 2002 through to January to March 2003.
16. Exchange rates are average daily rates for September 2002; PPPs are based on private consumption deflators for September 2002.
17. There are some technical problems in measuring the impact of the NMW. Not only is there the problem of using the derived hourly wage variable, but also the Family Expenditure Survey dataset, used in the chapter, includes some data from 1999/00, when the NMW had been introduced. This might therefore show up in the 'before measures' case and add noise to the results.
18. The 97 per cent MDR is calculated in the following way: a £1 increase in gross earnings would yield a £0.70 rise in post tax and NICs income; 70% of this (£0.49) would be withdrawn through a reduced Family Credit award. The remaining net income (£0.21) could then be withdrawn at a rate of 85% through the Housing and Council Benefit tapers.
19. Family Credit's withdrawal rate was 70 per cent; in addition, Housing Benefit is withdrawn at a rate of 65 per cent and Council Tax Benefit at a rate of 20 per cent.

20. An equally valid way of explaining Point E is to note that, because of the social security system, out-of-work incomes will be positive. To simplify the presentation, both the structure of the social security system and National Insurance Contributions are ignored.
21. As noted, tax credits are awarded to families, not individuals. In this discussion we are abstracting from the issues of modelling labour supply choices where there are two adults in the family.
22. The chart abstracts from the rules of the childcare element of the WTC, which is only available to lone parents working 16 or more hours per week and to couples where both partners work at least 16 or more hours per week. As a result, strictly speaking, the effect of the childcare element is to boost in work income, for a given level of childcare costs. But the effects on work incentives are equivalent: a lower level of earnings is required to generate a given gain to work.
23. Leisure is assumed to be a normal good so that an increase in income increases demand for it and correspondingly reduces willingness to supply labour.
24. See for example Lindsey (1987) and Bosworth and Burtless (1992)
25. While the results are very persuasive due to the robust design of the experiment, there are two caveats. First, the need to monitor families for five years induces the choice of relatively immobile households, which might introduce some sample selection bias. Second, programme participants might perceive the temporary nature of the programme, and will decide to re-allocate labour supply across their lifetimes, increasing labour supply for the duration of the programme to a level above the one chosen if the programme were in place permanently (the so called 'Hawthorne effect').
26. The illustration of the theoretical models of minimum wage is drawn from Card and Kruger (1995).
27. The US does not have a lower youth rate.
28. Youth sub-minima refer to lower rates of minimum wage paid to young people. For example, in the UK the lower rate paid to 18 to 21 year olds.

Chapter 11

1. Measured as children in households with less than 60 per cent of contemporary median income. Data are from Department for Work and Pensions (2003a).
2. Measured as the proportion of children living in households below 50 per cent median income before housing costs.
3. For example, see Bradshaw (2001).
4. PATs were set up at the end of 1998 as part of the National Strategy for Neighbourhood Renewal. They brought together civil servants from a range of departments and outside experts – including residents – with practical experience of living and working in deprived neighbourhoods.
5. This includes increasing the level of maternity pay from £75 to £100 a week and the duration of maternity leave from 18 to 26 weeks; increasing Ordinary Maternity Leave to 26 weeks and setting unpaid Additional Maternity Leave at 26 weeks (up to one year in total); the introduction of two weeks paternity leave and 26 weeks paid adoption leave (both paid at the same flat rate as

maternity pay); and the launch of a new right for parents of young and disabled children to request a flexible working pattern and a duty on employers to consider their applications seriously.

6. The aim of the Unit is to increase the availability of childcare for all children and work with parents to be, parents and children to promote the physical, intellectual and social development of babies and young children – particularly those who are disadvantaged – so that they can flourish at home and at school, enabling their parents to work and contributing to the ending of child poverty.
7. For further information see www.dti.gov.uk/work-lifebalance/

Chapter 12

1. In an open economy such as that of the UK, international capital flows – not just domestic saving – provide funds for investment.
2. Saving in this context is a net concept, i.e. acquisition of assets (gross saving) minus borrowing. It ignores unrealised capital gains on housing and other assets. Household saving should not be confused with national saving, which shows total UK funds available for investment.
3. Financial Services Consumer Panel (2000).
4. Financial Services Authority (2002)

Chapter 14

1. Department of International Development (2000)
2. Speech by Ed Balls (2003) 'Preventing Financial Crises: The Case for Independent IMF Surveillance', speech to Institute of International Economics, Washington DC, 6 March.
3. For more information on Poverty reduction Strategy Papers, visit the World Bank website: www.worldbank.org/poverty/strategies/index.htm
4. Under HIPC, low-income countries with unsustainable debt after traditional debt relief mechanisms (Paris Club) receive sufficient additional debt relief to return them to a sustainable level. Countries have to prove their commitment to poverty reduction and stay on track with their IMF programmes in order to receive HIPC relief. Up to 38 countries stand to benefit from HIPC. Further details can be found at www.worldbank.org
5. Total inflows stood at $203 billion in 1990 and rose to a peak of $1,491 billion in 2000, before falling back to a level of $735 billion in 2001 (UNCTAD 2002).
6. See World Bank and IMF (2003) 'Supporting Sound Policies with Adequate and Appropriate Financing'.
7. The full text of the report can be found at www.un.org/reports/financing/.
8. The full proposal document can be found at www.hm-treasury.gov.uk/documents/international_issues/int_gnd_intfinance.cfm.

Chapter 15

1. As outlined in HM Treasury (2003d).

2. Estimated Total Managed Expenditure 2001–02, excluding social security payments, central administration, public sector debt interest and other accounting adjustments. Sourced from HM Treasury (2003e).
3. Barr (1998) describes in greater depth the market failures that arise in key public services.
4. The problem of non-contractable quality is described more fully in Domberger and Jensen (1998).
5. Dolton (2003) discusses the multiple tasks facing teachers in greater detail, while Smith, Mannion and Goddard (2003) consider the numerous objectives of health care.

Chapter 16

1. Le Grand (2003) describes the command and control approach to the public services in greater depth. See also Balls (2002).
2. The advantages of greater local flexibility in the provision of public services were set out by Tiebout (1956). This approach has been developed and applied to the contemporary UK situation by Balls (2002) and Corry and Stoker (2002).
3. Discussions of institutional design exist within both economics and management theory but concur with principal-agent theory on the importance of objective setting, appropriate incentives and good information in achieving high performance. See, for example, Drucker (1955) and Cole (1996).
4. Chen (2003) describes the benefits of more active citizen participation in the management of public services in greater depth.
5. Findings for the review were published in January 2004 and are available on the Treasury website, www.hm-treasury.gov.uk.
6. Crime and Disorder Reduction Partnership areas were set-up by the Crime & Disorder Act (1998) and aim to reduce crime and disorder in their localities, through the co-ordination of police, fire and local authorities, and by health authorities from 2004.
7. www.hm-treasury.gov.uk/performance

Chapter 17

1. For further details see Balls and O'Donnell (2002).
2. HM Treasury (2003g); National Audit Office (2001b).
3. HM Treasury (2003b).

Glossary

Adverse Selection In a market place, a buyer may not be able to accurately judge the quality of a product, due to an asymmetry of information (see definition), and therefore the market is likely to be dominated by lower quality products.

Arms Tax A proposal, raised by Brazil's President Lula da Silva at the June 2003 G8 summit, to levy a tax on the international arms trade to finance development.

Asymmetry of Information Where information is unequally shared between individuals in the market, usually between buyers and sellers. For example, this information could include the identity of alternative suppliers or customers, or product quality and performance.

Barriers to Entry Any restrictions on the entry of firms into the market place, such as patents and copyrights, resource ownership, government regulation or restrictions and start-up costs.

Benchmarking Benchmarking involves comparisons of individual performances (be it firms, public services or, in the case of the EU, Member States) against qualitative and quantitative indicators and targets, taking into account the best practice of others. As an example, the European Employment Strategy – or Luxembourg Process – involves annual reporting by Member States on national employment policies, which leads to mutual evaluation of progress against the commonly agreed Employment Guidelines and the explicit Lisbon employment targets.

Budget Constraint The alternative combinations of two goods that can just be afforded given a certain level of income and prices.

Budget Set Baskets of goods that are affordable by the consumer, but are below the consumer's budget constraint (see definition).

Cluster A geographical concentration of interdependent and competing companies, connected through a system of market and non-market links.

Complimentarily Goods or services whose demand are interrelated, so that an increase in the price of one, for example, would reduce the demand for the other.

Contagion The cross-country transmission of shocks or the general cross-country spillover effects; for example an ongoing economic crisis in one country can spill over to others spreading like a contagious disease. Contagion does not need to be related to crises but has been emphasised during crisis times.

Cyclical Adjustment The method of adjusting public finance indicators by subtracting an estimate of the impact of the economic cycle so that the underlying or structural trend can be seen more easily. This is particularly important when assessing fiscal prospects. The economic cycle can have a large short-term impact on the public finances through the operation of the automatic stabilisers. Experience has shown that in the past serious policy errors can occur if purely cyclical, and thus temporary, improvements in the public finances are treated as though they represented structural improvements. The Code for Fiscal Stability commits the government to publishing cyclically adjusted fiscal indicators.

Elasticity The relative response of one economic variable to changes in another variable. For example, the price elasticity of demand considers the percentage change in quantity demanded to the percentage change in price, showing how much demand will change given a 1% change in the price level.

Externality An effect of using or producing a good or service, which is not incorporated into its market price and creates a positive or negative effect on welfare. This could be pollution, in the case of a negative externality, or additional skills gained from education, in the case of a positive externality. Externality is a type of market failure (see definition), which causes inefficiency.

Free Riding The tendency for individuals not to contribute towards the cost of a good, knowing that they will still receive the full benefit. Defence alliances are a good example; smaller countries know that they will receive a high level of defence due to the higher defence expenditures of large countries in the alliance.

Grandfathering Allocating property rights based on past behaviour, for example allocating rights to emit levels of pollutants based on previous emissions.

Gross Value Added (GVA) The value generated by any unit engaged in production, and the contributions of individual industries or sectors to gross domestic product. It is measured at basic prices, excluding taxes less subsidies on products.

Income Decile The division of a distribution of ranked scores into equal intervals where each interval contains one-tenth of the scores.

Income Effect Where a change in price gives an individual more purchasing power (real income) even though their nominal income remains the same. This affects the demand for a good and is one of two effects (the other being the substitution effect – see definition), which cause the negative slope of the demand curve.

Indifference Curve This shows the combinations of two goods that will provide the consumer with the same level of satisfaction, or utility.

Kyoto Protocol The Kyoto Protocol is an international treaty requiring the 170 signatory countries to cut greenhouse gas emissions by an average of 5% from 1990 levels by 2008–2012. It was drafted in December 1997, at the United Nations

Framework Convention on Climate Change, Kyoto, but it still waiting to be ratified by many countries, notably the United States.

Market Failure Where the market fails to yield an efficient, or indeed equitable, allocation of a good or service and so does not achieve an optimal level of welfare. The main causes of market failure are lack of competition, externality, the presence of public goods (see definition) and imperfect information.

Market Power The ability of buyers or sellers to exert influence over the price or quantity of a good or service in the market place. Under perfect competition, all competitors are assumed to have zero market power. However, if a market has relatively few buyers, but many sellers, this limited competition means buyers tend to have relatively more market power than sellers.

Median That value in a data set for which there is an equal number of items with values below it as above it.

Monopsony A market where there is only a single buyer of the goods sold, compared to a monopoly, which is characterised by a single seller. As the monopsonist is the single buyer in the market, they will have an impact on the price of the good sold.

Moral Hazard The tendency of individuals or firms, once insured against an event, to behave so as to make that event more likely to occur. For example, individuals may be less careful in protecting their home after obtaining an insurance policy against theft.

Natural Monopoly A special form of monopoly in which characteristics of the market mean that a single producer is the most efficient outcome. Utilities are a common example of this as they require a large, single network of pipes or cables, which is best provided by a single producer.

Output Gap The difference between observed GDP and potential GDP, expressed as percentage of potential GDP. A positive output gap implies inflationary pressures in the economy and a negative output gap implies deflationary pressures. The output gap is often used as a measure of the position of the economy in the economic cycle.

Potential GDP The sustainable maximum output of the economy, determined by the availability of factors of production and technology. If observed GDP rises temporarily above potential GDP, bottlenecks and other forces will soon reduce GDP to or below potential.

Progressive Universalism The principle of providing support for all but more help for those who need it most.

Public Good A good which is provided to society as a whole, rather than to individuals, such as the provision of a park area. It is non-rival, as the consumption of the good does not prevent another individual from consuming it in the future, and it is non-excludable, as individuals cannot restrict others from consuming it.

Purchasing Power Parity (PPP) The equality of the prices of a bundle of goods in two countries when valued at the prevailing exchange rate (absolute PPP), so that the exchange rate reflects the relative prices of goods purchased in the respective countries. This is also useful for making comparisons between GDP and wage rates, for example.

Retail Prices Index (RPI) An index derived from the prices of a basket of typical goods and services, purchased by consumers, used to measure inflation.

Ring-fenced Grants A grant that is specifically allocated to a particular policy measure. Generally, the grant is appropriately protected within a wider budget.

Soft Loans/Concessional Loans A loan which is subsidised so that the repayment rate is below the market rate. For example, IDA (International Development Association; the development arm of the World Bank Group) loans are interest-free, with borrowers liable only to pay a small service charge of 0.75%. IDA loans also have a 10-year grace period in which no repayment of the principal is required

Spare Capacity At the aggregate economy level, this is defined as the difference between the potential and observed GDP levels which, when divided by potential GDP, is defined by the output gap (see definition).

Spillover A cost or benefit resulting from a transaction or business activity that is borne by a third party not engaged in the transaction.

Structural (see Cyclical Adjustment)

Substitution Effect Where a change in the price of a good makes the price relatively higher or lower than other goods in the market place, which may act as substitutes. This affects the demand for the good and is one of two effects (the other being the income effect – see definition), which cause the negative slope of the demand curve.

Taper The reduction in a tax credit award, or state benefit income, as a result of the household or individual's increased personal income.

Tobin Tax A tax on international currency transactions first proposed by economist James Tobin in 1978.

Uprating The annual review of Social Security benefit rates by the Secretary of State in accordance with s150 – 154 of the Social Security Administration Act 1992. Rates of benefit are uprated each year by the Social Security Benefits Uprating Order. Generally, contributory and non-contributory benefits are increased in line with the Retail Prices Index (see definition) and income-related benefits increased by Rossi (RPI less housing costs). September RPI figures are used and new rates take effect in the following April.

Univariable Used to describe statistical techniques for analysing a single, dependent variable.

Yardstick Competition The idea that owners of firms are able to agree better informed and more efficient contracts (with suppliers and customers), if they are better able to observe the performance of managers of other similar firms.

List of Abbreviations

BCC – British Chamber of Commerce
BERD – Business Enterprise Research and Development
CAT – Charges, Access and Terms
CBI – Confederation of British Industry
CC – Competition Commission
CCL – Climate Change Levy
CDFI – Community Development Finance Institution
CGT – Capital Gains Tax
CHP – Cogeneration of Heat and Power
CITR – Community Investment Tax Relief
COSOP – Cabinet Office Statement of Practice
CPA – Comprehensive Performance Assessment
CTC – Child Tax Credit
CTF – Child Trust Fund
DEL – Departmental Expenditure Limit
DETR – Department of the Environment, Transport and the Regions
DfES – Department for Education and Skills
DISs – Departmental Investment Strategies
DoH – Department of Health
DTI – Department of Trade and Industry
DWP – Department for Work and Pensions
EEF – Engineering Employees' Federation
EER – Equilibrium Exchange Rate
EES – European Employment Strategy
EITC – Earned Income Tax Credit
EMA – Education Maintenance Allowance
EMU – European Monetary Union
FES – Family Expenditure Survey
FSA – Financial Services Authority
FSAP – Financial Services Action Plan
FTA – Fair Trading Act (1973)
GAAP – Generally Accepted Accounting Practices
GAD – Government Actuary's Department
GDP – Gross Domestic Product
GERD – Gross Domestic Expenditure on Research and Development

GVA – Groaa Value Added
HBAI – Households Below Average Income
HIPC – Heavily Indebted Poor Countries
HMT – Her Majesty's Treasury
ICT – Information and Communications Technology
IDA – International Development Association
IDeA – Improvement and Development Agency
IFF – International Finance Facility
IFS – Institute for Fiscal Studies
ILO – International Labour Organisation
IMF – International Monetary Fund
IPA – Integrated Policy Appraisal
ISA – Individual Savings Account
LEL – Lower Earnings Limit
LFS – Labour Force Survey
LGA – Local Government Association
LPC – Low Pay Commission
LSC – Learning and Skills Council
MA – Modern Apprenticeship
MDG – Millenium Development Goal
MDR – Marginal Deduction Rate
MIG – Minimum Income Guarantee
MPC – Monetary Policy Committee
NAIRU – Non-Accelerating Inflation Rate of Unemployment
NAO – National Audit Office
NAR – National Asset Register
NDDP – New Deal for Disabled People
NDLP – New Deal for Lone Parents
NDYP – New Deal for Young People
NEPAD – New Partnership for African Development
NGO – Non-Governmental Organisation
NHS – National Health Service
NICE – National Institute for Clinical Excellence
NICs – National Insurance Contributions
NIESR – National Institute for Economic and Social Research
NMW – National Minimum Wage
NTC – New Tax Credit
ODPM – Office of the Deputy Prime Minister
OECD – Organisation for Economic Co-operation and Development
Ofsted – Office for Standards in Education
OFT – Office of Fair Trading

OGC – Office of Government Commerce
OMC – Open Method of Co-ordination
ONS – Office of National Statistics
OST – Office of Science and Technology
PAT – Policy and Action Team
PCT – Primary Care Trust
PFI – Private Finance Initiative
PPP – Public Private Partnership
PSA – Public Service Agreement
PSNI – Public Sector Net Investment
R&D – Research and Development
RCME – Regional Centre for Manufacturing Excellence
RDA – Regional Development Agency
RPI – Retail Price Index
RTPA – Restrictive Trade Practices Act (1976)
RVCF – Regional Venture Capital Fund
S2P – Second State Pension
SBS – Small Business Service
SDRs – Special Drawing Rights
SERPS – State Earnings Related Pensions Scheme
SMEs – Small and Medium Enterprises
TFP – Total Factor Productivity
TUC – Trade Unions Congress
UNCTAD – United Nations Conference on Trade and Development
WFIs – Work Focused Interviews
WFTC – Working Family Tax Credit
WTC – Working Tax Credit
WTO – World Trade Organisation

List of Country Abbreviations

AU – Austria
BE – Belgium
CY – Cyprus
CZ – Czech Republic
DK – Denmark
EST – Estonia
EU – European Union
EU15 – The EU as currently constituted, i.e. 15 Member States
EU25 – The EU post-enlargement, i.e. 25 Member States
FN – Finland

FR – France
GE – Germany
GR – Greece
H – Hungary
IR – Ireland
IT – Italy
LT – Lithuania
LV – Latvia
LX – Luxembourg
MT – Malta
NL – Netherlands
P – Poland
PT – Portugal
SE – Sweden
SK – Slovak Republic
SL – Slovenia
SP – Spain
UK – United Kingdom
US – United States of America

Bibliography

Acemoglu, D. and Pischke, J. (forthcoming) 'Minimum Wages and on-the-job Training', *Research in Labour Economics.*

Acemoglu and Zilibotti (2001) 'Productivity Differences', *Journal of Labour Economics*, 116, May 2001.

Amiti, M. (1997) 'Specialisation Patterns in Europe', *Centre of Economic Performance*, DP 363, September 1997, London: LSE.

Armstrong and Taylor (2000) 'Regional Economics and Policy', London: Blackwell.

Arulampam, W. Booth, A. and Bryan, M. (2002) 'Work Related Training and the New National Minimum Wage in Britain', *Institute for Social and Economic Research*, Essex: University of Essex.

Atkinson and Stiglitz (1980) 'Lecturers in Public Economics' London: McGraw-Hill.

Audit Commission (2001) 'Managing to Improve Local Services', London: Audit Commission.

Audit Commission (2002a) 'Comprehensive Performance Assessment', London: Audit Commission.

Audit Commission (2002b) 'Recruitment and Retention: A Public Service Workforce for the 21st Century', London: Audit Commission.

Audretsch, D. (1998) 'Agglomeration and the Location of Innovative Activity', *Oxford Review of Economic Policy*, 14(2), Summer 1998.

Bailey, S. (2002) 'Public Sector Economics: Theory, Policy and Practice', Basingstoke: Palgrave.

Baily and Gersbach (1995) 'Efficiency in Manufacturing and the Need for Global Competition', *Brooking Papers on Economic Activity: Microeconomics.*

Baily, Hulten and Campbell (1992) 'The Distribution of Productivity in Manufacturing Plants', *Brooking Papers on Economic Activity: Microeconomics.*

Balls, E. (1998) 'Open Macroeconomics in an Open Economy', *Scottish Journal of Political Economy*, 45(2), May 1998.

Balls, E. (2002) 'The New Localism', Speech to CIPFA annual conference, Brighton, 12 June.

Balls and Healey (2000) 'Towards a New Regional Policy: Delivering Growth and Full Employment', London: Smith Institute.

Balls, E. and O'Donnell, G. (2002) 'Reforming Britain's Economic and Financial Policy', London: Palgrave.

Bank of England (2000) 'Finance for Small Businesses in Deprived Communities'.

Banks, J. Blundell, R. Disney, R. and Emmerson, C. (2002) 'Retirement, Pensions and the Adequacy of Saving: A Guide to the Debate', Briefing Note No. 29, London: IFS.

Banks, J. Smith, Z. and Wakefield, M. (2002) 'The Distribution of Financial Wealth in the UK: Evidence from 2000 BHPS Data', Working Paper 02/21, London: IFS.

Bannock, R., Baxter, R. E. and Davis, E. (1998) 'Dictionary of Economics, 6th ed.', London: Penguin.

Barker, K. (2003) 'Review of Housing Supply: Securing our Future Housing Needs', London: HM Treasury.

Barr, N. (1998) 'The Economics of the Welfare State', Oxford: Oxford University Press.

Barro and Sala-I-Martin (1991) 'Convergence Across States and Regions', *Brookings Papers on Economic Activity: Macroeconomics*.

Bartelsman and Dhrymes (1998) 'Productivity Dynamics: U.S. Manufacturing Plants 1972–86', *Journal of Productivity Analysis*, 9(1).

Bartelsman and Doms (2000) 'Understanding Productivity: Lessons from Longitudinal Microdata', *Journal of Economic Literature*, 38(3), September 2000.

Baumol, Willig and Panzer (1982) 'Contestable Markets and the Theory of Industry Structure', New York: Harcourt Brace Jovanovich Inc.

Baygan, G. and Freudenberg, M. (2000) 'The Internationalisation of Venture Capital Activity in OECD Countries: Implications for Measurement and Policy', STI Working Papers 2000/7, OECD, December 2000.

Becker, G. (1964) 'Human Capital', Chicago: The University of Chicago Press.

Benhabib and Spiegel (1994) 'The Role of Human Capital in Economic Development: Evidence from Aggregate Cross-Country Data', *Journal of Monetary Economics*, 34(2).

Besley, T. (2003) 'Making Government Responsive', in *Public Services Productivity seminar papers*, London: HM Treasury.

Black et. al. (1996) 'House Prices: The Supply of Collateral and the Enterprise Economy', *Economic Journal*, 106.

Blackaby, and Murphy (1991) 'Industry Characteristics and Inter-regional Wage Differences', *Scottish Journal of Political Economy*, 1991.

Blackaby, and Murphy (1995) 'Earnings, Unemployment and Britain's North-South Divide: Real or Imaginary?', *Oxford Bulletin of Economics and Statistics*, 57(4).

Blanden, Gregg and Machin (2001) 'Family Income and Children's Educational Achievement: Evidence from the NCDS and BCS', Paper presented at IPPR child poverty conference, November 2001.

Blundell, R. (2000) 'Work Incentives and 'In-Work' Benefit Reforms: A Review', *Oxford Review of Economic Policy*, Oxford: Oxford University Press.

Blundell, R. Duncan, A. McCrae, J. and Meghir, C. (2000) 'Evaluating In-Work Benefit Reform: The Working Families Tax Credit', *Fiscal Studies* 21.

Blundell, R. Griffith, R. and Van Reenan, J. (1995) 'Dynamic Count Data Models of Technological Innovation', *The Economic Journal*, 105, March 1995.

Bond, S. and Meghir, C. (1994a) 'Dynamic Investment Models and the Firm's Financial Policy', *Review of Economic Studies*, 61.

Bond, S. and Meghir, C. (1994b) 'Financial Constraints and Company Investment', *Fiscal Studies*, 15.

Borensztein, E. et. al. (1998) 'How Does Foreign Direct Investment Affect Economic Growth?', *Journal of International Economics*, 45.

Bosworth, B. and Burtless, G. (1992) 'Effects of Tax Reform on Labour Supply, Investment and Saving', *Journal of Economic Perspectives*, 6(1).

Bradbury, B. and Jantti, M. (1999) 'Child Poverty Across the Industrialised Nations', UNICEF Innocenti Occasional Paper, *Economic and Social Policy Series*, 71.

Bradshaw, J. (2001) 'Poverty: The Outcomes for Children', London: Family Policy Studies Centre.

Braunerhjelm, Fiani, Norman, Ruane and Seabright (2000) 'Integration and the Regions of Europe: How the Right Policies can Prevent Polarisation', *CEPR Monitoring European Integration 10*, February 2000.

Brown, C. (1999) 'Minimum Wages, Employment and the Distribution of Income' in Card and Ashenfelter (eds.), 'Handbook of Labour Economics', Amsterdam.

Bullock, Cosh and Hughes (2000) 'Survival, Size, Age and Growth', in Cosh and Hughes (eds.) 'British Enterprise in Transition', Cambridge: Centre for Business Research.

Burgess, S. and Metcalfe P. (1999) 'Incentives in the Public Sector: A Survey of the Evidence', CMPO Discussion Paper 99/016.

Cabinet Office (2000a) 'Winning the Generation Game: Improving Opportunities for People Aged 50–65 in Work and Community Activity', April 2000.

Cabinet Office (2000b) 'Good Policy Making: A Guide to Regulatory Impact Assessment'.

Cabinet Office (2002) 'The Energy Review'.

Cabinet Office (2003) 'Ethnic Minorities and the Labour Market', March 2003.

Calmfors, L. Forslund, A. and Helmström, M. (2002) 'Does Active Labour Market Policy Work? Lessons from the Swedish Experience', IFAU Working Paper, 2002.

Cameron, G. (1998) 'Innovation and Growth: A Survey of the Empirical Evidence', *Mimeo*, Nuffield College, Oxford, July 1998.

Campbell, Chapman and Hutchinson (2000) 'Spatial Skills Variations: Their Extent and Implications', Skill Task Force Research Paper 14.

Cappellari, L. and Jenkins, S. (2002) 'Who Stays Poor? Who Becomes Poor? Evidence from the British Households Panel Survey', *Economic Journal*, 112.

Card, D. and Kruger, A. (1995) 'Myth and Measurement: The New Economics of the Minimum Wage', New Jersey: Princeton University Press.

Caselli and Coleman (2000) 'The World Technology Frontier', *National Bureau of Economic Research*, WP 7904, September 2000.

Cave, M. (2002) 'Review of Radio Spectrum Management', <http://www.spectrumreview.radio.gov.uk>

CBI (2002) 'The Climate Change Levy: First Year Assessment', Confederation of British Industry and Engineering Employers Federation, October 2002.

Chancellor of the Exchequer (2000) Speech at the Royal Economic Society Conference 2000, 13 July.

Chancellor of the Exchequer (2001a) Speech to the Federal Reserve, New York, 16 November.

Chancellor of the Exchequer (2001b) Speech to the Press Club, Washington DC, 17 December.

Chancellor of the Exchequer (2003) Speech to Social Market Foundation, Cass Business School, London, 3 March.

Chen, S. (2003) 'The Fifth Pillar: Active Citizenship and Public Service Reform', London: Social Market Foundation.

CIPD (2001) 'Married to the Job, Survey', Brighton: Institute for Employment Studies.

Cohen, W. and Levinthal, D. (1989) 'Innovation and Learning: Two Faces of R&D', *Economic Journal*, 99.

Cole, G. (1996) 'Management Theory and Practice', London: Letts.

Commission for Health Improvement (2002) 'Emerging Themes from 175 Clinical Governance Reviews', London: The Stationery Office.

Corry, D. and Stoker, G. (2002) 'New Localism: Refashioning the Centre-Local Relationship', *New Local Government Network*, London.

Cosh, A. and Hughes, A. (2002) 'Innovation Activity and Performance in UK SMEs', in Cosh and Hughes (eds.) 'British Enterprise in Transition', Cambridge: Centre for Business Research.

Cosh, A. and Hughes, A. (2003) 'Enterprise Challenged: Policy and Performance in the British SME Sector 1999–2002', Cambridge: Centre for Business Research.

Council of the European Union (2003) 'Proposal for a Council Directive Restructuring the Community Framework for the Taxation of Energy Products and Electricity', 8084/03 FISC 59, March 2003.

Council for Excellence in Management and Leadership (2002) 'Managers and Leaders: Raising our Game', London: CEML.

Crafts and O'Mahony (2000) 'A Perspective on UK Productivity Performance', *Mimeo*, July 2000.

Crisculol, Chiara and Martin (2002) 'Multinationals, Foreign Ownership and Productivity in the UK Businesses', *Centre for Research into Business Activity*, London: ONS.

Cruickshank, D. (2000) 'Competition in Retail Banking, A Report to the Chancellor of the Exchequer' London: The Stationery Office.

Davies, H. (2002) 'Review of Enterprise and the Economy in Education', <http://www.daviesreview.org/index1024.html>

Davies, S. and Majumdar, A. (2002) 'The Development of Targets for Consumer Savings Rising from Competition Policy', OFT research paper No. 4.

Deci, E. and Ryan, R. (1985) 'Intrinsic Motivation and Self-determination in Human Behaviour', New York: Plenum Press.

DeLong and Summers (1991) 'Equipment Investment and Economic Growth', *Quarterly Journal of Economics*, 106(2).

Department of Health (2000) 'The NHS Plan: A Plan for Investment, a Plan for Reform', London: The Stationery Office.

Department for Education and Skills (2003a) '21st Century Skills: Releasing our Potential: Individuals, Employees, Nations', London: The Stationery Office.

Department for Education and Skills (2003b) 'The Future of Higher Education', London: The Stationery Office.

Department of the Environment, Transport and the Regions (1998) 'Modernising Planning', London: The Stationery Office.

Department of the Environment, Transport and the Regions (2000) 'Transport 2010: The 10 Year Plan', London: The Stationery Office.

Department for International Development (2000) 'Eliminating World Poverty: Making Globalisation Work for the Poor', London: The Stationery Office

Department of Social Security (1998) 'New Contract for Welfare: Partnership in Pensions', London: The Stationery Office.

Department of Trade and Industry (2002) 'Our Energy Future – Creating a Low Carbon Economy', London: The Stationery Office.

Department for Work and Pensions (2002) 'Pathways to Work: Helping People into Employment', London: The Stationery Office

Department for Work and Pensions (2002b) 'A Simpler Way to Better Pensions – An Independent Report by Alan Pickering', London: The Stationery Office.

Department for Work and Pensions (2003a) 'Measuring Child Poverty', <www.dwp.gov.uk/consultations/consult/2003/childpov/final.asp>

Department for Work and Pensions (2003b) 'Households Below Average Income: An Analysis of the Income Distribution from 1994/95–2001/02', London: The Stationery Office.

Department for Work and Pensions (2003c) 'Action on Occupational Pensions', London: The Stationery Office.

Department for Work and Pensions and University of Bath (2003) 'New Deal for Lone Parents: 2nd Synthesis Report of the National Evaluation', London: The Stationery Office

Department for Work and Pensions, HM Treasury and Inland Revenue (2002) 'Simplicity, Security and Choice: Working and Saving for Retirement', London: The Stationery Office.

Department for Work and Pensions and HM Treasury (2003) 'Proposed Product Specifications for Sandler "Stakeholder" Products', London: The Stationery Office.

Desai, T. Gregg, P. Steer, J. and Wadsworth, J. (1999) 'Gender and the Labour Market', in Gregg and Wadsworth (eds.), 'The State of Working Britain', Manchester University Press.

Dewatripont, M. Jewitt, I. and Tirole, J. (1999) 'The Economics of Career Concerns', *Review of Economic Studies*, 66(1).

Dickens and Ellwood (2003) 'Whither Poverty in Great Britain and the United States? The Determinants of Changing Poverty and Whether Work Will Work?', February 2003, Cambridge MA: National Bureau of Economic Research.

Dignan, T. (1995) 'Regional Disparities and Regional Policy in the European Union', *Oxford Review of Economic Policy*, 11(2), Summer 1995.

Disney, Haskel and Heden (2003) 'Restructuring and Productivity Growth in UK Manufacturing', *Economic Journal*, June 2003.

Dixit, A. (1996) 'The Making of Economic Policy: A Transaction Cost Politics Perspective', Cambridge MA: MIT Press.

Dixit, A. (2000) 'Incentives and Organizations in the Public Sector: An Interpretative Review', New Jersey: Princeton University Press.

Dobson, W. and Hufbauer, G. (2001) 'World Capital Markets – Challenge to the G-10', Washington DC: Institute for International Economics.

Dollar, D. and Kraay, A. (2001) 'Trade, Growth and Poverty', *Development Research Group*, The World Bank, June 2001.

Dolton (2003) 'Performance Related Pay for Teachers', in *Public Services Productivity seminar papers*, London: HM Treasury.

Domberger, S. and Jensen, P. (1998) 'Contracting Out by the Public Sector', Oxford: Oxford University Press.

Doms, Dunne and Troske (1997) 'Workers, Wages and Technology', *Quarterly Journal of Economics*, 112(1).

Drucker, P. (1955) 'The Practice of Management', Oxford: Butterworth Heinemann.

Duncan and Chase-Landsdale (2000) 'Welfare Reform and Child Well-being', Northwestern University.

Duncan, Chase-Lansdale and Lindsay (eds.) (2001) 'For Better and For Worse: Welfare Reform and the Well-Being of Children and Families', New York: Russell Sage Foundation.

Economic Policy Committee (2002) 'Annual Report on Structural Reforms 2002', No. 167, March 2002.

Eissa, N. (1995) 'Taxation and the Labour Supply of Married Women: The Tax Reform of 1986 as a Natural Experiment', NBER Working Paper 5023, Cambridge MA: NBER.

Eissa, N. (1996) 'Tax Reforms and Labor Supply', *Tax Policy and the Economy*, 10.

Eissa, N. and Liebman, J. (1996) 'Labour Supply Response to the Earned Income Tax Credit', *Quarterly Journal of Economics*, 111.

Ermisch, J. Francesconi, M. and Pevalin, D. (2001) 'Outcomes for Children of Poverty', Research Report 158, London: DWP.

European Commission (2001) 'Internal Market Scoreboard 2001'.

European Commission (2002a) 'Internal Market Scoreboard, No.11'.

European Commission (2002b) 'Towards a European Research Area: Science, Technology and Innovation. Key Figures 2002', <http://europa.eu.int/comm/research/era/pdf/benchmarking2002_en.pdf>

European Commission (2002c) 'The Internal Market – Ten Years without Frontiers'.

European Commission (2003) 'Green Paper: Entrepreneurship in Europe'.

Feinstein, L. (1998) 'Pre-school Educational Inequality? British Children in the Cohort', *Centre for Economic Performance*, Discussion Paper No.404, London: LSE.

Feinstein, Matthews and Odling-Smee (1982) 'British Economic Growth, 1856 – 1973', Stanford University Press.

Financial Services Authority (2000) 'Better Informed Consumers: Assessing the Implications for Consumer Education of Research by BRMB', London: FSA.

Financial Services Authority (2002) 'Reforming Polarisation: Making the Market Work for Consumers', London: FSA.

Financial Services Consumer Panel (2000) 'Consumers in the Financial Market: FSCP Annual Survey of Consumers 2000', London: Financial Services Consumer Panel.

Forth, J. and O'Mahony, M. (2003) 'The Impact of the National Minimum Wage on Labour Productivity and Unit Labour Costs', Research report for the Low Pay Commission's Fourth Report.

Francois, J. and Nelson, D. (2003) 'Globalisation and Relative Wages: Some Theory and Evidence', Leverhulme Centre for Research on Globalisation and Economic Policy, Research Paper 2003/15.

Frankel, J. and Romer, D. (1996) 'Trade and Growth: An Empirical Investigation', NBER Working Paper No. 5476, London: NBER.

Frankel, J. and Rose, A. (2000) 'Estimating the Effect of Currency Unions on Trade and Output', NBER Working Paper No. 7857, London: NBER.

Fujita, Krugman and Venables (1999) 'The Spatial Economy', Cambridge MA: MIT Press.

Galinsky, E. (1999) 'Ask the Children', US study cited in Daycare Trust, 2001.

Girma, Greenaway and Wakelin (1999) 'Wages, Productivity and Foreign Ownership in UK Manufacturing', *Centre for Research on Globalisation and Labour Markets*, Research Paper 99/14.

Girma and Wakelin (2000) 'Are there Regional Spillovers from FDI in the UK?', *Centre for Research on Globalisation and Labour Markets*, 6(1).

Global Entrepreneurship Monitor (2001) 'GEM Global 2001 Executive Report', <http://www.gemconsortium.org/download/1059044507175/GEMGlobal2001 report.pdf>

Global Entrepreneurship Monitor (2002) 'GEM Global 2002 Executive Report', <http://www.gemconsortium.org/download/1059044507175/GEMGlobal2002 report.pdf>

Goddon, D. (2001) 'Investment Appraisal in UK Manufacturing: Has it changed since the mid-1990s?', London: CBI.

Gosling, A. and Lemieux, T. (2001) 'Labour Market Reforms and Changes in Wage Inequality in the United Kingdom and United States', Cambridge MA: National Bureau of Economic Research.

Gosling, A. Machin, S. and Meghir, C. (1998) 'The Changing Distribution of Male Wages in the UK', Institute for Fiscal Studies Working Paper Series No. W98/9, London: IFS.

Green Alliance (2001) 'Signed, Sealed and Delivered? The Role of Negotiated Agreements in the UK', London: Green Alliance.

Gregg, P. Hansen, K. and Wadsworth, J. (1999) 'The Rise of the Workless Household', in Gregg and Wadsworth (eds.) 'The State of Working Britain', Manchester: Manchester University Press.

Gregg, Johnson and Reed (1999) 'Entering Work and the British Tax and Benefit Sysytem', London: IFS.

Gregg, P. Knight, G. and Wadsworth, J. (1999) 'The cost of job loss', in Gregg and Wadsworth (eds.) 'The State of Working Britain', Manchester: Manchester University Press.

Gregg, P. and Machin, S. (2000a) 'Childhood Disadvantage and Success or Failure in the Labour Market Performance', in Blanchflower, D. and Freeman, R. (eds.) 'Youth Employment and Joblessness in Advanced Countries', Chicago: Chicago University Press.

Gregg, P. and Machin, S. (2000b) 'Childhood Experiences: Educational Attainment and Adult Labour Market Performance', in Vleminckx, K. and Smeeding, T. (eds.) 'Child Well Being in Modern Nations: What do we know?', Chicago: Chicago University Press.

Gregg, P. and Wadsworth, J. (1999) 'The State of Working Britain', Manchester: Manchester University Press.

Griffith, R. (2000) 'How Important is Business R&D for Economic Growth and Should the Government Subsidise it?', Institute for Fiscal Studies, Briefing Note No.12.

Griffith, R. Redding, S. and Van Reenan, J. (2000) 'Mapping the Two Faces of R&D: Productivity Growth in a Panel of OECD Countries', *Centre of Economic Policy Research*, DP 2457, London: CEPR.

Griliches, Z. (1992) 'The Search for R&D Spillovers', *Scandinavian Journal of Economics*, 94.

Griliches, Z. (1994) 'R&D and Productivity: The Econometric Evidence', Chicago: Chicago University Press.

Grossman, S. and Hart, O. (1986) 'The Costs and Benefits of Ownership', *Journal of Political Economy*, August 1986.

Haaland, Kind, Knarvik and Torstensson (1999) 'What Determines the Economic Geography of Europe?', *Centre for Economic Policy Research*, DP 2072, February 1999, London: CEPR.

Hall, B. and van Reenen, J. (1999) 'How Effective are Fiscal Incentives for R&D? A New Review of the Evidence', NBER Working Papers 7098, National Bureau of Economic Research, Inc.

Harris and Trainor (1997) 'Productivity Growth in the UK Regions 1968–91', *Oxford Bulletin of Economics and Statistics*.

Hart, O. (1995) 'Firms, Contracts and Financial Structure', Oxford: Oxford University Press.

Hart, O. (2003) 'Incomplete Contracts and Public Ownership: Remarks, and an Application to Public-Private Partnerships', in *Public Services Productivity seminar papers*, London: HM Treasury.

Hart, Shleifer and Vishny (1997) 'The Proper Scope of Government: Theory and an Application to Prisons', *Quarterly Journal of Economics*, 112(4).

Harvey and Jaeger (1993) 'Detrending, Stylised Facts and the Business Cycle', *Journal of Applied Econometrics*.

Haskel, J. and Criscuolo, C. (2002) 'Innovation and Productivity Growth in the UK', paper presented at ONS / DTI productivity workshop, 2 November 2002.

Haskel and Martin (2002) 'The UK Productivity Spread', Working paper from CERIBA, <www.ceriba.org.uk>

Haskel and Pereira (2002) 'Skills and Productivity in the UK Using Matched Establishment and Worker Data', Centre for Research into Business Activity.

Hasluck, C. Elias, P. and McKnight, A. (2000) 'Evaluation of the New Deal for Lone Parents: Early Lessons from the Phase One Prototype – Cost-benefit and Econometric Analyses', DSS Research Report No. 110, Leeds: CDS.

Helg, Peri and Viesti (2000) 'Catching Up and Lagging Behind', in Hurst (ed.) 'Regional Development in Europe: An Assessment of Policy Strategies', *European Investment Bank*, Cahiers Papers, 5(1).

HM Treasury (1997a) *Fiscal Policy: Lessons from the Last Economic Cycle*, November 1997.

HM Treasury (1997b) 'Tax Measures to Help the Environment', *HM Treasury News Release*, 2 July 1997.

HM Treasury (1997c) *Employment Opportunity in a Changing Labour Market: The Modernisation of Britain's Tax and Benefit System, No.1.*

HM Treasury (1998a) *Delivering Economic Stability: Lessons from Macroeconomic Policy Experience*, November 1998.

HM Treasury (1998b) *The Working Families Tax Credit and Work Incentives.*

HM Treasury (1998c) *Comprehensive Spending Review: New Public Spending Plans 1999–2002.*

HM Treasury (1998d) *The Code for Fiscal Stability.*

HM Treasury (1998e) *The Modernisation of Britain's Tax and Benefit System: Work Incentives.*

HM Treasury (1999a) *Fiscal Policy: Public Finances and the Cycle.*

HM Treasury (1999b) *Trend Growth: Prospects and Implications for Policy.*

HM Treasury (1999c) *Enterprise and Social Exclusion.*

HM Treasury (1999d) *Supporting Children Through the Tax and Benefit System, The Modernisation of Britain's Tax and Benefit System, No.5.*

HM Treasury (1999e) *Budget 1999.*

HM Treasury (2000a) *Planning Sustainable Public Spending: Lessons from Previous Policy Experience*, November 2000.

HM Treasury (2000b) *Helping People to Save: The Modernisation of Britain's Tax and Benefit System, No.7.*

HM Treasury (2000c) *Productivity in the UK: The Evidence and the Government's Approach.*

HM Treasury (2000d) *2000 Spending Review: Public Service Agreements.*

HM Treasury (2001a) *Productivity in the UK: The Regional Dimension.*

HM Treasury (2001b) *The Changing Welfare State: Employment Opportunity for All.*

HM Treasury (2001c) *Tackling Child Poverty: Giving Every Child the Best Possible Start in Life*, December 2001.

HM Treasury (2001d) *Savings and Assets for all: The Modernisation of Britain's Tax and Benefit System, No.8.*

HM Treasury (2001e) *Delivering Savings and Assets: The Modernisation of Britain's Tax and Benefit System, No.9.*

HM Treasury (2001f) *The National Asset Register*, July 2001.

HM Treasury (2002a) *Enterprise Britain: A Modern Approach to Meeting the Enterprise Challenge.*

HM Treasury (2002b) *Investing in Innovation: A Strategy for Science, Engineering and Technology.*

HM Treasury (2002c) *2002 Spending Review, Public Service Agreements 2003–2006.*

HM Treasury (2002d) *Tax and the Environment: Using Economic Instruments.*

HM Treasury (2002e) *Realising Europe's Potential: Economic Reform in Europe.*

HM Treasury (2002f) *Reform of Corporation Tax: A Consultation Document.*

HM Treasury (2002g) *Departmental Investment Strategies – A Summary*, December 2002.

HM Treasury (2002h) *The Modernisation of Britain's Tax and Benefit System: Child and Working Tax Credits.*

HM Treasury (2002i) *Spending Review 2002: Opportunity and Security for All.*

HM Treasury (2003a) *UK Membership of the Single Currency.*

HM Treasury (2003b) *The Green Book: Appraisal and Evaluation in Central Government.*

HM Treasury (2003c) *Meeting the Challenge: Economic Reform in Europe.*

HM Treasury (2003d) *Public Services: Meeting the Productivity Challenge.*

HM Treasury (2003e) *Public Expenditure Statistical Analyses 2002–03.*

HM Treasury (2003f) *PFI: Meeting the Investment Challenge: An Assessment of the PFI Programme.*

HM Treasury (2003g) *Productivity in the UK: 4 – The Local Dimension.*

HM Treasury (2003h) *Euro 2003: Associated Studies* <http://www.hm-treasury.gov.uk/documents/the_euro/assessment/studies/euro_assess03_studindex.cfm>

HM Treasury (2003i) *Economic and Fiscal Strategy Report, Budget 2003.*

HM Treasury (2003j) *Budget 2003.*

HM Treasury (2003k) *A Modern Regional Policy for the United Kingdom.*

HM Treasury (2003l) *Pre-Budget Report 2003.*

HM Treasury (2003m) *Corporation Tax Reform: The Next Steps.*

HM Treasury, DFES (2002) 'Developing Workforce Skills: Piloting a New Approach', London: The Stationery Office.

HM Treasury, DTI, DWP (2002) 'Towards Full Employment in the European Union', London: The Stationery Office.

HM Treasury, Inland Revenue (2002) 'Simplifying the Taxation of Pensions: Increasing Choice and Flexibility for all', London: The Stationery Office.

HM Treasury, Inland Revenue (2003) 'Simplifying the Taxation of Pensions: The Government's Proposals', London: The Stationery Office.

Higgs, D. (2003) 'Review of the Role and Effectiveness of Non-Executive Directors: A Consultation Paper', London: The Stationery Office.

Hodrick, R. and Prescott, E. (1980) 'Postwar US Business Cycles: An Empirical Investigation', Pittsburgh: Carnegie-Mellon University.

Holmstrom, B. (1979) 'Moral Hazard and Observability', *Bell Journal of Economics and Management Science*, 10(1).

Holmstrom, B. (1982) 'Moral Hazard in Teams', *Bell Journal of Economics and Management Science*, 13(2).

Holmstrom, B. (2000) 'Managerial Incentive Problems: A Dynamic Perspective', *Review of Economic Studies*, 66(1).

Holmstrom, B. and Milgrom, P. (1991) 'Multi-task Principal Agent Analyses', *Journal of Law, Economics and Organization*, 7(1).

Home Office (2002a) 'The Migrant Population in the UK: Fiscal Effects', RDS Occasional Paper No.77, <http://www.homeoffice.gov.uk/rds/pdfs/occ77migrant.pdf>

Home Office (2002b) 'Migrants in the UK: Their Characteristics and Labour Market Impacts', RDS Occasional Paper No. 82, <http://www.homeoffice.gov.uk/rds/pdfs2/occ82migrantuk.pdf>

Hurst, Thisse and Vanhoudt (2000) 'What Diagnosis for Europe's Failing Regions?', in Hurst (ed.) 'Regional Convergence in Europe, *European Investment Bank*, Cahiers Papers 5(1).

Iacovou and Berthoud (2000) 'Parents and Employment', Department for Work and Pensions Research Report No.107, London: DWP.

Institute for Employment Research (2002) 'The Re-engineered ND25+: A Summary of Recent Evaluation Evidence', September 2002, Warwick: IER.

Institute of Fiscal Studies (2002a) 'The Distribution of Financial Wealth in the UK: Evidence from 2000 BHPS Data', IFS Working Paper 02/21, November 2002.

Institute of Fiscal Studies (2002b) 'Retirement, Pensions and the Adequacy of Saving: A Guide to Debate', IFS Briefing Note No. 29, October 2002.

Institute of Fiscal Studies (2003) 'What do the Child Poverty Targets Mean for the Child Tax Credit? An Update', IFS Briefing Note No. 41.

Johnson and Winterton (1999) 'Skills Taskforce Research Paper 3: Management Skills', September 1999, London: DfES.

Jones (1991) 'Employment Change in Small Firms: A Cohort Analysis from 1985, 1988 and 1991 Survey Findings', paper presented at the 14th Small Firms Policy and Research Conference, Blackpool, November 20–22 1991.

Joshi, H. and Verropoulou, G. (2000) 'Maternal Employment and Child Outcomes', London: Smith Institute.

Kempson, E. and McKay, S. (forthcoming) 'Saving & Life Events', London: DWP.

Le Grand, J. (2003) 'Models of Public Service Provision: Command and Control, Networks or Quasi-Markets?' in *Public Services Productivity seminar papers*, London: HM Treasury.

Le Grand, J., Propper, C. and Robinson, R. (1992) 'The Economics of Social Problems', London: Macmillan.

Learning Skills Council (2003), 'Exploring Local Areas, Skills and Unemployment', London: LSC

Lichtenberg, F. (1992) 'Corporate Takeovers and Productivity', Cambridge MA: MIT Press.

Lichtenberg and Siegel (1991) 'The Impact of R&D Investment on Productivity – New Evidence Using Linked R&D-LRD Data', *Economic Inquiry*, 29(2).

Lindsey, L. (1987) 'Individual Taxpayer Response to Tax Cuts: 1982–84', *Journal of Public Economics*, 33.

Lipsey, R. and Lancaster, K. (1956) 'The General Theory of Second Best', *Review of Economic Studies*, 24.

London Business School (1999) 'Global Entrepreneurship Monitor 1999 UK Executive Report'.

London Stock Exchange (1998) 'The Principles of Good Governance and Code of Best Practice'.

Low Pay Commission (2003) 'Building on Success: The Fourth Report of the Low Pay Commission', London: The Stationery Office.

Lucas, R. (1988) 'On the Mechanics of Economic Development', *Journal of Monetary Economics*, 22(1).

Machin, S. Manning, A. and Rahman, L. (2002) 'Care Home Workers and the Introduction of the UK National Minimum Wage', *Mimeo*, London: LSE.

Mankiw, Romer and Weil (1992) 'A Contribution to the Empirics of Economic Growth', *The Quarterly Journal of Economics*, May 1992.

Martin, R. (2000) 'The Role of Public Policy in the Process of Regional Convergence', in Hurst (ed.) 'Regional Convergence in Europe: Theory and Empirical Evidence', *European Investment Bank*, Cahiers Papers, 5(2).

Mason and Harrison (1999) 'Public Policy and the Development of the Informal Venture Capital Market', Cowling (ed.) 'Industrial Policy in Europe', London: Routledge.

McCormick, B. (1997) 'Regional Unemployment and Labour Mobility', *European Economic Review*, 41.

McCormick and Redding (2001) 'Productivity, Unemployment and Employment Rates, Within and Between UK Regions', *Mimeo*, Southampton: Southampton University.

McGuckin and Nguyen (1995) 'On Productivity and Plant Ownership Change: New Evidence from the LRD', *RAND Journal of Economics*, 26(2).

McGuckin, Streitweiser and Doms (1998) 'Advanced Technology Usage and Productivity Growth', *Economic Innovation New Technology*, 7(1).

McMorrow, K. and Roger, W. (2002) 'Production Function Approach to Calculating Potential Growth and Output Gaps – Estimates for the EU Member States and the US', EC Economics Papers, 176.

Midelfart-Knarvick, Overman, Redding and Venables (2000) 'The Location of European Industry', *Centre for Economic Performance*, London: LSE.

Milgrom, P. and Roberts, J. (1992) 'Economics, Organisation and Management', New Jersey: Prentice Hall.

Mirrlees, J. (1976) 'The Optimal Structure of Incentives and Authority within an Organisation', *Bell Journal of Economics and Management Science*, Spring.

Moucque (2000) 'A Survey of Socio-economic Disparities between the Regions of the EU', in Hurst (ed.) 'In Regional Convergence of Europe', *European Investment Bank*, Cahiers Papers 5(2).

Myners, P. (2001) 'Review of Institutional Investment in the UK', <http://www.hm-treasury.gov.uk/Documents/Financial_Services/Securities_and_Investments/fin_sec_mynfinal.cfm>

National Audit Office (2001a) 'Modern Policy-Making: Ensuring Policies Deliver Value for Money', London: The Stationery Office.

National Audit Office (2001b) 'Modernising Construction', London: The Stationery Office.

National Institute for Economic and Social Research (2000a) 'New Deal for Young People: Implications for Employment and the Public Finances' December 2000, London: NIESR.

National Institute for Economic and Social Research (2000b) 'New Deal for Young People: National Follow-Through', April 2000, London: NIESR.

Nelson, E. and Nikolov, K. (2001) 'UK Inflation in the 1970S and 1980s: The Role of the Output Gap Mismeasurement', *Centre for Economic Policy Research*, DP 2999, October 2001, London: CEPR.

Neumark, D. and Wascher, W. (1995) 'The New Jersey Minimum Wage Experiment: A Re-evaluation using Payroll Records', National Bureau of Economic Research Working Paper.

Neumark, D. Wascher, W. (1998) 'Minimum Wage and Training Revisited', National Bureau of Economic Research Working Paper.

Neumark, D. Wascher, W. (1999) 'A Cross-National Analysis of the Effects of Minimum Wages on Youth Employment', National Bureau of Economic Research Working Paper.

Neumark, D. and Wascher, W. (2002) 'Do Minimum Wages Fight Poverty?', *Economic Enquiry*, 40.

Nickell, S. (1996) 'Competition and Corporate Performance', *Journal of Political Economy*, 104(4).

Nickell, S. (2003) 'Poverty and Worklessness in Britain', Speech given at the RES Conference at Warwick University.

Nickell and Nicolitas (2000) 'Human Capital, Investment and Innovation: What are the Connections?', in Barrel, Mason and O'Mahony (eds.) 'Productivity, Innovation and Economic Performance', Cambridge: Cambridge University Press.

Nickell S.and Quintini G. (2002) 'The Recent Performance of the UK Labour Market', *Oxford Review of Economic Policy*, 18(2).

Nicoletti et al (2001) 'Product and Labour Market Interactions in OECD Countries', ECO/WKP(2001)38, OECD.

O'Mahony, M. (1999) 'Britain's Productivity Performance 1950–96: An International Perspective', London: NIESR.

O'Mahony, M. and de Boer, W. (2001) 'Britain's Relative Productivity Performance: Updates to 1999', Final Report to DTI/Treasury/ONS, November 2001.

O'Mahony, M. (2002) 'Index of Productivity', London: NIESR

OECD (2001) 'Product and Labour Market Interactions', Paris.

OECD (2002a) 'OECD Employment Outlook', July 2002, Paris.

OECD (2002b) 'OECD Health Data 2002', Paris.

OECD (2003) 'OECD Employment Outlook – Towards More and Better Jobs', Paris.

Office of National Statistics (2001a) 'Regional Trends', No.36.

Office for National Statistics (2001b) 'Measuring Productivity in the Provision of Public Services', *Economic Trends*, May 2001.

Office of National Statistics (2002a) 'Labour Force Survey, Quarterly Supplement', October 2002.

Office of National Statistics (2002b) 'National Accounts 2002'.

Office of National Statistics (2003) 'National Accounts 2003'.

Office of Fair Trading (Jan 2002) 'The Control of Entry Regulations and Retail Pharmacy Services in the UK: A Report of an OFT Market Investigation', London: The Stationery Office.

Office of the Deputy Prime Minister (2001) 'The Government's Response to the Planning Green Paper Consultation', London: The Stationery Office.

Ottaviano and Puga (1997) 'Agglomeration in the Global Economy: A Survey of the New Economic Geography', *Centre for Economic Performance*, DP 356, August 1997, London: LSE.

Oulton, N. (1996) 'Competition and the Dispersion of Labour Productivity Amongst UK Companies', DP 103, London: NIESR.

Oulton, N. (2000) 'Why do Foreign Owned Firms in the UK have Higher Productivity?, in Pain (ed.) 'Inward Investment, Technological Change and Growth', London: Macmillan.

Pissarides, C.(2002) 'Unemployment in Britain: A European Success Story ', *Paper written for the conference* 'Unemployment in Europe: Reasons and Remedies', Munich, December 2002.

Pocock, B. (2001) 'The Effect of Long Hours on Family and Community Life', A Report for the Queensland Department of Industrial Relations.

Porter (1985) 'Competitive Advantage: Creating and Sustaining Superior Performance', New York: Free Press.

Porter, M. and Ketals, C. (2003) 'UK Competitiveness: Moving to the Next Stage', DTI economics paper, No. 3.

Public Services Productivity Panel (2000a) 'Improving Police Performance – A New Approach to Measuring Police Efficiency', London: HM Treasury.

Public Services Productivity Panel (2000b) 'Public Services Productivity: Meeting the Challenge', London: HM Treasury.

Public Services Productivity Panel (2001) 'Customer-focused Government', London: HM Treasury

Public Services Productivity Panel (2002) 'Accountability for Results', London: HM Treasury.

Quah, D. (1996) 'Regional Convergence Clusters Across Europe', *European Economic Review*, 40.

Quah, D. (1997) 'Regional Cohesion from Located Isolated Actions: I. Historical Outcomes', *Centre for Economic Performance*, London: LSE.

Ramey and Ramey (1995) 'Cross-Country Evidence on the Link Between Volatility and Growth', *American Economic Review*, 85(5).

Reynolds, P. Bygrave, W. Autio, E. Cox, L. and Hay, M. (2002) 'Global Entrepreneurship Monitor 2002 Executive Report', <www.gemconsortium.org>

Robert, G. (2002) 'SET for success: The Supply of People with Science, Technology, Engineering and Mathematical Skills', London: The Stationery Office.

Rodreiguez-Pose, A. (2001) 'Economic Convergence and Regional Development Strategies in Spain: The Case of Galicia and Navarre', in Hurst (ed.) 'Regional Development in Europe: An Assessment of the Policy Strategies', *European Investment Bank*, Cahiers Papers, 5(1).

Rowthorn, R. (1999) 'Unemployment, Wage-bargaining and Capital Labour Substitution', *Cambridge Journal of Economics*, July 1999.

Sandler, R (2002) 'Medium and Long-term Retail Savings in the UK', London: HM Treasury.

Sargent, J. (2002) 'Towards a New Economy? Recent Inflation and Unemployment in the United Kingdom ', *National Institute Economic Review*, 181, July 2002.

Schliefer, A. (1998) 'State versus Private Ownership', *Journal of Economic Perspectives*, Autumn 1998.

Short, C. (2001) 'Making Globalisation Work for the Poor: A Role for the United Nations', Speech at the Rockefeller Foundation, New York, February 2001.

Small Business Service (2002) 'Small Business and Government, The Way Forward', London: The Stationery Office.

Smith, P. Mannion, R. and Goddard, M. (2003) 'Performance Management in Health Care; Information, Incentives and Culture', *Public Service Productivity seminar papers*, London: HM Treasury

Social Exclusion Unit (2000) 'National Strategy for Neighbourhood Renewal, Policy Action Team Audit Number 12: Young People', March 2000.

Stewart, M. (2002a) 'The Impact of the Introduction of the UK Minimum Wage on the Employment Probabilities of Low Wage Workers', Working Paper, University of Warwick.

Stewart, M. (2002b) 'Estimating the Impact of the Minimum Wage using Geographical Wage Variations', Working paper, University of Warwick.

Storey, D. (1994) 'Understanding the Small Business Sector', London: Routledge.

Storey, Watson and Wynarczyk (1987) 'The Performance of Small Firms', London: Routledge.

Tiebout, C. (1956) 'A Pure Theory of Local Expenditures', *Journal of Political Economy*, 64(5).

Tirole, J. (1986) 'Hierarchies and Bureaucracies: On the Role of Collusion in Organizations', *Journal of Law, Economics and Organisation*, 2.

Turner, D. Boone, L. Giorno, C. Meacci, M. Rae, D. and Richardson, P. (2001) 'Estimating the Structural Rate of Unemployment for the OECD Countries', *OECD Economic Studies*, 33.

Turner, D. Richardson, P. and Rauffet, S. (1996) 'Modelling the Supply Side of the Major OECD Economies', OECD Economics Working Paper No. 167.

UNCTAD (2002) 'World Investment Report, 2002 – Transnational Corporations and Export Competitiveness', New York and Geneva: United Nations.

Urban Task Force (1999) 'Towards an Urban Renaissance', *LGA Briefing*, June 1999.

Van Reenan, J. (2001) 'No more skivvy schemes? Active Labour Market Policies and the British New Deal for the Young Unemployed in Context', Cambridge MA: NBER.

Vanhoudt, Matha and Smid (2000) 'Regional Convergence in Europe: Theory and Empirical Evidence', *European Investment Bank*, Cahiers Papers, 5(2).

Walton, D. and Binsbergen, J. V. (2002) 'Focus: UK, A Question of Slack', European Weekly Analyst, Goldman Sachs, 25 January 2002.

Wanless, D. (2002) 'Securing our Future Health: Taking a Long-term View', London: HM Treasury.

Wickens, M. (1995) 'Trend Extraction: A Practitioner's Guide', GES Working Paper, No. 125.

World Bank (2002) 'Global Economic Prospects Report 2002', <http://www.worldbank.org/prospects/gep2002/full.htm>

World Bank and IMF (2003) 'Supporting Sound Policies with Adequate and Appropriate Financing', 13 September 2003.

World Health Organisation (2001) 'The World Health Report 2001', Geneva: WHO.

Zedillo, E. (2001) 'Financing for Development: Report of the High Level Panel on Financing for Development', <http://www.un.org/reports/financing/summary.htm>

Zoltan and Armington (2003) 'Endogenous Growth and Entrepreneurial Activity in Cities', *US Bureau of the Census, 2003,* University of Baltimore.

Index

Compiled by Sue Carlton

Access Agreements 83
Action Teams 203–4, 206–7
adjustment mechanisms 13, 168
adoption leave 253, 385
Advisory Centre on WTO Law 312
Advisory Committee on Business and the Environment 134
aggregate household saving ratio 266–8
air travel 79–80, 86
airspace 154
Allsopp Review 89
Analysis of European and UK business cycles and shocks 167
Arms Tax 318
arms trade 313, 320
Artis, Michael 167
Atkinson Review 328
Audit Commission 330–1, 338, 342, 360

Bank of England
  independence 18, 194–5, 348, 381
  method of estimating trend output 50
  Monetary Policy Committee (MPC) 46, 348
Barcelona European Council 149, 155
Barker Review 79, 109, 259–61
Barnhill Community School, Middlesex 341
Basic Command Units (BCUs) 352
benchmarking 146, 332, 348, 352, 357–8
benefit system *see* tax and benefit system
Besley, T. 326
Blundell, R. 226
Bradbury, B. 242
Bridges Community Development Venture Fund 119–20
British Agrochemicals Association 134
British Chambers of Commerce (BCC) 52
British Cohort Survey (BCS) 243, 244
British Household Panel Survey (BHPS) 214–15, 268, 269
British Youth Panel 243
budget set analysis 227–8
business assets, definition of 72
business cycles 45, 167, 170
Business Links 119
Business Planning Zones 79
business tax 70–1, 86
Business Volunteer Mentors Association 75

Cabinet Office Statement of Practice (COSOP) 373
Cambridge (UK) 112
Camdessus, Michel 306
Canadian Self-Sufficiency Program (SSP) 232
Cancun, WTO conference 311, 313
Capital Gains Tax (CGT) 72
capital markets
  EU and 145, 153, 162–3, 165–6
  flexibility 13, 92, 165, 166
  promoting economic growth 38
  small business and 72
carbon dioxide emissions 137, 139, 144
Card, D. 233
Cardiff European Council 146
cars
  carbon dioxide emissions 137, 139
  new cars market 153
CAT standards 277, 292
Cave, M. 77
Child Benefit 15, 250–1, 385
child poverty 241–65
  causes of 245–7
  and educational attainment 243, 245

effect on children 242, 243–4
European comparisons 246
extent of 242, 245–6
impact of financial support 243–4, 249
and increasing wage differentials 245–6
intergenerational effects 243
strategy to eradicate 15, 198, 247–54
impact of 263–4
public service provision 254–62, 264
Child Poverty Review 264
Child Tax Credit (CTC) 15, 212, 213, 215, 250–2, 265
Child Trust Fund 276, 277, 279–80, 291, 384
Child and Working Tax Credits 249
childcare 14, 198, 209, 249, 252, 253–4, 385
and tax credits 14, 200, 212–13, 229, 251, 254, 383–4
children
disabled 251, 254
investment in early lives 252–4, 256–7
in workless households 208–9
Children at Risk review 262
Children's Centres 253–4
choices, over lifecycle 383–5
churches, role in poverty reduction 322
civil society, and poverty reduction strategies 306
Clementi, David 68
climate change 130, 131, 133
Climate Change Levy (CCL) 132, 134–5, 136–8, 143–4
Cobb-Douglas production function 50
Code for Fiscal Sustainability 381
Combined Code 73–4
combined heat and power (CHP) 135, 138
Commission for Health Improvement 342
Community Development Finance Institutions (CDFIs) 119–20
Community Investment Tax Relief (CITR) 120
Community Patent 154
competition 6, 7–8, 42
in banking 68, 86
and environmental policy 124–5, 129
EU policy 67, 153, 154, 159–60
imperfect 124–5
and innovation 9, 37, 38, 39–40, 70
policy 66–7, 86, 120, 159–60, 382, 383
and productivity of firms 28, 35, 36–8, 42
regional variations 104–5, 120
and regulation 68, 72, 160
utilities and 69
Competition Act 1998 66–7
Competition Commission (CC) 67, 68
Comprehensive Performance Assessment (CPA) 330–1, 359, 360
Confederation of British Industry (CBI) 52, 66
Connexions service 82, 262
constrained discretion model 18, 346–8, 350, 352, 381–2
Consumer Direct 70
consumer information 8, 67, 70
financial services 275–7, 279
public services 334–5, 339
Corporate Venturing Scheme 78
corporation tax 71, 78, 117, 278
Council Tax Benefit 210, 288
Crafts, N. 33
Crime and Disorder Reduction Partnerships 352, 355
crime reduction 352, 354, 355
Customs and Excise 119

Davies Review 74
De Boer, W. 33
Debt Management Office 382
debt relief 302, 313–14, 315
rescheduling 306, 321
Deci, E. 338
Delivering through Planning 79
Department of International Development 304–5

Department of Transport and Industry (DTI)
  Innovation Review 75
  programmes 77
  regional development 118
Departmental Expenditure Limits (DELs) 351, 370
Departmental Investment Strategies (DISs) 368
developing countries
  access to medicines 311–12, 318
  capacity building 312, 320
  codes and standards of transparency 303, 304–5
  eliminating corruption 303, 304, 308, 320
  and foreign investment 307–9
  and military expenditure 313
  participation in global economy 302, 303–5
  poverty reduction strategies 306–7, 308, 317, 319–20
  and primary education 299, 302, 318
  and trade liberalisation 303, 309, 310–12, 317, 320–1
development aid 313–19
  disbursement 319
  effective targeting 315–16
  effective use of 317, 320
  see also debt relief
Devolved Decision Making Review 355
disabled people *see* sick and disabled people
Disabled Person's Tax Credit 201–2, 251
Disney, R. 104
Dixit, A. 342
Docklands Light Railway 341
Doha Development Agenda 146, 311–12
Dollar, D. 310

Earned Income Tax Credit (EITC) 211, 232
ECOFIN 162
economic cycles 45–7, 51, 53, 60, 193, 231
economic performance *see* productivity; productivity growth; regional economic performance
economic shocks 12, 13, 167, 168
education
  expenditure 207, 351
  further 83–4, 352, 385
  higher 76, 82–3, 181, 205, 385
  incentive schemes 358
  new schools 341, 373
  raising standards 9, 30–2, 82–4, 87, 116, 257, 384–5
  reform 116, 354, 355, 356
  regional variations 98–9
  school league tables 352, 358, 361
  secondary 82
  targets 115, 116, 257, 353–4, 355, 387
Education Maintenance Allowances (EMAs) 82, 257–8
Eissa, N. 231
Employer Training Pilots 84, 385
Employment Opportunity in a Changing Labour Market 208
employment policy
  EU and 146, 147–50, 153
  and local flexibility 13, 206–7
  making work pay 12, 13, 188, 198, 207, 208–38, 249
  managed migration 13
  opportunity for all 5, 11–13, 14, 25, 175, 188–207, 379
  see also New Deals; Welfare to Work
employment rates 58–9, 176–7, 193–4
  in EU 147–50, 153
  female 147, 148, 253
  and hours worked 196
  older workers 148–9, 153, 179–80
  regional variations 92–7, 185–6
  and regulation 160–1
  see also labour productivity
Employment Taskforce 155–6
Employment Zones 193
EMU and business sectors 28, 78, 169
EMU and the cost of capital 92, 169
EMU entry
  and adjustment mechanisms 13, 168, 175
  and cost of capital for UK 169

EMU entry *continued*
- effect on business 28, 78, 169
- effect on trade 28, 170
- and exchange rates 167–8, 169
- and fiscal stabilisation 171
- five tests assessment 13, 28, 167–71
- investment test 78, 167
- and market flexibility 13, 92, 145, 147, 167
- studies 167–71
- transition costs 168
- and UK productivity 27, 28

EMU and labour market flexibility 92, 109, 168–9, 175
EMU and the monetary transmission mechanism 168
EMU and Trade 28, 170
End Year Flexibility 368
energy use 132, 134, 135, 136–8
- energy labelling 137, 139
- *see also* Climate Change Levy

enterprise 7, 9, 37, 42, 70–4, 86
- barriers to 156–7
- business start-up rates 104, 106
- and business support 70, 72, 86, 118–19
- in deprived areas 74, 86, 120, 156
- and equal opportunities 74
- EU policy 156–7
- exploiting regional strengths 9, 88
- regional variations 103–4, 106, 118–19
- and regulation 72, 160–1
- and role of non-executive directors 73–4, 87

Enterprise Act 2002 67
Enterprise Bill 120
Enterprise Capital Funds 72
enterprise gap 156
Enterprise Insight initiative 75
Enterprise Investment Scheme 72, 78
environmental policy 10–11, 122–43
- and consultation 129, 130, 134
- costs and benefits of 129–33
- development of 123–4, 130–3, 134–5
- environmental market failure 10, 122, 123, 124–9
- evaluating progress of 139–43
- evidence-based approach 129, 130
- and externalities 124, 125, 143–4
- information campaigns 137, 139
- measures introduced 136–9
- recycling of revenue 132–3, 134, 135
- regulation 129, 137
- setting targets 130–1, 136
- subsidies 128
- sustainable development indicators 140–3
- taxation 127, 131–2, 133, 134–5, 136–8
- trading schemes 127–8, 131, 132, 133, 137, 138–9
- transboundary problems 133–6
- voluntary agreements 129, 132, 134–5, 139, 144

equilibrium exchange rates (EERs) 167–8
Estimates of equilibrium exchange rates for sterling against the euro 167–8
Ethical Trading Initiative (ETI) 310
ethnic minorities
- and labour market 202–4
- and National Minimum Wage 222

European Action for Growth Initiative 158
European Central Bank 168
European Charter for Small Businesses 154
European Commission, methods of estimating trend output 49, 50, 64
European Employment Strategy (EES) (Luxembourg Process) 146, 149–50, 155
European Investment Bank 158, 165
European Investment Fund Start-Up facility 157
European Union
- and ageing population 289, 291
- and capital markets 145, 153, 162–3, 165–6
- carbon dioxide emissions agreement 137, 139
- Cohesion Funds 165
- competition and mergers policy 67, 153, 154, 159–60

and development aid 315, 316
eco-label scheme 137, 139
economic reform 145–71
goals 145, 147
priorities 149–59
progress on 152–4, 166
recent history of 146–7
UK approach to 151
and education 147, 157
emissions trading scheme 132, 136
and employment 146, 147–50, 153
and energy liberalisation 153
enlargement 145, 164
enterprise policy 154, 156–7
and environmental issues 133, 136, 147
Financial Policy Committee 162
and labour markets 145, 149–50, 153, 166, 168–9
and pensions 289
and product markets 145, 154, 166
productivity 147–50
and R&D 147, 158
regional policy 115, 165
and regulation 153, 156–7, 160–1
Single Market 145, 146–7, 151, 153, 162, 169
for services 148, 161–2
and state aid rules 163–4, 165
Structural Funds 114, 157, 165
and sustainable development 147, 148–9
taxation of energy products 136
trade with developing countries 312
unemployment 148, 150–1
European Working Time Directive (1999) 58, 197
Eurostat 152
The exchange rate and macroeconomic adjustment 169
Extractive Industries Transparency Initiative (EITI) 310

Fair Deal for Staff Pensions 373
Fair Trading Act 1973 (FTA) 66
families
financial support for 250–2
public sector support for 255
see also children; parents
Family Credit 210, 211–12, 213, 225
Family Income Supplement 212
financial crises 306, 321
financial services
consumer information and education 275–7, 279, 291
impact of EMU entry on 169–70
independent advice 276–7
market failures 266, 272–3, 280
regulation 68, 273–4, 293, 294–5, 381
Financial Services Action Plan (FSAP) 147, 148, 162–3
Financial Services Agency 381
Financial Services Authority (FSA) 68, 81, 274, 276–7, 291, 293, 294
Financial Services Consumer Panel 275–6
Financial Services and Markets Act 2000 68, 272–3
Financial Stability Forum 305, 321
Financing for Development Conference, Monterrey 315
firms
agglomeration 108, 110–11
employee training 39, 83–4
investment in public goods 39
location decisions 107–8, 110–11
R&D activity 39
fiscal policy
and estimates of trend growth 46, 47, 64
new framework 78, 380, 381
Fiscal stabilisation and EMU 171
The five tests framework 167
foreign direct investment 100, 307–9
Forth, J. 221
France
and ICT 77
investment 30, 100
labour productivity 25, 26, 30, 56
labour quality 30–1
lone parents employment 179
working hours 57
fuel duty 136, 137
Funding Councils 76
Future of Higher Education 83

G7 302, 318
G8 308, 318
G20 302
gains to work 210, 211, 212, 216, 224–5
Gateway reviews 376–7
generally accepted accounting practices (GAAP) 369
Germany
  and ICT 77
  investment 30, 100
  labour productivity 25–7
  labour quality 30–1, 31, 33–4, 42
  working hours 57
Global Compact 310, 322
global economy
  codes and standards of transparency 304–5
  crisis prevention and management 306, 321
  and foreign direct investment 307–9
  international institutions 302, 303, 306–7
  surveillance 305
Global Reporting Initiative 310, 322
globalisation
  benefits of 300
  and economic development 300–1
  UK Government's approach to 300–1, 302–3
Goldman Sachs 50
Gothenburg European Council 149
government
  environmental intervention 10–11, 123, 126–9, 130
  and market failures 7, 8, 9, 10, 16, 86
  role and limits of 6–7, 19, 65
Government Actuary's Department (GAD) 60
Green Book 375–6, 379
Green Fuel Challenge 136
greenhouse gases 135, 138, 140, 144, 147
Gregg, P. 226
Griliches, Z. 40

Haskel, J. 34, 104
health, and inequality 258–9, 352
health care
  choice 340
  and equity 334, 336
  expenditure 16–17, 328–9, 351
  and information problems 335, 342
  new hospitals 341, 373
  outcome-focused approach 346, 352, 382
  waiting times 382
Heavily Indebted Poor Countries (HIPC) initiative 307, 313–14
Heden, Y. 104
Higgs Review 73–4
Higher Education Innovation Fund 76, 118
Highly Skilled Migrant Scheme 85
HIV/AIDS 318
HM Treasury, EMU studies 167, 168–9
Hodrick-Prescott (H-P) filter 49, 64
hours worked 56–8, 62, 186, 187, 195–7, 226, 227–30
housing 78–9, 109
  home ownership 109, 271
  investment in 259–61
  and labour mobility 109
  on previously developed land 143
  PSA targets 114, 354
Housing Benefit 210, 216, 225, 288
Housing, consumption and EMU 109, 168

Improvement and Development Agency (IDeA) 360
inactivity 11, 175–6, 177–86, 189–90
  and gender 182–4
  lone parents 178–9, 205
  over 50's 179–80, 205
  regional variations 95, 97, 185–6
  sick and disabled 181
  and social housing estates 186
  and voluntary retirement 180, 182
  see also unemployment; worklessness
Incapacity Benefit (IB) 182, 192
Income Support (IS)
  and disabled people 181
  families 15, 251
  lone parents 178
  older workers 192
  pensioners 282, 283

Independent Evaluation Office (IEO) 306
Independent Financial Advisers 276
Individual Savings Accounts (ISAs) 277, 280, 292, 384
inflation 41, 176, 348
  and trend growth rate 45–6, 47, 59–60, 63
Information and Communications Technology (ICT) 77, 86, 111–12
  impact on productivity 32, 54, 55, 77
Inland Revenue 119, 213
innovation 6, 7, 9, 32, 33, 42, 75–7
  competition and 9, 37, 38, 39, 70
  and environment 122
  EU and 158–9
  exploiting regional strengths 9, 88
  and productivity of firms 36
  regional variations 102–3, 117–18
  and regulation 68, 72, 160–1
  see also research and development (R&D); science
Innovation Forum 360
Institute for Employment Research 192
Institute for Fiscal Studies (IFS) 268, 269, 270
institutions
  local and regional 113–15
  see also international institutions
International Finance Facility (IFF) 302–3, 315, 318–19
international institutions, and poverty reduction 302, 306–7, 316, 319, 321
International Labour Organisation (ILO) 11
International Monetary Fund (IMF) 304–5, 307, 314, 318, 321
  method of estimating trend output 50, 64
  and Millennium Development Goals 302
  Poverty Reduction and Growth Facility 321
  transparency 306
Invalidity Benefit 180
investment
  foreign 100, 307–9
  in human capital 30–2, 35–6, 38, 40, 42, 82–4
  in ICT 55
  incentives for 72
  institutional 80, 86
  and macroeconomic stability 33, 41, 54, 78
  in physical capital 9, 29–30, 33, 35, 36, 42, 77–82, 100–1
  in R&D 36, 40, 42, 82–3, 86, 158–9
  regional variations 100–1, 117
  and regulation 161
  stakeholder products 274–5
  in training 39, 116, 183–4

Jantti, M. 242
Japan
  ageing population 291
  labour productivity 25, 26, 56
Job Brokers 201
job creation, regional differences 111
Jobcentre Plus 12, 16, 198, 204, 206, 382
Jobseeker's Allowance (JSA) 181, 191, 192, 200, 251, 383
Johnson, P. 226

Kempson, E. 269
Köhler, Horst 306
Kraay, A. 310
Krueger, A. 233
Kyoto Protocol 131, 133, 134, 139

Labour Force Survey (LFS) 62, 216
labour market 38, 226–7, 379
  developments in 176–7
  entry fees 211, 228, 249
  entry wages 226
  EU and 145, 148, 150, 166
  flexibility 12, 13, 149–50, 188, 189, 209–10
    EMU entry and 13, 92, 167, 168–9, 175
  improved performance 194
  labour supply decisions 227–32
  mobility 8, 108–9
  see also employment; inactivity; unemployment; Welfare to Work

labour productivity 24, 25–7, 33
  growth of 37–8, 42, 44, 49, 50, 53–6
  and human capital 35, 42
  see also productivity; productivity growth
lambda 49
Lambert Review of Business-University Interaction 75
Lamfalussy arrangements 162, 163
Lancaster, K. 337
landfill tax 134–5, 137
Leadership Incentive Grant 358
Learning and Skills Council (LSC) 84, 116
  Local (LLSCs) 84, 114, 116, 119, 386
Liebman, J. 231
life expectancy 259, 282, 290, 291, 296
Link scheme 77
Lipsey, R. 337
liquid financial wealth 268–9, 278
Lisbon European Council 146–8
  economic reform agenda 147–8, 150, 156, 166
  progress made 152–4
local authorities 109, 119, 120, 382, 386
  and PSA targets 114–15, 354, 355–6
  services' performance 330–1, 342, 358–9, 360
  support for businesses 119
Local Education Authorities 116
Local Government Association (LGA) 356, 360
Local Strategic Partnerships (LSPs) 115
The location of financial activity and the euro 169–70
London Development Agency 114
London Underground 352
lone parents
  and child poverty 245, 246
  employment rate 205
  help with childcare 198–9, 200, 209, 253
  and Income Support 178, 185, 199
  increase in 208, 253
  and labour market 178–9, 200
  labour supply decisions 227, 232
  New Deal for 12, 193, 198–200
Low Pay Commission (LPC) 216–17, 220–3
low-skilled workers
  and inactivity 181, 184–5, 208–9
  migrants 86
  and mobility 108
  wages 184, 208–9, 235
Luxembourg Process 146, 149–50, 155

Machin, S. 220
McKay, S. 269
macroeconomic policy
  and estimates of trend growth 45–7, 63
  new framework 54–5
macroeconomic stability 5, 11, 41, 54–5, 78, 113, 380
  and employment opportunity for all 188
  and investment 33, 41, 54, 78
  and productivity growth 41, 54–5, 78
  and saving decisions 273
Manufacturing Advisory Service 118
Marginal Deduction Rates (MDRs) 210–11, 224–5
market failure 8–9, 65, 86, 88, 380
  at regional and local level 107–11, 113
  environmental 10, 122, 123, 124–9
  and EU regulation 160
  and externalities 8, 10, 16, 39, 124–6, 137, 143–4
  government intervention 386–7
  impact on productivity 37–40, 163
  and poor regulation 40
  replacing with state failure 7, 19
  and state aid 163
  and workforce training 83
markets
  investigations into 67–8
  market power 8, 37, 39–40, 69
  and productivity growth 38
  and public interest 6–8, 16–19, 19, 65–6, 380
  regulation 9
  role and limits of 6–7, 19, 65–6
Marshall task force 134
Martin, R. 34

maternity leave 253, 385
maternity pay 14
microeconomic reform 5–6
  bottom-up approach 9, 88, 116
  building fairer society 6–8, 13–16, 19, 283, 379–80, 387
  and consultation 66
  principles 6–19
  raising productivity growth rate 7–11, 23, 41–2, 54, 56, 65–87
migration 13, 60, 85–6
Miles, David 109
Millennium Development Goals (MDGs) 299, 301–3, 307, 315, 317, 322
Milwaukee New Hope programme 244
Minimum Funding Requirement 294
Minimum Income Guarantee (MIG) 14, 223, 224, 283–4, 286, 287–8, 296
Minimum Pension Age 296
Ministry of Defence 374
Modelling shocks and adjustment mechanisms in EMU 168
Modelling the transition to EMU 168
Modern Apprenticeships (MA) scheme 83, 87, 385
Modernising Planning agenda 79
monetary policy
  and constrained discretion model 348, 380
  economic response to changes in 168
  and estimates of trend growth 46, 63
monopsony model 235–7
Monterrey Consensus 315
multinational companies 309, 322
Myners Review 80–1, 82

National Air Traffic Service (NATS) 373
National Asset Register (NAR) 369
National Audit Office 342
National Centre for Social Research 192
National Child Development Study (NCDS) 243
National Childcare Strategy 198, 249, 254
National Council for Graduate Entrepreneurship 75
National Curriculum 276, 279, 291, 352, 355
National Family and Parenting Institute (NFPI) 261
National Health Service (NHS) 336, 338–9
  Foundation Trusts 358
  incentive schemes 358
  local responsibility 356, 358
  performance information 357–8
  PSA targets 353, 354, 356
  reforms 351–3, 355, 356–7
  Ten-Year Plan 352, 355, 368
National Institute for Clinical Excellence (NICE) 357–8
National Institute of Economic and Social Research (NIESR) 50, 191–2
National Insurance Contributions (NICs) 13, 14, 209, 210–11, 227, 294
  employer contributions 58, 134, 135, 138, 294
  'entry fee' 211, 249
  reform 197, 223, 225
  and State Pension 283, 284, 297
National Minimum Wage (NMW) 12–13, 14, 209, 216–23, 227, 249
  aims and objectives 216
  design and implementation 216–17
  impact
    on competitiveness and productivity 220–2, 233–5
    coverage 219
    on employment 220, 232–7
    on poverty 222–3
  international comparisons 217–19
  and monopsony model 232, 235–7
  and neoclassical model 233–5
  rates 217
National Network of Centres of Expertise in Manufacturing 118
National Strategy for Neighbourhood Renewal 115
National Technology Strategy 75

National Vocational Qualification (NVQ) 83, 84, 98
Neighbourhood Renewal Fund 115
Nelson, E. 46
Neumark, D. 238
New Deals 12, 190–3, 206, 207, 383
  Gateway period 190
  and long-term unemployed 12, 190–2
  New Deal for Disabled People (NDDP) 12, 201
  New Deal for Lone Parents (NDLP) 12, 193, 198–200
  New Deal for over-25s (ND25+) 191, 192
  New Deal for over-50s (ND50+) 12, 192–3, 296
  New Deal for Partners 200–1
  New Deal for Young People (NDYP) 12, 190–2
New Partnership for Africa's Development (NEPAD) 308–9
New Regional Housing Boards 109
NGOs, role in poverty reduction 322
Nickell, S. 60, 104
Nikolov, K. 46
Non-Accelerating Inflation Rate of Unemployment (NAIRU) 59–60
Northern Ireland 89, 92, 97, 109, 113, 135, 138

Office of Fair Trading (OFT) 66–8, 69, 120
Office of Gas and Electricity Markets 69
Office of Government Commerce (OGC) 373, 377
Office for National Statistics 272
Office of Science and Technology (OST) 77
Office for Standards in Education (Ofsted) 75, 352, 357
old-age dependency ratio 291
older workers
  age discrimination 192
  employment opportunities 149, 180, 282, 295–6
  employment rate 148–9, 291
  inactivity 179–80, 192–3, 205
  Income Support 192
O'Mahony, M. 33, 221
open method of coordination (OMC) 146–7, 155
Organisation of African Unity Summit 2001, Lusaka 309
Organisation for Economic Co-operation and Development (OECD)
  and environmental issues 133
  Guidelines on Multinational Enterprises 310, 322
  International Regulation Database 72
  and market regulation 161
  method of estimating trend output 50, 64
  and Millennium Development Goals 302
Oulu (Finland) 112

Parenting and Education Support Forum (PESF) 261
parents
  flexible working practices 249, 252–3, 254, 385
  help in finding work 249, 265
  parenting support services 261–2, 265
  support during child's early years 253–4, 256–7
  and welfare system reforms 14
  and work-life balance 252–4, 265, 383–4, 385
Partnerships UK (PUK) 373, 377
paternity leave 253, 385
Pension Credit 14, 15, 281, 284, 286–9, 296, 385
Pension Service 16, 288–9
Pensions Commission 282, 297
Pensions Protection Fund 282, 295
Pensions Regulator 295
pensions/pensioners 14–15, 281–97
  additional payments 286
  contracting-out 294
  and demographic change 289, 290–1
  forecast tools 292
  impact of policies 289
  and Income Support 282, 283

income-related support 284
and informed choice 275–7, 282, 291–2, 293–4, 295
and Minimum Income Guarantee (MIG) 281, 283–4, 286, 287–8, 296
occupational pensions 282, 283, 287, 290, 292, 293–4, 295, 296
policy measures 283–9
position in 1997 282–3
private provision 269, 270, 291–2, 385
public service schemes 296
and Retail Price Index (RPI) 284–5
saving for retirement 268, 286–8, 290–3, 295, 297
and tax system reforms 14–15, 278, 282, 286, 293, 294, 384
underprovision 269, 271–2, 281
working beyond retirement age 286, 291, 292, 295–6, 297, 384
see also State Pension
Personal Equity Plans (PEPs) 277, 292
Pesticides Voluntary Agreement 134–5, 137, 139, 144
Phoenix Fund 119–20
Pickering, A. 294
polarisation 276
police, performance monitors 352, 358
Police Standards Unit 352
Policy and Action Team (PAT) 244
Policy frameworks in the UK and EMU 170–1
pollution 127–8, 132, 141, 142, 143–4
poverty
pensioners 281, 288, 296
and worklessness 176, 183, 187
see also child poverty
poverty reduction 298–322, 380, 383
and development aid 313–19
investment 303–5, 307–9, 321
Millennium Development Goals (MDGs) 299, 301–3, 307, 315, 317, 322
through trade liberalisation 310–12
UK Government's approach 300–1, 302–3, 307, 310, 313, 314, 316
see also global economy
poverty reduction strategies 306–7, 308
Poverty Reduction Strategy Paper (PRSP) 306
poverty trap 210, 212, 216, 223–4, 227, 383
Prices and EMU 28, 92, 170
Primary Care Trusts (PCTs) 352, 356
Prince's Trust 75
principal-agent theory 348–9
prisons 352
Private Finance Initiatives (PFIs) 6, 341, 366, 371–4
probation services 333
product markets
EU and 145, 148, 166
flexibility 13, 92, 166
productivity 24–8
impact of market failure 37–40, 65, 163
and labour quantity and quality 30–2, 33, 35–6, 42
measures of 24, 25–8
and physical capital 35, 36, 42
regional variations 89–97
and convergence 107–8, 111–12
and employment patterns 92–7
variation between firms 34–8, 42
see also labour productivity
productivity growth 7–11, 23, 27, 379, 382
differences between countries 32–4, 42
five drivers of 42, 66–86, 151
at regional level 97–104, 116–20
growth accounting 33
and macroeconomic stability 41, 54–5, 78
see also trend growth
protectionism 7, 300
Public Private Partnerships (PPPs) 18, 340–1, 366, 371, 373, 377
Public Sector Net Investment (PSNI) 364
Public Service Agreements (PSAs) 114–15, 259, 352, 353–6
extension of 354–5
Local 115, 354, 355–6, 360
targets 114–15, 353–6, 359, 382, 386

public services
  accountability 17–18, 342–3, 344, 347, 353
  asset base 363–4, 365, 369–71
  choice 340
  clear objectives 343, 344, 347, 348, 350, 352, 353–5
  commercial services 374
  and competition 333, 335, 338, 343, 366, 372
  customer focus 343, 344
  definitions of 326
  and efficiency 17–18, 327, 334–6
  and equity 17–18, 334, 336, 337, 339, 353
  ethos 337, 338
  and externalities 334, 335
  governance structures 347–50
  incentive systems 348, 351, 352, 358–9
  and information 343, 344, 347, 348–9
    about performance 350–1, 352, 357–8
    consumer 334–5, 339
  investment
    capital expenditure 365, 368, 372–3
    decline in 364–6
  investment strategy 30, 362–3, 366–74, 386–7
    asset management 369–71
    capital appraisal 374–6
    Gateway reviews 376–7
    long-term planning 368, 386
    private sector role 340–1, 371–4
    promoting best practice 377
    and reforms 351–3, 368–70, 380
    resource accounting and budgeting 369–70
    and sustainable investment rule 366–7
  local flexibility 17–19, 346–50, 352, 355–6, 382
  and market failure 16–18, 333–5, 337–8, 344
  performance assessments 359–60
  prioritisation 342, 343, 344, 347, 348
  productivity
    focus on outcomes 346, 353–5, 356
    importance of 327
    of individual service providers 331–3, 344
    international comparisons 328–9, 344
    local variations 330–1
    measuring 327–33
    raising 55, 325, 342–4, 345–51, 380, 382
  public sector provision 337–8
  reforms 6, 16–19, 351–60, 384–5
    and investment strategy 351–2, 368–70, 380
  role of markets 334–6, 340–1, 344
  to eradicate child poverty 254–62, 264
  voluntary sector 75, 262–3
  workforce strategies 359
  see also education; health care; National Health Service (NHS); Public Private Partnerships (PPPs)
Public Services Productivity Panel 342
Purchasing Power Parity (PPP) 219

Quintini, G. 60

radio spectrum 77
Reed, H. 226
Regional Centres for Manufacturing Excellence (RCMEs) 118
Regional Development Agencies (RDAs) 114, 116, 118, 119, 382, 386
regional economic performance 88–121
  competition 104–5, 110, 120
  convergence 107–8, 111–12
  employment patterns 92–7, 185–6
  enterprise 103–4, 114, 118–19
  institutional framework 113–15
  investment 101, 103, 107, 112–13, 117
  market failures 107–11
  science and innovation 102–3, 117–18
  skill levels 97–9, 103, 108–10, 116
  variations 93–6

Regional Economic Strategies 114, 117–18, 119
Regional Employment and Skills Frameworks 114, 116
Regional Planning Guidance 109, 259
regional policy 112–20, 382
  exploiting regional strengths 9, 88–9, 92
  microeconomic reforms 115–20
Regional Spatial Strategies 79
Regional Venture Capital Funds (RVCFs) 72, 117
Registered Social Landlords (RSLs) 332, 333
Regulatory Impact Assessment (RIA) 386
Regulatory reform Action Plan 386
relative price adjustment 13
Replacement Ratio 210
Research Councils 76
research and development (R&D)
  business-university interaction 75–6, 77, 117–18
  disincentives for 39, 40
  expenditure on 32, 33, 36, 76–7, 86
    regional variations 102–3
  private and social returns to 40
  tax incentives to businesses 76, 117, 158
  see also innovation; science
Restrictive Trade Practices Act 1976 (RTPA) 66
Retail Price Index (RPI), and pensions 284–5
retirement age 146, 155, 296, 384
  early retirement 180, 182, 291
  working beyond 286, 291, 292, 295–6, 297, 384
Retirement Planner 292
Risk Capital Action Plan 146
road traffic 141, 144
Royal Parks Agency 374
Ryan, R. 338

Sandler Review 81–2, 274–5, 277, 278, 293, 384
Saving Gateway 277, 279, 280, 291, 384
savings and assets 266–80
  aggregated household savings 266–8
  barriers to saving 272–3
  disaggregated data on 267, 268–72
  improving environment for 273–5
  incentives 278–80, 384
  independent advice 276–7
  informed choice 275–7, 279
  life stage sequence 280
  stakeholder products 274–5, 277, 384
  and tax regime 278
  see also pensions/pensioners, private provision
School Standards Grant 352, 356–7
schools *see* education
science 9, 75–6, 83, 86
  overseas students 85
  see also innovation; research and development (R&D)
Scotland 92, 104, 111, 113
Sector Skills Development Agency 84
Severe Disablement Allowance (SDA) 192
sick and disabled people
  and employment 12, 178, 181, 201–2
  and National Minimum Wage 222
sickness and disability-related benefits 11, 176, 180, 181–2, 192, 201
Silicon Valley (USA) 112
single currency 146, 166
  see also EMU entry
Single Sky 148
skills 8, 9, 30–2, 35–6, 42, 82–4
  exploiting regional strengths 9, 88
  and innovation 103
  and labour mobility 109
  lifelong learning 155
  migration 85–6
  Modern Apprenticeships (MA) 83
  regional variations 97–9, 116
  workforce training 83–4, 87, 383, 385
  see also education; investment, in human capital; low-skilled workers
Skills for Life strategy 84
Small Business Investment Company programme, US 72

Small Business Service (SBS) 70, 72, 114, 118
small businesses
 and EU legislation 148, 157
 and tax system 70–4, 76–7, 120
Small Firms Loan Guarantee Scheme 72
small and medium-sized enterprises (SMEs)
 banking services 69
 support for 386
 tax credit 117
Special Drawing Rights (SDRs) 318
stakeholder pension 15, 277, 280, 292–3, 384
 decision trees 276, 277
stamp duty 120
Start-Up Guide 72
State Earnings Related Pension Scheme (SERPS) 282–3, 284
State Pension 282–3, 289, 296, 384, 385
 age 296
 Basic 14, 284–5, 286, 287, 288, 289, 292, 385
 and National Insurance Contributions (NICs) 283, 284, 297
 Second 14, 284, 285
Stockholm European Council 148, 155
Strategic Rail Authority 352
Street Crime Initiative 354
structural adjustment programmes 306, 308
structural indicators 152
students
 fees 83
 overseas 85
 working hours 58
sub-Saharan Africa
 disease 300
 foreign direct investment 308
Submissions on EMU from leading academics 170–1
Sure Start 253, 256–7, 262, 384
Sure Start Maternity Grant 251
Sustainable Communities initiative 79
sustainable development 122, 139–40, 302, 306, 309

tax and benefit system
 encouraging inactivity 11, 184
 integration of systems 15–16, 212, 213, 265, 385
 and labour supply decisions 227–32
 means test approach 249
 and pensions/pensioners 14–15, 278, 282, 286, 293, 294
 reforms 13–16, 58, 197, 210, 278, 383
 and savings 278
 unemployment benefits 181–2
 and worklessness 200
 see also welfare system
tax credits 6, 198, 211–16, 385
 and changing family circumstances 214–15
 and childcare 14, 200, 212–13, 229, 251, 254
 for disabled people 201–2, 251
 on dividends 78
 environmental incentives 136
 impact on labour supply 209, 227–32
 income and substitution effects 230
 and lone parents 198
 and MDRs 224–5
 new 213–16, 223
 for R&D 76–7, 117, 158
 for small businesses 117
 see also Child Tax Credit (CTC); Working Families Tax Credit (WFTC); Working Tax Credit (WTC)
Tax-Exempt Special Savings Accounts (TESSAs) 277, 292
taxation
 10p income tax band 12–13, 223, 249, 286
 environmental 123, 127, 131–2, 134–5, 136–8, 143–4
 for pensions 278
 role of 10
 see also tax and benefit system
Taylor Review 212
Tobin Tax 318

total factor productivity (TFP) 24, 27, 28, 33, 50
training 39, 83–4, 116, 383, 385
transport
  expenditure 351–2
  falling costs 111
  links 79–80, 86, 107
  Ten-Year Plan 79, 341, 352
trend growth 44–64
  estimating
    decomposition 51–3, 62–3, 64
    importance of 45–7, 63
    methods of 47–53, 64
    on-trend points approach 47, 48–9, 51–3, 61, 62–3
    production function approach 50, 64
    statistical filtering techniques 48, 49, 64
    Treasury methodology 51–63, 61–2, 64
  projections 46, 49, 54–63
TUPE regulations 373

UK Online campaign 77
unemployment
  long-term 11, 12, 108–9, 153, 176, 189–90, 193, 195
  young people and 12, 178, 180–1, 189
  see also employment; inactivity
unemployment rate 11, 25, 176–7, 193–5
  NAIRU 59–60
  regional variations 93–7, 185–6
unemployment trap 209–10, 212, 216, 223, 227
United Kingdom
  capital to labour ratio 29, 30
  development aid 317–18
  labour market history 176–7
  productivity gap 9, 23, 24, 25–8, 42, 56, 66
    factors affecting 29–34, 42, 77, 100
United Nations
  and environmental issues 133
  Global Compact 310, 322
  and poverty reduction 299, 302, 315, 321
United States
  capital to labour ratio 30
  Earned Income Tax Credit (EITC) 211
  and ICT 32, 77
  labour mobility 108
  labour productivity 25–7, 32, 56
  labour quality 30–1, 42
  life expectancy 330
  lone parents' employment 179
  productivity 33, 147
The United States as a Monetary Union 28, 108, 170
Universal Banking Services 278
University Challenge 118
Urban Tax Force 120
utilities, and competition 69, 86

Van Reenan, J. 192
vehicle excise duty 136
venture capital funding 78, 81
  at regional level 100–1, 119–20
Venture Capital Trusts 72, 78
voluntary emissions trading scheme 132, 135, 136, 137, 138–9, 144

wages
  and child poverty 245–6
  flexibility 13, 194
  and labour mobility 108
Wales 89, 95, 104, 109, 113, 118
Wascher, W. 238
waste management 134–5, 143
welfare system
  basic principles 14
  past failure of 14
  progressive universalism 15–16, 249, 281, 283, 286, 385–6
  reform of 223–7, 241, 249–50, 385
  reforms 12
  rights and responsibilities 12, 14, 191, 200, 207, 385
  see also tax and benefit system
Welfare to Work 6, 188–205, 249, 383
  active policies 189–90
  Employment Zones 193
  increasing competition 189–90, 208
  introducing competition 193

Welfare to Work *continued*
  Jobcentre Plus 198
  making work pay 188, 198, 207, 208–38, 249
  and worklessness 197–205
  see also New Deals
Welsh Development Agency 118
Westaway, Peter 168
Windfall Tax 190
Winter Fuel Payment 286
Wolfensohn, Jim 306
women
  employment rate 147, 148, 253
  and National Minimum Wage 222
Work Permit system 85
work-focused interviews (WFIs) 199, 201
Work-Life Balance Campaign 254
workers, location decisions 107, 109
Working Families Tax Credit (WFTC) 13, 15, 212–13, 214, 223, 249
  child elements 200, 212–13, 251
  impact on labour supply decisions 226, 229
  and MDRs 225
Working Tax Credit (WTC) 13, 14, 15, 212, 213–16, 249–50, 265
  childcare element 200, 215, 223, 224, 251, 254
  and disabled people 202, 215
  for households without children 215
  impact on labour supply decisions 229–30
  and work incentives 223
workless households 183–4, 189, 197, 208–9
  and child poverty 184, 244–6
  geographical distribution of 185
  help for 200–1
worklessness 175–6, 177–8, 187, 189–0, 207
  local concentrations of 185–6, 197, 207
  policies to tackle 197–205
  and poverty 176, 183, 187
  see also inactivity; unemployment
World Bank 304–5, 306, 318, 321
  and aid disbursement 319
  and debt 314–15
  and Millennium Development Goals 302
  and trade liberalisation 310
  transparency 306
World Health Organisation (WHO) 328–9
World Trade Organisation (WTO) 321
  dispute-settlement procedure 312
  Doha Development Agenda 146, 311–12
Wren-Lewis, Simon 167

Young Enterprise initiative 75
young people
  inactivity rates 180–1
  New Deal for 12, 190–2
  post 16 learning 257–8
  unemployment 12, 178, 189

Zedillo Report 315, 318